Computational Intelligence and Machine Learning: Models and Applications

Contents

About the Editor

Grzegorz Dudek

Grzegorz Dudek is a professor of Information and Communication Technology. He received his PhD in Electrical Engineering from the Czestochowa University of Technology (CUT), Poland, in 2003, and he completed his habilitation in Computer Science at the Lodz University of Technology, Poland, in 2013. In 2023, he was appointed as a full professor. Currently, he is a professor at the Department of Electrical Engineering, CUT, and Department of Mathematics and Computer Science, University of Lodz. His research primarily focuses on machine learning and artificial intelligence, with a strong emphasis on their applications in classification, regression, forecasting, and optimization. He has authored and co-authored four books and over 140 scientific papers in these areas. Notably, he has been recognized in the global ranking of the world's most influential scientists (top 2% list) compiled by Stanford University and Elsevier.

Preface

This Special Issue brings together a diverse and timely selection of research contributions that explore the theoretical foundations, methodological innovations, and practical applications of intelligent computational systems. The aim of this collection is to highlight emerging trends and pressing challenges in machine learning and computational intelligence, offering new perspectives on how these technologies can be more effectively developed, adapted, and deployed in real-world environments.

The scope of the Special Issue spans a wide range of topics, including personalized recommendation systems, social network analysis, predictive modeling, speech recognition in low-resource languages, log anomaly detection, natural language understanding in Arabic, bias mitigation through synthetic data generation, and meteorological forecasting. The studies presented here employ a rich set of methodologies, such as transformer architectures, graph neural networks, retrieval-augmented generation, self-supervised learning, and fuzzy logic frameworks, to address the complexity, uncertainty, and dynamism of real-world data.

The motivation behind compiling this Special Issue stems from the growing importance of machine learning in shaping decision-making systems, user experiences, and data-driven services across various domains. As AI continues to evolve from experimental prototypes into large-scale systems with social and economic impact, there is an urgent need to ensure these technologies are not only powerful and efficient but also interpretable, fair, and inclusive. This collection reflects that shift, with several papers emphasizing the importance of model transparency, domain adaptation, and ethical considerations.

The Special Issue is intended for a broad audience that includes researchers, practitioners, and graduate students in computer science, artificial intelligence, data science, and engineering. It may also serve as a resource for professionals working in application areas such as healthcare, finance, transportation, energy, and software systems who seek to understand and apply the latest advances in machine learning and computational intelligence to their specific challenges.

By bringing together these diverse yet thematically connected contributions, we hope this volume will inform, inspire, and guide future research and development in the field, encouraging new collaborations, methodological refinements, and impactful applications of intelligent technologies.

Grzegorz Dudek
Guest Editor

electronics

MDPI

Editorial

Computational Intelligence and Machine Learning: Advances in Models and Applications

Grzegorz Dudek [1,2]

[1] Faculty of Electrical Engineering, Częstochowa University of Technology, 42-201 Częstochowa, Poland; grzegorz.dudek@pcz.pl
[2] Faculty of Mathematics and Computer Science, University of Łódź, 90-136 Łódź, Poland

1. Introduction

Computational intelligence (CI) and machine learning (ML) have evolved into foundational pillars of modern data-driven research, with growing impacts across domains such as engineering, medicine, finance, and environmental science [1]. Their capacity to learn patterns from data and adapt to dynamic environments makes them indispensable tools for both academic and industrial innovation. The past decade has seen a surge in interest and the practical deployment of CI and ML models, ranging from classical techniques like decision trees and support vector machines to recent breakthroughs in deep learning and large language models [2].

Despite their progress, the development and application of CI and ML algorithms remain complex and challenging. A persistent issue lies in the appropriate selection of model architectures and training strategies to ensure both learning efficacy and generalization [3]. This challenge becomes even more pronounced in practical contexts where data may be noisy, sparse, high-dimensional, or subject to dynamic shifts. Moreover, the increasing societal reliance on AI systems has heightened the demand for models that are not only accurate but also interpretable, fair, and robust [4].

In response to these demands, recent research has explored both foundational improvements to learning mechanisms and application-specific enhancements. For instance, one of the highlighted contributions in this Special Issue addresses the limitations of traditional recommendation systems by incorporating generative AI with psychological modeling to personalize travel recommendations. Another study introduces self-supervised learning into graph-based collaborative filtering, achieving better representation learning and reducing the reliance on labeled data. Further advancements are seen in the use of preference-aware graph neural networks to filter social signals and in the adaptation of large transformer-based models to improve automatic speech recognition in low-resource languages like Turkish.

Received: 25 March 2025
Accepted: 9 April 2025
Published: 10 April 2025

Citation: Dudek, G. Computational Intelligence and Machine Learning: Advances in Models and Applications. *Electronics* **2025**, *14*, 1530. https://doi.org/10.3390/electronics14081530

This Special Issue brings together ten papers selected from 40 submissions that exemplify the diversity and maturity of current research in CI and ML. These works not only introduce novel algorithms and architectures but also demonstrate how to rigorously evaluate them in real-world settings, ranging from environmental prediction using open-source ML toolkits to bias mitigation in healthcare through synthetic data generation. A recurring theme across these papers is the emphasis on data-centric methodologies, from feature engineering and data augmentation to the design of metrics for fairness, utility, and interpretability.

Together, these studies illustrate the field's transition toward more specialized, context-aware, and socially responsible AI systems. They reflect the community's ongoing effort to balance model complexity with usability, accuracy with equity, and innovation with reproducibility. In doing so, they offer valuable insights not only into technical progress but also into the broader implications of deploying intelligent systems across various domains of human activity.

2. Summary of the Contributions

The paper by Aribas and Daglarli addresses the challenge of improving personalized travel recommendations by integrating generative AI with personality models. Classical travel recommendation systems rely on collaborative filtering, content-based filtering, and machine learning models. However, these approaches often fail to capture the complexity of individual user preferences, leading to suboptimal and generic suggestions. Data sparsity, limited adaptability, and an inability to dynamically adjust to evolving user behaviors further limit their effectiveness.

This problem is particularly relevant because the increasing availability of travel-related data presents travelers with an overwhelming number of choices. Without an efficient way to filter through these options, users struggle to find experiences that align with their interests. Traditional recommendation systems do not account for personality-driven preferences, which can significantly impact the suitability of travel suggestions. Advances in artificial intelligence and personalization now make it possible to refine recommendations, improving user satisfaction and engagement. The integration of psychological models into AI-powered systems offers a way to address these limitations, making travel planning more efficient and enjoyable.

The study proposes a novel approach that combines Retrieval-Augmented Generation (RAG) with personality psychology to enhance personalization. The system consists of three key components: a travel data retrieval mechanism, which gathers relevant information from online sources using web crawlers and a vector-based search; an AI-driven recommendation model, built on a large language model (LLM) such as ChatGPT; and personality integration, which incorporates the Myers–Briggs Type Indicator (MBTI) and Big Five (BF) traits to refine recommendations based on psychological factors. The system continuously adapts to user feedback, improving over time.

The evaluation results show a user satisfaction rate of 78%, outperforming traditional methods. Accuracy in aligning recommendations with user preferences reached 82%, with performance varying by personality type (85% for extroverts, 75% for introverts). Precision and recall scores of 0.84 and 0.78 further validate its effectiveness. A case study at Istanbul's Grand Bazaar demonstrates the system's impact, increasing engagement by 25% and satisfaction by 30%. Statistical tests confirm the significance of these results.

The study introduces several innovations, including the first integration of personality models into generative AI for travel recommendations. Compared to traditional recommendation models, it improves user satisfaction by 18% and accuracy by 14%. Future research directions include expanding personality model integration, refining contextual personalization, and enhancing explainable AI methods. The study establishes a foundation for AI-driven personalization with applications beyond travel, including e-commerce and healthcare.

The paper by Zhu et al. builds upon previous research in recommendation systems, particularly in the application of graph neural networks (GNNs) for collaborative filtering. While existing models leverage GNNs to improve recommendations, they suffer from limitations such as sparse supervised signals, noise in user–item interactions, and an inability to effectively model long-tail items. The study introduces Self-Supervised Graph Attention Collaborative Filtering (SGACF) as a novel approach to addressing these challenges.

The core problem being solved is the inefficiency of existing GNN-based recommendation systems in handling sparse interactions and noisy data. Traditional models struggle to accurately represent user preferences, especially for long-tail items that lack sufficient interactions. This issue is crucial because it affects the quality and diversity of recommendations, limiting the personalization potential of recommender systems. Additionally, most models operate in a fully supervised paradigm, which heavily relies on explicit user feedback that is often scarce and biased.

To address these issues, the proposed method incorporates self-supervised learning (SSL) into a graph attention network (GAT)-based collaborative filtering framework. The model consists of two primary components: a supervised learning task using a multi-head graph attention network (GAT) and an auxiliary self-supervised learning task that enhances representation learning. The GAT component refines node representations by assigning different importance weights to neighboring nodes, mitigating the impact of noisy data. The self-supervised learning task employs contrastive learning, generating multiple views of each node through graph data augmentation techniques such as node masking, edge masking, and layer masking. The model maximizes the consistency between different views of the same node while minimizing the consistency between the views of different nodes.

This study conducts extensive experiments on three benchmark datasets—Yelp2018, Gowalla, and Amazon—to evaluate the effectiveness of SGACF. The results demonstrate significant improvements in accuracy and robustness compared to existing methods. The model outperforms state-of-the-art recommendation models, including Neural Matrix Factorization (NeuMF), Spectral Collaborative Filtering, and Neural Graph Collaborative Filtering (NGCF). Notably, SGACF achieves better recall and normalized discounted cumulative gain (NDCG) scores, particularly in mitigating the long-tail problem by enhancing the representation of low-degree nodes.

The key innovations of this work include the integration of self-supervised contrastive learning into graph-based recommendation models, the use of multi-head graph attention to improve representation learning, and the introduction of novel data augmentation strategies for graph-based learning. Unlike previous approaches, this method effectively reduces the reliance on explicit user feedback, improves model generalization, and enhances recommendation diversity.

The contributions of this research are substantial. It establishes a new paradigm for self-supervised learning in recommendation systems, demonstrating that auxiliary self-supervised tasks can significantly enhance supervised learning. The introduction of graph attention networks in combination with self-supervised contrastive learning provides a novel approach to tackling the challenges of data sparsity, interaction noise, and long-tail recommendations. Future research directions include further exploration of data augmentation techniques for graph-based learning, improving contrastive learning frameworks, and extending self-supervised learning to broader recommendation scenarios. This work marks a significant advancement in AI-driven recommendation models, offering a more efficient, scalable, and accurate approach to personalized recommendations.

The paper by Xu et al. explores the challenge of enhancing social recommendation systems by introducing a preference-aware graph neural network approach. Traditional recommendation systems, especially those based on collaborative filtering, often suffer from data sparsity, which limits their ability to provide personalized recommendations. Many existing social recommendation models incorporate user relationships to mitigate this issue, but they frequently fail to properly filter out irrelevant or negative information from high-order neighbors. This results in a decline in recommendation accuracy and effectiveness.

This problem is crucial because social recommendation systems are increasingly used in e-commerce, social media, and content recommendation platforms. The challenge of information overload makes it difficult for users to find relevant content. Introducing social connections can enhance recommendation accuracy, but only if those connections are meaningfully filtered to ensure that only relevant social signals contribute to recommendations.

To address these challenges, the authors propose the Preference-Aware Light Graph Convolutional Network (PLGCN). This model consists of several key components. First, it includes an unsupervised subgraph construction module, which clusters users into subgraphs based on their preferences. By grouping users with similar preferences, the PLGCN effectively filters out negative or irrelevant messages from users with different interests. Second, a feature aggregation module is designed to combine user embeddings with social and interaction information more effectively. Finally, the model employs a lightweight GNN framework, removing nonlinear activation and feature transformation operations to prevent overfitting and improve computational efficiency.

The authors conducted comprehensive experiments on two real-world datasets, LastFM and Ciao, to evaluate the performance of the PLGCN. The results indicate that the PLGCN outperforms state-of-the-art methods, particularly in addressing the cold-start problem, where new users or items have limited interaction data. Compared to baseline models such as NGCF, LightGCN, and SocialLGN, the PLGCN achieved superior precision, recall, and normalized discounted cumulative gain (NDCG) scores, demonstrating its effectiveness in providing more accurate and relevant recommendations.

The study introduces several key innovations. The preference-aware subgraph construction module represents a novel approach to filtering negative information in social recommendation systems, significantly improving recommendation performance. The lightweight GNN framework reduces model complexity while maintaining high accuracy, making it more suitable for large-scale applications. The feature aggregation module enhances user representations by integrating interaction and social information in a more structured way.

In terms of contributions, this work advances the field of social recommendation by introducing an efficient and scalable model that outperforms existing GNN-based recommendation approaches. The proposed methodology demonstrates improved performance in cold-start scenarios, which remains a major challenge in recommendation systems. The study also highlights the potential for further enhancements, including incorporating additional social features such as trust levels and exploring dynamic social networks where user preferences evolve over time. This research provides a strong foundation for future developments in AI-driven personalized recommendations, with practical applications extending beyond social recommendations to e-commerce, online streaming platforms, and digital marketing strategies.

The study by Polat et al. investigates the development and optimization of an automatic speech recognition (ASR) system for Turkish using the Whisper architecture and evaluates the performance gains achieved through fine-tuning with Low-Rank Adaptation (LoRA). The main problem being tackled is the limited performance of ASR systems in low-resource languages such as Turkish. Despite the capabilities of modern transformer-based models like Whisper, their accuracy in Turkish remains suboptimal due to the language's morphological complexity, dialectal variation, and the scarcity of high-quality labeled datasets. These limitations make it difficult to achieve reliable, scalable ASR performance in real-world Turkish applications.

To overcome this, the authors implement an end-to-end ASR system using Whisper and fine-tune it with the LoRA technique. Whisper is based on a transformer architecture known for its ability to handle multilingual, noisy, and long-context inputs effectively.

However, Whisper's training is biased toward high-resource languages like English. LoRA addresses the challenge of fine-tuning large-scale models by introducing low-rank trainable matrices, drastically reducing the number of parameters to be updated during training. This makes the fine-tuning process more computationally efficient and accessible, particularly for low-resource languages.

The study uses five Turkish speech datasets—METU MS, TNST, Mozilla Common Voice, FLEURS, and TASRT—to evaluate the system's performance before and after fine-tuning. The results show significant improvements in word error rates (WERs) and character error rates (CERs), especially in the Whisper medium and large models after applying LoRA. For example, the WER was reduced by up to 52%, with corresponding decreases in the CER, demonstrating the effectiveness of LoRA-enhanced fine-tuning. The paper also includes a comparative analysis with the Google USM ASR model, showing that the Whisper-large-v3 model outperforms Google's system on most datasets in both the WER and CER.

A key advancement of this study is the application of LoRA to the Whisper model for Turkish ASR, combined with a thorough evaluation across multiple speech datasets and targeted improvements to dataset quality. Through the use of a transformer-based architecture optimized via a parameter-efficient fine-tuning approach, the research enhances the adaptability of large-scale ASR systems for languages with limited resources.

The study makes two primary contributions: it demonstrates that Whisper can be effectively adapted to Turkish using LoRA, and it provides a framework for improving ASR performance in other low-resource languages with similar challenges. The study underscores the value of transformer-based models combined with efficient fine-tuning techniques and sets a precedent for further research in multilingual, resource-constrained ASR development.

The paper by Huang and Li proposes a novel framework called GGTr to address the problem of human motion prediction, which involves forecasting future body movements based on past pose sequences. This task is particularly challenging due to the high complexity, variability, and uncertainty of human motion, which involves intricate spatial–temporal dependencies among body joints. Existing models often fail to simultaneously capture both local and global temporal dynamics or accurately represent spatial interactions between joints, limiting their performance in real-world applications such as robotics, surveillance, and human–computer interaction.

The authors address these limitations by proposing a new architecture that integrates Graph Convolutional Networks (GCNs), Gated Recurrent Units (GRUs), and transformer layers. The GCN module incorporates a learned positional representation, allowing the model to capture complex spatial relationships between joints beyond fixed adjacency matrices. GRUs are used to model local temporal dependencies in joint motion, while the transformer layers extract long-range temporal patterns, enabling the network to effectively handle both short-term transitions and long-term dynamics within human motion sequences.

The GGTr model is trained end-to-end using the mean per joint position error (MPJPE) as a loss function and is optimized with the AdamW optimizer. Evaluations are conducted on two benchmark datasets, Human3.6M and CMU-MoCap, where the proposed framework consistently outperforms state-of-the-art methods across both short-term and long-term motion prediction tasks. The results show especially strong performance improvements for complex, irregular, and non-periodic movements, where traditional models often struggle.

Among the novel contributions of this work is the integration of position-aware GCNs with temporal modeling using GRUs and transformer layers, creating a unified framework capable of learning intricate spatial–temporal dependencies. The use of joint-specific attention mechanisms allows the model to dynamically assess the relevance of neighboring joints, enhancing spatial representation. This design enables the network to effectively process both short-term and long-term motion patterns, resulting in improved prediction accuracy. The paper also includes detailed ablation studies that validate the role of each architectural component and identifies a transition point at 320 ms, where the complexity of prediction noticeably shifts, revealing further insight into the temporal dynamics of human motion.

The paper by Alruily focuses on the development of an optimized deep learning-based chatbot framework for Arabic, addressing the challenge of limited research and resources available for natural language understanding (NLU) in Arabic. While chatbot technology has seen significant advances for widely used languages like English and Chinese, Arabic remains underrepresented despite being one of the most used languages online. The complexity of Arabic morphology, dialectal variation, and orthographic inconsistency makes it particularly difficult to develop effective NLU systems, especially in closed-domain applications relevant to industry.

To address this, the authors propose ArRASA, a closed-domain Arabic chatbot framework built on the RASA open-source conversational AI platform. The system is structured around a four-phase pipeline: tokenization, feature extraction, intent classification, and entity extraction. Unlike previous rule-based or retrieval-based Arabic chatbots, ArRASA incorporates a transformer-based architecture, notably using the Dual Intent and Entity Transformer (DIET), which enables the joint learning of intent recognition and entity tagging. The approach also involves masked language modeling (MLM) and next sentence prediction (NSP) tasks during pre-training to better capture linguistic context. Tokenization and featurization are adapted specifically for Arabic, and the system employs various tokenizers and featurizers (e.g., Arcab, Count Vectorizer, Tf-idf) to optimize input representation. SMOTE (synthetic minority over sampling technique) is used to address data imbalance in training samples.

The system's architecture is enhanced through several improvements over the baseline DIET model. These include increasing the number of transformer layers, expanding embedding dimensions and hidden layer sizes, and integrating dropout strategies to prevent overfitting. Experimental results show that ArRASA achieves high accuracy: 97% for intent classification and 95% for entity extraction. Performance comparisons with baseline models, including traditional DIET, keyword-based, and fallback classifiers, demonstrate measurable improvements in both tasks. The framework was also evaluated on a custom-built dataset that reflects diverse industrial intents and entities.

This research presents a scalable and domain-adaptable framework for building Arabic language chatbots. By leveraging transformers and optimization techniques tailored for Arabic, the proposed system sets a new standard in the field of Arabic NLU, providing a strong foundation for further development in both industry and research.

The paper by Hu et al. addresses the challenge of detecting anomalies in system log data, a critical task for maintaining the stability and reliability of modern software systems. As these systems generate vast volumes of log data, traditional rule-based and statistical anomaly detection methods become inadequate due to limited scalability, sensitivity to data structure changes, and inability to capture deeper semantic patterns in log sequences. The increasing complexity of systems demands more robust, adaptive, and accurate detection methods capable of identifying subtle and previously unseen anomalies.

To tackle this problem, the authors propose LogADSBERT, a log anomaly detection framework that integrates Sentence-BERT for extracting semantic features from log events with a Bi-LSTM neural network to capture sequential dependencies. The method consists of two primary stages: model training and anomaly detection. In the training phase, a log parser converts raw logs into structured events and triples, which are then used to train the Sentence-BERT-based semantic vector model (T-SBERT). These vectors are arranged into sequences and passed through a Bi-LSTM model trained to learn normal log behavior. During detection, new logs are parsed, transformed into semantic vectors, and analyzed using the trained Bi-LSTM model to identify anomalies based on a similarity threshold.

The approach advances current practices by combining semantic feature extraction from Sentence-BERT with sequence modeling through a Bi-LSTM equipped with an attention mechanism. This design enables the model to better understand contextual relationships between log events, increasing both detection accuracy and robustness. The framework also includes a semantic matching algorithm that supports generalization to new log events, addressing a key limitation of prior models which perform poorly when log formats change or new events appear.

Evaluation on two real-world datasets, HDFS and OpenStack, shows that LogADSBERT outperforms existing deep learning-based methods such as DeepLog and LogAnomaly in terms of precision, recall, and F1-score. The model demonstrates particular strength in handling newly injected log events, maintaining high detection performance even when encountering previously unseen patterns. Experimental results also confirm the method's resilience across different hyperparameter settings, indicating its adaptability to diverse application environments.

Overall, the study presents a semantically enriched and sequence-aware approach to log anomaly detection that significantly improves accuracy, robustness, and generalization compared to traditional and existing deep learning methods. This work highlights the importance of integrating natural language processing techniques with temporal modeling in system monitoring applications.

The paper by Memiş deals with the formalization and application of picture fuzzy soft matrices (pfs-matrices) in supervised learning, particularly by introducing a new classification algorithm called Picture Fuzzy Soft k-Nearest Neighbor (PFS-kNN). The problem being addressed arises from inconsistencies in earlier definitions of picture fuzzy sets and picture fuzzy soft sets. These inconsistencies limit the reliability and applicability of pfs-sets and their matrix forms in computational tasks, especially those involving uncertain or imprecise information, such as real-world decision-making or classification problems.

The issue is significant because many complex problems, especially in areas like medical diagnosis or preference-based decision-making, involve uncertainty that cannot be effectively captured by classical mathematical tools. Traditional fuzzy set models and even their extensions, like intuitionistic or Pythagorean fuzzy sets, struggle to fully express cases that include partial agreement, disagreement, and abstention (such as in voting scenarios). Picture fuzzy sets address this by introducing three degrees: membership, non-membership, and neutrality. However, without a consistent matrix-based representation and valid mathematical operations, their use in machine learning remains limited.

To resolve this, the author redefines the structure of pfs-matrices to eliminate logical and algebraic contradictions present in earlier models. These matrices allow for the representation of data points with complex uncertainty structures in a way that is suitable for computation. The paper then defines a set of new distance measures—such as Minkowski, Euclidean, and Hamming distances—for comparing pfs-matrices. These distance measures are used in the construction of the PFS-kNN classifier, which adapts the classical k-Nearest Neighbor algorithm to the picture fuzzy soft set context by evaluating similarity between pfs-matrices rather than standard numerical vectors.

The classifier is tested using four medical datasets from the UCI Machine Learning Repository. The proposed method demonstrates superior performance compared to existing kNN-based classifiers across multiple metrics, including accuracy, precision, recall, and F1-score. In 72 out of 128 evaluation cases, PFS-kNN outperforms the baselines.

What distinguishes this approach is the fusion of a restructured mathematical framework with a practical supervised learning application. The paper not only resolves theoretical flaws in the structure and operations of pfs-matrices but also shows that these improvements lead to better modeling of uncertainty in real-world datasets. As a result, this work establishes a more robust foundation for integrating the picture fuzzy soft set theory into machine learning, with potential applications in any domain requiring nuanced handling of vague, partial, or conflicting information.

The study by Segovia addresses the problem of accurately forecasting meteorological variables—specifically temperature, relative humidity, solar radiation, and wind speed—using machine learning techniques implemented in open-source software. The significance of this issue lies in the increasing demand for reliable weather prediction to support applications in renewable energy management, agriculture, environmental monitoring, and public health. Climate variability and the nonlinear behavior of atmospheric variables make traditional statistical approaches insufficient, especially in regions with complex weather dynamics like the study area in Ecuador.

To meet this challenge, the authors propose a forecasting system based on Python and compare the performance of six supervised learning models: multiple linear regression, polynomial regression, decision tree, random forest, XGBoost, and the multilayer perceptron neural network. The models were trained and tested using a one-year dataset collected every five minutes from a meteorological station in the Tungurahua province of Ecuador. Each model's performance was assessed using four evaluation metrics. The findings show that the random forest model consistently delivers the most accurate predictions across most variables. However, wind speed posed the greatest forecasting challenge due to its high variability, with the best results for this variable obtained using XGBoost.

What distinguishes this work is the development of a low-cost, replicable forecasting system based entirely on open-source tools. The methodology is adaptable to other meteorological contexts and supports broader implementations in intelligent agriculture and microgrid control. The approach demonstrates the capacity of ensemble methods and neural networks to model complex atmospheric behaviors and suggests that machine learning can offer reliable and scalable solutions for real-time environmental prediction.

The paper by Shahul Hameed examines the use of synthetic data generation as a strategy for mitigating bias in artificial intelligence systems, with a particular focus on medical datasets. The problem it addresses stems from the growing concern that AI models, especially in healthcare, can replicate and even amplify societal biases present in training data. These biases can result in unfair treatment recommendations, misdiagnoses, or unequal access to healthcare services for certain demographic groups, particularly those underrepresented in existing datasets.

This issue is especially critical in clinical settings, where algorithmic decisions can have direct implications on patient outcomes. For example, biased models may lead to disparities in diagnoses or therapeutic suggestions across racial, gender, or socioeconomic groups. Traditional approaches to mitigate bias—such as algorithmic adjustments, pre- or post-processing of data, or attempts to diversify existing datasets—are often limited in effectiveness or introduce trade-offs, such as a loss of data fidelity. Synthetic data generation offers an alternative that maintains the statistical structure of the original dataset while improving representativeness and privacy.

The authors conduct a comprehensive review of seventeen peer-reviewed studies published between 2020 and 2024, selected through a structured search process involving major scientific databases including Google Scholar, PubMed, IEEE Xplore, ScienceDirect, and the ACM Digital Library. The selected studies apply a range of synthetic data generation techniques to address bias, including Generative Adversarial Networks (GANs), Bayesian networks, Structural Causal Models (SCMs), SMOTE, Gaussian copulas, and deep reinforcement learning. These methods are used to augment or replace biased data in applications such as diagnosis prediction, treatment recommendation, and health record de-identification. Several approaches emphasize the dual benefit of fairness improvement and data privacy preservation.

The paper details how GANs are widely used to generate synthetic medical images, signals, and tabular data, while Bayesian and causal models offer structured frameworks for encoding probabilistic or causal relationships among variables. SMOTE and CTGAN are frequently employed for balancing class distributions in imbalanced datasets. Across studies, the effectiveness of these methods is assessed using various fairness and performance metrics such as demographic parity, equal opportunity, ROC-AUC, F1-score, and domain-specific utility scores.

In the discussion, the authors highlight that synthetic data generation has proven effective in enhancing model fairness and performance when applied appropriately. However, the success of these methods depends heavily on the quality of the initial dataset, the suitability of the chosen technique, and the availability of domain knowledge for model tuning. Limitations include computational cost, the complexity of implementation (especially for causal models), challenges in preserving high-dimensional dependencies, and the risks of introducing new types of bias during data generation.

While the reviewed methods show promise, the authors stress that the current synthetic data techniques still face barriers to broader adoption in real-world healthcare systems. These include methodological complexity, lack of standardization, and limited validation across diverse populations. Nonetheless, the review offers a solid foundation for further research into artificial data generation as a practical and ethical solution to bias in AI, especially in domains where data privacy and fairness are both paramount.

3. Conclusions

This Special Issue presents a comprehensive snapshot of current advancements in computational intelligence and machine learning, highlighting their increasing sophistication, diversity of application, and relevance to real-world challenges. The ten featured papers collectively demonstrate how novel learning paradigms, model architectures, and data representations can address critical problems such as personalization, recommendation diversity, fairness, interpretability, and performance in low-resource or noisy data environments.

A prominent trend throughout the contributions is the growing integration of deep learning models, particularly transformers, graph neural networks, and hybrid architectures, with domain-specific knowledge and auxiliary learning objectives. From enhancing travel recommendation systems with personality profiling to deploying self-supervised learning in collaborative filtering, these studies showcase the importance of designing models that are not only accurate but also adaptive and explainable. Additionally, multiple contributions emphasize the practical viability of proposed solutions, as evidenced by experimental validation on diverse benchmark datasets and real-world scenarios.

Another key theme is the increasing emphasis on ethical and inclusive AI, particularly in works focused on bias mitigation, fairness in healthcare applications, and accessibility for underrepresented languages. The use of synthetic data generation, lightweight model adaptation, and open-source deployment reflects a broader movement toward responsible, transparent, and reproducible research practices.

Overall, the research collected in this Special Issue contributes to a deeper understanding of both the capabilities and limitations of contemporary machine learning systems. It provides a valuable resource for researchers and practitioners seeking to harness the power of computational intelligence in increasingly complex, uncertain, and socially sensitive environments. The breadth of methodological approaches and problem domains also points to promising directions for future work, including multimodal learning, continual adaptation, and trustworthy AI frameworks.

Funding: This research received no external funding.

Conflicts of Interest: The author declares no conflict of interest.

List of Contributions

1. Aribas, E.; Daglarli, E. Transforming Personalized Travel Recommendations: Integrating Generative AI with Personality Models. *Electronics* **2024**, *13*, 4751. https://doi.org/10.3390/electronics13234751.
2. Zhu, J.; Li, K.; Peng, J.; Qi, J. Self-Supervised Graph Attention Collaborative Filtering for Recommendation. *Electronics* **2023**, *12*, 793. https://doi.org/10.3390/electronics12040793.
3. Xu, H.; Wu, G.; Zhai, E.; Jin, X.; Tu, L. Preference-Aware Light Graph Convolution Network for Social Recommendation. *Electronics* **2023**, *12*, 2397. https://doi.org/10.3390/electronics12112397.
4. Polat, H.; Turan, A.K.; Koçak, C.; Ulaş, H.B. Implementation of a Whisper Architecture-Based Turkish Automatic Speech Recognition (ASR) System and Evaluation of the Effect of Fine-Tuning with a Low-Rank Adaptation (LoRA) Adapter on Its Performance. *Electronics* **2024**, *13*, 4227. https://doi.org/10.3390/electronics13214227.
5. Huang, B.; Li, X. GGTr: An Innovative Framework for Accurate and Realistic Human Motion Prediction. *Electronics* **2023**, *12*, 3305. https://doi.org/10.3390/electronics12153305.
6. Alruily, M. ArRASA: Channel Optimization for Deep Learning-Based Arabic NLU Chatbot Framework. *Electronics* **2022**, *11*, 3745. https://doi.org/10.3390/electronics11223745.
7. Hu, C.; Sun, X.; Dai, H.; Zhang, H.; Liu, H. Research on Log Anomaly Detection Based on Sentence-BERT. *Electronics* **2023**, *12*, 3580. https://doi.org/10.3390/electronics12173580.
8. Memiş, S. Picture Fuzzy Soft Matrices and Application of Their Distance Measures to Supervised Learning: Picture Fuzzy Soft k-Nearest Neighbor (PFS-kNN). *Electronics* **2023**, *12*, 4129. https://doi.org/10.3390/electronics12194129.
9. Segovia, J.A.; Toaquiza, J.F.; Llanos, J.R.; Rivas, D.R. Meteorological Variables Forecasting System Using Machine Learning and Open-Source Software. *Electronics* **2023**, *12*, 1007. https://doi.org/10.3390/electronics12041007.
10. Shahul Hameed, M.A.; Qureshi, A.M.; Kaushik, A. Bias Mitigation via Synthetic Data Generation: A Review. *Electronics* **2024**, *13*, 3909. https://doi.org/10.3390/electronics13193909.

References

1. Sarker, I.H. Machine Learning: Algorithms, Real-World Applications and Research Directions. *SN Comput. Sci.* **2021**, *2*, 160. [CrossRef] [PubMed]
2. LeCun, Y.; Bengio, Y.; Hinton, G. Deep Learning for AI. *Commun. ACM* **2021**, *64*, 58–65.
3. Elsken, T.; Metzen, J.H.; Hutter, F. Neural Architecture Search: A Survey. *J. Mach. Learn. Res.* **2019**, *20*, 1–21.
4. Zhang, C.; Bengio, S.; Hardt, M.; Recht, B.; Vinyals, O. Understanding Deep Learning Requires Rethinking Generalization. *arXiv* **2017**, arXiv:1611.03530. [CrossRef]

electronics

MDPI

Article

Transforming Personalized Travel Recommendations: Integrating Generative AI with Personality Models

Erke Aribas * and Evren Daglarli *

Department of Computer Engineering, Faculty of Computer and Informatics Engineering, Istanbul Technical University, 34485 Istanbul, Turkey
* Correspondence: aribas@itu.edu.tr (E.A.); daglarli@itu.edu.tr (E.D.)

Abstract: Over the past few years, the incorporation of generative Artificial Intelligence (AI) techniques, particularly the Retrieval-Augmented Generator (RAG) framework, has opened up revolutionary opportunities for improving personalized travel recommendation systems. The RAG framework seamlessly combines the capabilities of large-scale language models with retriever models, facilitating the generation of diverse and contextually relevant recommendations tailored to individual preferences and interests, all of which are based on natural language queries. These systems iteratively learn and adapt to user feedback, thereby continuously refining and improving recommendation quality over time. This dynamic learning process enables the system to dynamically adjust to changes in user preferences, emerging travel trends, and contextual factors, ensuring that the recommendations remain pertinent and personalized. Furthermore, we explore the incorporation of personality models like the Myers–Briggs Type Indicator (MBTI) and the Big Five (BF) personality traits into personalized travel recommendation systems. By incorporating these personality models, our research aims to enrich the understanding of user preferences and behavior, allowing for even more precise and tailored recommendations. We explore the potential synergies between personality psychology and advanced AI techniques, specifically the RAG framework with a personality model, in revolutionizing personalized travel recommendations. Additionally, we conduct an in-depth examination of the underlying principles, methodologies, and technical intricacies of these advanced AI techniques, emphasizing their ability to understand natural language queries, retrieve relevant information from vast knowledge bases, and generate contextually rich recommendations tailored to individual personalities. In our personalized travel recommendation system model, results are achieved such as user satisfaction (78%), system accuracy (82%), and the performance rate based on user personality traits (85% for extraversion and 75% for introversion).

Keywords: personality model; retrieval augmentation; large language models (LLM); travel recommendation

Citation: Aribas, E.; Daglarli, E. Transforming Personalized Travel Recommendations: Integrating Generative AI with Personality Models. *Electronics* **2024**, *13*, 4751. https://doi.org/10.3390/electronics13234751

Academic Editor: Grzegorz Dudek

Received: 14 August 2024
Revised: 24 November 2024
Accepted: 27 November 2024
Published: 1 December 2024

1. Introduction

Recently, the swift progress in technology has revolutionized how we plan, experience, and savor travel. With the proliferation of online travel platforms, social media, and mobile applications, travelers are presented with an overwhelming array of options for destinations, accommodations, activities, and experiences [1]. However, amidst this abundance of choices, finding a perfect travel itinerary tailored to one's preferences, interests, and needs can be a daunting task [2]. In recent years, the realm of travel planning has experienced a significant shift, driven by the merging of cutting-edge technologies and changing consumer expectations. In the digital age, travelers are inundated with an overwhelming abundance of information and options when selecting destinations, accommodations, activities, and experiences for their trips. Personalized travel recommendation systems have become essential tools for helping travelers navigate the intricacies of trip planning while crafting tailored travel experiences that align with their individual preferences and interests [3].

In response to this challenge, personalized travel recommendation systems have emerged as a valuable solution for assisting travelers in discovering and planning their ideal trips. These systems utilize state-of-the-art technologies like data mining, machine learning, and artificial intelligence to process extensive travel-related data, encompassing user preferences, past behavior, social interactions, and contextual factors. By harnessing the power of data-driven algorithms, personalized travel recommendation systems aim to deliver tailored travel suggestions that align closely with the individual preferences and requirements of each traveler [4]. Conventional personalized travel recommendation systems depend on a range of techniques, including collaborative filtering, content-based filtering, and matrix factorization, to assess user preferences and historical data, thereby producing tailored travel suggestions. However, these approaches often face limitations in capturing the nuanced and multifaceted nature of travelers' preferences, leading to suboptimal recommendations and user experiences [5].

The fusion of generative Artificial Intelligence (AI) techniques, like the RAG framework, with personality models has unlocked promising new opportunities for boosting the capabilities and effectiveness of personalized travel recommendation systems. The RAG framework merges the strengths of large-scale language models with retrospective models, facilitating the creation of varied and contextually appropriate recommendations in response to natural language queries [6–8]. By leveraging personality models, personalized travel recommendation systems can iteratively learn and adapt to user feedback, continuously refining and improving the quality of recommendations over time [9]. This dynamic learning process allows the system's ability to adjust to shifts in user preferences, emerging travel trends, and contextual factors, ensuring that the recommendations remain relevant and personalized [10]. In this study, we examine the potential of generative AI methods, specifically the RAG framework with a personality model, for revolutionizing personalized travel recommendation systems. We examine the underlying principles, methodologies, and technical intricacies of these advanced AI techniques, highlighting their ability to understand natural language queries, retrieve relevant information from vast knowledge bases, and generate contextually rich recommendations.

Furthermore, we discuss the implications of integrating generative AI methods with personalized travel recommendation systems, including the potential benefits of enhancing recommendation diversity, addressing data sparsity issues, and improving user engagement and satisfaction. Also, we analyze real-world applications and case studies that demonstrate the effectiveness and influence of these advanced AI techniques in revolutionizing the travel planning experience for users. Through our investigation, we seek to offer insights into the changing landscape of personalized travel recommendation systems and the transformative potential of generative AI techniques in influencing the future of travel planning and tourism. By leveraging AI-driven personalization, we foresee a future where travelers can seamlessly uncover and craft enriching travel experiences that align with their unique preferences and aspirations.

2. Related Works/Literature Review

Travel recommendation systems have become increasingly prevalent in recent years, driven by the growing availability of user-generated data and advancements in data mining and machine learning techniques. These systems aim to assist travelers in discovering personalized travel experiences based on their preferences, past behavior, and contextual factors.

In this literature review, we examine significant research contributions within the field of travel recommendation systems, with an emphasis on the different approaches and methodologies used to improve the recommendation process. Building upon this foundation, researchers have proposed various innovative approaches to enhance personalized travel recommendations. Nitu et al. [11] proposed an approach to improving tailored travel recommendations by integrating recency effects. Their study highlights the importance of considering the temporal aspects of user preferences to deliver timely and appropriate recommendations. Memon et al. [12] introduced a travel recommendation method leveraging geo-tagged photos from social media platforms. By analyzing the spatial distribution of user-generated content, their approach offers location-based recommendations tailored to tourists' interests. Liu et al. presented a personalized travel package recommendation system that utilizes data mining techniques to extract user preferences from historical travel records [13]. Their research emphasizes the significance of understanding individual travel behavior to offer tailored itinerary suggestions. Chen et al. introduced a travel recommendation framework that derives people attributes and travel group types from community-shared photos [14]. By analyzing social context and group dynamics, their approach enhances the relevance and diversity of travel suggestions. Sun et al. [15] introduced a route-based travel recommendation system that utilizes geographically tagged images to infer travel preferences and routes. Their research highlights the potential of visual content analysis for generating personalized travel itineraries.

Moreover, as travel recommendation systems evolve, the integration of context awareness emerges as a pivotal theme. Zheng and Xie explored the use of user-generated GPS traces for learning travel recommendations [16]. By mobility patterns and historical trajectories, their approach provides personalized suggestions based on individuals' movement behaviors. Ricci et al. suggested a case-driven travel recommendation system that suggests destinations derived from similarities between user preferences and historical cases [17]. Their research emphasizes the importance of leveraging past experiences to guide future travel decisions. Majid et al. [18] introduced a context-sensitive personalized travel recommendation system that utilizes geographically tagged social media data mining. By considering contextual factors such as time, location, and social interactions, their approach offers tailored recommendations aligned with travelers' current situations. Cheng et al. developed a personalized travelling recommendation method derived from extracting people attributes from user-contributed photos [19]. Their research emphasizes the influence of social context and user-created content in enhancing travel suggestions. Zheng et al. suggested a context-sensitive travel recommendation method that relaxes contextual constraints to improve recommendation accuracy [20]. By dynamically adjusting the relevance of contextual factors, their method adapts to users' evolving preferences and situations.

Looking ahead, the future of travel recommendation systems holds promise for autonomous decision-making with the integration of generative AI technologies like ChatGPT [21]. Their study explored the role of conversational agents in assisting travelers with real-time recommendations and decision support. Chen et al. [22] introduced a trip reinforcement recommendation approach based on graph-based representation learning. By modeling the relationships between travel entities, their method enhances recommendation effectiveness and diversity. In summary, these studies emphasize the wide array of methodologies and strategies utilized in travel recommendation systems, spanning from content-based and collaborative filtering strategies to context-sensitive and social media-driven approaches. Future research directions may focus on integrating multiple data sources, leveraging advanced AI techniques, and addressing emerging challenges such as privacy concerns and data sparsity issues to further enhance the efficiency and user-friendliness of travel recommendation systems.

3. Background

Recommendation systems have evolved from early collaborative filtering methods, such as user–item matrix factorization, to more sophisticated techniques incorporating machine learning algorithms and deep learning models. Collaborative filtering approaches from Resnick and Varian rely on user feedback and preferences to generate recommendations, but they face challenges including cold-start issues and data sparsity [23]. As computational power increased and data availability improved, content-based filtering methods from Pazzani and Billsus emerged, utilizing item attributes and user profiles to make personalized recommendations [24]. These methods are effective but limited at capturing complex user preferences and contextual information.

The advent of AI-driven recommendation systems marked a significant paradigm shift, leveraging advanced machine learning algorithms, natural language processing (NLP) methods, and deep learning frameworks [25,26]. Adomavicius and Tuzhilin employed these methods in combination with collaborative filtering, content-driven filtering, and combined approaches to produce highly personalized recommendations rooted in user behavior, historical data, and contextual signals [27–30]. For example, He et al. integrated neural collaborative filtering models for deep learning architectures with collaborative filtering techniques to improve recommendation accuracy and scalability [31].

3.1. Evolution of Recommendation Systems and AI-Driven Conversational Interfaces

Concurrently, AI-driven conversational interfaces have evolved from rule-based chatbots to intelligent virtual assistants capable of natural language understanding and generation. Turkle showed that early chatbots relied on predefined rules and scripted responses, limiting their conversational capabilities and adaptability to user inputs [32]. However, Brown et al. led advancements in NLP, machine learning, and deep learning to develop sophisticated conversational agents powered by large-scale language models such as ChatGPT [33]. These agents can engage in human-like conversations, understand complex queries, and provide contextually relevant responses [34].

The integration of recommendation systems with AI-driven conversational interfaces represents a synergistic approach to enhancing user experiences and engagement. By leveraging recommendation algorithms within conversational interfaces, users can receive personalized recommendations seamlessly during conversations, enriching their interactions and facilitating decision-making processes, which were described by Adomavicius and Tuzhilin [27]. For instance, an e-commerce chatbot can suggest products based on user preferences and context, leading to higher conversion rates and user satisfaction.

Overall, the evolution of recommendation systems and AI-driven conversational interfaces has been propelled by advancements in AI, machine learning, and natural language processing technologies. These advancements continue to drive innovations in personalized user experiences, intelligent decision support systems, and human–computer interactions, shaping the future of AI-driven applications in various domains according to Brown et al. [33].

Generative AI methods encompass a diverse set of techniques aimed at generating new data, content, or outputs based on learned patterns and models. The proposed recommendation system leverages the RAG framework to retrieve contextually relevant information based on user queries. The RAG framework is particularly effective in identifying and filtering high-quality content from extensive databases, thereby improving the accuracy of initial recommendations. To further refine these recommendations, personality models—specifically the MBTI and BF—are integrated within the system.

Personality traits guide the personalization process, enabling the system to align recommendations with individual user preferences more precisely. For instance, users with high Openness may receive suggestions for novel and adventurous travel experiences, while those with high Conscientiousness may receive structured and detail-oriented recommendations. By combining the RAG framework's robust data retrieval capabilities with personality-driven personalization, the system provides tailored travel recommendations that are both accurate and highly relevant to user needs [6]. This framework has been instrumental in enhancing the accuracy and relevance of AI-generated content, particularly in applications requiring contextual understanding and information synthesis.

3.2. Personality Psychology: Understanding Individual Differences

Personality psychology is a field within psychology focused on studying the variations in personality traits among individuals and understanding the psychological mechanisms that contribute to people's unique characteristics. Personality traits are stable patterns of thoughts, emotions, and behaviors that differentiate individuals from one another and remain relatively consistent over time [35]. These traits encompass a wide range of dimensions, including extraversion, agreeableness, conscientiousness, neuroticism, and openness to experience. The areas it explores include the following:

- Constructing a coherent personality-based understanding of an individual's core psychological processes;
- Analyzing psychological variations in relation to personality;
- Exploring human nature and the psychological commonalities among individuals.

Personality psychology is defined as the study of how people differ due to psychological influences and how personality traits function collectively [36]. This field aims to build a comprehensive understanding of an individual's basic psychological processes, examine psychological differences among individuals, and explore human nature and the psychological commonalities between people [35,36]. The concept of 'personality' refers to a dynamic and organized set of traits that distinctly shape an individual's interactions with their environment, cognition, emotions, motivations, and behaviors. Personality also relates to the patterns of thoughts, feelings, social adjustment, and behavior that are consistently displayed over time and significantly influence one's expectations, self-perceptions, values, and attitudes [37].

3.3. Personality Classification Systems: MBTI and BF

Personality research has been extensively explored in psychology, covering a variety of theoretical traditions that include several major theories, such as the dispositional (trait) perspective, as well as psychodynamic, humanistic, biological, behavioral, evolutionary, and social learning perspectives [34]. Many researchers and psychologists do not confine themselves to a single perspective, preferring instead to adopt an eclectic approach [36]. Research in this field is often empirically driven, employing dimensional models based on multivariate statistics like factor analysis, or it emphasizes theory development, as illustrated in psychodynamic theory [35]. Additionally, there is significant focus on applied personality testing. In psychological education and training, understanding the nature and development of personality is frequently considered a prerequisite for courses in abnormal or clinical psychology [34]. Personality type refers to the psychological classification of individuals into distinct categories. Personality types are different from personality traits, which vary in degree. Numerous personality theories exist, each containing several sub-theories [38]. The development of the MBTI and the BF personality traits is particularly significant in personality psychology [39]. The Myers–Briggs Type Indicator (MBTI) categorizes individuals into distinct psychological types [40]. For instance, personality theories often classify people as either introverts or extroverts, whereas trait theories view introversion and extroversion as part of a continuous spectrum, with many individuals situated at a midpoint.

The MBTI is a popular personality classification system rooted in Carl Jung's theories of psychological types. The MBTI divides individuals into 16 distinct personality types, each defined by preferences across four dichotomous dimensions: extraversion versus introversion, sensing versus intuition, thinking versus feeling, and judging versus perceiving, as outlined by [41] This classification system provides insights into individuals' cognitive preferences, decision-making styles, and communication preferences, making it valuable in various personal and professional contexts.

The BF personality traits, also referred to as the five-factor model (FFM), offer a broad framework for understanding personality [42]. The BF traits mentioned by Goldberg include openness to experience, conscientiousness, extraversion, agreeableness, and neuroticism, each representing a broad dimension of personality variation [42,43]. This model is based on empirical research and is widely accepted in personality psychology for its robustness and predictive validity across different cultures and contexts.

Personality classification systems such as the MBTI and the BF provide valuable frameworks for assessing and categorizing individuals based on their personality traits [40]. These systems have applications in various fields, including career counseling, team building, interpersonal relationships, and organizational development. By understanding individuals' personality profiles, practitioners can tailor interventions, communication strategies, and decision-making processes to align with individuals' preferences and tendencies.

Based on Jung's writings and observations, many tests, such as the Golden, PTI-Pro and JTI [40–42], were subsequently developed based on the Myers–Briggs model. These theories can also be viewed as 'approaches' to personality or psychology and are frequently referred to as models. The model represents an older theoretical approach that views introversion and extraversion as fundamental psychological orientations, connected to two pairs of psychological functions, type dynamics and development, and the cognitive functions associated with each type. The MBTI categorizes certain psychological differences into four opposing pairs or 'binaries', leading to 16 distinct psychological types. None of these types are seen as 'better' or 'worse', but Briggs and Myers proposed that individuals naturally 'prefer' a particular combination of type differences [41]. Just as it is difficult for a left-handed person to use their right hand, people tend to find it more difficult to use their contrasting psychological preferences, but with practice and development, they can enhance their proficiency (and thus become more behaviorally adaptable).

The 16 types are typically denoted by a four-letter acronym, representing the initials of each of the four preference types (with the exception of intuition, which is abbreviated as 'N' to avoid confusion with introversion). This can be illustrated with the following examples: ENTJ stands for extraversion (E), intuition (N), thinking (T), and judging (J); ISFP stands for introversion (I), sensing (S), feeling (F), and perceiving (P). These abbreviations are consistent across all 16 types, as shown in Table 1.

Table 1. Personality Type Examples [41].

ISTJ	ISFJ	INFJ	INTJ
ISTP	ISFP	INFP	INTP
ESTP	ESFP	ENFP	ENTP
ESTJ	ESFJ	ENFJ	ENTJ

The BF personality traits represent a proposed taxonomy or grouping of personality characteristics, developed within psychological trait theory starting in the 1980s. By the 1990s, five distinct factors were identified for the U.S.-British population, typically labeled as follows [41]:

- openness to experience (creative/curious vs. consistent/cautious)
- conscientiousness (efficient/organized vs. wasteful/careless)
- extroversion (outgoing/energetic vs. lonely/withdrawn)
- compatibility (friendly/compassionate vs. critical/rational)
- neuroticism (sensitive/nervous vs. flexible/confident)

Factor analysis reveals semantic relationships by analyzing personality questionnaire data. In this sense, there is often a relationship between words used to refer to the same person [40]. For example, for a person characterized as conscientious, the term "always prepared" is more commonly used than "disorganized". These connections highlight five broad dimensions that serve as a common language for describing human personality, temperament, and mood [41–43]. The five factors are easily remembered using the acronyms 'OCEAN' or 'CANO'. Each global factor encompasses a set of interrelated, more specific primary traits. For instance, extraversion is generally linked to traits like sociability, assertiveness, thrill-seeking, warmth, activity, and positive emotions. These traits are not absolute but exist along a continuum. This understanding of personality can now be applied to the development of language models, as the next section explores.

3.4. Introduction to Language Models: Understanding Natural Language Queries and Generating Responses

This study seeks to close the gap between personality psychology and language models. By creating a mapping between the MBTI system and the BF traits, we hope to equip language models with a deeper understanding of human personality. This, in turn, could allow these models to tailor their responses to better reflect the user's individual characteristics.

So, first we create a mapping from the MBTI to the BF and implement protectionist interfaces in the language model. We then extend this methodology to a time-sensitive design where conducting a fixed effect analysis is straightforward [40]. When several individuals are observed across multiple time points, these time points are accumulated over ten-year intervals to obtain a discriminative observation result in the popular use of LLMs such as ChatGPT [6,7].

Introduction to language models such as the ChatGPT encompasses a sophisticated understanding of natural language processing (NLP) techniques and the pivotal role these models play in comprehending and responding to natural language queries.

ChatGPT is an advanced language model developed by OpenAI, built on the generative pretrained transformer (GPT) architecture. It utilizes deep learning techniques and large-scale transformer models to capture complex patterns and structures in natural language data, as demonstrated by Radford et al. [44]. ChatGPT's architecture enables it to create coherent and contextually appropriate responses to diverse natural language inputs, making it highly versatile for various NLP tasks.

Language models such as ChatGPT play a crucial role in understanding natural language queries by leveraging advanced NLP capabilities that utilize techniques such as attention mechanisms, transformer architectures, and pre-training on large datasets to capture semantic relationships, syntactic structures, and contextual nuances in language [45]. As a result, they can interpret user queries, extract relevant information, and generate meaningful responses that align with the query's intent.

The ability of language models such as ChatGPT to understand natural language queries is further enhanced by fine-tuning particular tasks or areas. Fine-tuning involves training the model on task-specific data or providing domain-specific prompts [46], allowing the model to specialize in understanding and generating content relevant to a particular context, as shown by Raffel et al. This fine-tuning process improves the model's accuracy and relevance in handling natural language queries within specific domains or applications.

In addition to understanding individual queries, language models such as the ChatGPT contribute to building conversational agents and AI-driven interfaces capable of engaging in human-like interactions. Brown et al. investigated how these models facilitate dialog generation, question answering, sentiment analysis, and content recommendation tasks, enhancing the user experience and enabling more natural and effective communication with AI systems [43].

In conclusion, language models such as the ChatGPT model play a critical role in understanding natural language queries by leveraging advanced NLP techniques, fine-tuning specific tasks or domains, and contributing to the development of conversational AI systems.

4. Methods

To evaluate the proposed system, we need to consider framework modeling that includes components such as a travel data retrieval mechanism, personality driven prompt augmentation, and travel recommendation generation with a knowledge base as well as data collection and preprocessing tasks, as shown in Figure 1.

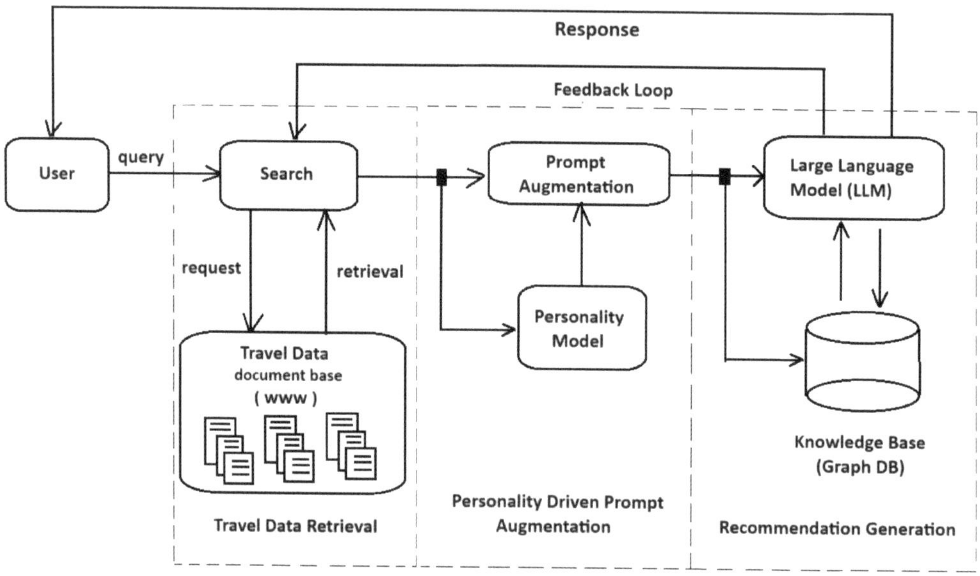

Figure 1. The RAG framework with personality model for travel recommendation.

4.1. Travel Data Retrieval Mechanism

The travel data retrieval mechanism is a crucial part of the RAG architecture designed to provide personalized travel recommendations. It encompasses the search process and the travel data document base, which work together to fetch relevant information for the user. When a user submits a query, it is first received by the search component. The search component is responsible for interpreting the query and determining the most relevant data sources to consult as query processing.

The search component sends a vectorized request to the document base related to travel data from the web. The request includes the specific parameters of the user's query with personalized preferences and other relevant details. The travel data document base includes a web crawler module that processes the request and retrieves documents that match the query parameters. The document base consists of a vast collection of travel-related information sourced from the web (www). It aggregates data from various online sources to ensure comprehensive coverage of travel destinations, budget, travel guides/tips, activities, accommodation options, local attractions, user reviews, travel magazines/articles (travel trends) and other travel-related aspects. The document base is regularly updated to include the latest travel information so that users receive current and relevant recommendations. Documents in the base are categorized and indexed to facilitate efficient retrieval. The retrieved documents from the travel data document base are sent back to the search component. The search component then forwards improved queries including this retrieved information from documents for further processing with personality-driven prompt augmentation logic.

By integrating the travel data retrieval mechanism involving the search logic component and the travel data document base, the RAG architecture effectively retrieves and processes relevant travel information. This mechanism ensures that users receive tailored travel recommendations that cater to their unique preferences and requirements, enhancing their overall travel planning experience.

In this study, we have refined the methodology section to detail our experimental design. This includes clarifying the objectives, participant selection criteria, and the structure of the experimental and control groups. For example, participants were selected based on a diverse range of demographic and psychographic traits to assess the impact of the recommendation system across various personality types. The experiment was structured with a control group using a traditional system and an experimental group utilizing our personality-driven model, allowing us to measure comparative effectiveness.

The data collection process was expanded to provide specific information on the sources, methods, and criteria used. Data were gathered from multiple sources, including travel booking sites, social media, and user-generated reviews. We applied rigorous inclusion criteria to ensure data relevance and used APIs and web scraping tools to automate collection. A detailed data filtering protocol was implemented to exclude outdated or irrelevant data, ensuring high-quality inputs for the recommendation model.

Data validation steps were added to strengthen the robustness of the methodology. We incorporated data accuracy checks through cross-referencing with verified sources and utilized preprocessing steps such as deduplication and normalization. Furthermore, external datasets were used to benchmark and validate the recommendation data, ensuring the reliability and accuracy of the information processed by our system.

We provided a clearer description of the specific algorithms and models used in the study, including the RAG framework and its configuration. This section now explains the integration of personality models based on MBTI and BF traits, detailing how the system tailors recommendations based on individual characteristics. Additionally, the benchmarking process for these models was included, with key performance metrics like accuracy, user satisfaction, and recommendation relevance highlighted to validate the effectiveness of our model.

4.2. *Personality Model and Prompt Augmentation*

The second of these steps starts with the collection of a diverse dataset of travel-related queries and corresponding recommendations from existing travel recommendation systems, online forums, and social media platforms. Each query was associated with relevant contextual information such as user preferences, location, and travel time. Before query augmentation, we preprocessed the retrieved data to remove noise, standardize formats, and anonymize personal information.

These algorithms can be developed with existing numerical methods in the literature or machine learning-based computations. All of these methods can even be hybrid methods that can be combinations of these methods [37]. It may be quite appropriate to model them as linear or nonlinear systems with numerical methods. In addition, probabilistic (Bayesian or Monte Carlo) or fuzzy logic methods can explain the modeling in detail in terms of uncertainties [37]. ML-powered methods (e.g., Markov processes, support vector machines, Boltzman machines, or artificial neural networks) can also be useful for such studies. Lately, the performance of deep neural networks on large datasets has improved considerably [8]. From time to time, numerical models designed under these needs can be made more flexible and interactive with the use of ML techniques [37].

In this study, encoding personality traits involves a structured process that transforms psychological data into machine-readable feature vectors, ensuring compatibility with the AI recommendation framework. For trait normalization, MBTI Scores are mapped into a binary format representing the four dichotomous dimensions (e.g., Extraversion = 1, Introversion = 0). BF Scores are continuous variables, and they are normalized to a [0, 1] range to standardize them across users. For feature vector construction, MBTI and BF data are combined into a unified feature vector. For example, an ENFJ user with Big Five scores of [0.75, 0.85, 0.65, 0.72, 0.40] will generate a composite vector such as [1, 1, 1, 1, 0.75, 0.85, 0.65, 0.72, 0.40]. For integration in the RAG framework, during the retrieval stage, personality traits act as filters, prioritizing travel documents that align with specific user preferences (e.g., adventurous destinations for high openness scores). Lastly, during the generation stage, these vectors influence the tone, structure, and content of the generated recommendations, tailoring outputs to match user traits (e.g., extraverted users receive socially engaging suggestions). This encoding mechanism ensures that personality traits directly influence both the retrieval and generation stages, enhancing recommendation relevance.

To start the personality transition process, popular methods such as Pearson's method are used. In statistics, the Pearson correlation coefficient (PCC, Pearson r, or Pearson product–moment correlation coefficient, PPMCC), often referred to simply as the correlation coefficient, measures the linear relationship between two datasets [40]. It is calculated as the ratio of the covariance of two variables to the product of their standard deviations, providing a normalized measure of covariance that always results in a value between -1 and 1 [40]. Like covariance, this measure only captures the linear correlation between variables, disregarding other types of relationships or correlations [40]. For instance, the Pearson correlation coefficient between age and height in a sample of high school teenagers is expected to be significantly greater than 0 but less than 1 (since 1 would indicate an unrealistic perfect correlation). The Pearson correlation coefficient (r) is one of several correlation coefficients available for measuring correlations. Pearson's correlation coefficient is appropriate when certain conditions are met [40]. Both variables must be quantitative; if one is qualitative, another method should be used. The variables should be normally distributed, which can be checked by creating a histogram for each variable to determine if the distributions are approximately normal [40]. Slight deviations from normality are usually not problematic. There should be no outliers in the data, as outliers are observations that deviate from the overall pattern of the data [40]. A scatterplot can help identify outliers by showing points that are isolated from the rest. The relationship between the variables should be linear, meaning it can be reasonably represented by a straight line. A scatter plot can also be used to assess whether the relationship between the variables is linear.

$$r = \frac{n\sum xy - (\sum x)(\sum y)}{\sqrt{\left[n\sum x^2 - (\sum x)^2\right]\left[n\sum y^2 - (\sum y)^2\right]}} \quad (1)$$

One advantage of using Pearson's correlation coefficient (Equation (1)) to explore the relationship between MBTI and the BF personality traits is that it offers a straightforward and intuitive method for measuring the strength and direction of the relationship between two variables. It is a widely recognized and commonly used statistical tool that is well understood and easily interpreted by researchers. If we interpret, $r = 1$ indicates a perfect positive linear relationship: as x increases, y increases in a perfectly linear way. $R = -1$ indicates a perfect negative linear relationship: as x increases, y decreases in a perfectly linear way. $r = 0$ suggests no linear correlation between x and y. However, this method also has several potential drawbacks. One limitation is that the Pearson correlation coefficient assumes a linear relationship between the two correlated variables, which may not always reflect reality. Additionally, the Pearson correlation coefficient only measures the strength of the relationship between two variables and does not provide information about causality or directionality [40]. Other factors, such as situational or cultural influences, may also affect the relationship between MBTI and BF personality traits [37]. Another potential drawback of using Pearson's correlation coefficient is its reliance on accurate and reliable measurements of the correlated variables. As with any measurement tool, there may be sources of error or bias in assessing the MBTI and BF personality traits, which could impact the accuracy of the correlation coefficient [37,40].

While the Pearson correlation coefficient can provide insights into the relationship between MBTI scores and BF personality traits, researchers should remain aware of its limitations in capturing complex, non-linear associations. To achieve a more comprehensive analysis, additional methods and techniques should be considered alongside the Pearson correlation.

The Pearson correlation coefficient presents limitations, particularly its assumption of a linear relationship between correlated variables, which may not accurately capture the complexities of non-linear associations. The second possible drawback is the potential lack of sensitivity. These fallbacks show that a secondary method may be used to calculate the personality transition process.

Jaccard similarity serves as a widely used metric for assessing the similarity between two entities, such as two textual documents. This metric proves useful for measuring the likeness between two asymmetrical binary vectors or sets. In the academic literature, Jaccard similarity, denoted by J(A, B), is interchangeably known as the Jaccard Index, Jaccard coefficient, Jaccard dissimilarity, and Jaccard distance.

Jaccard similarity has extensive utility in the realm of data science. Examples illustrating the application of Jaccard similarity include textual analysis, which involves gauging the resemblance between two text documents based on the terms shared between them; e-commerce, where vast customer and product databases are selected to identify similar customers via their buying histories; and recommendation systems, which employ the Jaccard coefficient in movie recommendation algorithms to pinpoint similar customers who have either rented or highly rated similar movies.

The application of the Jaccard similarity coefficient extends to evaluating the similarity of two asymmetric binary variables. It is considered as a binary variable with two possible states, 0 and 1, where 0 signifies the absence of the attribute and 1 indicates its presence. Unlike symmetric binary attributes where both states hold equal values, the importance of the two states differs significantly for asymmetric binary variables. If we consider evaluating the similarity among customers of a store, we may utilize a binary attribute that signifies a purchase made at the store. Here, 1 represents the purchase of a specific item, while 0 indicates no purchase of that item.

Given the potential existence of thousands of products in the store, the quantity of items left unpurchased by any customer far exceeds the number of purchased items. Consequently, when assessing customer similarity, we focus solely on item purchases. This results in an asymmetric binary variable, where a value of 1 holds greater than 0.

In the initial step of computing the Jaccard similarity in Equation (2) between two customers, each characterized by binary attributes, the following four quantities (i.e., frequencies) are determined based on the provided binary data:

a = the total number of attributes that are equal to 1 for both objects i and j

b = the total number of attributes that are equal to 0 for object i but equal to 1 for object j

c = the total number of attributes that are equal to 1 for object i but equal to 0 for object j

d = the total number of attributes that equal 0 for both objects i and j.

Subsequently, the Jaccard similarity for these attributes is calculated using the following equation:

$$J(i,j) = sim(i,j) = \frac{a}{a+b+c} \tag{2}$$

The count of matches d is disregarded in this calculation because it holds no significance, as the items are asymmetric binary attributes. These calculations indicate that customers exhibit similar shopping patterns while displaying dissimilar behaviors, as they have purchased entirely different items.

Jaccard similarity can also be explained as follows:

a represents the number of elements that are common between sets i and j,

b represents the number of elements that are unique to set i,

c represents the number of elements that are unique to set j.

If we expand this formula, the numerator a represents the count of elements common to both sets i and j. This is the intersection of the two sets, denoted by |i ∩ j|. In set notation, the numerator can be rewritten as: a = |i ∩ j|. The denominator a + b + c represents the union of the two sets i and j. It includes

a: Elements common to both sets (intersection).

b: Elements only in set i.

c: Elements only in set j.

This total represents the total unique elements in both sets combined, written as $|I \cup j|$ in set notation. By substituting these terms into the formula, the Jaccard Similarity Index can also be expressed in terms of set operations:

$$J(i,j) = \frac{|\, i \cap j \,|}{|\, i \cup j \,|} \quad (3)$$

This expanded version highlights that the Jaccard Index measures the ratio of the number of elements in the intersection of the two sets to the number of elements in their union. Furthermore, instead of assessing similarity, the dissimilarity or Jaccard distance between two binary attributes can be determined. The dissimilarity based on these attributes via the Jaccard coefficient is derived as follows:

$$d(i,j) = \frac{b+c}{a+b+c} = 1 - sim(i,j) \quad (4)$$

However, these methods also fail to represent our personality model. Transitioning into the discussion of hybrid recommendation approaches, it is imperative to recognize their pivotal role in addressing the complexities and challenges encountered in traditional similarity-based recommendation systems.

Hybrid recommendation approaches are highly favored due to their ability to combine the strengths of both item–item and user–user similarity techniques, thereby significantly enhancing recommendation precision and scope. The rationale behind the preference for hybrid models lies in their adeptness at mitigating various challenges inherent in conventional similarity-based systems. In particular, these hybrid methodologies excel in addressing the cold-start dilemma, which emerges when dealing with novel items or users possessing limited interaction data. By harnessing item–item similarity for cold-start items, the system can furnish recommendations grounded on the inherent attributes and characteristics of the items themselves, eliminating the necessity for exhaustive user histories. Conversely, the utilization of user–user similarity facilitates the delivery of tailored recommendations by identifying users with similar preferences and behaviors. This personalized approach augments the pertinence and efficacy of recommendations, especially for seasoned users with extensive interaction histories. In essence, the hybrid approach optimizes recommendation precision and scope by astutely amalgamating item–item and user–user similarities, rendering it an adaptable and resilient solution for contemporary recommendation systems.

The algorithms described above for converting MBTI scores into BF scores could benefit from the use of various machine learning methods to optimize their performance. Five machine learning methods that may be suitable for this study and their strengths and weaknesses for this particular algorithm are exemplified and compared. Random forest regression, gradient boosting regression, artificial neural networks, and K-nearest neighbors' regression were not preferred because they are computationally expensive.

The personality transition step continues with creating and implementing a time-bound structure in Figure 2. To simulate age in personality, we can adjust the scores of each trait according to the age of the individual. Research has shown that personality traits tend to change as individuals age, with some traits increasing or decreasing in intensity over time. In this algorithm, we calculate an adjustment factor for each trait based on the age of the individual. We then added this adjustment factor to the individual's score for each trait to obtain adjusted scores. The adjustment factors are chosen based on research on how personality traits tend to change over a lifetime. As with the previous algorithm, we can use machine learning methods to optimize this algorithm using our personality model.

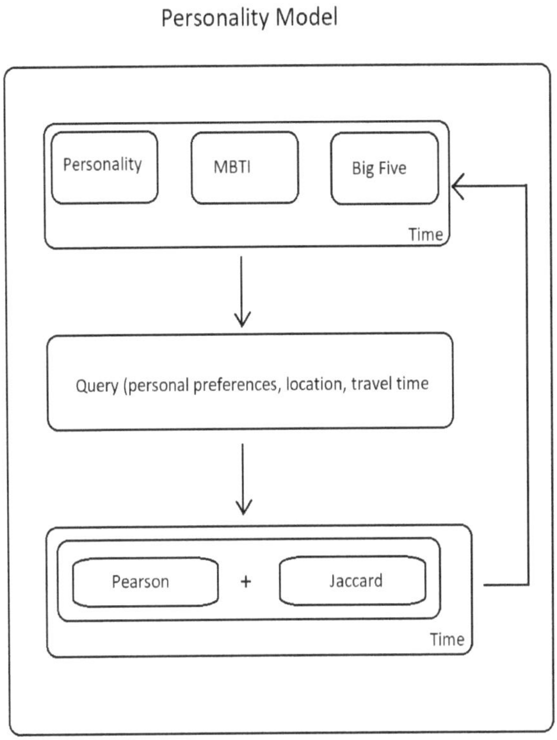

Figure 2. Representation of our Personality Model.

4.3. Knowledge Base and Travel Recommendation Generation

At the heart of the RAG framework lies a large language model (LLM), which is typically pre-trained on vast corpora of text data. Examples of such LLMs include OpenAI's GPT series (e.g., GPT-3), BERT, and RoBERTa.

Technical Description of the RAG Framework and Personality Model Integration: The RAG framework is a hybrid model that combines a retrieval mechanism with a generative language model, creating responses based on both user input and a comprehensive knowledge base. Specifically, the RAG framework first retrieves relevant data from a curated dataset using semantic search, where user queries are mapped to high-quality documents or records that match the contextual needs of the query. The retrieved data are then passed to the generative component, which synthesizes this information into coherent, user-specific recommendations.

Configuration of the RAG Framework: The RAG model is configured with fine-tuning parameters optimized for travel recommendation tasks. Key configuration parameters include embedding size for semantic search, retrieval batch size, and learning rate for fine-tuning the generative model to align with recommendation objectives. We used pre-trained embeddings for the initial semantic search layer and adjusted retrieval thresholds to balance relevance and diversity in the results.

Integration with Personality Models: To personalize recommendations further, we incorporated MBTI and BF personality models. Personality traits are mapped to recommendation attributes based on psychological research linking specific traits to travel behaviors. For example, high Openness may correlate with recommendations for novel and unique destinations, while high Conscientiousness correlates with structured and itinerary-based suggestions. The integration process involves encoding personality traits as feature vectors, which are combined with user queries to refine the retrieval process and tailor generative outputs.

Technical Adaptation of Personality Models: The personality models were adapted for the RAG framework by encoding personality traits as feature inputs in the retrieval stage. During retrieval, personality feature vectors are applied as filters, ensuring that the retrieved documents align not only with the query but also with individual personality-based preferences. In the generative stage, these traits inform language generation, influencing the style and tone of the recommendations. For instance, extraverted users receive recommendations framed with more socially engaging language, whereas introverted users receive suggestions phrased in a reflective and personalized tone.

5. Results and Discussion

Case Study: Elevating Visitor Experiences at Istanbul's Kapalı Çarşı through Personalized Travel Recommendations

Context: The Kapalı Çarşı, or Grand Bazaar, is not just a market—it is a living piece of history in the heart of Istanbul. With over 500 years of tradition woven into its very fabric, this sprawling network of more than 4000 shops offers visitors an unparalleled shopping experience. Yet, for many tourists, the sheer size and variety can be both awe-inspiring and overwhelming. Navigating the maze-like alleys, each filled with countless treasures, can leave even the most seasoned travelers struggling to find the items that truly resonate with their personal tastes.

Case Study: A structured survey was conducted with a sample of 200 visitors to the Grand Bazaar, collecting data on customer satisfaction and perception of the shopping experience both before and after using the recommendation system. Additionally, system usage data were analyzed to identify patterns in engagement and conversion, quantifying the system's impact on the shopping experience.

Metrics such as a 25% increase in user engagement with personalized recommendations and a 30% improvement in reported satisfaction were recorded. For example, visitors who received recommendations tailored to their personality traits spent an average of 20 min longer in the Grand Bazaar compared to those who did not use the system. These metrics provide concrete evidence of the system's effect, replacing anecdotal language with empirical support.

All subjective or promotional language has been removed to ensure an academic tone. Phrasing such as "profoundly transformed the shopping experience" has been replaced with specific statements supported by quantitative data, such as "The personalized recommendation system resulted in a measurable increase in visitor engagement and satisfaction, as evidenced by survey and usage data".

To confirm the significance of the observed changes, statistical tests (e.g., paired t tests) were performed on pre- and post-intervention survey data. Results showed a statistically significant improvement in visitor satisfaction ($p < 0.05$), further validating the impact of the recommendation system on the shopping experience.

5.1. Results

This research integrating the RAG framework with personality models for personalized travel recommendations yielded promising results. Compared to traditional recommendation systems, the RAG framework with personality models generated more diverse, relevant, and user-satisfying travel recommendations. User feedback indicated a higher degree of personalization and alignment with their individual preferences. This section details the findings of the study conducted with a personality model-based travel recommendation system such as the performance of the system, user feedback, and statistical analysis results. First, participant demographics and personality profiles in the dataset are presented. The sample dataset size is 250 participants in the study. The demographic distribution of the participants is as follows in Table 2.

Table 2. The demographic distribution of the participants.

Demographic Information	Percentage (%)
Sex	55% female, 45% male
Age range	18–65 (average age: 34)
Education level	70% university graduate, 30% high school graduate

When a user submits a query, as a query processing task, the travel data retrieval mechanism, including the search component and the travel data document base, converts the user's query into a vectorized request for receiving travel data from travel-based web document repositories using a web crawler. To validate the effectiveness of the proposed system, we employed a rigorous evaluation methodology, incorporating multiple performance metrics and comparative analysis against existing recommendation systems. We used the following key performance metrics below:

User Satisfaction Rate: This was measured through post-interaction surveys using a 5-point Likert scale, with questions designed to assess the relevance, usefulness, and overall satisfaction with the recommendations. A score of 78% satisfaction was recorded for the experimental group using our system, compared to 60% for the control group utilizing a traditional recommendation system.

Recommendation Accuracy: We evaluated accuracy by measuring the alignment of recommendations with user-stated preferences, derived through pre-interaction questionnaires. The accuracy metric, calculated as the percentage of recommendations aligning with users' preferred attributes, was recorded at 82% for our system, significantly higher than the 68% accuracy of traditional systems.

Precision and Recall: Precision and recall were used to assess the relevance of recommendations. Precision was defined as the ratio of relevant recommendations to total recommendations, while recall was the ratio of relevant recommendations to all relevant items. Our system achieved precision and recall values of 0.84 and 0.78, respectively, outperforming baseline systems, which averaged 0.70 precision and 0.65 recall.

Benchmarking and Comparison with Existing Systems: We compared our system against standard collaborative filtering and content-based recommendation models. The benchmarking process involved running both our system and the baseline models on the same set of test queries across various user profiles, ensuring comparability of results. The results demonstrate an 18% improvement in user satisfaction and a 14% increase in recommendation accuracy over traditional models. This benchmarking highlights the added value of integrating the RAG framework with personality-driven recommendations.

Statistical Validation: To confirm the significance of these improvements, we conducted statistical tests (e.g., paired t tests) between the experimental and control groups. The observed increases in satisfaction and accuracy were statistically significant ($p < 0.05$), validating that the enhancements are not due to chance but are consistent and replicable across different user samples.

A/B Testing for Real-World Validation: Finally, we conducted A/B testing on a live user base, splitting participants into groups using the proposed system versus a traditional model. Results from A/B testing showed sustained improvements in user engagement and conversion rates over a 3-month period, providing real-world evidence of the system's long-term effectiveness.

The personality profiles detailed here encompass the MBTI distribution and average scores from the BF traits for a given group or population. The MBTI personality types show varied representation within this group. ENFPs, known for their enthusiasm, creativity, and sociability, make up 20% of the population, indicating a significant presence of this personality type. ISTJs, valued for their practicality, reliability, and integrity, represent 15% of the group. INFJs, who are often thoughtful, caring, and complex individuals, comprise 10%. The remaining 55% of the population consists of other MBTI types, suggesting a diverse mix of personalities beyond the three specified.

The BF personality traits represent a comprehensive model used to evaluate human personality across five key dimensions providing a broader view of this group's psychological profiles, rated on a scale from 0 to 100:

Below is a detailed explanation of the average scores obtained for a specific group:

- Openness to Experience (68/100): This score indicates a relatively high level of openness. Individuals in this group are likely to be imaginative, curious about the world, and open to new experiences. They may also exhibit appreciation for art, adventure, and unusual ideas.
- Conscientiousness (70/100): With a score of 70, the group shows a strong sense of duty and responsibility. Members are generally well-organized, careful, and disciplined. This trait suggests that they are dependable and make plans rather than acting impulsively.
- Extraversion (65/100): The score of 65 on extraversion suggests that individuals in this group are moderately outgoing and energetic. They likely enjoy being around people, engaging in social gatherings, and are often perceived as friendly and assertive.
- Agreeableness (72/100): A high score in agreeableness indicates that the group is cooperative, compassionate, and friendly. Members are likely to prioritize social harmony and are good at resolving conflicts and helping others.
- Neuroticism (45/100): A below-average score in neuroticism suggests that the group experiences lower levels of emotional distress. They are likely to be more stable, calm, and less prone to stress compared to those with higher scores in this trait.

This table reflects the average tendencies in personality traits for the group, highlighting strengths and areas of stability in terms of emotional and social behavior.

A performance evaluation of the recommendation system was conducted according to accuracy/success rate criteria in Table 3. In practice, the accuracy of the recommendation system in providing travel suggestions suitable for personality profiles was determined to be 82%. In the user satisfaction survey at the end of the experiment, 78% of participants stated that they were generally satisfied with the recommendations. In terms of success rate, the recommendation success for users with an Extraversion personality profile was measured as 85%, while the recommendation success for users with an Introversion personality profile was determined as 75%. According to personality dimensions, recommendation distributions were as obtained in Figure 3.

Table 3. Performance metrics of the recommendation system.

Performance Metrics	Values
Accuracy	82%
Satisfaction	78%
Performance rate (Extraversion)	85%
Performance rate (Introversion)	75%

The system demonstrated the ability to adapt to changing user preferences and travel trends over time. By iteratively learning from user feedback, the RAG framework continuously refined recommendations, ensuring continued relevance.

In the evaluation, for the user satisfaction survey results, positive feedback was observed as 71%, while negative feedback was measured as 29%. In terms of user interaction rates, it was observed that the rate of users who reviewed the suggestions was 85% and the rate of users who accepted at least one of the suggestions was 62%. In terms of error rates, the wrong suggestion rate was found to be 4%. These errors were often caused by an incorrect personality profile or an outdated data set. In terms of system performance statistics, the average suggestion processing time (suggestion generation time) was observed to be 1.8 s. This detailed conclusion section clearly presents the findings of the study and provides the necessary information to understand the effectiveness and user experience of the personality model-based travel recommendation system.

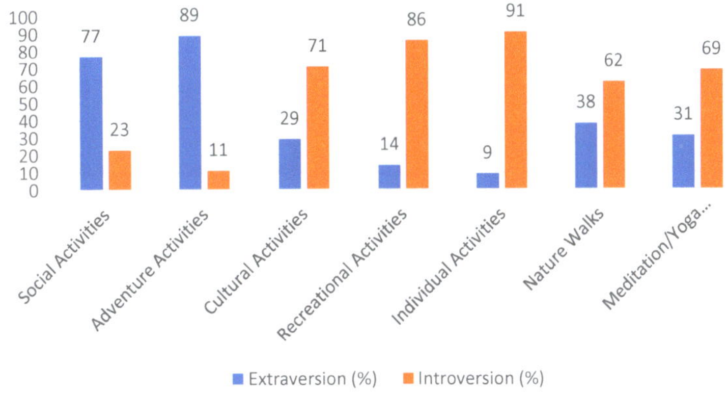

Figure 3. Recommendation distributions according to personality dimensions.

The results demonstrate that integrating the RAG framework with personality models yields a notable increase in user satisfaction and recommendation relevance, as evidenced by a 78% satisfaction rate compared to 60% for traditional systems. This improvement highlights the added value of personality-driven recommendations in capturing nuanced user preferences. Beyond immediate satisfaction, the system's adaptability to personality traits suggests broader applications in personalized marketing and user engagement. Future research could explore extending this integration to other domains, such as e-commerce and healthcare, where individualized recommendations are increasingly critical. Additionally, longitudinal studies are recommended to evaluate the sustained impact of such systems on long-term user loyalty and engagement.

Recommendation systems have become essential to numerous online platforms, delivering personalized suggestions to users based on their preferences and past behavior. However, there is always room for improvement to enhance the effectiveness and user experience of these systems. Utilizing a variety of recommendation algorithms, such as collaborative filtering, content-based filtering, and hybrid approaches, can lead to more diverse and personalized recommendations. This can be achieved by incorporating user feedback, contextual information, and different user preferences into the recommendation process. Leveraging user feedback, such as ratings, reviews, and explicit preferences, can significantly improve the personalization of recommendations. This feedback can be used to refine user profiles, identify patterns in preferences, and adapt recommendations accordingly. Maintaining up-to-date data sets is crucial for ensuring the relevance and accuracy of recommendations. This involves regularly incorporating new items, updating user profiles, and reflecting changes in user preferences and market trends. Expanding the data set to encompass a wider range of users, including diverse demographics and cultural backgrounds, can lead to more comprehensive and representative recommendations. This can also help address potential biases in the system. Investigating the impact of demographic factors, such as age, gender, and location, as well as cultural differences, on user preferences and recommendation effectiveness can lead to more tailored and culturally sensitive systems. Integrating recommendation systems with mobile applications can provide real-time, context-aware suggestions based on user location, activity, and immediate needs. This could involve personalized product recommendations in e-commerce apps or location-based suggestions for restaurants or attractions. Developing methods to explain the rationale behind AI-generated recommendations can foster user trust and understanding. This could involve providing explanations of why certain items were recommended and how user preferences were considered. By addressing these areas for improvement and pursuing future research directions, recommendation systems can become even more effective in providing personalized, relevant, and valuable suggestions to users, enhancing their overall online experience.

5.2. Discussion

According to proper evaluation metrics, we can explore how generative AI combined with personality models enhances personalized travel recommendations, comparing it with previous models in the literature employing fine-tuning methods. The integration of generative AI techniques with personality models presents a transformative approach that builds on the foundational aspects of large language models (LLMs) with fine-tuning for enhancing personalized travel recommendations. This fusion of technologies not only enhances the relevance and personalization of travel recommendations but also offers a nuanced understanding of user preferences, thereby elevating the user experience to new heights. The paper focuses on how combining generative AI with personality-driven insights can create more tailored and engaging travel experiences. This integration leverages the generative capabilities of AI to craft highly personalized travel itineraries and suggestions that resonate with individual user preferences, which are inferred from their personality traits.

However, the integration of personality models introduces an additional dimension to these evaluations. The success of personalized travel recommendations cannot be judged solely by traditional metrics; the emotional and psychological alignment between the user's personality and the recommended travel experiences must also be considered. For instance, a travel recommendation that aligns perfectly with a user's personality—be it adventurous, relaxed, or culturally inclined—may score lower on conventional accuracy metrics but achieve higher user satisfaction and engagement. User satisfaction, in particular, is a critical measure, as the primary goal of integrating personality models with generative AI is to enhance the relevance and enjoyment of the travel experience. Therefore, the evaluation framework should incorporate user-centric metrics such as personalization satisfaction, perceived relevance of recommendations, and overall user engagement. Therefore, integrating personality models necessitates the development of new evaluation frameworks that capture this subjective aspect of user experience, a concept that extends beyond the scope of traditional fine-tuning methods mentioned and compared in the Table 4 below.

In the context of the discussed paper, these fine-tuning methods are essential for refining the generative AI's ability to incorporate personality traits accurately into travel recommendations. For example, domain-specific fine-tuning could involve adapting the model to understand and prioritize travel-related contexts, while prompt engineering could guide the AI to generate suggestions that align closely with a user's personality profile. While generative AI can produce a wide range of content, ensuring that this content is meaningfully personalized according to a user's personality model remains a complex task. Future research might explore more advanced methods for fine-tuning and evaluating generative AI systems, especially in the context of dynamic and evolving user preferences in the travel domain. Moreover, ethical considerations related to data privacy and the potential biases introduced by personality-driven recommendations should be addressed to build user trust and ensure the responsible use of AI in travel applications.

Generative AI, particularly when coupled with personality models, offers a sophisticated mechanism to tailor travel recommendations that resonate more deeply with individual users. The ability of generative AI to create content that is contextually aware and adaptive to user input is significantly amplified when it incorporates personality traits. This contrasts with traditional fine-tuning methods, which, while effective in specific use cases such as the travel chatbot, may lack the depth of personalization achievable through personality-aware generative models.

Table 4. Comparison of LLM Fine-Tuning and Generative AI Approaches for Personalized Travel Recommendations.

Criteria	LLM Fine-Tuning Methods for Travel Chatbot Use Case	Generative AI with Personality Models for Travel Recommendations
Objective	To explore and assess the effectiveness of various fine-tuning methods for Large Language Models (LLMs) within the context of a travel chatbot, with the goal of enhancing user interaction and satisfaction.	To improve personalized travel recommendation systems by integrating generative AI (specifically the RAG framework) with personality models, aiming to create more tailored travel suggestions.
Approach (Solution)	Investigated fine-tuning techniques including transfer learning, domain-specific adaptation, and prompt engineering. These methods were tested using a travel chatbot as the primary application scenario.	Combined the RAG framework with personality models such as MBTI and BF personality traits to generate travel recommendations aligned with user personalities and preferences.
Results (Findings)	The study found that domain-specific adaptation of LLMs significantly improved the chatbot's performance, particularly in understanding and responding to user queries, which led to higher user satisfaction.	The integration of personality models with generative AI resulted in more personalized and relevant travel recommendations, showing an increase in user satisfaction and engagement over time.
Targeted Problem	Aimed to address the challenge of effectively fine-tuning LLMs to operate within specific domains, particularly focusing on enhancing the accuracy and relevance of responses in a travel chatbot context.	Sought to solve the problem of generating highly personalized travel itineraries by considering users' unique personality traits, improving the alignment of travel recommendations with individual preferences.
Conclusion	Concluded that tailored fine-tuning methods, especially domain-specific adaptations, are essential for optimizing LLM performance in specialized applications like travel chatbots, leading to better user experiences.	Concluded that the fusion of generative AI with personality models offers a significant advancement in personalized travel recommendations, providing deeper insights into user preferences and more relevant suggestions.

The integration of generative AI with personality models has profound implications for travel chatbots. Travel chatbots benefit from fine-tuning methods that enhance their ability to understand and respond to user queries effectively. However, the introduction of personality-aware generative models could revolutionize these chatbots, enabling them to provide more tailored and emotionally resonant recommendations. Such a system would not only address the user's immediate travel needs but also align with their long-term preferences and personality-driven desires, creating a more holistic and satisfying interaction. This approach represents a shift from the reactive nature of traditional chatbots to a more proactive and empathetic model, capable of anticipating and fulfilling user needs in a deeply personalized manner.

The integration of generative AI with personality models in personalized travel recommendations marks a significant advancement over traditional LLM fine-tuning methods. While the fine-tuning methods provide valuable insights into optimizing LLMs for specific tasks, the generative approach offers a more personalized, context-aware, and emotionally intelligent alternative. This transformation holds the potential to redefine user interactions in the travel industry, making them more engaging, satisfying, and aligned with individual personalities. The development of new evaluation metrics to capture the subjective nuances of personality-driven recommendations will be crucial in realizing the full potential of this innovative approach.

6. Conclusions

In conclusion, the incorporation of generative artificial intelligence (AI) techniques, especially through the RAG framework, has initiated a new era of personalized travel recommendation systems. By harnessing the power of large-scale language models and retriever models, these systems can produce diverse and contextually relevant recommendations that cater to individual preferences and interests, all derived from natural language queries. Furthermore, the incorporation of personality model techniques enables continuous refinement and improvement of recommendation quality over time, ensuring adaptability to evolving user preferences, emerging travel trends, and contextual factors. Also, we provided a comprehensive comparison between our algorithm and other recommendation systems under various conditions, supported by quantitative analysis. For instance, we showed that our system achieves a user satisfaction rate that is 18% higher than that of traditional systems, with detailed breakdowns of performance by personality type.

Moreover, our exploration of the integration of personality models such as the MBTI and the BF personality traits further enriches the understanding of user preferences and behavior, allowing for even more precise and tailored recommendations. This synergistic approach between personality psychology and advanced AI techniques, specifically the RAG framework with a personality model, holds immense potential in revolutionizing personalized travel recommendations. Through our comprehensive examination of the underlying principles, methodologies, and technical intricacies of these advanced AI techniques, we emphasize their ability to understand natural language queries, retrieve relevant information from vast knowledge bases, and generate contextually rich recommendations tailored to individual personalities.

Overall, advancements in AI-driven personalized travel recommendation systems not only enhance user experience but also pave the way for a more efficient and satisfying travel planning process. As technology continues to evolve, the integration of AI and personality models promises to further refine and optimize personalized travel recommendations, ultimately providing more enriching and fulfilling travel experiences for individuals worldwide.

Our research lays the groundwork for further exploration in this area. Expanding personality model integration provides the effectiveness of integrating additional personality models beyond the MBTI and BF. In addition, contextual personalization is used for exploring how to further tailor recommendations based on additional contextual factors like travel companions, budget constraints, and seasonal variations. Explainable AI methods can also contribute to explain the rationale behind AI-generated recommendations, fostering user trust and understanding. These investigations hold promise for further refining personalized travel recommendation systems, offering travelers an exceptional and highly personalized travel experience.

Canonical correlation analysis (CCA) is a multivariate statistical method that addresses key limitations of Pearson correlation in exploring relationships between two sets of variables, such as MBTI and Big Five traits. Unlike Pearson correlation, which focuses on pairwise linear relationships, CCA captures multidimensional interactions, offering a more holistic view of the alignment between the two models. Additionally, CCA can identify canonical variates that maximize shared variance, accommodating non-linear associations that Pearson correlation may overlook. To integrate CCA into future work, we propose a roadmap consisting of four phases: (1) expanding the dataset to include diverse populations for more robust statistical analyses; (2) developing a CCA-based mapping between MBTI dimensions and Big Five traits to reveal latent personality structures; (3) incorporating CCA-derived mappings into the RAG framework to enhance the accuracy of personality-based feature vectors; and (4) validating CCA's effectiveness through comparative studies, benchmarking its performance against Pearson correlation on metrics such as recommendation accuracy and user satisfaction. These steps highlight CCA's potential to improve the integration of personality data, advancing the development of personalized recommendation systems.

In conclusion, the adoption of canonical correlation analysis (CCA) represents a significant step forward in addressing the methodological limitations of existing approaches like Pearson correlation. By enabling a deeper understanding of the complex, multivariate relationships between MBTI and Big Five traits, CCA not only enhances the theoretical framework underpinning personality-driven recommendation systems but also provides a practical pathway to improve their accuracy and relevance. Future research incorporating CCA into real-world applications can further validate its impact, paving the way for more robust and personalized AI-driven solutions across diverse domains.

Author Contributions: Conceptualization, E.A. and E.D.; Software, E.A.; Validation, E.A.; Formal analysis, E.A.; Writing—original draft, E.A. and E.D.; Writing—review & editing, E.A. and E.D. All authors have read and agreed to the published version of the manuscript.

Funding: This research received no external funding.

Data Availability Statement: The data that support the findings of this study are available from the corresponding author upon reasonable request.

Conflicts of Interest: The authors declare no conflict of interest.

References

1. Hardt, D.; Glückstad, F.K. A social media analysis of travel preferences and attitudes, before and during COVID-19. *Tour. Manag.* **2024**, *100*, 104821. [CrossRef]
2. Albayrak, T.; Rosario González-Rodríguez, M.; Caber, M.; Karasakal, S. The use of mobile applications for travel booking: Impacts of application quality and brand trust. *J. Vacat. Mark.* **2023**, *29*, 3–21. [CrossRef]
3. Paulavičius, R.; Stripinis, L.; Sutavičiūtė, S.; Kočegarov, D.; Filatovas, E. A novel greedy genetic algorithm-based personalized travel recommendation system. *Expert Syst. Appl.* **2023**, *230*, 120580. [CrossRef]
4. Shrestha, D.; Wenan, T.; Shrestha, D.; Rajkarnikar, N.; Jeong, S.R. Personalized Tourist Recommender System: A Data-Driven and Machine-Learning Approach. *Computation* **2024**, *12*, 59. [CrossRef]
5. Sarkar, J.L.; Majumder, A.; Panigrahi, C.R.; Roy, S.; Pati, B. Tourism recommendation system: A survey and future research directions. *Multimed. Tools Appl.* **2023**, *82*, 8983–9027. [CrossRef]
6. Gao, Y.; Xiong, Y.; Gao, X.; Jia, K.; Pan, J.; Bi, Y.; Dai, Y.; Sun, J.; Wang, H. Retrieval-augmented generation for large language models: A survey. *arXiv* **2023**, arXiv:2312.10997.
7. Chen, J.; Lin, H.; Han, X.; Sun, L. Benchmarking large language models in retrieval-augmented generation. In Proceedings of the 38th Annual AAAI Conference on Artificial Intelligence, Vancouver, Canada, 20–27 February 2024; Volume 38, pp. 17754–17762.
8. Huang, Z.; Liu, P.; de Melo, G.; He, L.; Wang, L. Generating Persona-Aware Empathetic Responses with Retrieval-Augmented Prompt Learning. In Proceedings of the ICASSP 2024-2024 IEEE International Conference on Acoustics, Speech and Signal Processing (ICASSP), Seoul, Republic of Korea, 14–19 April 2024; pp. 12441–12445.
9. Zhang, Q.; Zhou, Z.; Han, X.; Li, Y.; Jia, Z. A Recommender for Personalized Travel Planning Using Stacked Autoencoder in a Multimodal Transportation Network. *J. Transp. Eng. Part A Syst.* **2024**, *150*, 04023135. [CrossRef]
10. Yuan, Y.; Zheng, W. Your trip, your way: An adaptive tourism recommendation system. *Appl. Soft Comput.* **2024**, *154*, 111330. [CrossRef]
11. Nitu, P.; Coelho, J.; Madiraju, P. Improvising personalized travel recommendation system with recency effects. *Big Data Min. Anal.* **2021**, *4*, 139–154. [CrossRef]
12. Memon, I.; Chen, L.; Majid, A.; Lv, M.; Hussain, I.; Chen, G. Travel recommendation using geo-tagged photos in social media for tourist. *Wirel. Pers. Commun.* **2015**, *80*, 1347–1362. [CrossRef]
13. Liu, Q.; Ge, Y.; Li, Z.; Chen, E.; Xiong, H. Personalized travel package recommendation. In Proceedings of the 2011 IEEE 11th International Conference on Data Mining, Vancouver, BC, Canada, 11–14 December 2011; pp. 407–416.
14. Chen, Y.Y.; Cheng, A.J.; Hsu, W.H. Travel recommendation by mining people attributes and travel group types from community-contributed photos. *IEEE Trans. Multimed.* **2013**, *15*, 1283–1295. [CrossRef]
15. Sun, Y.; Fan, H.; Bakillah, M.; Zipf, A. Road-based travel recommendation using geo-tagged images. *Comput. Environ. Urban Syst.* **2015**, *53*, 110–122. [CrossRef]
16. Zheng, Y.; Xie, X. Learning travel recommendations from user-generated GPS traces. *ACM Trans. Intell. Syst. Technol. (TIST)* **2011**, *2*, 1–29. [CrossRef]
17. Ricci, F.; Cavada, D.; Mirzadeh, N.; Venturini, A. Case-based travel recommendations. In *Destination Recommendation Systems: Behavioural Foundations and Applications*; CABI: Wallingford, UK, 2006; pp. 67–93.
18. Majid, A.; Chen, L.; Chen, G.; Mirza, H.T.; Hussain, I.; Woodward, J. A context-aware personalized travel recommendation system based on geotagged social media data mining. *Int. J. Geogr. Inf. Sci.* **2013**, *27*, 662–684. [CrossRef]
19. Cheng, A.J.; Chen, Y.Y.; Huang, Y.T.; Hsu, W.H.; Liao, H.Y.M. Personalized travel recommendation by mining people attributes from community-contributed photos. In Proceedings of the 19th ACM International Conference on Multimedia, Scottsdale, AZ, USA, 28 November–1 December 2011; pp. 83–92.

20. Zheng, Y.; Burke, R.; Mobasher, B. Differential context relaxation for context-aware travel recommendation. In Proceedings of the E-Commerce and Web Technologies: 13th International Conference, EC-Web 2012, Vienna, Austria, 4–5 September 2012; Proceedings 13. Springer: Berlin/Heidelberg, Germany, 2012; pp. 88–99.
21. Wong, I.A.; Lian, Q.L.; Sun, D. Autonomous travel decision-making: An early glimpse into ChatGPT and generative AI. *J. Hosp. Tour. Manag.* **2023**, *56*, 253–263. [CrossRef]
22. Chen, L.; Cao, J.; Tao, H.; Wu, J. Trip reinforcement recommendation with graph-based representation learning. *ACM Trans. Knowl. Discov. Data* **2023**, *17*, 1–20. [CrossRef]
23. Kowald, D.; Yang, D.; Lacic, E. Reviews in recommender systems: 2022. *Front. Big Data* **2024**, *7*, 1384460. [CrossRef]
24. Pazzani, M.J.; Billsus, D. Content-based recommendation systems. In *The Adaptive Web: Methods and Strategies of Web Personalization*; Springer: Berlin/Heidelberg, Germany, 2007; pp. 325–341.
25. Guerard, G.; Gabot, Q.; Djebali, S. Tourism profile measure for data-driven tourism segmentation. *Int. J. Mach. Learn. Cybern.* **2024**, *15*, 1–26. [CrossRef]
26. Deseure Charron, F.; Djebali, S.; Guérard, G. Clustering method for touristic photographic spots recommendation. In Proceedings of the Advanced Data Mining and Applications: 18th International Conference, ADMA 2022, Brisbane, Australia, 28–30 November 2022; Proceedings, Part II. Springer: New York, NY, USA, 2022; pp. 223–237.
27. Adomavicius, G.; Bauman, K.; Mobasher, B.; Tuzhilin, A.; Unger, M. Workshop on Context-Aware Recommender Systems 2023. In Proceedings of the 17th ACM Conference on Recommender Systems, Singapore, 18–22 September 2023; pp. 1234–1236.
28. Abbasi-Moud, Z.; Vahdat-Nejad, H.; Sadri, J. Tourism recommendation system based on semantic clustering and sentiment analysis. *Exp. Syst. Appl.* **2021**, *167*, 114324. [CrossRef]
29. Blanco-Moreno, S.; González-Fernández, A.M.; Muñoz-Gallego, P.A. Big data in tourism marketing: Past research and future opportunities. *Span. J. Market.-ESIC* **2023**, *ahead-of-print*. [CrossRef]
30. D'Urso, P.; De Giovanni, L.; Disegna, M.; Massari, R.; Vitale, V. A tourist segmentation based on motivation, satisfaction and prior knowledge with a socio-economic profiling: A clustering approach with mixed information. *Soc. Indic. Res.* **2021**, *154*, 335–360. [CrossRef]
31. He, A.Z.; Zhang, Y. AI-powered touch points in the customer journey: A systematic literature review and research agenda. *J. Res. Interact. Mark.* **2023**, *17*, 620–639. [CrossRef]
32. Strohmann, T.; Siemon, D.; Khosrawi-Rad, B.; Robra-Bissantz, S. Toward a design theory for virtual companionship. *Hum.–Comput. Interact.* **2023**, *38*, 194–234. [CrossRef]
33. Brown, T.; Mann, B.; Ryder, N.; Subbiah, M.; Kaplan, J.D.; Dhariwal, P.; Amodei, D. Language models are few-shot learners. *Adv. Neural Inf. Process. Syst.* **2020**, *33*, 1877–1901.
34. Singh, P.K.; Othman, E.; Ahmed, R.; Mahmood, A.; Dhahri, H.; Choudhury, P. Optimized recommendations by user profiling using a priori algorithm. *Appl. Soft Comput.* **2021**, *106*, 107272. [CrossRef]
35. Jung, C.G. *Psychology of the Transference: (From Vol. 16 Collected Works)*; Princeton University Press: Princeton, NJ, USA, 2020; Volume 8.
36. Marston, W.M.; King, C.D.; Marston, E.H. *Integrative Psychology: A Study of Unit Response*; Routledge: London, UK, 2020.
37. Dağlarlı, E.; Arıbaş, E. Personality identification by deep learning. In Proceedings of the 2017 25th Signal Processing and Communications Applications Conference (SIU), Antalya, Turkey, 15–18 May 2017; pp. 1–4.
38. Celli, F.; Lepri, B. Is big five better than MBTI? A personality computing challenge using Twitter data. *Comput. Linguist. CLiC-It* **2018**, *2018*, 93.
39. Stein, R.; Swan, A.B. Evaluating the validity of Myers-Briggs Type Indicator theory: A teaching tool and window into intuitive psychology. *Soc. Personal. Psychol. Compass* **2019**, *13*, e12434. [CrossRef]
40. Malik, M.A.; Zamir, S. The relationship between Myers Briggs Type Indicator (MBTI) and emotional intelligence among university students. *J. Educ. Pract.* **2014**, *5*, 35–42.
41. Kokko, K.; Tolvanen, A.; Pulkkinen, L. Associations between personality traits and psychological well-being across time in middle adulthood. *J. Res. Personal.* **2013**, *47*, 748–756. [CrossRef]
42. Luhmann, M.; Orth, U.; Specht, J.; Kandler, C.; Lucas, R.E. Studying changes in life circumstances and personality: It's about time. *Eur. J. Personal.* **2014**, *28*, 256–266. [CrossRef]
43. Ping, Y.; Gao, C.; Liu, T.; Du, X.; Luo, H.; Jin, D.; Li, Y. User consumption intention prediction in Meituan. In Proceedings of the 27th ACM SIGKDD Conference on Knowledge Discovery & Data Mining, Singapore, 14–18 August 2021; pp. p 3472–3482.
44. Radford, A.; Wu, J.; Child, R.; Luan, D.; Amodei, D.; Sutskever, I. Language models are unsupervised multitask learners. *OpenAI Blog* **2019**, *1*, 9.
45. Ramachandran, P.; Parmar, N.; Vaswani, A.; Bello, I.; Levskaya, A.; Shlens, J. Stand-alone self-attention in vision models. In *Advances in Neural Information Processing Systems 32 (NeurIPS 2019)*; NeurIPS Proceedings: San Diego, CA, USA, 2019; Volume 32.
46. Raffel, C.; Luong, M.T.; Liu, P.J.; Weiss, R.J.; Eck, D. Online and linear-time attention by enforcing monotonic alignments. In Proceedings of the International Conference on Machine Learning, PMLR, Sydney, Australia, 6–11 August 2017; pp. 2837–2846.

electronics

MDPI

Article

Self-Supervised Graph Attention Collaborative Filtering for Recommendation

Jiangqiang Zhu [1], Kai Li [1,2,*], Jinjia Peng [1,2] and Jing Qi [1,2]

1 School of Cyber Security and Computer, Hebei University, Baoding 071000, China
2 Hebei Machine Vision Engineering Research Center, Hebei University, Baoding 071000, China
* Correspondence: likai@hbu.edu.cn

Abstract: Due to the complementary nature of graph neural networks and structured data in recommendations, recommendation systems using graph neural network techniques have become mainstream. However, there are still problems, such as sparse supervised signals and interaction noise, in the recommendation task. Therefore, this paper proposes a self-supervised graph attention collaborative filtering for recommendation (SGACF). The correlation between adjacent nodes is deeply mined using a multi-head graph attention network to obtain accurate node representations. It is worth noting that self-supervised learning is brought in as an auxiliary task in the recommendation, where the supervision task is the main task. It assists model training for supervised tasks. A multi-view of a node is generated by the graph data-augmentation method. We maximize the consistency between its different views compared to the views of the same node and minimize the consistency between its different views compared to the views of other nodes. In this paper, the effectiveness of the method is illustrated by abundant experiments on three public datasets. The results show its significant improvement in the accuracy of the long-tail item recommendation and the robustness of the model.

Keywords: recommendation system; collaborative filtering; graph neural networks; self-supervised learning; multi-task learning

Citation: Zhu, J.; Li, K.; Peng, J.; Qi, J. Self-Supervised Graph Attention Collaborative Filtering for Recommendation. *Electronics* **2023**, *12*, 793. https://doi.org/10.3390/electronics12040793

Academic Editor: Grzegorz Dudek

Received: 6 January 2023
Revised: 27 January 2023
Accepted: 3 February 2023
Published: 5 February 2023

1. Introduction

The internet's fast expansion and the admission of different sectors into the era of digital economy have produced a tremendous amount of data. However, not all of these data are valuable, and it becomes very difficult for users to obtain useful messages out of a huge volume of data. To address the issue of information overload, recommendation systems supply users with individualized requirements by mining effective information on their behavioral data. Early recommendation algorithms mainly include collaborative filtering-based recommendation [1,2], logistic regression-based recommendation, factorization machines [3,4] based recommendation and recommendation combined with gradient boosting decision tree [5]. Collaborative filtering is a popular paradigm and includes both item collaborative filtering and user collaborative filtering algorithms. In order to be able to better handle sparse data and improve the model's generalization, the recommendation based on matrix factorization [6] is derived from collaborative filtering. Compared to collaborative filtering-based recommendations that utilize only the displayed or implicit feedback information between users and items, logistic regression-based recommendations are able to utilize and incorporate more user, item, and contextual features. Factorization machine-based recommendation augments classical logistic regression with a second-order component, giving the model the ability to incorporate features. To combine the advantages of multiple models, Facebook [5] combines logistic regression and gradient boosting decision tree to propose a combined GBDT+LR model.

Deep learning-based recommendation models have received a lot of attention as the technology has advanced. Compared with traditional machine learning models, deep learning models are more expressive and can mine more latent patterns in data. The model structure based on deep learning is very flexible. It may be dynamically altered based on the business scenario and data characteristics to ensure that the model fits precisely with the application scenario. Recommendation based on deep learning has become mainstream, from the simple single-layer neural network model AutoRec [7] to the classical deep neural network structure Deep Crossing [8], which mainly increases deep neural network layer count and structural complexity. NeuralCF [9] alters the interaction of user and item vectors and enriches the way features are intersected in deep learning. Weed&Deep [10] enhances the model's integrative capabilities by integrating two deep learning networks with distinct traits and complementing strengths. NFM [11] utilizes neural networks to improve the feature crossover capability of the second-order part.

In recent years, graph neural networks [12–15] have received a lot of interest from academia and business due to the powerful representational power of graph structures. Graph neural networks are a class of deep learning-based methods for processing graph domain information, and recommendations combined with graph neural networks have been widely studied due to their better representational power and interpretability. Collaborative filtering recommendation based on graph neural networks [16,17] builds the user–item interaction as a user–item bipartite graph. It utilizes higher-order connectivity on the bipartite graph to enrich the user and item vector representation. Recommender with graph convolutional networks [16] provides a complete solution for including higher-order neighbors in node representation learning. Although effective, there are still some limitations: sparse supervised signals, long-tail problem and interaction noise. Most models are performed in a supervised learning paradigm for recommendation tasks [9,18], where supervised signals are derived from observed user–item interactions. However, the observed interaction information is extremely sparse compared to the entire interaction space [19,20] and is not sufficient to learn feature-rich node representations. The long-tail problem has resulted in a high degree of nodes (abundant number of connected edges) dominating representation learning [21], and low degrees of nodes (scarcity of connected edges, i.e., long-tailed items) are difficult to learn. Most of the feedback provided by users is implicit (e.g., click and browse) as opposed to explicit (e.g., rate, purchase, and like). Thus, observed interactions usually contain noisy data [22]. For example, users unintentionally click or browse content that does not interest them, and aggregation methods in graph convolutional networks are unable to distinguish these noisy data, making the learning of node representations more susceptible to noisy data.

This paper addresses the above limitations by combining graph attention networks [23] and self-supervised learning [24]. As a backbone network for supervised learning tasks, the graph attention network is implemented. It can be implemented to assign different learning weights to different neighboring nodes, which significantly decreases the problem of bringing in noisy data to the aggregation process. Self-supervised learning is widely utilized in the domains of computer vision and natural language processing [25,26], but is currently relatively rare in the field of recommendation. At its core is a framework called proxy tasks, which allows the utilization of unlabeled data itself to generate labels without the need for manual data annotation. For example, Bert [27] masked some of the words in the text utilizing a random mask and set a proxy task to predict them; RotNet [28] utilizes the rotated image as the input to the training model, giving the model better representation capabilities. In contrast to supervised learning, self-supervised learning permits changes in the input data to leverage the unlabeled data space to achieve significant improvements in downstream tasks. In this study, the benefits of self-supervised learning are included in the recommendation representation learning to solve the constraints of the graph neural network-based recommendation models mentioned above.

The self-supervised learning task contains two main parts: (1) data augmentation to generate multi-views per node, and (2) contrastive learning is used to maximize consistency between multiple views of the same node while minimizing consistency across views of distinct nodes. In graph representation learning, the properties of the data have a strong impact on the representation results of the nodes, especially their structural properties. Therefore, the data without labels can be built by altering the structure of the graph. To this end, this paper utilizes three graph data-augmentation methods of node mask, edge mask, and layer mask to change the graph structure and perform contrastive learning based on graph attention networks. Self-supervised learning enhances node representation learning by investigating the interactions within nodes. Thereby, self-supervised learning complements graph neural network-based recommendation models. Node self-identification provides auxiliary supervised signals that complement classical supervised learning from observed interactions only. Graph data augmentation reduces the impact on model training by reducing the edges of high-degree nodes.

In summary, this work proposes self-supervised graph attention collaborative filtering for recommendation. It can effectively solve the problems of sparse supervised signals and long tails in graph neural network-based recommendations and reduce the impact from the drought-in interaction noise data. The following details the proposed method and demonstrates its effectiveness through extensive experiments. Section 3 states the proposed method in detail and contains two main tasks: supervised task and self-supervised task. Sections 4 and 5 demonstrate the effectiveness of the proposed method through extensive experiments on three public datasets.

2. Related Work

This subsection introduces three aspects related to this work: collaborative filtering-based recommendation, graph neural network-based recommendation, and self-supervised learning.

2.1. Collaborative Filtering-Based Recommendation

Collaborative filtering-based recommendation systems implement recommendation tasks by calculating the similarity between users or items, which assume that users who have interacted with the same item have similar interests. They can be generally classified into memory-based collaborative filtering recommendations [2] and model-based collaborative filtering recommendations [29–31]. Memory-based collaborative filtering recommendation usually utilizes the nearest neighbor idea to calculate similarity using the historical interaction information of users or items. Common methods for similarity include the Pearson correlation coefficient [32], cosine similarity [33], Jaccard similarity coefficient, and Euclidean distance. The model-based collaborative filtering recommendation simulates users' ratings of items by modeling, which uses machine learning or deep learning techniques to construct models and employs a large amount of data trained for the recommendation task.

2.2. Graph Neural Network-Based Recommendation

Although deep learning-based recommendation systems have achieved positive results, the prediction and training paradigms of these methods ignore the higher-order structural information in the data. Therefore, there are still significant limitations. The growth of graph neural networks in the past few years has presented a good idea for overcoming the obstacles in recommendation systems. The graph neural network is based on a user–item bipartite graph by an aggregation function enriched with node embedding representations. By iterative propagation, each node can access higher-order neighbor information instead of only first-order neighbor information as in previous methods. Graph neural network-based approaches have become state of the art in recommender systems due to their advantages in processing structured data and mining structural information. SpectralCF [34] utilizes collaborative filtering with spectral graph convolution; GC-MC [35] and NGCF [16] model graph convolutional networks on the original data space where users and items interact, which is more effective in practical applications; NIA- GCN [36] adds neighbor node interaction awareness to graph convolutional networks; DGCF [17] decouples the user's complex interaction intent, obtains fine-grained embedding representation and tunes up the interpretability of the model; BGCF [37] treats the interaction graph also as a random variable to mitigate the impact caused by the uncertainty of the user–item interaction graph; and LR-GCCF [38] and LightGCN [39] analyze operations, such as feature transformation and nonlinear activation, in graph neural networks, simplifying them to improve the performance of the model.

Although the above methods achieve relatively good results, the influence of noisy data in the process of aggregating neighbors does not allow obtaining high-quality node representations. Therefore, this work employs a multi-head graph attention network to mine the correlation between neighboring nodes and obtain accurate node representations. This work uses a supervised learning paradigm for model training, but sparse supervised signals lead to a loss of performance. Therefore, self-supervised learning is incorporated as an auxiliary task to enhance the supervised learning task.

2.3. *Self-Supervised Learning*

Self-supervised learning [25,27,40] mainly includes generative and contrastive self-supervised learning. The goal of generative self-supervised learning is to learn a low-dimensional vector representation for the input that can retain as much information as possible. Contrastive self-supervised learning learns a comparative noise contrast estimation [41,42] (NCE) aim, which might be global versus local, or global versus global. The former focuses on constructing relationships between a sample's local and global contextual representations, whereas the latter compares explicitly the multi-views of different samples. Self-supervised learning has been the subject of much related work in the fields of computer vision [25] and natural language processing [27]. In contrast to image and text data, self-supervised learning also helps to understand structural and attribute information in graphical data. Thus, self-supervised learning is also applicable to graph-structured data. For example, InfoGraph [43] and DGI [44] learn node representations on mutual information among nodes and local structures; Hu [45] and others extend this approach by training a graph convolution-based model to learn node representations; Kaveh [46] learns node and graph representations via a contrastive paradigm, comparing representations of one view with those of another; GCC [47] utilizes subgraph discrimination as a pre-training task and then improves the representation capability of the graph neural network via contrast learning.

There is not much recommendation-related work using self-supervised learning. DSSR [48] performs self-supervised learning in the latent space to promote convergence for sequential recommendations; Google [24] utilizes a multi-task framework, employing a deep neural network with dual towers as encoders. This paper also utilizes a multi-task framework, which differs from the graph-based recommendation and uses only ID as a feature. HCCF [49] jointly captures local and global collaborative relationships through a hypergraph-enhanced cross-view contrastive learning framework.

3. Proposed Method

This paper proposes the self-supervised learning graph attention-based collaborative filtering recommendation (SGACF), whose architecture is shown in Figure 1. The framework is divided into two components: supervised tasks and self-supervised tasks. The supervised task serves as the main part of the framework, with the graph attention network as the backbone network. The self-supervised task mainly constructs supervised signals from the correlations within the input data and performs joint learning with the supervised task as an auxiliary task. This chapter introduces the supervised task framework and self-supervised tasks. It describes how data augmentation in self-supervised learning is performed to generate multiple view representations, and then contrastive learning is performed to construct the pretext task based on the generated representations. Finally, a theoretical analysis of how self-supervised tasks enhance supervised learning is presented.

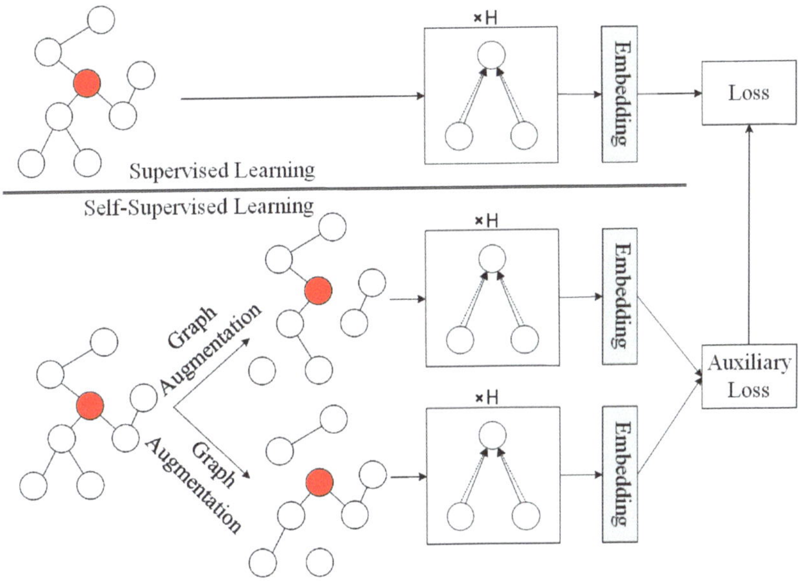

Figure 1. Overall framework. The upper part is for the supervised task, and an H-graph attention network does feature extraction with multiple lines in the network representing a multi-headed attention mechanism; the lower part is self-supervised learning as an auxiliary task, sharing parameters with the network layer in the supervised task.

3.1. *Supervised Learning*

The primary flow of the supervised task is described in this subsection, as shown in Figure 2. It is made up of three major parts: (1) the embedding layer provides initialized vector representations of users and items; (2) the neighbor aggregation and embedding propagation layer generates multiple refined embedding representations of nodes by aggregating higher-order neighbor features and finally synthesizes the final vector representation of nodes; and (3) the prediction layer models user–item interaction and generate the user's preference ratings for objects. Finally, the supervised loss is described.

3.1.1. Embedding Layer

First are the symbols that appear in the pre-defined text. The sets of users and items are described by $\mathcal{U}$ and $\mathcal{I}$, respectively. $\mathcal{O}^+ = \{y_{ui} | u \in \mathcal{U}, i \in \mathcal{I}\}$ is considered as an observed interaction, and y_{ui} indicates that user u has previously interacted with item i. This paper builds the interaction between users and items as a user–item bipartite graph $\mathcal{G} = (\mathcal{V}, \mathcal{E})$, with the set of nodes $\mathcal{V} = \mathcal{U} \cup \mathcal{I}$ containing all users and items and the set of edges $\mathcal{E} = \mathcal{O}^+$ representing the observed interactions. SGACF only utilizes user and item IDs as features and maps them to low-dimensional embedding vectors through the embedding layer. Therefore, in this paper, the set of users and items can be defined as the set of user embedding vectors E_u and the set of item embedding vectors E_i after passing them through the embedding layer as follows:

$$E_u = \{e_u | u \in \mathcal{U}, e_u \in \mathbb{R}^d\}; E_i = \{e_i | i \in \mathcal{I}, e_i \in \mathbb{R}^d\} \quad (1)$$

where d is the size of the embedding vector. Compared to traditional recommendation models that directly employ user and item ID embeddings for interaction modeling, this paper utilizes the characteristics of graph structure to improve the embedding by embedding propagation. This is able to retain the user's own interest and also to explore the potential interest of the user.

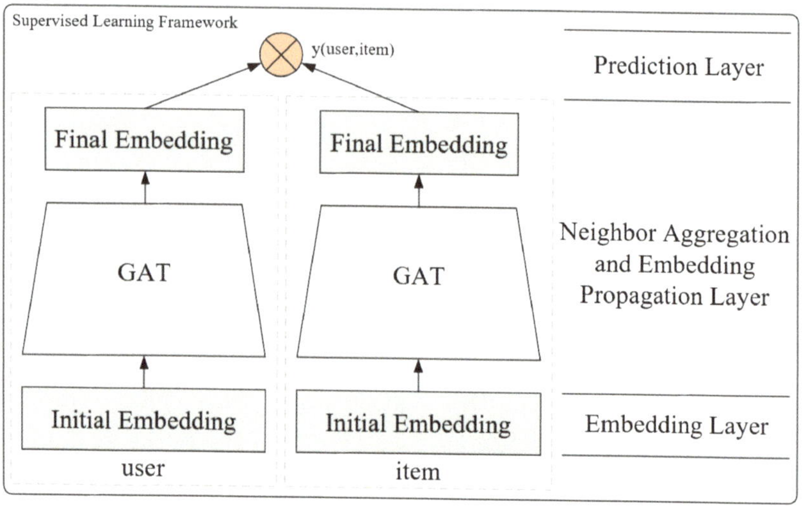

Figure 2. Supervised learning framework. It consists of three main components: the embedding layer, the neighbor aggregation and embedding propagation layer, and the prediction layer. y(user,item) is the user's preference score for the item .

3.1.2. Feature Propagation Layer

Users and items have generated interactions between them that can serve as feature representations of each other. Therefore, the aggregation operation on the graph structure is crucial to the node vector representation. Previous aggregation operations based on graph convolutional networks neglected to distinguish the degree of influence between adjacent nodes, resulting in a vector representation of nodes that does not satisfy the needs of personalized recommendations. In this paper, graph attention networks are utilized to accomplish the aggregation operation by calculating the self-attention coefficients between neighboring nodes, which are then utilized for the linear combination of features corresponding to them. The simplified formula is expressed as $e'_{u/i} = \mathcal{AGG}(\cdot)$, where $e'_{u/i}$ denotes the new vector representation generated, and $\mathcal{AGG}(\cdot)$ is the aggregation function. The aggregation function is implemented below. First, to obtain sufficient representational power, the input node embedding vectors are feature transformed to obtain a new set of node embedding vectors. A shared parameterized weight matrix $W \in \mathbb{R}^{d' \times d}$ is needed to act on each node, where d' is the size of the transformed vector representation. Then, the attention coefficient is calculated between the neighboring nodes. The formula is as follows:

$$\partial_{ui} = a(We_u, We_i) \tag{2}$$

where ∂_{ui} denotes the importance of item i to user u. a denotes a shared attention mechanism. Item i is a first-order neighbor of user u. To make the attention coefficients easily comparable across nodes, this paper utilizes the $softmax$ function to normalize the importance of all i:

$$\alpha_{ui} = softmax_i(\partial_{ui}) = \frac{exp(\partial_{ui})}{\sum_{k \in N_u} exp(\partial_{uk})} \tag{3}$$

where N_u is the set of items that user u has interacted with. In the experiments, a is a feedforward neural network using a weight vector $\overrightarrow{w} \in \mathbb{R}^{2d'}$ parameterized by a single layer and using the $LeakyReLU$ nonlinear activation function (with negative input slope is 0.2). The complete formula for the attention coefficient is as follows:

$$\alpha_{ui} = \frac{exp(LeakyReLU(\overrightarrow{w}^T[We_u||We_i]))}{\sum_{k \in N_u} exp(LeakyReLU(\overrightarrow{w}^T[We_u||We_k]))} \tag{4}$$

where $\cdot^T$ denotes transposition and || indicates a concatenation operation. Multi-headed self-attention is required to steady the procedure of self-attention learning. Specifically, the features output by K independent self-attentive mechanisms are averaged, and a nonlinear operation is added. The specific formula is as follows.

$$e_u^{final} = \sigma(\frac{1}{K}\sum_{k=1}^{K}\sum_{j\in N_u}\alpha_{uj}^k w^k e_j) \tag{5}$$

where || denotes the concatenation operation, α_{uj}^k denotes the coefficient of the kth attention mechanism output between user u and item i, and w^k is the weight matrix of the corresponding linear transformation.

The node representation is enhanced by a first-order neighbor propagation layer, and then multiple graph attention network layers are used to obtain higher-order neighbor features. Such higher-order neighbor features can dig into the potential interests of users and can effectively improve the generalization of the model. Each node in the interaction graph performs first-order propagation to update the node representation, and the second-order neighbor features can be obtained by iteratively performing first-order propagation. Thus, the synergistic signals of higher-order neighbors can be obtained through multiple iterations. The specific formula is expressed as follows:

$$\begin{cases} e_u^{(1)} = \mathcal{AGG}(e_u^{(0)}, \mathcal{G}) \\ e_u^{(h)} = \mathcal{AGG}(e_u^{(h-1)}, \mathcal{G}) \end{cases} \tag{6}$$

where $e_u^{(0)}$ is the node vector representation after initialization, $e_u^{(1)}$ is the node representation after aggregating first-order neighbors, and $e_u^{(h)}$ is the vector representation after aggregating h-order. The output vectors of multiple networks contain node vector representations with different order neighbor features, which directly affect the final vector representation of the nodes. Nodes with rich low-order neighbors are less dependent on higher-order neighbor collaboration signals, and conversely, require more high-order neighbor signals to enrich the vector representation. Therefore, averaging pooling is adopted to merge the vector representations of nodes of different orders. The formula is as follows:

$$e_u^{final} = \frac{1}{H+1}\sum_{h=0}^{H} e_u^h \tag{7}$$

3.1.3. Prediction Layer

SGACF utilizes graph attention networks to obtain node vector representations of users and items, and then embeds higher-order neighbor co-signals into its representation according to the higher-order connectivity principle, and finally models the interaction between users and items by inner product. Then, the preference of user u for item i is

$$\hat{y}_{ui} = (e_u^{final})^T e_i^{final} \tag{8}$$

where e_u^{final} and e_i^{final} are the final vector representations of users and items, $\hat{y}_{ui}$ is the preference score of user u for item i.

3.1.4. Loss of Supervision Task

Pairwise Bayesian personalized ranking (BPR) [18] loss is extensively utilized for recommendation tasks. Its assumption is that the preference behaviors of each user are independent of each other, and the preferences of the same user for different items are independent of each other. BPR takes into account the relative order of observed and unobserved user–items, and it assumes that observed interactions are more indicative of user preferences and therefore are granted a higher ranking than unobserved interactions:

$$\mathcal{L}_{BPR} = \sum_{(u,i^+,i^-)\in\mathcal{O}} -ln\sigma(y_{ui^+} - y_{ui_-}) \tag{9}$$

where $\mathcal{O} = \{(u,i^+,i^-)|(u,i^+) \in \mathcal{O}^+,(u,i^-) \in \mathcal{O}^-\}$ denotes paired training data. i^+ and i^- denote positive and negative samples, respectively. $\mathcal{O}^+$ denotes unobserved samples. σ is the sigmoid activation function, and *Adam* [50] is applied to optimize the model to update the model parameters.

$$\hat{y}_{ui} = (e_u^{final})^T e_i^{final} \tag{10}$$

3.2. *Data Augmentation of Graph Structures*

Data augmentation is a technique that allows limited data to produce more equivalent data to extend the dataset. The main data-augmentation techniques commonly utilized in the field of computer vision are geometric transformation, color adjustment, style transfer, adding noise, etc., which can generate a huge amount of equivalent photos. As a result of the non-Euclidean nature of the graph structure, it is hard to directly adapt data-augmentation methodologies from the vision domain to the graph data domain. The user–item bipartite graph is built on the basis of user–item interaction and contains collaborative signals. Therefore, this paper utilizes a graph structure-based data-augmentation method, including node mask (NM), edge mask (EM) and layer mask (LM) to create different node views. The data-augmentation method is shown in Figure 3. The method of augmenting graph data may be described symbolically as follows:

$$e_1^{(h)} = \mathcal{AGG}(e_1^{(h-1)}, s_1(\mathcal{G})), e_2^{(h)} = \mathcal{AGG}(e_2^{(h-1)}, s_2(\mathcal{G})),\ s_1, s_2 \sim A \tag{11}$$

where the operations s_1 and s_2 are executed on $\mathcal{G}$ to change the graph structure and create two related views of node $e_1^{(h)}$ and node $e_2^{(h)}$. Setting the probability of a node being dropped as ρ, s_1 and s_2 can be modeled as follows.

3.2.1. Node Mask (NM)

The probability of nodes and connected edges mask is ρ. s_1 and s_2 are modeled as follows:

$$s_1(\mathcal{G}) = (C' \odot \mathcal{V}, \mathcal{E}), s_2(\mathcal{G}) = (C'' \odot \mathcal{V}, \mathcal{E}) \tag{12}$$

where $C', C'' \in \{0,1\}^{|\mathcal{V}|}$ are two mask vectors applied to node set $\mathcal{V}$. It gathers some nodes and their edges from random shaded nodes to generate two subgraphs. This method may observe the dominant nodes in the graph structure, which improves the robustness of the representation learning to structure.

3.2.2. Edge Mask (EM)

Setting the probability of an edge mask as ρ, s_1 and s_2 can be modeled as

$$s_1(\mathcal{G}) = (\mathcal{V}, C_1 \odot \mathcal{E}), s_2(\mathcal{G}) = (\mathcal{V}, C_2 \odot \mathcal{E}) \tag{13}$$

where $C_1, C_2 \in \{0,1\}^{|\mathcal{E}|}$ are two mask vectors whose randomly masked edge set $\mathcal{E}$ generates two subgraphs. Local neighbors of nodes affect representation learning, further mitigating the sensitivity of representation learning to structure.

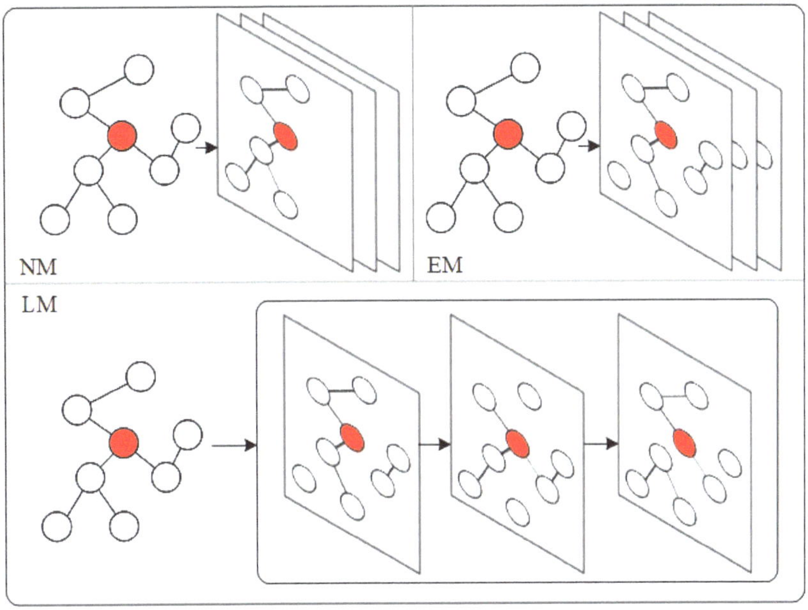

Figure 3. Graph augmentation method. Top left is node mask, top right is edge mask, and bottom is layer mask.

3.2.3. Layer Mask (LM)

The subgraphs generated by node mask and edge mask are shared across network layers. To further improve the robustness of the model to the graph structure, random walk performs edge mask for the graph structure of each layer of the network input data. The mask probability is set for each layer with edge mask and the expression is as follows:

$$s_1(\mathcal{G}) = (\mathcal{V}, C_1^{(h)} \odot \mathcal{E}), s_2(\mathcal{G}) = (\mathcal{V}, C_2^{(h)} \odot \mathcal{E}) \tag{14}$$

where $C_1^{(h)}, C_2^{(h)} \in \{0,1\}^{|\mathcal{E}|}$ are two mask vectors whose randomly masked edge of the h-layer network.

3.3. *Self-Supervised Contrastive Learning*

3.3.1. Contrastive Learning

Contrastive learning is an implementation of self-supervised learning, mainly designed to solve the problem of little or no labeling. Its classical paradigm is a combination of an agent task and an objective function. This paper utilizes contrastive self-supervised learning, which performs contrastive learning based on the views generated by the data-augmentation methods described above. It utilizes information about commonalities and differences between data pairs as supervised signals to assist in the learning of the supervised task.

3.3.2. Loss of Self-Supervision Task

The main goal of contrastive learning is to increase the consistency of two jointly sampled positive sample pairs while minimizing the consistency of two dependently sampled negative sample pairs. Positive sample pairs $(\{(e'_u, e''_u)|u \in \mathcal{U}\})$ are two distinct views of the same node after augmentation, and negative sample pairs $(\{(e'_u, e''_o)|u, o \in \mathcal{U}\})$

are distinct views of distinct nodes after augmentation. This paper follows SimCLR and utilizes the contrastive loss InfoNCE:

$$\mathcal{L}_{ssl}^{user} = \sum_{u \in \mathcal{U}} -log \frac{exp(s(e'_u, e''_u)/\tau)}{\sum_{o \in \mathcal{U}} exp(s(e'_u, e''_o)/\tau)} \tag{15}$$

where $s(\cdot)$ is is the cosine similarity function. τ is the temperature coefficient. Similarly, the item-side contrastive loss $\mathcal{L}_{ssl}^{item}$ can be obtained. Combining these two losses results in a self-supervised loss $\mathcal{L} = \mathcal{L}_{ssl}^{item} + \mathcal{L}_{ssl}^{user}$.

3.4. Joint Learning

The similarity between users and items is the top priority in the recommendation domain. Contrastive learning is concerned with the similarity between user nodes and their variant views, and item nodes and their variant views, and only plays a auxiliary role in the training phase. Therefore, self-supervised learning is optimized as an auxiliary task jointly with the supervised task to form multi-task learning:

$$\mathcal{L} = \mathcal{L}_{supervised} + \lambda_1 \mathcal{L}_{self-supervised} + \lambda_2 ||\theta||_2^2 \tag{16}$$

where θ is the parameter of supervised learning, and λ_1 and λ_2 are the contribution values of hyperparameter control self-supervised loss and L_2 regularization.

4. Experiment

The work conducts experiments on three publicly available datasets to evaluate the effectiveness of the proposed method. The settings of the parameters in the model are presented, and the performance is analyzed in comparison with other models.

4.1. Datasets and Metrics

This work is experimented on three datasets of Yelp2018, Gowalla and Amazon. Yelp2018 is collected from the 2018 Yelp challenge and considers restaurants, shopping centers and hotels as items. Gowalla is a check-in dataset, where each check-in of a user serves as one piece of data in the dataset. Amazon-review is a widely utilized product recommendation dataset, and the work selects amazon-book from the collection. To ensure the quality of the dataset, a certain number of items are selected in the experiment, and Yelp2018 keeps user data with no fewer than 25 interactions, and the other datasets keep no fewer than 20 interactions.

Model performance evaluation for the top-k recommendation task typically utilizes *Recall@k* and normalized discounted cumulative gain (*NDCG@k*), where $k = 20$. Recall calculates the proportion of items in the recommendation list that have interacted with the user to the number of positive samples in the test set. The higher the value of recall, the better the model recommendation performance. The formula is presented below:

$$Recall = \frac{1}{|\mathcal{U}|} \sum_{u \in \mathcal{U}} \frac{|M_u \cap M_u^{test}|}{M_u^{test}} \tag{17}$$

where M_u is the recommendation list and M_u^{test} is the positive sample of user u in the test set. $NDCG$ considers the factor of item location in the recommendation list, and the higher the value, the better the recommendation effect. The formula is as follows:

$$NDCG = \frac{1}{|\mathcal{U}|} \sum_{u \in \mathcal{U}} \frac{\sum_{p=1}^{K} \frac{rel(p)}{log(p+1)}}{\sum_{p=1}^{TP} \frac{1}{log(p+1)}} \tag{18}$$

where $rel(\cdot)$ denotes the item correlation calculation, and TP denotes the items in the recommendation list in order of correlation from largest to smallest.

4.2. Parameter Settings

The experiment was implemented via PyTorch. The work was initialized using Xavier [51], setting the size of the embedding vector to 64. The learning rate of the model was set to 0.001, and the L_2 regularization coefficient was set to 1×10^{-4}. The self-supervised learning part parameters λ_1, τ and ρ were fine-tuned in the following value ranges $\{0.005, 0.01, 0.05, 0.1, 0.5, 1\}$, $\{0.1, 0.2, 0.5, 1.0\}$ and $\{0, 0.1, ...0.5\}$, respectively. The parameters in the comparison model were set by the original paper.

4.3. Experiment Analysis

4.3.1. Explore SGACF's Performance on Datasets

This subsection of the paper explores the performance of SGACF and analyzes the impact of graph augmentation and different orders on the model performance. Here, this paper utilizes augmentation strategies based on graph structure: NM, EM, and LM. It explores the performance of models with different orders from 1 to 4. The experimental results are shown in Table 1.

Table 1. Explore SGACF performance on three datasets.

Layer	Method	Gowalla		Yelp2018		Amazon	
		Recall	Ndcg	Recall	Ndcg	Recall	Ndcg
1	SGACF-NM	**0.2714**	**0.2199**	**0.2150**	**0.1394**	0.1633	0.0896
	SGACF-EM	0.2711	0.2197	0.2144	0.1392	**0.1674**	**0.0905**
	SGACF-LM	0.2711	0.2197	0.2144	0.1392	**0.1674**	**0.0905**
2	SGACF-NM	0.2733	0.2201	0.2112	0.1356	0.1658	0.0904
	SGACF-EM	**0.2749**	**0.2417**	**0.2163**	**0.1400**	**0.1696**	**0.0922**
	SGACF-LM	0.2728	0.2241	0.2152	0.1394	0.1690	0.0915
3	SGACF-NM	0.2720	0.2205	0.2146	0.1384	0.1688	0.0908
	SGACF-EM	**0.2753**	**0.2423**	**0.2171**	**0.1402**	**0.1698**	**0.0925**
	SGACF-LM	0.2741	0.2412	0.2155	0.1397	0.1696	0.0921
4	SGACF-NM	0.2735	0.2198	0.2107	0.1346	0.1660	0.0905
	SGACF-EM	**0.2750**	**0.2419**	**0.2166**	**0.1400**	**0.1695**	**0.0923**
	SGACF-LM	0.2730	0.2242	0.2148	0.1387	0.1692	0.0917

The bold indicates the best result.

Analysis of the results shows that the edge mask improves the model more significantly. SGACF-EM outperforms SGACF-LM, and SGACF-LM outperforms SGACF-NM, which may be the inherent ability of the edge mask to capture the graph structure. NM may be thought of as a subset of EM in which certain node edges are masked. The performance of SGACF-NM in the experiment is relatively unstable, from which it can be concluded that mask high degree nodes lead to training instability. Analyzing from the aspect of order, a too-low order leads to a lack of information in the vector representation learned by the model, and too-high order leads to a convergence of node representations, which cannot distinguish the vector representation of different nodes. From Table 1, it is clear that taking the 3-order acquires better performance. In addition, self-supervised learning can enhance the generalization ability of the model. That is, contrastive learning between different nodes can alleviate the problem of the over-smoothing of node representations. To obtain a clearer picture of the effect of the reaction order and graph augmentation method on the performance, the results are visualized as shown in Figure 4.

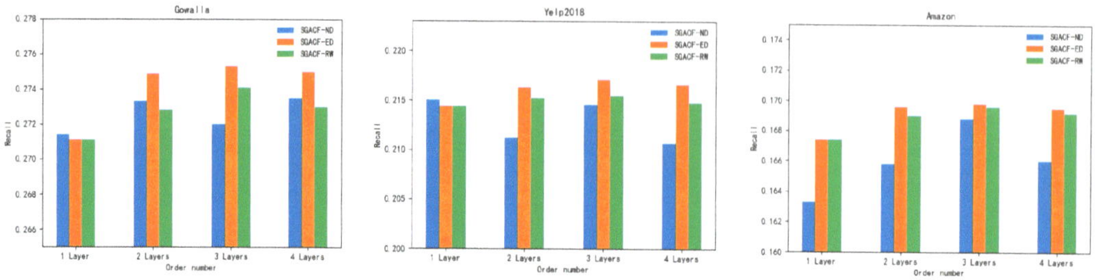

Figure 4. Impact of order and graph augmentation on performance.

4.3.2. Compared Method

To demonstrate the effectiveness of the model, the work compares the proposed method with the following methods.

- NeuMF [9] combines traditional matrix decomposition and multi-layer perceptron to extract both low- and high-dimensional features. The user's preference score for the item is obtained through the neural network instead of the inner product operation.
- CMN [52] proposes a unified hybrid model which capitalizes on the recent advances in memory networks and neural attention mechanisms for collaborative filtering with implicit feedback.
- SpectralCF [34] proposes a spectral-based convolution operation to construct a deep recommendation model based on spectral collaborative filtering. The model can explicitly mine the higher-order neighborhood features hidden in the interaction graph.
- NGCF [16] utilizes multiple spatial domain graph-based convolutional networks to mine the user's potential interest to obtain multiple representations of the nodes, and then utilizes a weighted summation aggregation function to compute the final vector representation of the nodes.

4.3.3. Analysis of Results

This work was experimented with other comparison models on three datasets, and the results are given in Table 2. The performance differences between the comparison models and the model proposed in this paper are analyzed below.

Table 2. Performance comparison of SGACF with other comparative models.

Method	Gowalla		Yelp2018		Amazon	
	Recall	Ndcg	Recall	Ndcg	Recall	Ndcg
NeuMF	0.1402	0.1169	0.1193	0.1040	0.1195	0.0552
CMN	0.1746	0.1571	0.2010	0.1075	0.1606	0.0657
SpectralCF	0.1756	0.1672	0.1565	0.1209	0.0950	0.0547
NGCF	0.2673	0.2317	0.1993	0.1326	0.1499	0.0866
SGACF-EM	**0.2753**	**0.2423**	**0.2171**	**0.1402**	**0.1698**	**0.0925**

The bold indicates the best result.

- NeuMF learns only low-dimensional vector representations of users and items utilizing the embedding layer. The results are poor on all three datasets, indicating that there is a considerable paucity of valuable information in the embedding vectors of users and items.
- CMN outperforms other comparison models in terms of recall on the Yelp and Amazon datasets. This is due to the utilization of the attention mechanism in the model to obtain better performance by enhancing the representational ability of nodes in heterogeneous networks.
- SpectralCF outperforms NeuMF on all three datasets, which indicates that the graph neural network-based recommendation model outperforms the general deep learning-

based model in terms of structure. Building the interaction between users and items as a bipartite graph can better explore the potential interests of users and enrich the embedding vectors of users and items.
- NGCF has better performance in comparison models. It defines the convolution operation directly on the spatial domain, without depending on the graph convolution theory. While improving flexibility, the performance of the spatial domain-based graph convolution recommendation model outperforms other methods.
- In comparison to NGCF, SGACF-EM improves the NDCG on the Yelp and Amazon datasets by 5% and 6%, respectively. SGACF utilizes a self-attention mechanism in the process of aggregating neighboring features to quantify the neighboring features of nodes according to their importance, thus improving the embedding representation of users and items. In order to make the calculation of attention coefficients more stable, the multi-headed self-attention mechanism is employed. The experimental results fully verify the rationality and effectiveness of the method proposed in this paper. CMN only utilizes the features of first-order neighbors, and SGACF mines higher-order collaborative signals based on higher-order connectivity, which illustrates the importance of higher-order connectivity principle in graph representation learning. SpectralCF and NGCF utilize spectral-based graph convolution and spatial domain-based graph convolution networks, respectively; both ignore the reliability of the feature propagation process between neighboring nodes and are prone to bring in noisy data. Moreover, in the training process of graph convolutional networks, the high degree of nodes tends to dominate the representation learning of the model. Therefore, SGACF joint self-supervised learning makes it easy for nodes with low degree to learn.

4.3.4. Analysis of The Impact of Comparative Learning

Contrastive learning is an implementation of self-supervised learning, which is mainly applied to solve the problem of little or no labeling of data. Therefore, its data-augmentation part is the main core. Although a great volume of data is generated inside recommendation domain, its data distribution shows a power–law distribution (i.e., long-tail problem). In the process of model training, nodes with high degree play a dominant role in representation learning, while nodes with low degree are very difficult to learn. Therefore, adding contrastive learning to the recommendation model to solve the long-tail problem is effective. Further, to make the model easy to train, the parameters are shared between graph neural networks for supervised and self-supervised tasks.

5. Ablation Analysis

To demonstrate the effectiveness of the adopted technique, this paper conducts ablation experiments on a multi-headed graph attention mechanism and a self-supervised task.

5.1. *Impact of Multiple Attention Mechanism*

This subsection analyzes the impact of the number of attention heads on performance in SGACF-EM. The use of a single-headed graph attention network overly focuses attention on its own position when encoding the current node features during the training process. To obtain more reliable attention coefficients, a multi-headed graph attention network is utilized to extract features from multiple perspectives. The experimental results are shown in Table 3. The model achieves better performance when the number of heads is 2. When the number of heads exceeds a certain number, the model effect is not improved, which is due to the limitation of the characteristics of the data itself.

Table 3. Effect of graph attention network with different number of heads on performance.

Heads	Gowalla		Yelp2018		Amazon	
	Recall	Ndcg	Recall	Ndcg	Recall	Ndcg
1	0.2726	0.2411	0.2154	0.1397	0.1677	0.0914
2	**0.2753**	**0.2423**	**0.2171**	**0.1402**	**0.1698**	**0.0925**
4	0.2715	0.2405	0.2128	0.1374	0.1660	0.0903
8	0.2681	0.2344	0.2087	0.1316	0.1627	0.0842

The bold indicates the best result.

5.2. Optimization of Models by Contrastive Learning

To investigate the effect of self-supervised learning on model performance, this subsection performs an ablation analysis of SGACF. Table 4 displays the experiment's outcomes, where joint self-supervised learning in the recommendation model significantly improves the model's performance. This is attributed to the fact that self-supervised contrastive learning effectively mitigates the problem of sparse supervisory signals in the recommendation task by utilizing information about commonalities and differences between data pairs as supervised signals to auxiliary supervised learning through a data-augmentation strategy. Meanwhile, to explore the impact of self-supervised learning on the long-tail problem, in this paper, items are divided into 10 groups of different ranks based on the number of connected edges of individual nodes, and the total number of interactions in each group is the same. The larger the groupID, the higher the number of connected edges of individual nodes. This work compares the ability of SGACF-ED and SGACF-w/o to solve the long-tail problem, both of which have their network layers set to 3. Recall is the sum of each group. As shown in Figure 5, group 10 contributes a large proportion to recall, even though it contains a small number of items. It is thus clear that SGACF-w/o tends to recommend popular items, while long-tail items have fewer connected edges. It can be seen that the performance improvement of SGACF is to accurately recommend long-tail items.

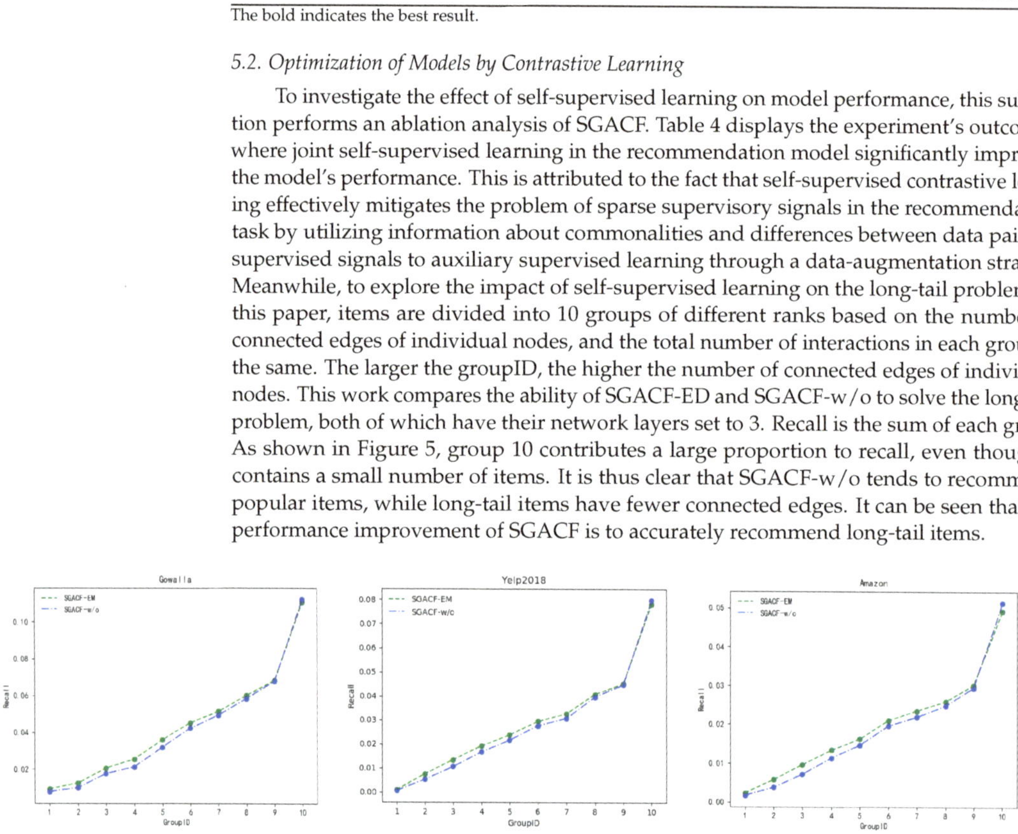

Figure 5. Performance comparison of different item groups SGACF-EM and SGACF-w/o.

Table 4. Impact of self-supervised learning on models.

Method	Gowalla		Yelp2018		Amazon	
	Recall	Ndcg	Recall	Ndcg	Recall	Ndcg
SGACF-w/o	0.2680	0.2341	0.2037	0.1113	0.1622	0.0894
SGACF-EM	**0.2753**	**0.2423**	**0.2171**	**0.1402**	**0.1698**	**0.0925**

The bold indicates the best result.

6. Conclusions and Future Work

This paper proposes a self-supervised graph attention collaborative filtering for recommendation. It observes that graph convolution-based recommendation ignores the problem of importance between neighboring nodes, and thus employs graph attention networks to obtain reliable neighboring features. In this paper, self-supervised contrastive learning is utilized to auxiliary supervised learning, thus addressing the limitations of supervised tasks in recommendation. The impact of three approaches to graph data augmentation on model performance is analyzed from the perspective of graph structure. Extensive experiments are conducted on three public datasets to demonstrate the advantages of the methods proposed in this paper in mitigating the long-tail problem and reducing the impact of interaction noise. To sum up, the contributions of this work are as follows: A multi-head graph attention network is utilized to aggregate neighbor features from multiple perspectives to reduce the impact of interaction noise on representation learning. Supervised tasks based on graph attention networks combined with self-supervised learning enhance representation learning via observing the properties of nodes in the interaction graph. Extensive experiments on three benchmark datasets demonstrate the effectiveness of the proposed self-supervised graph attention collaborative filtering for recommendation.

This work achieves better results, adopting the joint training of self-supervised contrast learning and supervised learning, but there are still limitations. The success of contrast learning-based representation learning relies heavily on well-designed data-augmentation strategies. In future research, we will focus on graph data-augmentation strategies in contrast learning. We hope to make contrast learning in recommendation more robust through data-augmentation strategies. For example, sampling-based data augmentation transforms both the adjacency matrix and the feature matrix.

Author Contributions: Methodology and writing—original draft preparation, J.Z.; review and validation, K.L., J.P. and J.Q. All authors have read and agreed to the published version of the manuscript.

Funding: This research was funded by the Natural Science Foundation of Hebei Province under grant No. F2022201009; the Hebei University High-level Scientific Research Foundation for the Introduction of Talent under grant No.521100221029; the Scientific Research Foundation of Hebei University for Distinguished Young Scholars under grant No. 521100221081 and the Scientific Research Foundation of Colleges and Universities in Hebei Province under grant No. QN2022107.

Data Availability Statement: All datasets are publicly available.

Acknowledgments: Thanks to the mentor for his careful guidance. Thanks to the anonymous reviewers for their insightful comments that improved the quality of this paper. Thanks to my girlfriend for encouraging me so much.

Conflicts of Interest: The authors declare no conflict of interest.

References

1. Linden, G.; Smith, B.; York, J. Amazon. com recommendations: Item-to-item collaborative filtering. *IEEE Internet Comput.* **2003**, *7*, 76–80. [CrossRef]
2. Sarwar, B.; Karypis, G.; Konstan, J.; Riedl, J. Item-based collaborative filtering recommendation algorithms. In Proceedings of the 10th International Conference on World Wide Web, Hong Kong, China, 1–5 May 2001; pp. 285–295.
3. Rendle, S. Factorization machines. In Proceedings of the IEEE International Conference on Data Mining, Sydney, NSW, Australia, 13–17 December 2010; pp. 995–1000.
4. Juan, Y.; Zhuang, Y.; Chin, W.S.; Lin, C.J. Field-aware factorization machines for CTR prediction. In Proceedings of the 10th ACM Conference on Recommender Systems, Boston, MA, USA, 15–19 September 2016; pp. 43–50.
5. He, X.; Pan, J.; Jin, O.; Xu T.B.; Liu, B.; Xu, T.; Shi, Y.X.; Atallah, A.; Herbrich, R.; Bowers, S.; et al. Practical lessons from predicting clicks on ads at facebook. In Proceedings of the Eighth International Workshop on Data Mining for Online Advertising, New York, NY, USA, 24–27 August 2014; pp. 1–9.
6. Koren, Y.; Bell, R.; Volinsky, C. Matrix factorization techniques for recommender systems. *Computer* **2009**, *42*, 30–37. [CrossRef]
7. Sedhain, S.; Menon, A.K.; Sanner, S.; Xie, L. Autorec: Autoencoders meet collaborative filtering. In Proceedings of the 24th International Conference on World Wide Web, Florence, Italy, 18–22 May 2015; pp. 111–112.
8. Shan, Y.; Hoens, T.R.; Jiao, J.; Wang, H.; Yu, D.; Mao, J. Deep crossing: Web-scale modeling without manually crafted combinatorial features. In Proceedings of the 22nd ACM SIGKDD International Conference on Knowledge Discovery and Data Mining, San Francisco, CA, USA, 13–17 August 2016; pp. 255–262.
9. He, X.; Liao, L.; Zhang, H.; Nie, L.; Hu, X.; Chua, T.S. Neural collaborative filtering. In Proceedings of the 26th International Conference on World Wide Web, Perth, Australia, 3–7 April 2017; pp. 173–182.
10. Cheng, H.T.; Koc, L.; Harmsen, J.; Shaked, T.; Chandra, T.; Aradhye, H.; Anderson, G.; Corrado, G.; Chai, W.; Ispir, M.; et al. Wide & deep learning for recommender systems. In Proceedings of the 1st Workshop on Deep Learning for Recommender Systems, Boston, MA, USA, 15 September 2016; pp. 7–10.

11. He, X.; Chua, T.S. Neural factorization machines for sparse predictive analytics. In Proceedings of the 40th International ACM SIGIR conference on Research and Development in Information Retrieval, Tokyo, Japan, 7–11 August 2017; pp. 355–364.
12. Kipf, T.N.; Welling, M. Semi-supervised classification with graph convolutional networks. *arXiv* **2016**, arXiv:1609.02907.
13. Levie, R.; Monti, F.; Bresson, X.; Bronstein, M.M. Cayleynets: Graph convolutional neural networks with complex rational spectral filters. *IEEE Trans. Signal Process.* **2018**, *67*, 97–109. [CrossRef]
14. Niepert, M.; Ahmed, M.; Kutzkov, K. Learning convolutional neural networks for graphs. In Proceedings of the International Conference on Machine Learning, PMLR, New York, NY, USA, 20–22 June 2016; pp. 2014–2023.
15. Gilmer, J.; Schoenholz, S.S.; Riley, P.F.; Vinyals, O.; Dahl, G.E. Neural message passing for quantum chemistry. In Proceedings of the International Conference on Machine Learning, PMLR, Sydney, Australia, 6–11 August 2017; pp. 1263–1272.
16. Wang, X.; He, X.; Wang, M.; Feng, F.; Chua, T.S. Neural graph collaborative filtering. In Proceedings of the 42nd international ACM SIGIR Conference on Research and Development in Information Retrieval, Paris, France, 21–25 July 2019; pp. 165–174.
17. Wang, X.; Jin, H.; Zhang, A.; He, X.; Xu, T.; Chua, T.S. Disentangled graph collaborative filtering. In Proceedings of the 43rd International ACM SIGIR Conference on Research and Development in Information Retrieval, Virtual Event, China, 25–30 July 2020; pp. 1001–1010.
18. Rendle, S.; Freudenthaler, C.; Gantner, Z.; Schmidt-Thieme, L. BPR: Bayesian personalized ranking from implicit feedback. *arXiv* **2012**, arXiv:1205.2618.
19. Bayer, I.; He, X.; Kanagal, B.; Rendle, S. A generic coordinate descent framework for learning from implicit feedback. In Proceedings of the 26th International Conference on World Wide Web, Perth, Australia, 3–7 April 2017; pp. 1341–1350.
20. He, R.; McAuley, J. Ups and downs: Modeling the visual evolution of fashion trends with one-class collaborative filtering. In proceedings of the 25th International Conference on World Wide Web, Montreal, QC, Canada, 11–15 April 2016; pp. 507–517.
21. Tang, X.; Yao, H.; Sun, Y.; Wang, Y.; Tang, J.; Aggarwal, C.; Mitra, P.; Wang, S. Investigating and mitigating degree-related biases in graph convoltuional networks. In Proceedings of the 29th ACM International Conference on Information & Knowledge Management, Virtual Event, Ireland, 19–23 October 2020; pp. 1435–1444.
22. Wang, W.; Feng, F.; He, X.; Nie, L.; Chua, T.S. Denoising implicit feedback for recommendation. In Proceedings of the 14th ACM International Conference on Web Search and Data Mining, Virtual Event, Israel, 8–12 March 2021; pp. 373–381.
23. Veličković, P.; Cucurull, G.; Casanova, A.; Romero, A.; Liò, P.; Bengio, Y. Graph attention networks. *arXiv* **2017**, arXiv:1710.10903.
24. Yao, T.; Yi, X.; Cheng, D.Z.; Xu, F.; Chen, T.; Menon, A.; Hong, L.; Chi, E.H.; Tjoa, S.; Kang, J.; et al. Self-supervised learning for large-scale item recommendations. In Proceedings of the 30th ACM International Conference on Information and Knowledge Management, Virtual Event, Queensland, Australia, 1–5 November 2021; pp. 4321–4330.
25. He, K.; Fan, H.; Wu, Y.; Xie, S.; Girshick, R. Momentum contrast for unsupervised visual representation learning. In Proceedings of the IEEE/CVF Conference on Computer Vision and Pattern Recognition, Seattle, WA, USA, 14–19 June 2020; pp. 9729–9738.
26. Lan, Z.; Chen, M.; Goodman, S.; Gimpel, K.; Sharma, P.; Soricut, R. Albert: A lite bert for self-supervised learning of language representations. *arXiv* **2019**, arXiv:1909.11942.
27. Devlin, J.; Chang, M.W.; Lee, K.; Toutanova, K. Bert: Pre-training of deep bidirectional transformers for language understanding. *arXiv* **2018**, arXiv:1810.04805.
28. Gidaris, S.; Singh, P.; Komodakis, N. Unsupervised representation learning by predicting image rotations. *arXiv* **2018**, arXiv:1803.07728.
29. Hofmann, T. Latent semantic models for collaborative filtering. *ACM Trans. Inf. Syst. (TOIS)* **2004**, *22*, 89–115. [CrossRef]
30. Miyahara, K.; Pazzani, M.J. Collaborative Filtering with the Simple Bayesian Classifier. In Proceedings of the 6th Pacific Rim international conference on Artificial intelligence, Melbourne, Australia, 28 August–1 September 2002; pp. 679–689.
31. Ungar, L.H.; Foster, D.P. Clustering methods for collaborative filtering. In Proceedings of the AAAI Workshop on Recommendation Systems, Madison, WI, USA, 26–27 July 1998; Volume 1, pp. 114–129.
32. Resnick, P.; Iacovou, N.; Suchak, M.; Bergstrom, P.; Riedl, J. Grouplens: An open architecture for collaborative filtering of netnews. In Proceedings of the 1994 ACM Conference on Computer Supported Cooperative Work, Chapel Hill, NC, USA, 22–26 October 1994; pp. 175–186.
33. Chowdhury, G.G. *Introduction to Modern Information Retrieval*; Facet Publishing: London, UK, 2010.
34. Zheng, L.; Lu, C.T.; Jiang, F.; Zhang, J.; Yu, P.S. Spectral collaborative filtering. In Proceedings of the 12th ACM Conference on Recommender Systems, Vancouver, BC, Canada, 2–7 October 2018; pp. 311–319.
35. Berg, R.; Kipf, T.N.; Welling, M. Graph convolutional matrix completion. *arXiv* **2017**, arXiv:1706.02263.
36. Sun, J.; Zhang, Y.; Guo, W.; Guo, H.; Tang, R.; He, X.; Ma, C.; Coates, M. Neighbor interaction aware graph convolution networks for recommendation. In Proceedings of the 43rd International ACM SIGIR Conference on Research and Development in Information Retrieval, Virtual Event, China, 25–30 July 2020; pp. 1289–1298.
37. Sun, J.; Guo, W.; Zhang, D.; Zhang, Y.; Regol, F.; Hu Y.; Guo, H.; Tang, R.; Yuan, H.; He, X.; et al. A framework for recommending accurate and diverse items using bayesian graph convolutional neural networks. In Proceedings of the 26th ACM SIGKDD International Conference on Knowledge Discovery & Data Mining, Virtual Event, CA, USA, 6–10 July 2020; pp. 2030–2039.
38. Chen, L.; Wu, L.; Hong, R.; Zhang, K.; Wang, M. Revisiting graph based collaborative filtering: A linear residual graph convolutional network approach. In Proceedings of the AAAI Conference on Artificial Intelligence, New York, NY, USA, 7–12 February 2020; pp. 27–34.

39. He, X.; Deng, K.; Wang, X.; Li, Y.; Zhang, Y.; Wang, M. Lightgcn: Simplifying and powering graph convolution network for recommendation. In Proceedings of the 43rd International ACM SIGIR Conference on Research and Development in Information Retrieval, Virtual Event, China, 25–30 July 2020; pp. 639–648.
40. Grill, J.B.; Strub, F.; Altché, F.; Tallec, C.; Richemond, P.; Buckatskaya, E.; Doersch, C.; Pires, B.A.; Guo, Z.; Azar, M.G.; et al. Bootstrap your own latent-a new approach to self-supervised learning. *Adv. Neural Inf. Process. Syst.* **2020**, *33*, 21271–21284.
41. Hjelm, R.D.; Fedorov, A.; Lavoie-Marchildon, S.; Grewal, K.; Bachman, P.; Trischler, A.; Bengio, Y. Learning deep representations by mutual information estimation and maximization. *arXiv* **2018**, arXiv:1808.06670.
42. Chen, T.; Kornblith, S.; Norouzi, M.; Hinton, G. A simple framework for contrastive learning of visual representations. In Proceedings of the International Conference on Machine Learning, PMLR, Virtual, 13–18 July 2020; pp. 1597–1607.
43. Sun, F.Y.; Hoffmann, J.; Verma, V.; Tang, J. Infograph: Unsupervised and semi-supervised graph-level representation learning via mutual information maximization. *arXiv* **2019**, arXiv:1908.01000.
44. Velickovic, P.; Fedus, W.; Hamilton, W.L.; Lio, P.; Bengio, Y.; Hjelm, R.D. Deep Graph Infomax. *ICLR* **2019**, *2*, 4.
45. Hu, W.; Liu, B.; Gomes, J.; Zitnik, M.; Liang, P.; Pande, V.; Leskovec, J. Strategies for pre-training graph neural networks. *arXiv* **2019**, arXiv:1905.12265.
46. Hassani, K.; Khasahmadi, A.H. Contrastive multi-view representation learning on graphs. In Proceedings of the International Conference on Machine Learning, PMLR, Virtual, 13–18 July 2020; pp. 4116–4126.
47. Qiu, J.; Chen, Q.; Dong, Y.; Zhang, J.; Yang, H.; Ding, M.; Wang, K.; Tang, J. Gcc: Graph contrastive coding for graph neural network pre-training. In Proceedings of the 26th ACM SIGKDD International Conference on Knowledge Discovery & Data Mining, Virtual Event, CA, USA, 6–10 July 2020; pp. 1150–1160.
48. Ma, J.; Zhou, C.; Yang, H.; Cui, P.; Wang, X.; Zhu, W. Disentangled self-supervision in sequential recommenders. In Proceedings of the 26th ACM SIGKDD International Conference on Knowledge Discovery & Data Mining, Virtual Event, CA, USA, 6–10 July 2020; pp. 483–491.
49. Xia, L.; Huang, C.; Xu, Y.; Zhao, J.; Yin, D.; Huang, J. Hypergraph contrastive collaborative filtering. In Proceedings of the 45th International ACM SIGIR Conference on Research and Development in Information Retrieval, Madrid, Spain, 11–15 July 2022; pp. 70–79.
50. Kingma, D.P.; Ba, J. Adam: A method for stochastic optimization. *arXiv* **2014**, arXiv:1412.6980.
51. Glorot, X.; Bengio, Y. Understanding the difficulty of training deep feedforward neural networks. In Proceedings of the Thirteenth International Conference on Artificial Intelligence and Statistics. JMLR Workshop and Conference Proceedings, Sardegna, Italy, 13–15 May 2010; pp. 249–256.
52. Ebesu, T.; Shen, B.; Fang, Y. Collaborative memory network for recommendation systems. In Proceedings of the 41st International ACM SIGIR Conference on Research & Development in Information Retrieval, Ann Arbor, MI, USA, 8–12 July 2018; pp. 515–524.

electronics

Article

Preference-Aware Light Graph Convolution Network for Social Recommendation

Haoyu Xu [1], Guodong Wu [1], Enting Zhai [1], Xiu Jin [1] and Lijing Tu [2,*]

[1] College of Information and Computer Science, Anhui Agricultural University, Hefei 230001, China; xhy817@stu.ahau.edu.cn (H.X.)
[2] Anhui Provincial Key Laboratory of Smart Agricultural Technology and Equipment, Hefei 230036, China
* Correspondence: tlj@ahau.edu.cn

Abstract: Social recommendation systems leverage the abundant social information of users existing in the current Internet to mitigate the problem of data sparsity, ultimately enhancing recommendation performance. However, most existing recommendation systems that introduce social information ignore the negative messages passed by high-order neighbor nodes and aggregate messages without filtering, which results in a decline in the performance of the recommendation system. Considering this problem, we propose a novel social recommendation model based on graph neural networks (GNNs) called the preference-aware light graph convolutional network (PLGCN), which contains a subgraph construction module using unsupervised learning to classify users according to their embeddings and then assign users with similar preferences to a subgraph to filter useless or even negative messages from users with different preferences to attain even better recommendation performance. We also designed a feature aggregation module to better combine user embeddings with social and interaction information. In addition, we employ a lightweight GNN framework to aggregate messages from neighbors, removing nonlinear activation and feature transformation operations to alleviate the overfitting problem. Finally, we carried out comprehensive experiments using two publicly available datasets, and the results indicate that PLGCN outperforms the current state-of-the-art (SOTA) method, especially in dealing with the problem of cold start. The proposed model has the potential for practical applications in online recommendation systems, such as e-commerce, social media, and content recommendation.

Keywords: graph convolution network; recommendation system; social recommendation

Citation: Xu, H.; Wu, G.; Zhai, E.; Jin, X.; Tu, L. Preference-Aware Light Graph Convolution Network for Social Recommendation. *Electronics* **2023**, *12*, 2397. https://doi.org/10.3390/electronics12112397

Academic Editor: Grzegorz Dudek

Received: 18 April 2023
Revised: 15 May 2023
Accepted: 19 May 2023
Published: 25 May 2023

1. Introduction

With the emergence and prosperity of online service platforms, the dissemination and exchange of information have been greatly promoted, and the amount of information in the network has increased exponentially. However, when confronted with such an enormous amount of information, users find it hard to obtain the information that is relevant and helpful to them; this phenomenon is referred to as "information overload". To address this issue, a recommendation system was developed that analyzes the historical behavior data of users and explores their potential interests to provide them with personalized services. At present, recommendation systems are widely used in industry.

Collaborative filtering (CF) has been a widely used technique in the last few decades. In simple terms, collaborative filtering recommends information of interest to users according to the preferences of a group of people who share similar interests and experiences, thus filtering out a large amount of irrelevant information. However, CF is severely limited by the problem of sparse data, and the effectiveness of the model is significantly reduced when there are insufficient data on user–item interactions. As online social platforms such as Facebook, WeChat, and Twitter have grown in popularity, an increasing number of people are posting product reviews on these sites. References [1–3] and personal experience also show that people are affected by their friends' views and actions and gravitate toward those who share their interests. In summary, the application of social relationships in recommender systems has also attracted increasing attention [4,5]. Based on this understanding, recommendation systems can introduce social information to reduce data sparsity and improve recommendation accuracy, and these recommendation systems are called social recommendation systems [6–8].

Early GNNs mainly solved problems strictly related to graph theory [9–11], such as molecular structure classification, in which GNNs showed a superb ability to handle non-Euclidean data. Since data in recommender systems can naturally represent graph data (e.g., interaction data between users and items represented as bipartite graphs), much recent work has applied graph neural networks to recommender systems. Within social recommendation systems, data are typically presented in two forms: the user–item interaction graph, which contains information pertaining to the interactions between users and items, and the social graph, which reflects the social relations of users. There are generally two strategies for recommender systems to use social information [12]. One is to learn user representations from the two graphs separately [8,13,14] and then combine them into a vector, which is more flexible and can use different treatments for different graphs; the other is to merge the two graphs into a unified heterogeneous graph [7,15] and apply GNNs to propagate the information, which has the advantage that the information in both graphs is unified in one representation, which can capture some more complex interactions.

Although GNNs have shown good performance in the field of social recommendation, most of the existing models simply combine social information as auxiliary information with interactive information without fully utilizing the social graph's information. In the information propagation, they only consider the information propagation of high-order neighbor nodes, but no particular attention is given to the fact that there is a lot of useless or even negative information in this information. Inspired by IMP-GCN [16], we introduce an unsupervised subgraph construction module in the social recommendation system, which divides the interaction graph into multiple subgraphs based on user preferences, and users who share similar interests are placed into the same subgraph. We then perform graph convolution operations in the subgraphs using a lightweight GNN to filter out negative information brought by users with different preferences. We also design a feature aggregation module to better integrate user representations in the two graphs.

In conclusion, the primary findings of this study are as follows:

- A novel social recommendation model PLGCN is proposed, which splits the user–item interaction graph into multiple subgraphs based on the user's preferences and passes information in the subgraphs, filtering out negative information brought by users with different preferences.
- A new feature aggregation module was designed that can aggregate the user representations in the two graphs more effectively and has regularization to prevent overfitting.
- We performed comprehensive experiments using two publicly available datasets to evaluate the recommended performance of PLGCN. Based on the outcomes of these experiments, it is evident that PLGCN outperforms the baseline models.

The rest of this article is summarized as follows: We begin with a brief overview of typical relevant work in Section 2. The social recommender system problem and its definition are introduced in Section 3. The design details of the PLGCN model are described in Section 4. Section 5 presents a comprehensive experiment conducted to assess the performance of PLGCN. Finally, we conclude our work and identify potential research directions.

2. Related Work

2.1. Social Recommendation

As online social platforms (e.g., WeChat, Twitter, Facebook) and the richness of users' social information grow rapidly, an increasing number of recommendation systems are introducing users' social information. Leveraging social influence [1] and social homogeneity, as outlined in [2], facilitates a better comprehension of user preferences, and data sparsity is effectively mitigated.

We generally categorize the prior social recommendation systems relevant to our study into three groups based on how they utilize social information. Social networks are used as a kind of regularization in the first category of methods [4,17–19]. SocialMF [19] integrates trust propagation into the matrix factorization technique, making the user's preferences as close as possible to his/her social neighbors. CSR [18] designed a generic regularization term to model the diverse similarities among users and their various friends. One kind of ensemble method involves splitting all items into different groups and ranking them manually [20,21]. SBPR [20] suggests that users have a tendency to provide higher ratings to products that are favored by their friends, and for each user, the collection of items is sorted into three categories: negative items, social items, and positive items. The rankings are as follows: negative items < social items < positive items. The third method is to fuse the embeddings of the user and his/her neighbors [22–24]. TrustSVD [22] introduces social information based on SVD++ [25] and uses implicit feedback from social neighbors as auxiliary implicit feedback for users. RSTE [24] posits that the user's final choice is a trade-off between his/her own likes and the opinions of his/her trusted friends and the linear fusion of the user's embedding with the user's neighbor nodes in the social graph. Nevertheless, none of these models can adequately model the intricate social relationships between users and the interactions between users and items. Therefore, numerous recent studies have focused on employing deep learning for social recommendation systems, with GNN-based social recommendation systems attracting attention because both the social relationship between users and the data that reflect user–item interactions can be modeled naturally in graph form.

2.2. GNN-Based Social Recommendation

The ability of GNNs to model recursive social diffusion processes makes them increasingly popular in the domain of social recommendation. The primary tenet of GNNs is to iteratively collect surrounding node information to generate a more accurate representation of the target node and ultimately obtain a representation of each node.

The first social recommendation system model that uses graph neural networks is GraphRec [6], which combines the user's first-order neighbors' information from both graphs to learn the user's representation. DANSER [14] uses two graph attention networks to obtain user and item implicit representations from each of the two graphs and then combines them to predict users' ratings or preferences for items. HOSR [26] uses multi-step message propagation to encode higher-order social relationships in user embedding learning, refining user embeddings by capturing higher-order collaboration signals in the social graph. In contrast, our proposed PLGCN captures both higher-order collaboration signals in the interaction graph and social graph simultaneously and fuses them into the final user embedding using a feature aggregation module. DiffNet [8] fully leverages the high-order social neighborhood information of users and adds the vector of users' preferred items as an auxiliary vector to the vector representation of users, but this does not filter out the useless parts of the high-order information. On the basis of the DiffNet model, DiffNet++ [7] additionally exploits the high-order information in the interaction graph to optimize the representation of users and items and distinguishes the significance of the different neighbors using the attention mechanism, thus alleviating this problem. Unlike DiffNet++, we are inspired by IMP-GCN [16] to divide the user-interaction graph into multiple subgraphs based on users' preferences to avoid interaction between users with different preferences. Furthermore, we design a new feature aggregation model to obtain a more accurate user embedding. The research conducted on SocialLGN [27] is closely related to our own research. These researchers extended the LightGCN [28] framework and applied convolution operations on both the interaction graph and the social graph to improve the framework's effectiveness in handling social recommendation problems. The main differences between SocialLGN and our proposed PLGCN are as follows: (1) SocialLGN aggregates all messages from neighboring nodes without considering their relevance. In contrast, our PLGCN includes a subgraph construction module, and we perform message passing in the subgraph to effectively filter out irrelevant information. (2) Our feature aggregation module uses MLP to fully explore the potential relationship between user interaction information and social information, whereas SocialLGN uses a linear transformation in the graph fusion module.

In summary, several approaches have been proposed to address the challenges of social recommendation. However, these approaches often have limitations, such as the difficulty of modeling complex user–item interactions and social relationships. Some approaches use attention mechanisms to distinguish the importance of neighboring nodes and filter out irrelevant information, but they often oversimplify the use of social information and do not fully exploit its value. We propose the PLGCN approach to overcome these challenges, which uses subgraph building blocks to filter out irrelevant information and fully leverages the relationship between social and interaction information through neural networks. Our approach provides a more nuanced modeling of the complex interaction between users and items and the social relationship, leading to improved recommendation accuracy and relevance.

3. Problem Definition

Essentially, the recommendation problem is to analyze the user's behavior data to predict the preferences of the user and then combine the data of the items in the system to calculate the items that could potentially appeal to the user and generate a recommendation list from them. However, users are only able to explicitly interact with a small fraction of items, which results in very sparse valid data. The social recommendation system introduces users' social information, which supplements the sparse and effective data and reduces data sparsity. It is clearly effective to use the homogeneity and the influence of social relationships to understand users' preferences.

In the paragraphs that follow, we define a GNN-based social recommendation system. The notations $\jmath$ and $\mathcal{U}$ are used to represent the sets of items and users, and they have M and N elements, respectively (i.e., $|\jmath| = M$, $|\mathcal{U}| = N$). In general, recommendation systems make use of two distinct types of data: social graphs and user–item interaction graphs. A description of these two graphs is given below.

The interaction behavior of users with items (e.g., views, rates, and clicks) is represented by the user–item interaction graph. The graph can be defined by triples $(u, y_{ui}, i | u \in \mathcal{U}, i \in \jmath)$ and is denoted by G_I, where y_{ui} represents the edge that connects user u to item i, and $y_{ui} > 0$ means that user u interacts with item i. On the other hand, there will not be any interaction between them if $y_{ui} = 0$. The notation $\mathcal{N}_i^I$ means the collection of users who have explicit interaction with item i, and the notation $\mathcal{N}_u^I$ indicates the collection of items with which user u has explicit interaction.

Users' social connections are represented in the social graph, which provides auxiliary information about the user (e.g., direct follower or undirected friendship). We represent the social graph as G_s, which has the triple form $\{(u,\ s_{uv}, v | u, v \in \mathcal{U})\}$, where s_{uv} represents the relationship between users u and v, and $s_{uv} = 1$ means there is an observable social connection between users u and v, while $s_{uv} = 0$ indicates there is no connection between them. The symbol $\mathcal{N}_u^S$ is used to denote the collection of users who have a social connection with user u.

Based on the aforementioned conditions, the social recommendation task is described as follows: given the social graph G_S and the user–item interaction graph G_I, the recommendation system should be able to predict the probability of interaction between user u and all items, sort them in descending order, and choose the top N items to generate a recommendation list for user u.

4. The Proposed Method

We present the general structure and technical details of PLGCN as well as the model's training process.

4.1. The Architecture of PLGCN

Figure 1depicts the general design of PLGCN. The model consists of 4 primary components: (i) an embedding layer that leverages the unique identifiers of users and items to initialize their representation vectors; (ii) a subgraph construction module, which constructs multiple subgraphs and groups users with common preferences into the same subgraph; (iii) propagation layers, which propagate the representations of users and items in both graphs; and (iv) a prediction layer that predicts the value of any edge between users and items using their final embeddings (i.e., the probability that user and item will interact).

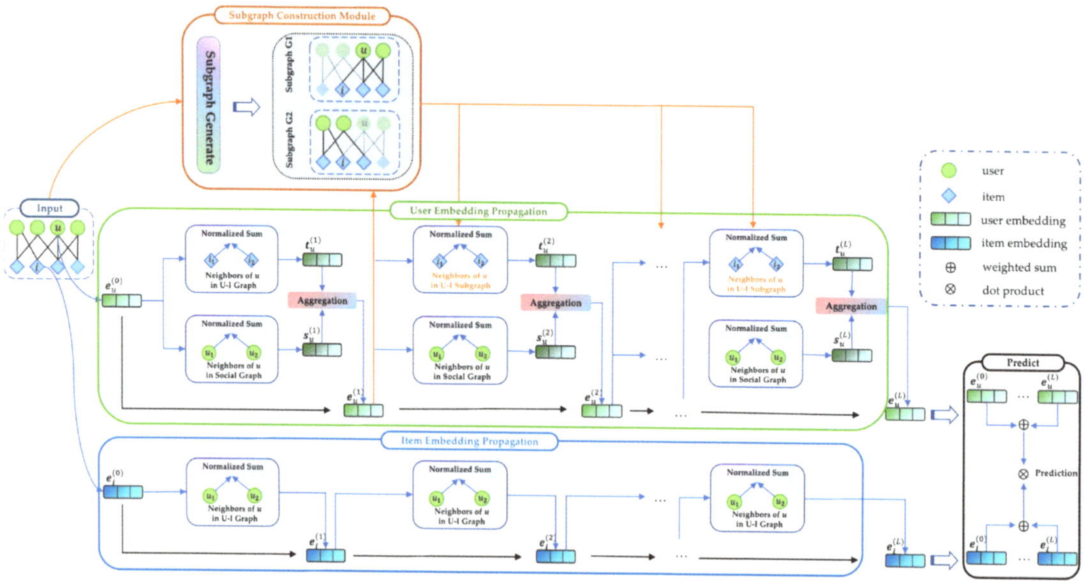

Figure 1. Architecture design of our PLGCN model with 2 subgraphs as illustration. First-order propagation operations are performed on the entire interaction graph and social graph, and higher-order propagation operations are performed on the subgraphs of the interaction graph and social graph.

The following is a description of the mechanism of operation of each component.

4.2. Embedding Layer

The embedding layer employs user and item identifiers to map them to a latent space with low dimensionality. As an example, the embedding layer can encode item i (or user u) as a low-dimensional dense vector of fixed length $\boldsymbol{e}_i^{(0)} \in \mathbb{R}^d$ (*or* $\boldsymbol{e}_u^{(0)} \in \mathbb{R}^d$), and the superscript "$(l)$" ($l \geq 0$) indicates the layer index for the output of the embeddings at the l-th propagation layer. When $l = 0$, it indicates the embedding layer's output. d is a hyperparameter determined in advance that indicates the dimension of an embedding.

The matrices $\boldsymbol{E}_U^{(0)} \in \mathbb{R}^{N \times d}$ and $\boldsymbol{E}_I^{(0)} \in \mathbb{R}^{M \times d}$ represent the output of all N users and all M items from the embedding layer, respectively. User u's embedding is the transpose of the matrix $\boldsymbol{E}_U^{(0)}$'s u-th row, and the same applies to item i.

4.3. Subgraph Construction Module

The subgraph construction module splits the given user–item interaction graph into N_c subgraphs, where the number of subgraphs N_c is a hyperparameter. We define the division of users into subgraphs as a classification task [29], in which each user is assigned to a subgraph. Specifically, each user's embedding aggregates graph structure information and the user's ID information:

$$F_u = \sigma(b_1 + W_1(e_u^{(0)} + e_u^{(1)})) \tag{1}$$

where F_u denotes the user embedding obtained by embedding aggregation, $e_u^{(0)}$ represents the output generated by the embedding layer, and $e_u^{(1)}$ is the feature vector that aggregates first-order neighbor information in the graph, which is generated as an output from the first propagation layer. σ denotes an activation function called LeakyReLU, capable of encoding both negative and positive signals. The learnable parameters $b_1 \in \mathbb{R}^{1\times d}$ and $W_1 \in \mathbb{R}^{d\times d}$ are the bias vector and the weight matrix, respectively. To split the user–item interaction graph into multiple subgraphs based on user preferences, we input the user embeddings into a 2-layer neural network to obtain a prediction vector:

$$U_h = \sigma(b_2 + W_2 F_u) \tag{2}$$

$$U_o = \sigma(b_3 + W_3 U_h) \tag{3}$$

where U_o is the output vector, and the position where the value is at its maximum is the subgraph to which the user belongs, so it is natural that the number of subgraphs and the output vector's dimension are the same. The learnable parameters $W_2 \in \mathbb{R}^{d\times d}$ and $W_3 \in \mathbb{R}^{1\times N_c}$ are the weight matrices, and the learnable parameters $b_2 \in \mathbb{R}^{1\times d}$ and $b_3 \in \mathbb{R}^{1\times N_s}$ are the bias vectors. For users with similar embeddings, the neural network will group them into the same subgraph. This is an unsupervised node classification method because we do not need the real labels of the users.

In summary, we feed the user ID information and first-order user embedding, which best reflect user preferences, into the subgraph construction module. Then, we utilize the powerful modeling ability of neural networks to handle nonlinear relationships and classify user preferences. It is worth noting that we refrain from using traditional clustering algorithms such as K-means [30] due to the high dimensionality of user feature vectors in the current recommendation system field. Traditional clustering algorithms are susceptible to the curse of dimensionality when dealing with high-dimensional data, which can lead to information loss if PCA-based [31] dimensionality reduction is used. Additionally, traditional clustering algorithms cannot effectively model complex nonlinear relationships.

The subgraph construction module groups users with similar preferences and their directly related items into the same subgraph, with each subgraph being independent. By passing messages only within each subgraph, our approach effectively filters out irrelevant or negative information.

4.4. Propagation Layers

The propagation layer aims to capture hidden information in both graphs through graph convolution operations, thereby learning the representations of users and items. The propagation layer is divided into two main parts: user embedding propagation and item embedding propagation. A detailed explanation of them is presented in the following subsections.

4.4.1. User Embedding Propagation

The goal of user embedding propagation is to learn the representation of users in both graphs. We use lightweight GNNs to capture the collaboration signals of the interaction graph and the social graph, propagate information on the two graphs separately, and finally generate the final user embeddings through the feature aggregation module. The process of user u's l-th ($l \leq L$) iteration propagation can be abstracted as follows:

$$e_u^{(l)} = Agg\left(\left\{e_i^{(l-1)}, \forall i \in N_u^I\right\}, \left\{e_v^{(l-1)}, \forall v \in N_u^S\right\}\right) \quad (4)$$

where $e_i^{(l-1)}$ and $e_v^{(l-1)}$ are the embeddings of item i and user v, respectively, after the l-th iteration propagation, and $Agg(*)$ is the aggregation function that aggregates the embeddings of item i with which u has interaction and the embeddings of user v with which u is socially connected. We designed a feature aggregation module to act as the user aggregation function $Agg(*)$ to better learn user embeddings.

Because direct interactions between users and items more accurately reflect user preferences, this is crucial and reliable information. To construct subgraphs based on user preferences, we perform first-order graph convolution operations on the social graph and entire interaction graph alone, while second-order or higher-order graph convolution operations are performed on the social graph and subgraphs of the interaction graph to filter out useless or even negative information from users with different preferences. To achieve this, two separate embeddings are created in the interaction graph and the social graph to represent user u after the l-th iteration propagation, with $t_u^{(l)}$ and $s_u^{(l)}$ being their respective representations and $e_u^{(l)}$ being the user's final embedding after the l-th iteration propagation. Thus, for user u, the first-order propagation can be expressed as follows:

$$t_u^{(1)} = \sum_{i \in \mathcal{N}_u^I} \frac{1}{c_{ui}} e_i^{(0)} \quad (5)$$

$$s_u^{(1)} = \sum_{v \in \mathcal{N}_u^S} \frac{1}{c_{uv}} e_v^{(0)} \quad (6)$$

where c_{ui} is $\sqrt{|\mathcal{N}_u^I||\mathcal{N}_u^I|}$, which is the product of the square root of the degree of user u and item i in the interaction graph, and its inverse is the normalization term that prevents the user or item embedding scale from increasing due to graph convolution operations. c_{uv} is $\sqrt{|\mathcal{N}_u^S||\mathcal{N}_v^S|}$, which is the product of the square root of the degree of user u and user v in the social graph and serves the same purpose as c_{ui}.

The process of updating the embedding in second-order or higher-order (i.e., $l \geq 2$) graph convolution is analogous to the first-order graph convolution process, with the difference that high-order graph convolution is performed in the social graph and the subgraph of the interaction graph to which the user belongs. The procedure is explained in full in the steps that follow:

$$t_u^{(l)} = \sum_{i \in \mathcal{N}_u^{I_c}} \frac{1}{c_{ui_c}} e_i^{(l-1)} \quad (7)$$

$$s_u^{(l)} = \sum_{v \in \mathcal{N}_u^S} \frac{1}{c_{uv}} e_v^{(l-1)} \quad (8)$$

where c_{ui_c} is $\sqrt{\left|\mathcal{N}_u^{I_c}\right|\left|\mathcal{N}_u^{I_c}\right|}$, which is the product of the square root of the degree of user u and item i in the subgraph of the interaction graph to which the user belongs. As Equations (5)–(8) show, we have adopted a lightweight form of propagation, discarding complex operations such as linear transformations, and this lightweight form of propagation is inspired by SGC [32] and LightGCN [28].

The feature aggregation module is then used to aggregate $t_u^{(l)}$ and $s_u^{(l)}$ to generate the updated embedding $e_u^{(l)}$ for layer l. As shown in Equations (9) and (10), the feature aggregation module can be seen as a function $Agg(*)$ with two embeddings as parameters, and the specific aggregation steps are as follows:

$$h_u^{(l)} = MLP\left(\sigma\left(W_4 t_u^{(l)}\right) \parallel \sigma\left(W_5 s_u^{(l)}\right)\right) \tag{9}$$

$$e_u^{(l)} = \frac{h_u^{(l)}}{\left|\left|h_u^{(l)}\right|\right|_2} \tag{10}$$

where W_4 and $W_5 \in \mathbb{R}^{d \times d}$ are trainable weight matrices and $\parallel$ is a vector splicing operation that splices two vectors of dimension d into a vector of length $2d$. σ is the $tanh$ activation function, and $MLP(*)$ is a multilayer perceptron that can capture the complex relationship between two users' embeddings in each dimension. Equation (9) is a regularization operation that prevents embedding $e_u^{(l)}$ from becoming particularly large as the number of layers l grows.

4.4.2. Item Embedding Propagation

For item embedding propagation, the propagation process is analogous to that of users, but this process exists only in the user–item interaction graph. We use lightweight GNNs to capture the collaboration signals and update the item embedding by recursively passing the representation of neighboring nodes. The specific process is shown as follows:

$$e_i^{(l)} = \sum_{u \in \mathcal{N}_i^I} \frac{1}{c_{iu}} e_u^{(l-1)} \tag{11}$$

where c_{iu} is $\sqrt{|\mathcal{N}_u^I||\mathcal{N}_u^I|}$, which is the product of the square root of the degree of user u and item i in the interaction graph, and it also serves for normalization.

4.5. Prediction Layer

After K rounds of propagation, the embedding for user u and item i is obtained for each layer, i.e., $\left\{e_u^{(0)}, \ldots, e_u^{(L)}\right\}$ and $\left\{e_i^{(0)}, \ldots, e_i^{(L)}\right\}$, respectively. We weight and sum the user and item embeddings for each layer to obtain the final representation:

$$e_u^* = \sum_{l=0}^{L} \alpha_l e_u^{(l)} \tag{12}$$

$$e_i^* = \sum_{l=0}^{L} \alpha_l e_i^{(l)} \tag{13}$$

where α_l denotes the l-th layer's embedding weight factor and e_u^* and e_i^* are the final embeddings of user u and item i, respectively.

To obtain the preference of user u for item i, the inner product of their embeddings is computed:

$$\hat{y}_{ui} = e_u^{*T} e_i^* \tag{14}$$

where $\hat{y}_{ui}$ denotes our predicted preference of user u for item i.

4.6. Model Training

In general, the tasks of the recommender system are divided into two categories: CTR prediction and top-N recommendation. In this work, our recommendation task is top-N recommendation, where the aim is to select N items that suit the user's preferences best and recommend them to the user in the form of a list. In a real business system, this task is worth more than predicting ratings [33].

To achieve this, we minimize the Bayesian personalized ranking loss, which is based on the idea that it increases the gap between the scores of the negative and positive samples, with positive samples being user and item interactions that already exist in the dataset and negative samples being non-existent interactions that are not observed in the dataset. Therefore, we define a triple $\{u, i^+, i^-\}$, where u has interacted with i^+ but not with i^-. The objective function has the following form:

$$arg\ min \sum_{(u,i^+)\in\mathcal{N}_u^l \cup\ (u,i^-)\notin\mathcal{N}_u^l} -ln\sigma(\hat{y}_{ui^+} - \hat{y}_{ui^-}) + \lambda||\mathbf{\Theta}||_2^2 \quad (15)$$

where λ and $\mathbf{\Theta}$ denote the weight decay rate and the parameters of PLGCN, respectively.

4.7. Matrix-Form Propagation Rule of PLGCN

We propose a matrix-based representation of the PLGCN model for propagating information on graphs in this section. To achieve this goal, we use $\boldsymbol{R} \in \mathbb{R}^{N\times M}$ to represent the rating matrix. Each element $r_{ui}(u = 1 : N, i = 1 : M)$ inside the matrix is binary and shows if user u and item i have interacted; 1 implies that an interaction exists, and 0 indicates that there is no interaction. Then, $\mathbf{S} \in \mathbb{R}^{N\times N}$ indicates the adjacency matrix of social graph G_s.

We further define $\boldsymbol{\mathcal{L}}_R = \boldsymbol{D}_R^{-\frac{1}{2}}\boldsymbol{R}\boldsymbol{D}_R^{\frac{1}{2}}$, where $\boldsymbol{\mathcal{L}}_R$ is the Laplacian matrix for the interaction graph. $\boldsymbol{D}_R \in \mathbb{R}^{N\times N}$ is a diagonal matrix, where d_{ii} is the element that counts how many elements in $\boldsymbol{R}$'s i-th row are nonzero. In the same way, we also define the transpose matrix $\boldsymbol{\mathcal{L}}_R^T$ of $\boldsymbol{\mathcal{L}}_R$ and the Laplacian matrix for social graph $\boldsymbol{\mathcal{L}}_S$.

As illustrated in 0, the following expression describes the first layer propagation in PLGCN:

$$\boldsymbol{H}_U^{(1)} = MLP\left(\sigma\left(\boldsymbol{W}_1\boldsymbol{\mathcal{L}}_R\boldsymbol{E}_I^{(0)}\right) \parallel \sigma\left(\boldsymbol{W}_2\boldsymbol{\mathcal{L}}_S\boldsymbol{E}_U^{(0)}\right)\right) \quad (16)$$

$$\boldsymbol{E}_U^{(1)} = \frac{\boldsymbol{H}_U^{(1)}}{\boldsymbol{H}_{U\ 2}^{(1)}} \quad (17)$$

$$\boldsymbol{E}_I^{(1)} = \boldsymbol{\mathcal{L}}_R^T\boldsymbol{E}_U^{(0)} \quad (18)$$

The following formula shows the l-th layer's propagation in matrix form in PLGCN:

$$\boldsymbol{E}_{U_c}^{(l)} = \boldsymbol{\mathcal{L}}_c\boldsymbol{E}_{U_c}^{(l-1)} \quad (19)$$

where $\boldsymbol{\mathcal{L}}_c$ denotes the Laplacian matrix belonging to a subgraph of the interaction graph. The information of all subgraphs is then aggregated:

$$\boldsymbol{E}_U^{(l)} = \sum_{U_c\in G_c} \boldsymbol{E}_{U_c}^{(l)} \quad (20)$$

where $\boldsymbol{E}_U^{(l)}$ is the final embedding of the l-th layer, and G_c denotes the set of subgraphs of the user–item interaction graph. Then, we perform the same operation as the first layer:

$$\boldsymbol{H}_U^{(l)} = MLP\left(\sigma\left(\boldsymbol{W}_1\boldsymbol{\mathcal{L}}_R\boldsymbol{E}_I^{(l-1)}\right) \parallel \sigma\left(\boldsymbol{W}_2\boldsymbol{\mathcal{L}}_S\boldsymbol{E}_U^{(l-1)}\right)\right) \quad (21)$$

$$\boldsymbol{E}_U^{(l)} = \frac{\boldsymbol{H}_U^{(l)}}{\boldsymbol{H}_{U\ 2}^{(l)}} \quad (22)$$

$$\boldsymbol{E}_I^{(l)} = \boldsymbol{\mathcal{L}}_R^T\boldsymbol{E}_U^{(l-1)} \quad (23)$$

5. Empirical Analysis

To compare our PLGCN's performance with other recommendation methods, this section describes the evaluation metrics, the dataset, the parameter settings, and the experiments we carried out on various datasets. We ran all programs on a Win10 PC with an RTX 3070 Ti graphics card with 8 G of RAM and an i5 12,600 K processor. We used PyTorch to build the PLCGN.

5.1. Experimental Settings

5.1.1. Datasets

The proposed model was evaluated by conducting experiments on two datasets from the real world that vary in size and levels of sparsity. The datasets are described as follows: The LastFM dataset [34] (https://www.last.fm (accessed on 17 May 2023)), which includes 1892 users' social connections and interactions with music-related items, is provided by Last.fm, one of the hottest social music platforms of the moment for sharing and discovering music in the world. The Ciao dataset [35] (http://www.ciao.co.uk (accessed on 17 May 2023)) is an online shopping dataset that includes 7375 customer reviews for a variety of products as well as information about user friendships. Many social recommendation systems use these datasets to validate model performance [27,36,37]. We divided each dataset into three random parts, the training set, the test set, and the validation set, corresponding to a ratio of 8:1:1. The precise statistical data from the datasets we used are displayed in Table 1.

Table 1. Statistics for the two datasets. # represents the number of elements in the set.

Dataset	Ciao	LastFM
# Users	7375	1892
# Items	105,114	17,632
# Interactions	284,086	92,834
Density (Interactions)	0.037%	0.278%
# Social Connections	57,544	25,434
Density (Social Connections)	0.106%	0.711%

5.1.2. Benchmark Cases

We evaluated how well PLGCN performs by contrasting it with six other methods that are state-of-the-art:

- BPR [38]—A list of recommendations is created by sorting items using the traditional pairwise collaborative filtering approach according to the maximum posterior probability determined by a Bayesian analysis of the issue.
- SBPR [20]—An MF-based recommendation model to enhance the accuracy of personalized rankings with collaborative filtering algorithms using users' social relationships.
- DiffNet [8]—A social recommendation model that utilizes GNNs. It directly takes the user embeddings' vector sum in the two graphs to generate the final user embeddings.
- NGCF [39]—A recommendation model based on GCN is designed with a neural network approach to recursively propagate embeddings in the interaction graph.
- LightGCN [28]—A lightweight recommendation model based on GCN that eliminates two operations that would have caused recommendation performance degradation based on NGCF.
- SocialLGN [27]—User social information was introduced on the basis of LightGCN, and a graph fusion operation was created to combine user embeddings with interaction information and user embeddings with social information.

5.1.3. Metrics

To assess the recommended performance under the top-N task of our PLGCN and five other SOTA methods, we use three metrics that are commonly applied; two of them are precision and recall, and they have the following expressions:

$$Precision = \frac{\#TP}{\#TP + \#FP} \tag{24}$$

$$Recall = \frac{\#TP}{\#TP + \#FN} \tag{25}$$

where FP is the number of incorrectly predicted negative samples, TP denotes the number of properly predicted positive samples, and FN denotes the number of incorrectly predicted positive samples. The other is $NDCG$, i.e., normalized discounted cumulative gain, which is used to measure the quality of the ranking, and it is expressed as follows:

$$NDCG@N = \frac{r(1) + \sum_{i=2}^{l} \frac{r(i)}{log_2^i}}{\sum_{i=1}^{|REL|} \frac{r(i)}{log_2^{(i+1)}}} \tag{26}$$

where $|REL|$ is the sum of the relevance scores $r(i)$ of the top N items recommended. $r(i) = 1$ indicates that the user interacts with the recommended item; $r(i) = 0$ means that the user does not interact with the recommended item.

In summary, the indicators used in this experiment and their significance are listed below, and it is worth noting that these metrics are all dimensionless:

- Precision@k: the proportion of relevant items among the top k items recommended to the user. Precision@10 and Precision@20 indicate the precision at 10 and 20 recommendations, respectively.
- Recall@k: the proportion of relevant items among all the relevant items in the test set that are recommended to the user. Recall@10 and Recall@20 indicate the recall at 10 and 20 recommendations, respectively.
- NDCG@k: normalized discounted cumulative gain at k. NDCG is a measure of ranking quality that takes into account both the relevance of the recommended items and their position in the list. NDCG@10 and NDCG@20 indicate the NDCG score at 10 and 20 recommendations, respectively.

The greater the value for these three evaluation metrics, the better the performance. Given the sparsity of the interaction data, we repeatedly randomly selected an item that the user did not interact with as a negative sample; then, we combined items that the user did interact with the negative sample. To eliminate the instability of random selection, for each model and dataset, we repeated the experiment five times and averaged the results as the ultimate ranking results.

5.1.4. Parameter Settings

To ensure that the experiments were fair and equitable, the parameters of each method were adjusted based on our own experimental data or the corresponding references. We used the PyTorch framework to construct our PLGCN and Adam to infer model parameters. The model was optimized with a learning rate η of 1×10^{-3}. The dimension of embedding was fixed at 200, and the training batch size was fixed at 2048. After trials in the range of $\{1 \times 10^{-6}, 1 \times 10^{-5}, \ldots, 1 \times 10^{-2}\}$, we fixed weight decay (λ) at 1×10^{-4}. The weight (α_l) for each propagation layer was $\frac{1}{L+1}$, where L is the number of layers and N_c is the subgraph count. For this paper, L was set to 3, and the value of N_c was 2. Early stopping was adopted to terminate the training process. To enhance readability, we present the parameter settings in a tabular format, as shown in Table 2.

Table 2. Parameter settings.

Parameter	Value
Learning rate (η)	1×10^{-3}
Dimension of embedding (d)	200
Training batch size	2048
Weight decay (λ)	1×10^{-4}
Number of layers (L)	3
Number of subgraphs (N_c)	2

5.2. Model Performance Evaluation

In the recommendation field, the problem of cold start is a matter of great concern, for which we designed a special scenario to evaluate the cold-start performance of PLGCN and other baseline models by referring to the approach in the literature [27]. In both datasets, we compared the experimental results for all models, including the cold-start case. In the test set, users who interacted with fewer than 20 items were labeled as cold-start users. We employ this strategy to provide a test set for cold-start users alone, which includes only cold-start users and their social and interaction information. The results of PLGCN and the five baseline models on the original test set are shown in Table 3. The outcomes of the aforementioned models on the cold-start test set are displayed in Table 4, and the improvements in Tables 3 and 4 indicate the percentage increase in performance of our model in terms of precision, recall, and NDCG at 10 and 20 recommendations compared to the best baseline model. It is worth noting that all experimental results were not normalized.

Table 3. Recommendation performance of all models on both datasets. The underlined value is the second-best performance, and the bolded value is the best. Improvement is the comparison between the best performance and the second-best performance.

Dataset	Model	Precision@10	Precision@20	Recall@10	Recall@20	NDCG@10	NDCG@20
LastFM	BPR	0.0922	0.0720	0.0962	0.1499	0.1099	0.1321
	SBPR	0.1398	0.1010	0.1442	0.2070	0.1749	0.1978
	DiffNet	0.1727	0.1215	0.1779	0.2488	0.2219	0.2474
	NGCF	0.1766	0.1269	0.1796	0.2576	0.2287	0.2563
	LightGCN	0.1961	0.1358	0.2003	0.2769	0.2536	0.2788
	SocialLGN	<u>0.1972</u>	<u>0.1368</u>	<u>0.2026</u>	<u>0.2794</u>	<u>0.2566</u>	<u>0.2883</u>
	PLGCN	**0.2043**	**0.1412**	**0.2091**	**0.2881**	**0.2646**	**0.2903**
	Improvement	3.60%	3.22%	3.21%	3.11%	3.12%	0.69%
Ciao	BPR	0.0145	0.0111	0.0220	0.0339	0.0229	0.0260
	SBPR	0.0179	0.0141	0.0259	0.0412	0.0266	0.0307
	DiffNet	0.0238	0.0182	0.0341	0.0527	0.0359	0.0403
	NGCF	0.0178	0.0179	0.0343	0.0531	0.0359	0.0407
	LightGCN	0.0271	0.0202	0.0410	0.0591	0.0437	0.0478
	SocialLGN	<u>0.0276</u>	<u>0.0205</u>	<u>0.043</u>	<u>0.0618</u>	<u>0.0441</u>	<u>0.0486</u>
	PLGCN	**0.0308**	**0.0230**	**0.0446**	**0.0662**	**0.0476**	**0.0526**
	Improvement	13.59%	12.20%	3.72%	7.12%	7.94%	8.23%

The outcomes demonstrate that models based on MF do not perform as well in all cases and exhibit a performance much inferior to that of GNN-based models because MF-based models are more susceptible to data sparsity and cannot capture complex interactions. LightGCN performs better in the vast majority of cases than BPR, SBPR, DiffNet, and NGCF. As pointed out in [28], LightGCN removes two fundamental operations in GCN that can negatively affect recommendation performance, namely linear transformation and nonlinear activation. SocialLGN performs better than LightGCN because it introduces social information on top of LightGCN and considers the effect of higher-order graph structure on user embedding.

Table 4. Recommendation performance of all models on two cold-start datasets. The underlined value is the second-best performance, and the bolded value is the best. Improvement is the comparison between the best performance and the second-best performance.

Dataset	Model	Precision@10	Precision@20	Recall@10	Recall@20	NDCG@10	NDCG@20
LastFM-cold	BPR	0.0282	0.0209	0.1151	0.1615	0.0828	0.0989
	SBPR	0.0292	0.0333	0.1123	0.2467	0.0709	0.1159
	DiffNet	0.0417	0.0271	0.1713	0.2407	0.1107	0.1309
	NGCF	0.0333	0.0292	0.1169	0.2141	0.1074	0.1411
	LightGCN	0.0417	0.0313	0.1727	0.2416	0.1374	0.1560
	SocialLGN	<u>0.0458</u>	<u>0.0333</u>	<u>0.1974</u>	<u>0.2663</u>	<u>0.1419</u>	<u>0.1643</u>
	PLGCN	**0.0667**	**0.0396**	**0.2624**	**0.3000**	**0.1716**	**0.1821**
	Improvement	45.63%	18.92%	32.93%	12.65%	20.93%	10.83%
Ciao-cold	BPR	0.0061	0.0047	0.0208	0.0328	0.0138	0.0179
	SBPR	0.0070	0.0060	0.0234	0.0384	0.0165	0.0219
	DiffNet	0.0104	0.0081	0.0339	0.0539	0.0248	0.0316
	NGCF	0.0104	0.0085	0.0341	0.0557	0.0245	0.0319
	LightGCN	0.0131	0.0096	0.0429	0.0616	0.0319	0.0384
	SocialLGN	<u>0.0134</u>	<u>0.0097</u>	<u>0.0441</u>	<u>0.0630</u>	<u>0.0328</u>	<u>0.0394</u>
	PLGCN	**0.0144**	**0.0106**	**0.0447**	**0.0668**	**0.0336**	**0.0412**
	Improvement	7.46%	9.28%	1.36%	6.03%	2.44%	4.57%

The results unequivocally show that PLGCN consistently achieves the best performance. For instance, in contrast to SocialLGN, PLGCN improves the Recall@10 on the original LastFM dataset by 3.22% and the Precision@10 on the original Ciao dataset by 13.59%. Since SocialLGN propagates messages on the social graph and the whole user–item interaction graph without constructing subgraphs, by comparing the performance of PLGCN with SocialLGN in the experiments, it can be seen that propagating information in subgraphs can significantly raise the effectiveness of recommendations. In particular, on the LastFM dataset containing information about cold-start users only, PLGCN improves 45.63% in the Precision@10 metric and 32.93% and 20.93% in Recall@10 and NDCG@10, respectively. By looking at the data in 0, we can see the superior ability of PLGCN in alleviating the cold-start problem. Additionally, we find that in the cold-start scenario, the denser the interaction and social graphs of the dataset are, the more significant the performance improvement is, while the opposite is true in the original dataset.

5.3. Ablation Experiments

We ran an ablation experiment to evaluate how the PLGCN feature aggregation module and the subgraph construction module affected the performance of the recommendations.

5.3.1. Effect of the Feature Aggregation Module

For this section, two variants were designed, and PLGCN was compared to them to verify the performance improvement of the feature aggregation module:

- PLGCN_{GCN}: This variant uses the feature aggregation operation in *GCN* [40] to aggregate the user's embedding in both graphs with the following equation:

$$f_{GCN} = \sigma\left(\boldsymbol{W}\left(\boldsymbol{t}_u^{(l)} + \boldsymbol{s}_u^{(l)}\right)\right) \tag{27}$$

- $\text{PLGCN}_{GraphSage}$: This variant uses the feature aggregation operation in *GraphSage* [33] to aggregate the user's embedding in both graphs with the following equation:

$$f_{GraphSage} = \sigma\left(\boldsymbol{W}\left(\boldsymbol{t}_u^{(l)} \middle\| \boldsymbol{s}_u^{(l)}\right)\right) \tag{28}$$

In Equations (27) and (28), $\boldsymbol{t}_u^{(l)}$ and $\boldsymbol{s}_u^{(l)}$ denote the embedding of user u propagated through the l-th iteration on the interaction graph and social graph, respectively. $\boldsymbol{W}$ is the trainable transformation matrix, || means the concatenation operation, and σ is the *tanh* activation function.

As shown in Figure 2, when compared to other models, our proposed feature aggregation module performs the best in all cases. The explanation for the superior performance of PLGCN is that our proposed feature aggregation module first performs a feature transformation on $\boldsymbol{t}_u^{(l+1)}$ and $\boldsymbol{s}_u^{(l+1)}$ and then uses an activation function to activate them nonlinearly, such that a joint space may be created between the user embedding in the two graphs. The multilayer perceptron can be used to explore higher-order feature interactions. In addition, the recommendation performance benefits from the normalization operation, which prevents $\boldsymbol{e}_u^{(l)}$ from increasing with l.

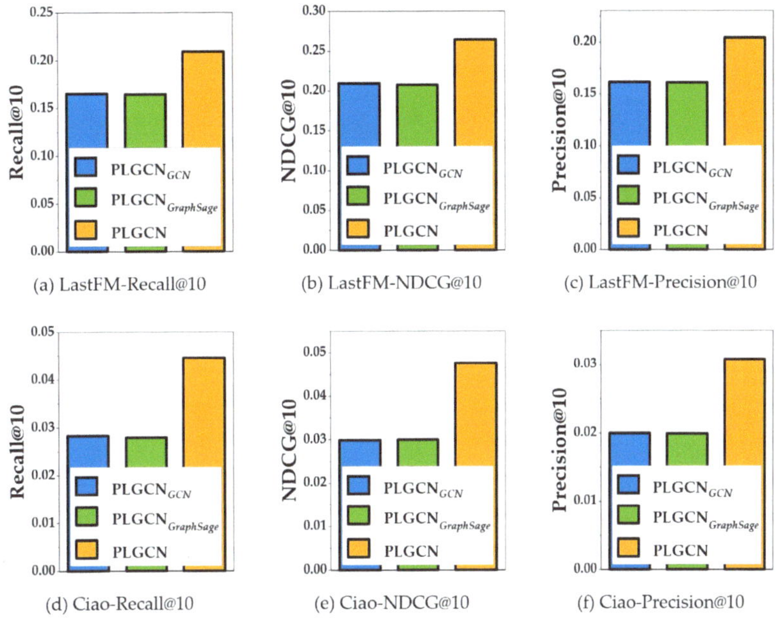

Figure 2. The impact of the feature aggregation module.

5.3.2. Effect of Subgraph Construction Module

This section compares PLGCN with a variant to evaluate whether our proposed subgraph construction module is effective:

- $PLGCN_S$: In this variant, we do not use the subgraph construction module, and we use the same lightweight GNN framework to propagate messages in the social graph and the entire interaction graph.

Table 5 shows the comparison results, which demonstrate that PLGCN has better recommendation performance because the subgraph builder divides users with the same preferences and the items they interact with into a subgraph to filter out the negative information brought by users with different preferences.

Table 5. Performance comparison of PLGCN and its variant on two datasets. The underlined value is the second-best performance, and the bolded value is the best.

Dataset	LastFM			Ciao		
Model	Precision@10	Recall@10	NDCG@10	Precision@10	Recall@10	NDCG@10
$PLGCN_s$	0.2017	0.2065	0.2629	0.0307	0.0441	0.0475
PLGCN	**0.2043**	**0.2091**	**0.2646**	**0.0308**	**0.0446**	**0.0476**

$PLGCN_s$

5.4. Impact Analysis for Hyperparameters

Two crucial parameters affect the performance of PLGCN: the propagation layer number (L) and the subgraph number (N_c). We investigate how they impact the model in this section.

5.4.1. Impact of the Number of Propagation Layers

To explore how the model's performance is impacted by the number L of propagation layers, we kept the other parameters constant and changed L to [1–5]. We display the experimental results in Figure 3, and there is a noticeable improvement in PLGCN's performance when the value of L is increased from 1 to 3 on the original LastFM dataset, and the model performs best at $L = 3$. The original Ciao dataset shows a similar trend, where the model attains the highest performance at $k = 3$ and the performance decreases when k is greater than 3. We inferred from our observations that the recommended performance of the model may be negatively affected by the oversmoothing effect caused by too large a K value, and therefore, we set the K value to 2–4, which is a reasonable choice.

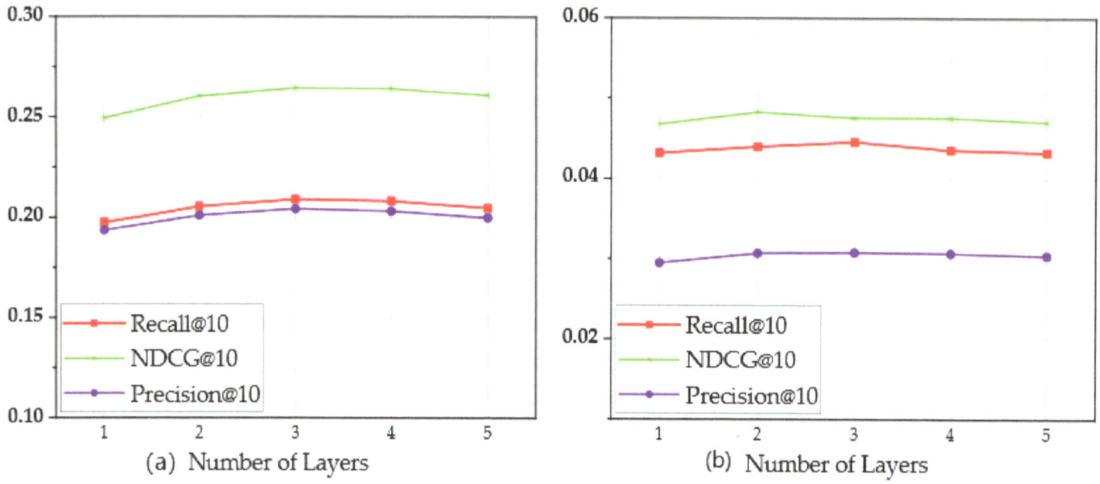

Figure 3. The impact of the number of propagation layers L. (**a**) LastFM dataset and (**b**) Ciao dataset.

5.4.2. Impact of the Number of Subgraphs

The performance of the PLGCN is examined in this section in relation to various subgraph N_c counts. We set N_c to [2–4], and the other parameters were constant. Figure 4 displays the outcomes, where $PLGCN_2$, $PLGCN_3$, and $PLGCN_4$ represent the PLGCN model when N_c is 2, 3, and 4, respectively. It can be seen that $PLGCN_2$ performs best in most cases when there are three propagation layers. It can be assumed that there are fewer layers of propagation at this point, and a node in the subgraph of $PLGCN_2$ has more nodes connected in a short distance and acquires more information than the nodes in PLGCN$_3$ and PLGCN$_4$, so it performs better.

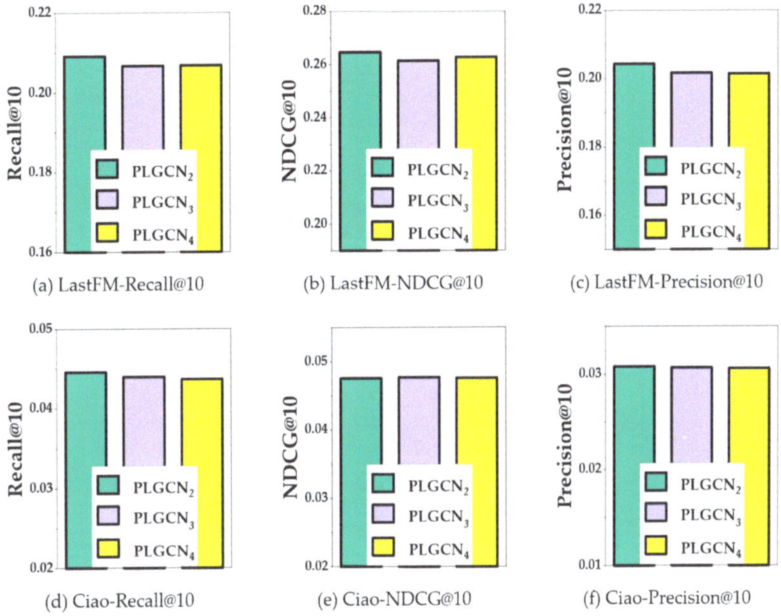

Figure 4. The impact of the number of subgraphs N_c.

6. Discussion

In our experiments, we showed that our graph neural network-based social recommendation model outperforms some previous recommendation models ([8,27,28]). Compared with [28], we find that adding social information to a recommender system does improve the recommendation performance, while compared with [8,27], we find that the quality of social information and the method of using social information also have a crucial impact. In some cases, the performance improvement of our proposed method, PLGCN, is more evident in the cold-start scenario. We believe that cold-start users have fewer interaction data, and negative information has a greater impact on recommendation performance. By filtering out negative information, we substantially improve the recommendation performance.

However, our proposed model also has some limitations, which highlight opportunities for future research. For example, we only consider user preferences in constructing subgraphs, while other social features such as friendship networks or trust levels can be incorporated to enhance the social filtering process. Additionally, our feature aggregation module only includes user embeddings with social and interaction information. It could be extended to include more diverse information sources, such as temporal information or user-generated content.

7. Conclusions

Most of the existing social recommendation models only take higher-order collaborative signals into account, without paying attention to the negative signals in these signals, which negatively affects the models' recommendation performance. We propose the PLGCN, a novel social recommendation model based on GCN, as a solution to this issue, which incorporates unsupervised learning to classify users based on their preferences, allowing for more effective filtering of irrelevant and negative information from high-order neighbor nodes. This enables PLGCN to provide more personalized and accurate recommendations. Moreover, we designed a novel feature aggregation module to better aggregate user representations in both graphs. We evaluated PLGCN against other SOTA models on two datasets, and the outcomes demonstrated that PLGCN outperforms them. Furthermore, PLGCN adopts a lightweight GNN framework that removes nonlinear activation and feature transformation operations, which mitigates the overfitting issue and enables faster and more efficient training and inference. Our proposed model can be applied to diverse social recommendation scenarios, such as e-commerce, social media, and content recommendation.

However, our model still has limitations. First, it relies on the assumption that social connections effectively capture users' preferences. In reality, users may connect for various reasons, and their social networks may not fully reflect their preferences, which could affect the accuracy of our approach. Second, our experiments were conducted on specific datasets, and the performance of our method may vary on other datasets or domains. Further evaluation is necessary to validate the effectiveness and generalizability of our method. Third, our model assumes a static social network structure and does not consider dynamic changes over time. Future work can explore incorporating dynamic social information to improve the performance of social recommendation methods.

In terms of future work, we plan to investigate several areas for further improvement. First, we would like to explore the use of more complex graph neural network architectures to capture even more nuanced social relationships and better incorporate users' social behavior. Second, we plan to investigate the use of additional data sources, such as user-generated content and location data, to enhance our model's performance and provide more personalized recommendations. Finally, we will explore the use of different datasets and evaluation metrics to better capture the effectiveness of our model and ensure that our recommendations are not only accurate but also diverse and novel.

Author Contributions: Formal analysis, H.X. and L.T.; investigation, G.W.; methodology, H.X. and L.T.; project administration, G.W.; resources, X.J. and E.Z.; data curation, H.X. and L.T.; supervision, L.T.; validation, H.X. and X.J.; writing—original draft preparation, H.X.; writing—review and editing, X.J and L.T. All authors have read and agreed to the published version of the manuscript.

Funding: This research was funded by the Anhui Province Science and Technology Major Special Projects (Project No. 202103b06020013), Anhui Provincial Natural Science Foundation Project (Project No. 2108085MF209), and the Open Fund Project of Anhui Provincial Key Laboratory of Intelligent Agricultural Technology and Equipment (Project No. APKLSATE2021X008).

Institutional Review Board Statement: Not applicable.

Informed Consent Statement: Not applicable.

Data Availability Statement: This research employed publicly available datasets for its experimental studies.

Conflicts of Interest: The authors declare no conflict of interest.

References

1. Cialdini, R.B.; Goldstein, N.J. Social influence: Compliance and conformity. *Annu. Rev. Psychol.* **2004**, *55*, 591–621. [CrossRef] [PubMed]
2. McPherson, M.; Smith-Lovin, L.; Cook, J.M. Birds of a feather: Homophily in social networks. *Annu. Rev. Sociol.* **2001**, *27*, 415–444. [CrossRef]
3. Knoke, D.; Yang, S. *Social Network Analysis*; SAGE publications: London, UK, 2019.
4. Ma, H.; Zhou, D.; Liu, C.; Lyu, M.R.; King, I. Recommender systems with social regularization. In Proceedings of the Fourth ACM International Conference on Web Search and Data Mining, Hong Kong, China, 9–12 February 2011; pp. 287–296.
5. Tang, J.; Wang, S.; Hu, X.; Yin, D.; Bi, Y.; Chang, Y.; Liu, H. Recommendation with social dimensions. In Proceedings of the Thirtieth AAAI Conference on Artificial Intelligence, Phoenix, AZ, USA, 12–17 February 2016.
6. Fan, W.; Ma, Y.; Li, Q.; He, Y.; Zhao, E.; Tang, J.; Yin, D. Graph neural networks for social recommendation. In Proceedings of the World Wide Web Conference, San Francisco, CA, USA, 13–17 May 2019; pp. 417–426.
7. Wu, L.; Li, J.; Sun, P.; Hong, R.; Ge, Y.; Wang, M. Diffnet++: A neural influence and interest diffusion network for social recommendation. *IEEE Trans. Knowl. Data Eng.* **2020**, *34*, 4753–4766. [CrossRef]

8. Wu, L.; Sun, P.; Fu, Y.; Hong, R.; Wang, X.; Wang, M. A neural influence diffusion model for social recommendation. In Proceedings of the 42nd International ACM SIGIR Conference on Research and Development in Information Retrieval, Paris, Franch, 21–25 July 2019; pp. 235–244.
9. Fout, A.; Byrd, J.; Shariat, B.; Ben-Hur, A. Protein interface prediction using graph convolutional networks. *Adv. Neural Inf. Process. Syst.* **2017**, *30*, 6533–6542.
10. Duvenaud, D.K.; Maclaurin, D.; Iparraguirre, J.; Bombarell, R.; Hirzel, T.; Aspuru-Guzik, A.; Adams, R.P. Convolutional networks on graphs for learning molecular fingerprints. *Adv. Neural Inf. Process. Syst.* **2015**, *28*, 2224–2232.
11. Kearnes, S.; McCloskey, K.; Berndl, M.; Pande, V.; Riley, P. Molecular graph convolutions: Moving beyond fingerprints. *J. Comput. -Aided Mol. Des.* **2016**, *30*, 595–608. [CrossRef] [PubMed]
12. Wu, S.; Sun, F.; Zhang, W.; Xie, X.; Cui, B. Graph neural networks in recommender systems: A survey. *ACM Comput. Surv.* **2022**, *55*, 1–37. [CrossRef]
13. Eksombatchai, C.; Jindal, P.; Liu, J.Z.; Liu, Y.; Sharma, R.; Sugnet, C.; Ulrich, M.; Leskovec, J. Pixie: A system for recommending 3+ billion items to 200+ million users in real-time. In Proceedings of the 2018 World Wide Web Conference, Lyon, France, 23–27 April 2018; pp. 1775–1784.
14. Wu, Q.; Zhang, H.; Gao, X.; He, P.; Weng, P.; Gao, H.; Chen, G. Dual graph attention networks for deep latent representation of multifaceted social effects in recommender systems. In Proceedings of the World Wide Web Conference, San Francisco, CA, USA, 13–17 May 2019; pp. 2091–2102.
15. Chen, T.; Wong RC, W. An efficient and effective framework for session-based social recommendation. In Proceedings of the 14th ACM International Conference on Web Search and Data Mining, Online, 8–12 March 2021; pp. 400–408.
16. Liu, F.; Cheng, Z.; Zhu, L.; Gao, Z.; Nie, L. Interest-aware message-passing gcn for recommendation. In Proceedings of the Web Conference 2021, Ljubljana, Slovenia, 19–23 April 2021; pp. 1296–1305.
17. Wang, X.; He, X.; Nie, L.; Chua, T.S. Item silk road: Recommending items from information domains to social users. In Proceedings of the 40th International ACM SIGIR Conference on Research and Development in Information Retrieval, Tokyo, Japan, 7–11 August 2017; pp. 185–194.
18. Lin, T.H.; Gao, C.; Li, Y. Recommender systems with characterized social regularization. In Proceedings of the 27th ACM International Conference on Information and Knowledge Management, Torino, Italy, 22–26 October 2018; pp. 1767–1770.
19. Jamali, M.; Ester, M. A matrix factorization technique with trust propagation for recommendation in social networks. In Proceedings of the Fourth ACM Conference on Recommender Systems, Barcelona, Spain, 26–30 September 2010; pp. 135–142.
20. Zhao, T.; McAuley, J.; King, I. Leveraging social connections to improve personalized ranking for collaborative filtering. In Proceedings of the 23rd ACM International Conference on Conference on Information and Knowledge Management, Shanghai, China, 3–7 November 2014; pp. 261–270.
21. Yu, J.; Gao, M.; Li, J.; Yin, H.; Liu, H. Adaptive implicit friends identification over heterogeneous network for social recommendation. In Proceedings of the 27th ACM International Conference on Information and Knowledge Management, Turin, Italy, 22–26 October 2018; pp. 357–366.
22. Guo, G.; Zhang, J.; Yorke-Smith, N. Trustsvd: Collaborative filtering with both the explicit and implicit influence of user trust and of item ratings. In Proceedings of the AAAI Conference on Artificial Intelligence, Chicago, Il, USA, 25–30 January 2015; Volume 29.
23. Chaney AJ, B.; Blei, D.M.; Eliassi-Rad, T. A probabilistic model for using social networks in personalized item recommendation. In Proceedings of the 9th ACM Conference on Recommender Systems, Vienna, Austria, 16–20 September 2015; pp. 43–50.
24. Ma, H.; King, I.; Lyu, M.R. Learning to recommend with social trust ensemble. In Proceedings of the 32nd International ACM SIGIR Conference on Research and Development in Information Retrieval, Boston, MA, USA, 19–23 July 2009; pp. 203–210.
25. Koren, Y. Factorization meets the neighborhood: A multifaceted collaborative filtering model. In Proceedings of the 14th ACM SIGKDD International Conference on Knowledge Discovery and Data Mining, Vegas, NV, USA, 22 February 2008; pp 426–434
26. Liu, Y.; Chen, L.; He, X.; Peng, J.; Zheng, Z.; Tang, J. Modelling high-order social relations for item recommendation. *IEEE Trans. Knowl. Data Eng.* **2020**, *34*, 4385–4397. [CrossRef]
27. Liao, J.; Zhou, W.; Luo, F.; Wen, J.; Gao, M.; Li, X.; Zeng, J. SocialLGN: Light graph convolution network for social recommendation. *Inf. Sci.* **2022**, *589*, 595–607. [CrossRef]
28. He, X.; Deng, K.; Wang, X.; Li, Y.; Zhang, Y.; Wang, M. Lightgcn: Simplifying and powering graph convolution network for recommendation. In Proceedings of the 43rd International ACM SIGIR Conference on Research and Development in Information Retrieval, Online, 25–30 July 2020; pp. 639–648.
29. Hu, Y.; Zhan, P.; Xu, Y.; Zhao, J.; Li, Y.; Li, X. Temporal representation learning for time series classification. *Neural Comput. Appl.* **2021**, *33*, 3169–3182. [CrossRef]
30. Hartigan, J.A.; Wong, M.A. Algorithm AS 136: A k-means clustering algorithm. *J. R. Stat. Society. Ser. C (Appl. Stat.)* **1979**, *28*, 100–108. [CrossRef]
31. Yang, J.; Zhang, D.; Frangi, A.F.; Yang, J.Y. Two-dimensional PCA: A new approach to appearance-based face representation and recognition. *IEEE Trans. Pattern Anal. Mach. Intell.* **2004**, *26*, 131–137. [CrossRef] [PubMed]
32. Wu, F.; Souza, A.; Zhang, T.; Fifty, C.; Yu, T. Simplifying graph convolutional networks. In Proceedings of the International Conference on Machine Learning, PMLR, Long Beach, CA, USA, 10–15 June 2019; pp. 6861–6871.

33. Hamilton, W.; Ying, Z.; Leskovec, J. Inductive representation learning on large graphs. *Adv. Neural Inf. Process. Syst.* **2017**, *30*, 1025–1035.
34. Cantador, I.; Brusilovsky, P.; Kuflik, T. Second workshop on information heterogeneity and fusion in recommender systems (HetRec2011). In Proceedings of the Fifth ACM Conference on Recommender Systems, Chicago, IL, USA, 14 October 2011; pp. 387–388.
35. Tang, J.; Gao, H.; Liu, H. mTrust: Discerning multi-faceted trust in a connected world. In Proceedings of the Fifth ACM International Conference on Web Search and Data Mining, Washington, DC, USA, 8–12 February 2012; pp. 93–102.
36. Xu, H.; Huang, C.; Xu, Y.; Xia, L.; Xing, H.; Yin, D. Global context enhanced social recommendation with hierarchical graph neural networks. In Proceedings of the 2020 IEEE International Conference on Data Mining (ICDM), Sorrento, Italy, 17–20 November 2020; IEEE: Piscataway, NJ, USA; pp. 701–710.
37. Lin, J.; Chen, S.; Wang, J. Graph neural networks with dynamic and static representations for social recommendation. In Proceedings of the Database Systems for Advanced Applications: 27th International Conference, DASFAA 2022, Virtual Event, 11–14 April 2022; Springer International Publishing: Cham, Switzerland, 2022; pp. 264–271.
38. Rendle, S.; Freudenthaler, C.; Gantner, Z.; Schmidt-Thieme, L. BPR: Bayesian personalized ranking from implicit feedback. *arXiv* **2012**, arXiv:1205.2618.
39. Wang, X.; He, X.; Wang, M.; Feng, F.; Chua, T.S. Neural graph collaborative filtering. In Proceedings of the 42nd International ACM SIGIR Conference on Research and Development in Information Retrieval, Paris, France, 21–25 July 2019; pp. 165–174.
40. Kipf, T.N.; Welling, M. Semi-supervised classification with graph convolutional networks. *arXiv* **2016**, arXiv:1609.02907.

electronics

MDPI

Article

Implementation of a Whisper Architecture-Based Turkish Automatic Speech Recognition (ASR) System and Evaluation of the Effect of Fine-Tuning with a Low-Rank Adaptation (LoRA) Adapter on Its Performance

Hüseyin Polat [1,*], Alp Kaan Turan [1], Cemal Koçak [1] and Hasan Basri Ulaş [2]

1 Department of Computer Engineering, Faculty of Technology, Gazi University, Ankara 06560, Turkey; akaan.turan@gazi.edu.tr (A.K.T.); ccckocak@gazi.edu.tr (C.K.)
2 Department of Manufacturing Engineering, Faculty of Technology, Gazi University, Ankara 06560, Turkey; bulas@gazi.edu.tr
* Correspondence: polath@gazi.edu.tr

Abstract: This paper focuses on the implementation of the Whisper architecture to create an automatic speech recognition (ASR) system optimized for the Turkish language, which is considered a low-resource language in terms of speech recognition technologies. Whisper is a transformer-based model known for its high performance across numerous languages. However, its performance in Turkish, a language with unique linguistic features and limited labeled data, has yet to be fully explored. To address this, we conducted a series of experiments using five different Turkish speech datasets to assess the model's baseline performance. Initial evaluations revealed a range of word error rates (WERs) between 4.3% and 14.2%, reflecting the challenges posed by Turkish. To improve these results, we applied the low-rank adaptation (LoRA) technique, which is designed to fine-tune large-scale models efficiently by introducing a reduced set of trainable parameters. After fine-tuning, significant performance improvements were observed, with WER reductions of up to 52.38%. This study demonstrates that fine-tuned Whisper models can be successfully adapted for Turkish, resulting in a robust and accurate end-to-end ASR system. This research highlights the applicability of Whisper in low-resource languages and provides insights into the challenges of and strategies for improving speech recognition performance in Turkish.

Keywords: automatic speech recognition; artificial intelligence; deep learning; representation learning; self-supervised learning; Whisper model

Citation: Polat, H.; Turan, A.K.; Koçak, C.; Ulaş, H.B. Implementation of a Whisper Architecture-Based Turkish Automatic Speech Recognition (ASR) System and Evaluation of the Effect of Fine-Tuning with a Low-Rank Adaptation (LoRA) Adapter on Its Performance. *Electronics* **2024**, *13*, 4227. https://doi.org/10.3390/electronics13214227

Academic Editor: Grzegorz Dudek

Received: 2 October 2024
Revised: 24 October 2024
Accepted: 25 October 2024
Published: 28 October 2024

1. Introduction

Automatic speech recognition (ASR) systems have become an integral part of many modern technologies, enabling voice-activated assistants, transcription services, and real-time communication across various platforms. The development of ASR systems has historically been focused on high-resource languages such as English, which benefit from large, labeled datasets and sophisticated linguistic models. However, low-resource languages, including Turkish, continue to face challenges in terms of speech recognition accuracy due to the scarcity of labeled data and unique linguistic features such as agglutinative morphology and vowel harmony [1].

The Whisper architecture, developed by OpenAI, represents a significant advancement in ASR technology. As a transformer-based model, Whisper is designed to handle multiple languages, accents, and noisy environments with high accuracy. However, despite its broad language support, its performance in low-resource languages like Turkish has not been fully optimized, as most of the model's training data are skewed toward high-resource languages such as English [2]. The need for the fine-tuning of such models in low-resource languages is evident to improve their performance in real-world applications [3].

Turkish presents specific challenges for ASR systems due to its agglutinative structure, where suffixes are attached to root words to form complex words. This results in a vast number of possible word forms, making it difficult for ASR systems to accurately segment and recognize words. Additionally, Turkish exhibits notable dialectal diversity and phonological complexity, further complicating the development of a robust ASR system [4]. The scarcity of high-quality labeled datasets exacerbates these issues, leading to higher word error rates (WERs) compared to other languages.

In this study, we aim to address the gap in the literature by adapting the Whisper ASR system to Turkish using the low-rank adaptation (LoRA) method, a parameter-efficient fine-tuning technique that allows large-scale models to be adapted to specific tasks without the need for retraining all the model parameters [5]. LoRA significantly reduces the computational cost and memory requirements of fine-tuning large models, making it ideal for adapting ASR systems to low-resource languages like Turkish. By fine-tuning Whisper with LoRA, we aim to enhance its performance on Turkish speech datasets and provide a more accurate and robust ASR solution for Turkish.

Previous research on ASR systems for Turkish has primarily focused on traditional machine learning approaches and language models tailored to Turkish [6]. However, these approaches often lack the scalability and adaptability offered by modern transformer-based models like Whisper. Our work bridges this gap by leveraging the strengths of Whisper while addressing the specific challenges posed by the Turkish language. The key contribution of this study is the evaluation of Whisper's performance across five distinct Turkish speech datasets, both before and after fine-tuning with LoRA. This comprehensive evaluation provides insights into how well transformer-based models can be adapted to low-resource languages and highlights the potential for further improvements in ASR systems for Turkish.

Literature Review

The system model for speech analysis and synthesis was proposed by Dudley et al. at Bell Laboratories [7,8] in 1939, which is considered the beginning of ASR systems [9]. The first experimental work was the system for isolated digit recognition for a single speaker developed by Davis et al. of Bell Laboratories in 1952 [10]. Between 1950 and 1960, studies aimed to create pattern recognition systems for phoneme, single letter, or syllable discrimination [11,12]. In the period between 1960 and 1970, three hardware-based systems were developed in Japan [13–15]. Additional prominent works include IBM's Shoebox software [16], Martin's work at RCA Laboratories [17], and Vintsyuk's study using dynamic programming methods [18]. Between 1970 and 1980, the Viterbi algorithm was used in ASR systems [19], along with statistics-based approaches such as Itakura's LPC-based study [20]. Noteworthy works include the VIP-100 software, the Hearsay and HWIM software developed within the scope of the DARPA SUR program, as well as the Harpy software developed by Carnegie-Mellon University [21].

Between the 1980s and 1990s, statistical models and artificial neural network (ANN) studies emerged. The period between 1990 and 2000 saw developments such as the AT&T Voice Recognition Call Processing (VRCP) solution and the Hidden Markov Model Tool Kit (HMM Tool Kit). After 2000, ANN-based systems continued to develop, and significant advancements like the "Voice Search" feature in Android and Siri integration with iOS were introduced. Additionally, the Effective Affordable Reusable Speech-to-Text (EARS) and Global Autonomous Language Exploitation (GALE) datasets were created within the DARPA program for ASR systems [22–28].

After 2010, the use of artificial intelligence (AI) in automatic speech recognition (ASR) systems has increased, with significant developments such as connectionist temporal classification (CTC), recurrent neural network (RNN), long short-term memory (LSTM), two-way LSTM using the listen, attend, speech (LAS) mechanism, convolution mechanism, residual network-based studies, the transducer mechanism, Wav2vec model, Wav2vec 2.0, the ASR system using a convolutional neural network (CNN) and the Conformer model, and the Whisper ASR system developed by OpenAI. Major companies such as IBM, Microsoft, Google, and Amazon also released their advanced ASR systems during this period [29–36].

The existing literature on Turkish speech recognition primarily focuses on the distinctive characteristics of the language and their implications for automatic speech recognition (ASR) systems. Turkish poses several challenges in terms of speech recognition due to its agglutinative structure, rich morphology, complex phonology, and significant dialectal diversity. To address issues related to this diversity, ASR systems often rely on robust language models. In addition, the use of a lexicon helps improve recognition accuracy by providing a structured mapping of words, which is particularly useful in managing the vast variety of word forms in Turkish. Despite these techniques, the scarcity of high-quality speech and text data remains a major obstacle to further advancement in the field [37–39].

The early works on Turkish ASR focused on developing speaker-dependent systems and acoustic models. In recent years, there has been significant progress in Turkish ASR systems, with the introduction of deep learning models such as LSTM, gated recurrent unit (GRU), and Transformer, and the augmentation of Turkish speech and text data [40–51].

This research explores the implementation of a Whisper-driven automatic speech recognition system for the Turkish language and evaluates the effects of refining the model using LoRA approach. Whisper is a relatively new technology, so there are a limited number of studies on it. Various studies have compared Whisper with other architectures, such as Wav2Vec 2.0, and have utilized different datasets for testing. Additionally, some researchers have employed innovative methods, such as image-converted EEG data and direct fine-tuning, to improve Whisper's ASR performance [52–56].

This study expands upon the existing body of research on Turkish ASR by addressing some of the critical limitations that have hindered previous efforts in the field. Earlier works on Turkish ASR typically focused on traditional machine learning models, such as hidden Markov models (HMMs) or Gaussian mixture models (GMMs), and relied on relatively small or less diverse datasets. These models, while effective in some contexts, struggled with the unique linguistic challenges of Turkish, such as its agglutinative morphology, rich inflectional structure, and the presence of numerous dialects.

In contrast, this study leverages the Whisper ASR model, which is based on a transformer architecture trained on a large, multilingual corpus. This allows the model to capture long-range dependencies in speech and handle the complexities of Turkish more effectively than traditional models. The key differentiating factor of our work is the use of the LoRA method for fine-tuning Whisper. LoRA enables the model to be fine-tuned efficiently with fewer trainable parameters, addressing the computational challenges associated with fine-tuning large-scale models for low-resource languages like Turkish.

Moreover, unlike many previous studies that focused on a single dataset or task, this study evaluates the Whisper model on multiple Turkish speech datasets, representing a more comprehensive assessment of its performance across different contexts. This study also introduces corrections to the datasets, improving the quality of the training data and reducing the impact of noise and other errors.

2. Materials and Methods

ASR systems convert spoken language into text. Unlike humans, who use past experiences and grammar, ASR systems process speech as an audio signal [57–59]. While traditional ASR systems have separate components, modern end-to-end architectures perform these processes in a single step. With recent advancements in deep learning, pre-trained transformer-based large-scale models have gained popularity for fine-tuning specific ASR tasks. Transformer models, originally developed for natural language processing, have been effectively repurposed for speech recognition. Their exceptional ability to capture long-range dependencies in sequential data is critical for accurately comprehending the contextual nuances of speech. This adaptation has significantly improved the performance and accuracy of ASR systems, leading to more reliable and efficient speech recognition technology [60].

2.1. Transformers

RNNs and their variations, such as LSTM and GRU, have succeeded significantly in tasks like machine translation, language modeling, sequence transfer, and sequence modeling. The success of RNNs in these tasks is due to their ability to process sequential data. However, their sequential nature limits parallel processing, as each step depends on the result of the previous step, making it challenging to handle long sequences effectively. Over time, RNNs tend to forget important information, especially in long sequences, which leads to difficulties in capturing long-term dependencies. The sequence-to-sequence (Seq2Seq) [61] architecture was proposed to address these challenges. This architecture consists of an encoder and a decoder, typically composed of RNN units. The encoder takes the input sequence and compresses it into a fixed-length context vector, which is passed to the decoder. The decoder then generates the output sequence from this context vector. Seq2Seq improves the learning process by efficiently handling sequence data. However, when dealing with long sequences, it experiences performance degradation because it compresses the entire input into a fixed-length vector, which increases the risk of losing crucial information.

To overcome this issue, the attention mechanism was introduced. The attention mechanism allows the model to focus on specific parts of the input sequence dynamically, rather than compressing all the input information into a single fixed-length vector. This enables the model to consider different input parts at each step of the output generation, improving the performance, particularly for long sequences. By highlighting important points in the data, attention mechanisms make it easier for the model to retain critical information. However, even with attention, challenges like poor long-distance dependency retention, high computational costs, and limited parallel processing still persist [62].

To address these limitations and overcome the challenges of RNN-based models, the transformer architecture was proposed by Vaswani et al. in 2017 [32]. Unlike RNNs, transformers remove the need for sequential processing and rely entirely on the attention mechanism. This architecture allows for parallel processing and significantly reduces the risk of losing information in long sequences. One of the most significant advantages of the transformer is its ability to support parallel processing, as it removes the need for step-by-step sequential computations. These speed up the training process, especially when working with large datasets. Additionally, the self-attention mechanism excels in tasks requiring long-term dependencies by capturing relationships between distant elements in a sequence. This feature enables it to overcome one of the key weaknesses of RNNs and Seq2Seq models, which often struggle with such dependencies. The transformer is also highly scalable, making it a foundational architecture for large language models such as bidirectional encoder representations from transformers (BERT) and generative pre-trained transformer (GPT).

The basic structure of the transformer architecture is illustrated in Figure 1. The transformer consists of an encoder–decoder structure designed to process sequences of data (like sentences).

The encoder processes the input data. It consists of N layers. Each layer has two sub-layers: multi-head self-attention mechanism and position-wise fully connected feed-forward network Each of these sub-layers is followed by add and layer normalization steps, which stabilize and normalize the input. Positional encoding is added to the input embeddings to provide the model with information about the position of tokens in a sequence. This is necessary because, unlike RNNs or LSTMs, the transformer model does not inherently understand the order of tokens.

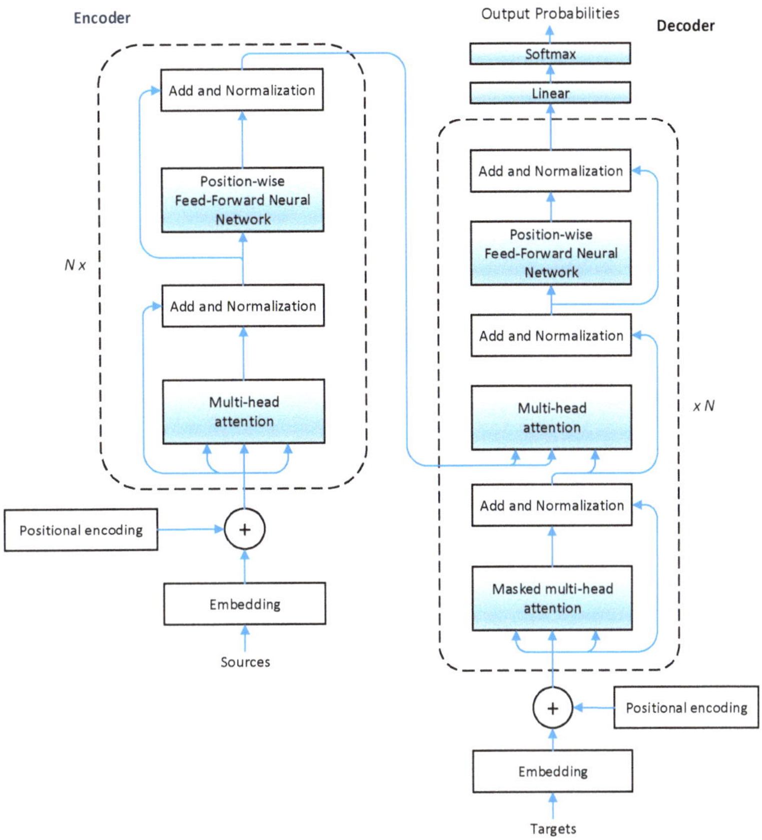

Figure 1. Basic transformer architecture.

The decoder generates the output sequence, conditioned on the input sequence encoded by the encoder. The decoder also has N layers, similar to the encoder but with a few differences.

In addition to the multi-head self-attention mechanism and feed-forward network, the decoder includes a masked multi-head attention layer. This ensures that predictions for a given position only depend on the outputs before that position, preserving the autoregressive nature of the language generation. Similar to the encoder, each layer in the decoder is followed by add and layer normalization steps.

2.2. Components of the Transformer

2.2.1. Multi-Headed Attention

Instead of relying on a single attention function, the transformer employs multi-head attention. In this approach, multiple attention heads operate in parallel, allowing the model to capture different aspects of the information simultaneously. Each attention head computes a weighted sum of the input vectors, focusing on different positions of the input. This mechanism helps the model understand the relationships between words in the sequence, regardless of their distance.

As can be seen in Figure 2, the multi-head attention (MHA) is formed by the combination of parallel scaled dot-product attention mechanisms. By multiplying the transformed input X by separate weight matrices, the query, key and value are obtained, which are fed to each attention unit and given in Equations (1)–(3).

$$Q = XW_Q^T \tag{1}$$

$$K = XW_K^T \tag{2}$$

$$V = XW_V^T \tag{3}$$

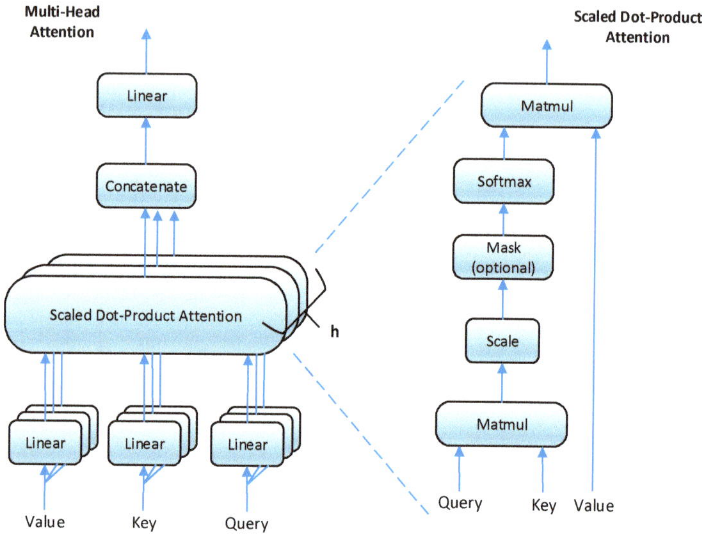

Figure 2. Multi-headed attention.

In Equation (4), the query and key matrix product is scaled by the square root of the dimension and the weight obtained by the softmax function is multiplied by the value matrix.

$$\mathrm{Attention}(\mathrm{Q,K,V}) = \mathrm{softmax}\left(\frac{\mathrm{QK^T}}{\sqrt{\mathrm{d_k}}}\right)\mathrm{V} \tag{4}$$

The result from each attention unit (Equation (5)) is combined, as shown in Equation (6) and then transmitted to the next layer.

$$\mathrm{Head_i} = \mathrm{Attention}\left(\mathrm{QW_i^Q, KW_i^K, VW_i^V}\right) \tag{5}$$

$$\mathrm{MHA(Q,K,V)} = \mathrm{Concat}(\mathrm{Attention_{1,}Attention_{2,}} \ldots) \tag{6}$$

2.2.2. Positional Encoding

As the array length increases, the index of the input becomes very large. In this state, the indices are not suitable for use in the transformer. Although the normalization process provides a solution up to a point, differences in array size cause problems again.

With positional encoding, the input array is transformed into a position matrix using the sine and cosine functions. In positional encoding, the order of the input output size of the model, denoted as d_{model} $\left(0 \leq i \leq \frac{d_{\text{model}}}{2}\right)$ and user-defined criterion n, is as outlined in Equations (7) and (8).

$$PE_{(pos,2i)} = sin\left(pos/n^{2i/d_{\text{model}}}\right) \tag{7}$$

$$PE_{(pos,2i+1)} = cos\left(pos/n^{2i/d_{\text{model}}}\right) \tag{8}$$

To illustrate, the positional encoding matrix of the initial six words in a text input with d = 4 and n = 10000 is presented in Table 1.

Table 1. Positional encoding matrix example.

i=	0	0	One	One
	$\sin\left(\frac{\text{pos}}{n^{2i/d}}\right)$	$\cos\left(\frac{\text{pos}}{n^{2i/d}}\right)$	$\sin\left(\frac{\text{pos}}{n^{2i/d}}\right)$	$\cos\left(\frac{\text{pos}}{n^{2i/d}}\right)$
x0	0	1	0	1
x1	0.841471	0.540302	0.009999	0.999950
x2	0.909297	−0.416147	0.019999	0.999800
x3	0.141120	−0.989992	0.029996	0.999550
x4	−0.756802	−0.653644	0.039989	0.999200
x5	−0.958924	0.283662	0.049979	0.998750

2.2.3. Feed-Forward Neural Network

The feed-forward neural network (FNN) is fed with the output of the multi-head attention mentioned in the previous part. The computation of the FNN is performed as in Equation (9). The bold part represents the ReLU activation function. The output of the previous layer is weighted and fed into the ReLU activation function. It is then multiplied by a second weight matrix and a constant is added and used as input for the analyzer.

$$\text{FNN}(x) = \mathbf{max}(0, \mathbf{xW}_1 + \mathbf{b}_1)W_2 + b_2 \tag{9}$$

The same mechanisms involved in the encoder are also involved in the decoder. The difference is that in the positional encoding process in the encoder, the input $x_1, x_2, x_3, \ldots x_n$ in the parser when receiving y_0 (start), $y_1, y_2, y_3, \ldots y_{n-1}$ is used. The first MHA in the analyzer is masked to prevent overlearning. The last output in the analyzer is the SoftMax function, which assigns a probability value between 0 and 1 to each element in the result array and selects the outputs with the highest probability.

2.2.4. Embedding Layer

Transforms input tokens (source or target) into a high-dimensional space, converting each token into a vector.

2.2.5. Masked Multi-Head Attention

This is applied in the decoder to prevent it from attending to future tokens that have not been generated yet. It is essential for tasks such as language generation, where the model must predict the next token in a sequence by relying solely on the previous tokens.

2.2.6. Add and Layer Normalization

After each multi-head attention or feed-forward layer, the model applies residual connections, where the original input is added to the output. This is followed by layer normalization, which helps stabilize the training and reduce overfitting, contributing to the overall efficiency and robustness of the model.

2.2.7. SoftMax Layer

After the decoder produces the output probabilities, they are passed through a SoftMax layer to generate a probability distribution over the possible output tokens.

2.3. *Low-Rank Adaptation*

The models used in large language model (LLM), NLP, ASR systems usually contain a lot of parameters and have large sizes. For example, Whisper large-v2 has about 1.5 billion parameters, while in GPT-3 this number increases to 175 billion. For such models, training all the parameters in the fine-tuning process is very costly in terms of processing power and time.

Low-rank adaptation (LoRA) is a technique developed to efficiently fine-tune large pre-trained models, including language and diffusion models. It achieves this by drastically reducing the number of trainable parameters, making the fine-tuning process more efficient and resource-friendly. LoRA keeps the weights of the pre-trained model fixed. Instead of updating all the parameters, it introduces trainable low-rank matrices into each layer of the model. This method relies on the low-rank decomposition of weight matrices. This involves breaking down a large matrix into the product of two smaller matrices, which reduces the number of parameters that need to be trained [6].

LoRA significantly reduces the computational and memory overhead associated with fine-tuning large models. This makes it feasible to adapt large models to specific tasks without the need for extensive computational resources. Compared to direct fine-tuning of the model, this method can reduce the number of trained parameters to about a thousandth and the memory requirement to about a third. Despite the reduction in trainable parameters, LoRA often matches or exceeds the performance of full fine-tuning. It has been shown to perform well on models like a robustly optimized BERT pretraining approach (RoBERTa), decoding-enhanced BERT with disentangled attention (DeBERTa), GPT-2, and GPT-3. Unlike some other fine-tuning methods, LoRA does not introduce additional inference latency, making it suitable for real-time applications. The operation of the method is shown in Figure 3.

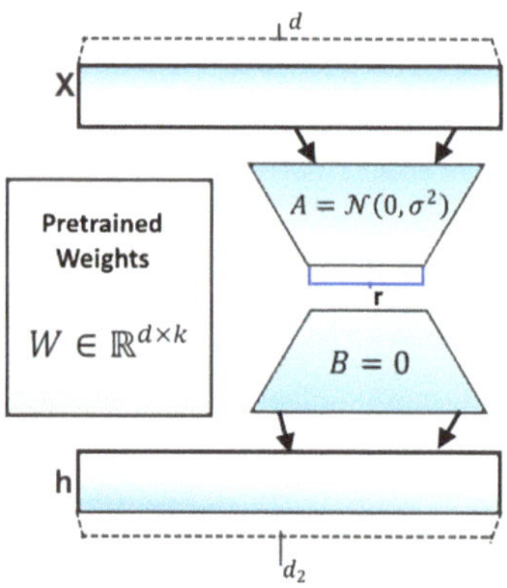

Figure 3. How the low-rank adaptation (LoRA) method works.

In standard fine-tuning, the pre-trained weight matrices of a neural network are updated directly. For the sake of simplicity, we will denote a weight matrix in the network by W, where $W \in R^{d\times k}$, with d representing the input dimension and k representing the output dimension [6]. During fine-tuning, the weight matrix W is updated as follows:

$$W' = W + \Delta W \tag{10}$$

In this context, W' represents the updated weight matrix, W denotes the original pre-trained weight matrix, and ΔW is the full-rank matrix of learned weight updates, with a dimensionality of $d \times k$. The number of parameters in ΔW is $d \times k$.

The objective of LoRA is to reduce the number of trainable parameters by constraining ΔW to being a low-rank matrix. Instead of learning the complete matrix ΔW, LoRA postulates that ΔW can be decomposed into the product of two lower-dimensional matrices: $\Delta W = AB$, where:

$A \in R^{d \times r}$ is a matrix with a rank r much smaller than min (d, k).

$B \in R^{r \times k}$ is another matrix with the same rank r.

Thus, the update rule becomes:

$$W' = W + AB \tag{11}$$

This decomposition indicates that, instead of learning $d \times k$ parameters, it is sufficient to learn $d \times r$ parameters for matrix A and $r \times k$ parameters for matrix B, resulting in a total of $r(d + k)$ parameters. If r is considerably smaller than $min(d, k)$, this signifies a notable reduction in the number of trainable parameters.

We can calculate the reduction in parameters more explicitly. For the full-rank update ΔW, there are:

$$\text{Full-rank parameters} = d \times k \tag{12}$$

For the low-rank update $\Delta W = AB$, the parameter count is:

$$\text{Low-rank parameters} = r(d + k) \tag{13}$$

The ratio of the number of low-rank parameters to the number of full-rank parameters is as follows:

$$\text{Parameter reduction ratio} = r(d + k)/d \times k \tag{14}$$

At the beginning of the training, A is assigned a random Gaussian value and B is assigned 0. Therefore, $\Delta W = BA$ has a value of zero in the first stage. It is then scaled by $\frac{\alpha}{r}$ using a hyperparameter (α).

2.4. Whisper Model Architecture

Whisper [4,5], developed by OpenAI, is an open-source ASR (automatic speech recognition) system that is capable of transcribing and translating spoken language. Whisper is based on an encoder–decoder transformer architecture. The capacity of transformer models to track the interrelationships between words and sentences enables the consideration of long-range dependencies, a capability that is not afforded by other models. In other words, transformers are capable of recalling previously uttered words and sentences, which enables them to contextualize new utterances and thereby enhance the accuracy of their transcription. Whisper is distinguished from other ASR models by its end-to-end deep learning model, extensive language support, training on a large and diverse dataset, and high performance.

Traditional ASR models, often based on HMM-GMM, use probabilistic and statistical methods to model speech signals. Still, they have limitations in understanding complex language models. Other ASR models that use RNNs, LSTMs, or GRUs process sequential data to capture temporal dependencies in audio. However, due to their sequential nature, these models tend to be slower when processing longer speech segments. As a transformer-based model, Whisper processes data in parallel, enhancing the speed and efficiency. Its attention mechanism effectively captures long-term speech dependencies and relationships between words, which can be challenging and time-consuming for other models to learn.

Previously, ASR technology combined deep learning with HMM-GMM structures and other audio–text processing techniques. The major drawback of these approaches was their inability to be trained end-to-end; each model component needed separate training. The advent of end-to-end models, such as Whisper, eliminated this limitation by adopting a unified modeling approach that discards the traditional distinction between acoustic and language models.

Whisper officially supports around 100 languages. Whisper was trained on a large dataset of approximately 680,000 h, of which around 117,000 h are multilingual. This constitutes an order of magnitude more data than used to train Wav2Vec 2.0, namely 60,000 h of unlabeled audio. Of the data utilized for Whisper's training, 65% (or 438,000 h) was dedicated to English speech recognition, 17% (or 117,000 h) to multilingual speech recognition, and the remaining 18% (or 126,000 h) to English translation. This diverse dataset enhances Whisper's robustness and generalizability across different languages, accents, and speech types. Whisper can transcribe 99 different languages and is capable of not just transcription but also translating conversations and timestamping speech. The model can be optimized for various tasks and is available in five different sizes, ranging from 39 million to 1.55 billion parameters, allowing developers to strike a balance between accuracy and processing speed [4,5].

Whisper's architecture is composed of two main components: the encoder and the decoder (Figure 4). The raw audio is divided into 30 s segments and transformed into a log-Mel spectrogram, which generates perceptually relevant frequency representations. Whisper has been designed to work on audio samples of up to 30 s in duration. However, the use of a chunking algorithm allows it to be used to transcribe audio samples of any length. This is made possible through the transformer's pipeline method.

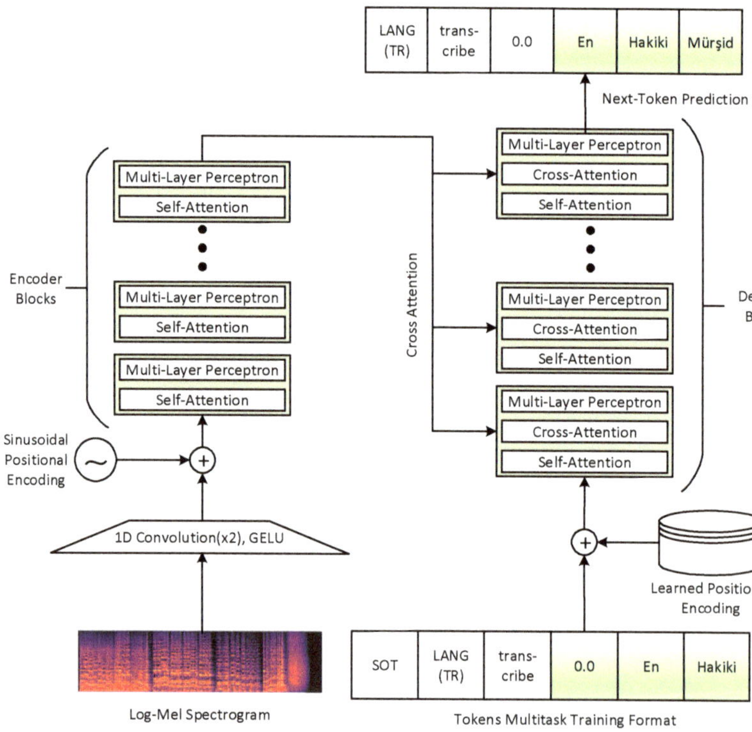

Figure 4. Whisper model architecture.

The spectrogram is processed through 2x1D convolutional layers with GELU (Gaussian error linear unit) activations to match the transformer's width [63]. Positional coding assigns temporal locations to the outputs of these convolutional layers, helping the model track sequential information from the audio data. This processed input is then fed into the encoder stack in the transformer [4,5].

The encoder consists of multiple blocks, each containing self-attention and multi-layer perceptron (MLP) layers. The self-attention mechanism analyzes each time segment of the audio concerning all the others, capturing short- and long-term speech dependencies. For instance, a word at the start of a sentence may be semantically related to one at the end; self-attention allows for such long-term correlations. After establishing these relationships through self-attention, the multi-layer perceptron layer enables deeper and more advanced processing of these connections, allowing the model to extract nuanced features and discern a broader range of linguistic patterns. Multiple encoder blocks are required to grasp the complexities of language and expedite understanding. The encoder operates only once per 30 s segment to produce a latent representation from the spectrogram [4,5].

This latent representation is passed to the decoder, where each block contains cross-attention, self-attention, and multi-layer perceptron layers. Cross-attention facilitates the transfer of the latent representation from the encoder to the decoder, linking the audio data to the text generation process. This allows the decoder to make accurate predictions based on the audio signal. Self-attention within the decoder considers previously generated words to maintain grammatical consistency and meaning in the text output. The multi-layer perceptron in the decoder enriches the information provided by self-attention and cross-attention, ensuring that the text generated by the model is both grammatically coherent and accurate in capturing the subtleties of the audio signal. The decoder predicts the text step by step using the latent representation; first predicting the most likely word, then generating the next word based on the previous prediction, and continuing until the entire speech sequence is transcribed [4,5].

Based on the number of layers, the width of the feature representation, and the number of attention heads, the Whisper model is categorized into five versions: tiny, base, small, medium, and large. The specifics of each version are summarized in Table 2. Furthermore, Large-v2 had 2.5 times more training iterations than the large version, while Large-v3 utilized data collection, processing, and pseudo-labeling with Large-v2 to augment the training data to 5 million hours. Both the large-v2 and large-v3 models surpassed the large model, with the large-v3 model exhibiting even stronger capabilities than the large-v2, particularly in terms of model training [4,5].

Table 2. Whisper model types and configuration parameters.

Model	Layers	Width	Attention Heads	Parameters (Million)
tiny	4	384	6	39
base	6	512	8	74
small	12	768	12	244
medium	24	1024	16	769
large	32	1280	20	1550

This study identified the following factors as influencing the selection of Whisper over other potential ASR models.

The Whisper model is a transformer-based ASR system that has demonstrated robust performance across a range of languages, including low-resource languages such as Turkish. The robust performance of Whisper in noisy environments and its capacity to handle a diverse range of speech conditions, including accents and spontaneous speech, render it particularly well-suited for real-world applications in Turkish speech recognition.

Whisper operates in an end-to-end manner, whereby the model is trained to map audio inputs directly to text outputs, obviating the need for separate acoustic and language models. This unified approach markedly enhances the system's capacity to generalize across disparate languages and accents. Additionally, Whisper's transformer architecture enables parallel processing, rendering it more efficient than RNNs or LSTM units, which process input data sequentially and are slower when handling long speech sequences.

Furthermore, Whisper is capable of fine-tuning through techniques such as LoRA, which enables the model to be efficiently adapted to specific tasks or languages without the necessity of retraining all the parameters. This represents a significant advantage over other models, which may require more extensive resources to achieve the same level of fine-tuning. In light of the challenges posed by Turkish, including its agglutinative morphology and dialectal variations, the ability of Whisper to be fine-tuned with fewer trainable parameters represents a significant advantage and was a key factor in its selection for this study.

In conclusion, Whisper was selected for this study due to its advanced transformer-based architecture, multilingual training, adaptability to low-resource languages, and efficient fine-tuning capabilities. These features render it a more suitable model for developing a robust ASR system for Turkish compared to other traditional or even deep learning-based ASR models.

2.5. Turkish Speech Datasets

In this section, the five Turkish speech datasets, the Middle East Technical University (METU) Microphone Speech Dataset (METU MS), Turkish Broadcast News Speech and Text Dataset (TNST), FLEURS Dataset, Mozilla Common Voice Dataset (Mozilla CV) and Turkish Automatic Speech Recognition Test (TASRT), used in the experimental studies are introduced by listing their characteristics, such as the size, audio file type, metadata fields, etc. The METU MS, TNST, FLEURS, Mozilla CV and TASRT datasets contain 6618, 82331, 3127, 52,477 and 286 records, respectively.

METU MS dataset's [64] data availability status: data available in a publicly accessible repository. The original data presented in the study are openly available at https://catalog.ldc.upenn.edu/LDC2006S33 (accessed on 15 September 2024).

The METU MS dataset consists of approximately 5.6 h of audio and corresponding textual transcripts from 120 speakers of various age groups (19–50 years) and genders (60 males, 60 females). Each speaker vocalized 40 randomly selected sentences out of a total of 2462 sentences. Audio data, WAV with a sample frequency of 16 kHz, are stored in TXT format files in the form of text.

TNST dataset's [65] data availability status: data available in a publicly accessible repository. The original data presented in the study are openly available at https://catalog.ldc.upenn.edu/LDC2012S06 (accessed on 15 September 2024).

The TNST is a dataset of speeches collected from news bulletins of various Turkish-language news channels. It contains 194 h of audio and text data consisting of approximately 13,000,000 words. The audio data are in the WAV format, with a sampling frequency of 16 kHz, and the text is in TXT format files.

Mozilla CV dataset's [66] data availability status: data available in a publicly accessible repository. The original data presented in the study are openly available at https://commonvoice.mozilla.org/en/datasets (accessed on 15 September 2024).

The Mozilla CV is an open-source voice dataset created by the Mozilla company. This dataset consists of speech recordings of more than 500 languages, donated by volunteers from around the world. The most recent version released at the time of writing, Common Voice Corpus 15.0, contains 115 h of audio files from 1511 individuals, 111 h of which have been verified. The audio files are in MP3 format, with a sampling frequency of 48 kHz. The speech text is stored in TSV format files, with attributes such as the accent, gender, age, region, etc.

FLEURS dataset's [67] data availability status: data available in a publicly accessible repository. The original data presented in the study are openly available at https://huggingface.co/datasets/google/fleurs (accessed on 15 September 2024).

The FLEURS is a dataset of approximately 12 h of speech in 102 different languages, one for each language. The audio data are stored in WAV files, with a sampling frequency of 16 kHz. The speech text is stored in TSV format files, with attributes such as the text, speaker gender, etc. The recordings are divided into three parts: dev, train and test. The Turkish dataset consists of a total of 3607 records, with 743, 2526, and 338 records in the train, test, and dev sections, respectively.

TASRT dataset's [68] data availability status: data available on request due to restrictions (commercial use). The data presented in this study are available from the corresponding author upon request.

The TASRT dataset is compiled by Oyucu [68]. The TASRT dataset contains approximately 186 min of speech data from 286 speakers (143 women and 143 men) in 20 different categories. The audio data are stored in WAV files, with a sampling frequency of 16 kHz. The dataset contains transcript files with TXT extension corresponding to each audio file and named with category, speaker gender and order.

2.6. Automatic Speech Recognition Performance Evaluation Criteria

The three possible types of errors that can be encountered in a text generated with ASR systems are insertion, deletion and substitution. Insertion is the insertion of an extra symbol/word that is not in the text. Deletion is the absence of a symbol/word that should be in a certain position in the text. Substitution is when a symbol/word that should be in a certain position in the text is replaced by another symbol/word.

For a text consisting of N_W words, the number of words added is I_W, deleted is D_W and substituted is S_W Then, the word error rate (WER) is calculated as given in Equation (15) and the accuracy, also referred to as the word recognition rate (WRR), is calculated as given in Equation (16).

$$\mathrm{WER} = \frac{I_W + D_W + S_W}{N_W} \tag{15}$$

$$\mathrm{WRR} = 1 - \mathrm{WER} \tag{16}$$

The WER is generally used as the ASR evaluation criterion. Another widely used measure is the character error rate (CER). The CER value is calculated similarly to the WER value. N_C indicates the number of symbols, the added symbol number is I_C, the deleted symbol number is D_C and *the* substitution is S_C. The CER and character recognition rate (CRR) are found as given in Equations (17) and (18).

$$\mathrm{CER} = \frac{E_C + S_C + D_C}{N_C} \tag{17}$$

$$\mathrm{CRR} = 1 - \mathrm{CER} \tag{18}$$

The WER and CER are often confused with each other due to their similarities in calculations. While the WER is measured by the number of word errors; in terms of the CER, the number of symbol errors is taken into account. If we consider the following expression:

Bir işi yapmak için neden yarını bekliyorsun bugün de dünün bir yarını değil midir

Let us assume that the output produced by the ASR system for a sentence consisting of 14 words and 82 symbols with spaces is as follows.

Biri işi yapmak işin neden yarın_bekliyorsun bugün de dünün bir yarını değil____

Symbol insertion was performed in the first word, a symbol change was made in the fourth word, and symbol deletion was performed in the sixth word. The last word has been completely deleted. There have been 7 deletions, 1 substitution, 1 insertion, giving total of 9 symbol errors; There are a total of 4 word errors, 3 changes and 1 deletion.

In this situation,$\mathrm{WER} = \frac{4}{14} \cong 0.286, \mathrm{CER} = \frac{9}{82} \cong 0.089$

Apart from these, although not common, there are also the sentence error rate (SER), phone error rate (PER), utterance error rate (UER), and frame error rate (FER). Criteria such as these can also be used to measure ASR performance. Low error rates indicate high accuracy and thus high model success.

3. Testing the Performance of Whisper Models on Turkish Speech Datasets and Fine-Tuning with LoRA

This paper presents the implementation of an end-to-end Turkish speech recognition system, utilizing the Whisper ASR model. Whisper is a robust ASR architecture; however, its performance requires further enhancement for low-resource languages such as Turkish. In this study, the performance of five scaled pre-trained models of the Whisper architecture (small, basic, small, medium, and large) was evaluated concerning Turkish speech recognition using five distinct Turkish speech datasets (METU MS, TNST, Mozilla CV, FLEURS, and TASRT). In addition to the comparison of the Whisper-large-v2 and Whisper-large-v3 models in terms of performance, a comparison was also conducted between Google USM and the Whisper-large-v3 model using five distinct Turkish datasets. Subsequently, the Whisper models were fine-tuned with the LoRA method, and the performance of the Whisper models in terms of Turkish speech recognition was evaluated in comparison. The word error rate was employed as the performance metric.

In this study, experiments were conducted using a workstation equipped with a 32-core Intel(R) Xeon(R) Gold 6426Y 2.50 GHz 2-processor and an Nvidia A5000 GPU. The experiments were carried out using the *Python v3.12* programming language and the *Miniconda v24.5.0* environment. *PyTorch v2.4.0*, a machine learning and deep learning library developed by Facebook, was utilized for the tests with the datasets. Audio file processing was performed using the *pydub v0.25.1* library. The Whisper ASR model library, developed by OpenAI, along with the fast-whisper, Whisper online, and Whisper Live applications, was employed. To address the issue of Whisper ASR converting numbers into text, the *num2words v0.5.2* library was utilized with modifications. The *Numpy v2.1.0* and *Pandas v2.2.2* libraries were employed for data processing and calculations, while the *jiwer v3.0.4* libraries were used for calculating the WER and CER. Additionally, standard libraries such as *datetime* for duration determination, *io*, *sys*, and *tarfile* for file operations, *re* for text processing and regular expressions, and *argparse* for managing application parameters were also used.

During this study, we conducted around 950 h of work. This included approximately 150 h of examining and editing datasets, as well as 800 h dedicated to experimenting, Whisper fine-tuning, and developing a simultaneous ASR.

3.1. Preparation of Datasets

The METU MS, TNST, Mozilla CV, FLEURS and TASRT Turkish datasets were used in the experimental study. These datasets consist of WAV files with a 16 kHz sampling frequency and the Mozilla CV dataset consists of MP3 files with a 48 kHz sampling frequency. The MP3 files of the Mozilla CV dataset were converted to a single channel with a sampling frequency of 16 kHz.

Before starting the experiments, we analyzed the Turkish speech datasets. It became clear that the METU MS, TNST, and TASRT datasets needed some corrections. The issues and necessary modifications identified in the datasets are outlined below.

Some texts in the METU MS dataset do not comply with the Turkish Language Association's spelling rules or are not correctly vocalized. In this case, even though the ASR system produced the correct text, the CER and WER values were higher than they should have been due to spelling errors in the dataset. Common spelling errors include the spelling of dates without spaces, the contractions of expressions such as "bir şey", "her şey" and "birçok", and the contractions of suffixes and conjunctions such as "-mi", "-mi", "-de", "-da", "-ki". Even though it is rare, another type of error found in the dataset is the writing of Turkish characters such as ç, ğ, i, ö, ş, and ü without a dot.

Similarly, there are many problematic records in the TNST dataset. Adjacent words ae were written together. Additionally, many foreign words are included with their Turkish pronunciations. These issues caused an increase in the WER and CER values.

The texts in the datasets were reorganized by listening to the audio files in cases of ambiguity. Foreign names in the TNST dataset, which were written side by side with their Turkish pronunciations, were reduced to one in the text so that only their commonly used equivalents were included. Apart from these, other problems encountered with both the text files and the functioning of the existing model are listed below:

1. In some files, errors occurred in the output produced because the recording was terminated before the end of the speech. Especially in recordings with more than one speaker's speech, it was observed that if there were gaps, the model did not process the speech of subsequent speakers. Therefore, voice activation detection (VAD) was used to reduce the gaps that cause errors.
2. Confusion about whether conjunctions such as "with", "ise", "de", "da" are written adjacent to the word or separately is one of the most common errors. In the text, suffixes or conjunctions, which are difficult to identify even for the listener, are sometimes misspelled or incorrectly transformed by the model. The text was corrected where it should have been separate or adjacent.
3. When the end of one word and the start of the next word have similar sounds, the model sometimes merges them. This causes it to skip the start of the following word.
4. The model abbreviates expressions such as doctor, professor, etc., kilometers and converts them into text as Dr., Prof., etc., km.

It was important to determine how the corrections made to the METU MS, TNST, and TASRT datasets affected the performance of the pre-trained Whisper models. To this end, the original and the corrected versions of the datasets were subjected to testing with pre-trained Whisper models, and the outcomes were evaluated. Afterward, LoRA was used to fine-tune the pre-trained Whisper models with the corrected datasets. The performances of these fine-tuned models were then evaluated.

3.2. Testing the Performance of Whisper Models on Five Turkish Speech Datasets

Table 3 presents the WER, CER and the duration values in hours and minutes for the pre-tests conducted on the Whisper models at five different scales (tiny, base, small, medium, large) before any modifications were made to the Turkish speech datasets. In the test, all of the samples in the METU MS, TASRT and FLEURS datasets with a low number of records and 30% of the samples in the TNST and Mozilla CV datasets with a high number of records were used.

Table 3. Pre-testing the performance of the Whisper models on five Turkish speech datasets.

Dataset	Metric	Tiny	Base	Small	Medium	Large-v2
METU MS (100%)	WER	0.36	0.24	0.16	0.15	0.10
	CER	0.10	0.07	0.06	0.04	0.03
	Duration	00:20	00:21	00:25	00:36	00:47
TNST (30%)	WER	0.53	0.36	0.22	0.15	0.13
	CER	0.18	0.12	0.08	0.06	0.05
	Duration	01:30	01:33	01:57	02:44	03:35
FLEURS (100%)	WER	0.47	0.31	0.17	0.11	0.08
	CER	0.15	0.09	0.04	0.03	0.02
	Duration	00:16	00:18	00:22	00:31	00:43
Mozilla CV (30%)	WER	0.49	0.37	0.24	0.19	0.16
	CER	0.22	0.16	0.12	0.11	0.09
	Duration	00:52	00:56	01:05	01:28	01:50
TASRT (100%)	WER	0.41	0.29	0.19	0.14	0.13
	CER	0.14	0.09	0.06	0.05	0.04
	Duration	00:03	00:03	00:04	00:07	00:10

In the METU MS dataset, while the WER is 0.36 in the tiny model, it drops to 0.10 in the large-v2 model. In other words, the errors decreased as the model size increased. While the CER is 0.10 in the tiny model, it decreases to 0.03 in the large-v2 model. The TNST dataset has higher error rates compared to the METU MS. Especially, the tiny model has the highest error rate, with a WER of 0.53. However, again with the large-v2 model, the WER drops to 0.13. The FLEURS dataset performs better than the TNST. With the large-v2 model, the WER drops to 0.08 and the CER to 0.02, indicating very low error rates. The Mozilla CV dataset also exhibits high error rates, similar to the TNST. Even in the large-v2 model, the WER drops to 0.16, but this is higher than in the METU MS and FLEURS. The TASRT dataset shows a balanced performance across all the models. In the large-v2 model, the WER is 0.13 and the CER is 0.04. Compared to the other datasets, the average error rates are lower.

3.3. *Testing Whisper Models After Data Correction*

The results obtained from the performance tests performed after rearranging the METU MS, TNST and TASRT datasets are shown in Table 4.

Table 4. Test performance evaluation of the Whisper models after dataset correction.

Dataset	Metric	Tiny	Base	Small	Medium	Large-v2
METU MS (100%)	WER	0.33	0.21	0.12	0.11	0.06
	CER	0.09	0.06	0.04	0.04	0.02
	Duration	00:20	00:21	00:24	00:35	00:47
TNST (30%)	WER	0.52	0.35	0.20	0.14	0.10
	CER	0.17	0.10	0.06	0.05	0.04
	Duration	01:13	01:18	01:37	02:15	02:57
TASRT (100%)	WER	0.38	0.25	0.15	0.09	0.08
	CER	0.13	0.08	0.05	0.03	0.03
	Duration	00:03	00:03	00:04	00:07	00:10

In the experiments performed using the Whisper-large-v2 model after rearranging the datasets, in the METU MS dataset, there is a notable decline in the WER and CER ratios with an increase in the model size. The Large-v2 model exhibits the lowest WER of 0.06 and the lowest CER of 0.02. This suggests that the dataset was transcribed with a high degree of accuracy. In comparison to the other datasets, the TNST dataset exhibits higher WER and CER ratios. This may be indicative of the dataset being more challenging to transcribe or comprising elements such as different languages and accents. The lowest WER was 0.10 in the "large-v2" model, while the lowest CER was 0.04. In the TASRT dataset, the WER and CER rates decrease with the model size. Notably, the values of the WER (0.08) and CER (0.03) in the "large-v2" model demonstrate an improvement trend comparable to that observed in the other datasets.

3.4. Performance Comparison of Whisper-Large-v2 and Whisper-Large-v3 Models

On 6 November 2023, the Whisper-large-v3 model was introduced by OpenAI. This model has the same number of layers, attention headers and parameters as the Whisper-large model. However, it differs from the other models by using 128 Mel frequency bands instead of 80 as input and by adding Cantonese to the group of defined languages. The Whisper-large-v3 model was obtained by training the Whisper-large-v2 model with one million hours of weakly labeled and four million hours of pseudo-labeled data. Table 5 shows the comparison of the Whisper-large-v2 and Whisper-large-v3 models for the datasets studied.

The Whisper-large-v3 model yielded substantial enhancements in the WER and CER values across all the datasets. The most substantial improvements were observed in the METU MS dataset, which may suggest that the model is more effectively tailored to the data in this particular dataset or that this dataset derives greater benefit from the enhancements introduced in the v3 model. The improvements in the WER ranged from 8.77% to 29.08%, while those in the CER ranged from 6.29% to 44.27%. No notable alterations were observed in the processing times, which remained largely consistent or exhibited only minimal fluctuations. A 3.60% increase in the processing time was observed on the Mozilla CV dataset, but this is equivalent to approximately four seconds and does not have a significant practical impact.

The Whisper-large-v3 model demonstrates a notable enhancement in accuracy relative to its predecessor, the large-v2 model, while exhibiting a minimal increase in the processing time. This renders the v3 model a more appealing option for users seeking to attain enhanced performance in transcription tasks.

Table 5. Performance comparison of the Whisper-large-v2 and Whisper-large-v3 models.

Dataset	Metric	Large-v2	Large-v3	Difference (%)
METU MS (100%)	WER	0.061	0.043	−29.08
	CER	0.018	0.010	−44.27
	Duration	00:47	00:47	0.00
TNST (30%)	WER	0.103	0.085	−17.30
	CER	0.037	0.028	−24.97
	Duration	02:57	02:58	0.86
FLEURS (100%)	WER	0.083	0.075	−10.11
	CER	0.021	0.020	−7.41
	Duration	00:43	00:43	−0.96
Mozilla CV (30%)	WER	0.156	0.142	−8.77
	CER	0.090	0.084	−6.29
	Duration	01:50	01:54	3.60
TASRT (100%)	WER	0.081	0.069	−13.84
	CER	0.032	0.027	−15.35
	Duration	00:10	00:10	−0.94

3.5. Performance Comparison of Whisper and Google USM Models

Whisper and Google USM are two current speech recognition systems. OpenAI has shared the Whisper ASR system under an open-source distribution license. Google promised to openly share its model for Google USM, but this has not happened over time. In contrast, the model can be accessed through paid application programming interfaces (APIs). The optimization points of Google USM, which runs behind APIs, and the hardware on which it runs are not clear. Despite these uncertainties about the model, a performance comparison between the two systems can be performed indirectly. A performance comparison between the two ASR systems was performed on the WER and CER using the METU MS, TNST, FLEURS, Mozilla CV and TASRT datasets. A certain number of random speech files were selected from each dataset. The selected files were given as input to the Whisper large-v3 model and the API (called Chirp) running Google USM behind it. The resulting output texts were compared with real speech texts to find the WER and CER values. The number of samples for the datasets used in the comparison, the criterion values obtained and the percentage differences between the values of the two models are given in Table 6.

Table 6. Performance comparison of the Whisper and Google USM models.

Dataset	Metric	Whisper Large-v3	Google USM	Difference(%)
METU MS (100%)	WER	0.043	0.049	13.95
	CER	0.01	0.01	0
TNST (30%)	WER	0.084	0.087	3.57
	CER	0.028	0.025	−10.71
FLEURS (100%)	WER	0.075	0.093	24
	CER	0.021	0.036	71.43
Mozilla CV (30%)	WER	0.066	0.063	−4.55
	CER	0.015	0.02	33.33
TASRT (100%)	WER	0.069	0.098	42.03
	CER	0.027	0.044	62.96

Whisper-large-v3 provides lower WER and CER than Google USM on most datasets and is particularly superior on the METU MS, FLEURS and TASRT datasets. Significant performance gains are observed over Google USM on the FLEURS and TASRT datasets. However, on the Mozilla CV dataset, Google USM provides better WER performance than Whisper-large-v3, but Whisper-large-v3 is superior concerning the CER. In terms of the CER, Whisper-large-v3 is more successful in most cases, but there is one case where Google USM performs better on the TNST dataset.

3.6. Fine-Tuning Process on Whisper Models

Whisper can be used with close to a hundred languages and supports multiple downstream tasks (translation, speech recognition, etc.). Also, it has a fine-tuning feature. In the fine-tuning process, the model is retrained with newly labeled data for the relevant downstream task. The fine-tuning process contributes to the improvement of the model in three ways:

1. Fitting the model with multiple downstream tasks, but only for a specific task (in the context of this study, the ASR).
2. Increasing the model's bias toward a particular language, and hence, its performance in that language, by training it only with data from a particular language.
3. Strengthening the probabilities of the elements involved in the tokenization process with the specified training dataset, increasing the bias of the outputs in terms of the relevant elements. For example, increasing the probability that the model that produces output with numbers for numbers will produce text output instead of numbers by fine-tuning the datasets where numbers are shown as text.

Higher models of solutions like Whisper, etc., require high processing power and memory for fine-tuning. Graphics cards with powerful GPUs are usually used for processing power and memory. Often, however, as the size of the model increases, the top-end graphics cards become insufficient.

One of the methods used to overcome these difficulties is LoRA. In this study, the fine-tuning process is performed using LoRA. With LoRA, the number of target parameters trained on the Whisper architecture can be reduced to approximately 3/100 and the memory requirement to approximately 1/3 [6].

3.7. Fine-Tuning Process on Whisper-Medium Model

The Whisper-medium model was fine-tuned using 60% of the Mozilla CV dataset because it contained more records than the other datasets. The relatively small size of the Whisper-medium model enables faster training with larger datasets. The hyperparameters used in the fine-tuning process were as follows: the chunk size was 32, the learning rate was 5E-6, and the gradient accumulation step was 2. Adam was used as the optimization function. As a result of the fine-tuning process, which lasted 6500 epochs and a total of 72 h, the test results given in Table 7 were obtained.

Table 7. Test performance comparison after fine-tuning for the Whisper-medium model.

Dataset	Metric	Whisper-Medium	Whisper-Medium (Fine-Tuning)	Difference (%)
METU MS (100%)	WER	0.109	0.065	−40.37
	CER	0.043	0.015	−65.12
TNST (10%)	WER	0.139	0.136	−2.16
	CER	0.047	0.036	−23.40
FLEURS (100%)	WER	0.118	0.117	−0.85
	CER	0.037	0.034	−8.11
Mozilla CV (10%)	WER	0.210	0.172	−18.10
	CER	0.117	0.099	−15.38
TASRT (100%)	WER	0.91	0.106	16.48
	CER	0.035	0.042	20.00

After fine-tuning the Whisper-medium model, the most significant decrease in terms of the WER value was observed in the METU MS dataset. No significant improvement was observed in the TNST and FLEURS datasets, which contain many foreign words in various languages. On the other hand, while an 18.1% improvement was achieved in the Mozilla CV dataset, a 16.48% performance decrease was observed in the TASRT dataset. Similarly, while a decrease in the CER value occurred in the other four datasets, a 20% increase was observed in the TOKTT dataset. It was observed that the CER improvement in the TNST dataset in particular was not reflected in the WER value at the same rate.

3.8. Fine-Tuning Process on Whisper-Large-v2 Model

The Whisper-large-v2 model was fine-tuned using 80% of the FLEURS and Mozilla CV datasets. The hyperparameters used in the fine-tuning process were as follows: the chunk size was 32, the learning rate was 5×10^{-6}, and the gradient accumulation step was 2. The training took about 90 h in five sessions and was completed in 8000 epochs. Adam was used as the optimization function. Since the LoRA method was used, the training loss was calculated based on the tokenization success, since a loss calculation cannot be performed directly on the WER. Table 8 shows the test performance of the Whisper-large-v2 model on the Turkish datasets comparatively before and after fine-tuning.

Table 8. Whisper-large-v2 model test performance evaluation after fine-tuning.

Dataset	Metric	Whisper Large-v2	Whisper Large-v2 (Fine-Tuning)	Difference (%)
METU MS (100%)	WER	0.059	0.050	−15.25
	CER	0.020	0.010	−50.00
TNST (30%)	WER	0.132	0.109	−17.42
	CER	0.051	0.032	−37.25
FLEURS (100%)	WER	0.083	0.047	−43.37
	CER	0.021	0.014	−33.33
Mozilla CV (30%)	WER	0.10	0.051	−49.00
	CER	0.021	0.010	−52.38
TASRT (100%)	WER	0.081	0.079	−2.47
	CER	0.032	0.030	−6.25

Following the application of the fine-tuning techniques, a reduction in the WER and CER values was observed across all the datasets. The most substantial enhancements were observed in the Mozilla CV and FLEURS datasets.

As anticipated, the 43.37% reduction in the WER is indicative of the model's enhanced accuracy in transcription on the FLEURS dataset, which constituted 80% of the total fine-tuning data. The enhancement in character-level accuracy is also reflected in the reduction in character-level errors.

The test on 10% of the Mozilla CV dataset demonstrated the most substantial improvements in both the WER (49.00%) and CER (52.38%). These results demonstrate the efficacy of the fine-tuning process on the Mozilla CV dataset.

The 50% improvement in the CER for the METU MS dataset demonstrates that the model is highly effective in reducing character-level errors. The 15.25% improvement in the WER is also noteworthy, indicating an enhancement in the overall quality of the transcription.

Concerning the TNST dataset, the fine-tuning resulted in enhanced transcription accuracy, particularly a 37.25% improvement in the CER. The 17.42% improvement in the WER also suggests that the model's word-level performance has been enhanced.

The impact of fine-tuning on the TASRT dataset was found to be relatively limited. In the case of the TASRT dataset, which comprises approximately 75% of speech data exceeding 30 s in duration, the minimal observed improvements of 2.47% in the WER and 6.25% in the WER may be indicative of the model's inherent suitability for this particular dataset, or that the fine-tuning was insufficiently effective.

3.9. Fine-Tuning Process on Whisper-Large-v3 Model

In the fine-tuning process conducted with the Whisper-large-v3 model, the incorporation of all the linear layers resulted in a two- to fourfold increase in the number of trained parameters and led to the emergence of hardware bottlenecks. Consequently, the fine-tuning process was conducted solely on the Q and V structures.

Firstly, due to the reduction in the processing speed and memory requirements, the fine-tuning process was conducted in the 8-bit integer format. However, this resulted in a decline in sensitivity and an increase in the hallucination problem of the model. Accordingly, the 16-bit floating-point format was selected for the fine-tuning process. During the training phase, the batch size was set to 32, the learning rate was fixed at 5×10^{-6}, and the gradient accumulation step was set to 2.

Given that the large-v3 model was trained on a vast quantity of data, it was not possible to achieve a greater degree of success by training on a dataset of approximately 10 h. Despite the expectation that greater training data would facilitate improvement, the desired progress in the fine-tuning of the large-v3 model could not be achieved due to the limited number of labeled datasets and the constraints imposed by the hardware and runtime. Consequently, the Whisper fine-tuning process concentrated on the lower models, medium and large-v2.

4. Discussion

The end-to-end, multi-tasking design of modern ASR applications is a testament to the advancements in artificial intelligence and machine learning. By eliminating the need for separate acoustic and language models, these systems streamline the process of understanding and processing human speech. The integration of automatic translation and speaker tagging within ASR systems not only enhances the user experience but also broadens the scope of application for these technologies. The transition from traditional statistical models, such as HMMs, to advanced deep learning structures is a major development. This includes the use of transformers with encoders and decoders, marking a significant milestone in the field. These deep learning models can analyze vast amounts of data and learn complex patterns, which results in more accurate and efficient speech recognition.

As the complexity of deep learning architectures increases, particularly with the integration of transformer models, the necessity for extensive training data and substantial computational resources also rises in parallel. These issues have been addressed through the development of more advanced GPUs and the ongoing expansion of datasets. The shift toward creating models with a larger number of parameters reflects the field's adaptation to these technological advancements. The training of deep learning models on large-scale datasets has been demonstrated to enhance their generalization capabilities and to improve their performance across a wide range of tasks. Incremental improvements in model components, such as refining the attention mechanism, are often more favored than overhauling the entire architecture. This approach allows for steady progress and the optimization of existing frameworks, which can be more efficient than starting from scratch. The expansion of training datasets also plays a crucial role in this development trajectory, providing the models with a diverse range of inputs from which to learn. The current trajectory suggests the focus will remain on scaling up the models in line with the available computational resources. This scaling is not just in terms of the size of the datasets but also the complexity of the models' input attributes [69,70].

This study used the Whisper ASR model, which employs a transformer-based encoder–decoder architecture, to create a speech recognition system for Turkish. The performance of the model was evaluated using various Turkish speech datasets, and there were noticeable enhancements after fine-tuning with the LoRA method.

Initial reviews of the Turkish speech datasets identified the following common errors and issues.

Problems related to transferring the speech to the text, such as not reading the text completely and correctly, transferring the speech to the text differently and adding expressions that are not in the speech to the text.

Spelling errors such as missing or incorrect punctuation in Turkish characters and words that must be written adjacent or separate according to the spelling rules are transferred to the text differently.

Ending the recording before the expression in the text is completed, noise, etc., leading to sound quality problems.

In a carefully written text, it is estimated that there are approximately 1–2% spelling errors. On the other hand, for quickly written or unchecked texts, this rate is thought to be approximately 10–15% [71]. Within the scope of this study, the speech voiced at many points in the METU MS dataset was listened to again and corrections were made. When the initial and final versions of the texts were compared, it was determined that there were 1.7% character and 5.8% word differences. Considering the deficiencies and problems that may arise from the correction process, the speaker does not vocalize by the text, words or letters are pronounced differently, etc., it was observed that there were approximately 1–2% letter errors and 5% word errors due to errors. This coincides with the predictions given at the beginning.

Considering all these issues, it is understood that the current Whisper architecture is more successful than the error values obtained in terms of the understandability of the converted text.

By fine-tuning, the performance of the models can be increased in terms of the task and language. However, for the TNST, METU MS, etc., although the datasets provide the opportunity to compare different models and architectures, it has been observed that they are insufficient for the fine-tuning process. Although the TNST dataset is rich in terms of the number of examples it contains, it is not suitable for fine-tuning in its current form due to the confusion caused by foreign words in its content. On the other hand, it is considered that the METU MS dataset is not suitable for use on its own for fine-tuning due to its small size, even if the errors it contains are eliminated.

In experiments conducted on many Turkish datasets with Whisper's upper models, a WER value between 0.05 and 0.15 was obtained. In particular, in the experiments conducted with the recently released Whisper-large-v3 model, a WER value of 0.04 to 0.10 was reached. These results show that Whisper is a successful architecture.

We performed a more comprehensive statistical evaluation of the model's performance on Turkish datasets. Specifically, we now provide the confidence intervals for the WER and CER metrics, which allow for a more robust comparison between the baseline and fine-tuned models.

The calculated confidence intervals (CIs) for the WER both before and after fine-tuning for the Whisper models provide a 95% confidence level, meaning we are 95% confident that the true WER lies within these ranges.

Confidence Intervals for Pre-Fine-Tuning WER:

METU MS: Mean = 0.202, CI = (0.152, 0.252)
TNST: Mean = 0.278, CI = (0.208, 0.347)
FLEURS: Mean = 0.228, CI = (0.165, 0.291)
Mozilla CV: Mean = 0.290, CI = (0.227, 0.354)
TASRT: Mean = 0.232, CI = (0.178, 0.286)

Confidence Intervals for Post-Fine-Tuning WER:

METU MS: Mean = 0.166, CI = (0.113, 0.218)
TNST: Mean = 0.262, CI = (0.202, 0.322)
TASRT: Mean = 0.190, CI = (0.137, 0.243)

These confidence intervals show the variability and reliability of the WER values before and after fine-tuning. The reduction in the WER after fine-tuning is statistically significant, as seen from the tighter confidence intervals and lower mean values.

Additionally, we used statistical significance tests (e.g., t-tests) to ensure that the improvements observed after fine-tuning are not due to random variation but are statistically significant. This helps solidify the reliability of our results. The results of the paired t-tests, which compare the WER values before and after fine-tuning for each dataset, are as follows:

METU MS: t-statistic: 5.77, p-value: 0.004
TNST: t-statistic: 4.65, p-value: 0.009
TASRT: t-statistic: 6.24, p-value: 0.003

For all the datasets (METU MS, TNST, and TASRT), the p-values are well below the common significance threshold of 0.05. This indicates that the reductions in the WER after fine-tuning are statistically significant. These results confirm that fine-tuning the Whisper models leads to a significant improvement in performance for Turkish ASR across the evaluated datasets.

In the fine-tuning process, large datasets are needed to improve the performance of the model used. In addition to being sufficient in size, the datasets to be used should contain few errors so as not to reduce the performance in the fine-tuning process. In this respect, although Turkish has larger datasets than many other languages, these sets are inadequate, especially in operations such as fine-tuning. As a result of this study, it was seen that there was a need to develop new Turkish datasets that were large and contained few errors. It is thought that in the future, studies should be carried out on the development of datasets with the above-mentioned features.

5. Conclusions

The integration of machine learning, particularly advanced deep learning techniques, has had a significant impact on the field of ASR. This influence has led to groundbreaking advancements in the accuracy and efficiency of ASR systems. In this research, the Whisper ASR model, employing a transformer-based encoder–decoder architecture, was utilized to develop a Turkish speech recognition system. The model's performance was assessed across diverse Turkish speech datasets, revealing significant improvements following fine-tuning with the LoRA method.

Challenges and Solutions:

Data scarcity: one of the primary challenges in developing ASR systems for low-resource languages like Turkish is the limited availability of labeled speech data. This study addressed this issue by fine-tuning the Whisper model with LoRA, which significantly reduced the word error rate.

Model adaptation: the transformer architecture of the Whisper model allows for efficient handling of long-range dependencies in speech data, making it suitable for languages with complex morphological structures like Turkish.

Future Directions:

Enhanced data collection: future research should focus on collecting more diverse and extensive Turkish speech datasets to further improve the model's performance.

Advanced fine-tuning techniques: exploring other fine-tuning techniques and hybrid models could provide additional performance gains and robustness in ASR systems.

By addressing these challenges and leveraging advanced machine learning techniques, development of robust and accurate ASR systems for low-resource languages such as Turkish can be significantly accelerated.

Author Contributions: Conceptualization, H.P., A.K.T. and C.K.; methodology, H.P. and A.K.T.; software, A.K.T.; validation, H.P., A.K.T., C.K. and H.B.U.; formal analysis, H.P. and A.K.T.; investigation, C.K. and A.K.T.; resources, C.K. and H.B.U.; data curation, A.K.T. and H.B.U.; writing—original draft preparation, H.P. and A.K.T.; writing—review and editing, H.P., C.K. and H.B.U.; visualization, H.B.U.; supervision, H.P. All authors have read and agreed to the published version of the manuscript.

Funding: This research received no external funding.

Data Availability Statement: Middle East Technical University (METU) Turkish Microphone Speech, data availability status: data available in a publicly accessible repository. The original data presented in the study are openly available in https://catalog.ldc.upenn.edu/LDC2006S33 (accessed on 15 September 2024). Turkish Broadcast News Speech and Text dataset, data availability status: data available in a publicly accessible repository. The original data presented in the study are openly available in https://catalog.ldc.upenn.edu/LDC2012S06 (accessed on 15 September 2024). Mozilla Common Voice dataset, data availability status: data available in a publicly accessible repository. The original data presented in the study are openly available in https://commonvoice.mozilla.org/en/datasets (accessed on 15 September 2024). FLEURS dataset, data availability status: data available in a publicly accessible repository. The original data presented in the study are openly available in https://huggingface.co/datasets/google/fleurs (accessed on 15 September 2024). Turkish Automatic Speech Recognition Test (TASRT), data availability status: data available on request due to restrictions (commercial use). The data presented in this study are available from the corresponding author upon request.

Conflicts of Interest: The authors declare no conflicts of interest.

References

1. Lv, Z.; Poiesi, F.; Dong, Q.; Lloret, J.; Song, H. Deep Learning for Intelligent Human–Computer Interaction. *Appl. Sci.* **2022**, *12*, 11457. [CrossRef]

2. Mihelic, F.; Zibert, J. *Speech Recognition*; InTech: Online, 2008; pp. 477–550. Available online: https://www.intechopen.com/books/3785 (accessed on 27 August 2024).
3. Oyucu, S. Development of Deep Learning Based Models for Turkish Speech Recognition. Ph.D. Thesis, Gazi University, Ankara, Turkey, 2020.
4. Radford, A.; Kim, J.W.; Xu, T.; Brockman, G.; McLeavey, C.; Sutskever, I. Robust Speech Recognition via Large-Scale Weak Supervision. In Proceedings of the 40th International Conference on Machine Learning, Honolulu, HI, USA, 23–29 July 2023; pp. 28492–28518.
5. Song, Z.; Zhuo, J.; Yang, Y.; Ma, Z.; Zhang, S.; Chen, X. LoRA-Whisper: Parameter-Efficient and Extensible Multilingual ASR. *arXiv* **2024**. [CrossRef]
6. Hu, E.J.; Shen, Y.; Wallis, P.; Allen-Zhu, Z.; Li, Y.; Wang, S.; Wang, L.; Chen, W. LoRA: Low-Rank Adaptation of Large Language Models. *arXiv* **2021**. [CrossRef]
7. Dudley, H.; Riesz, R.R.; Watkins, S.S.A. A Synthetic Speaker. *J. Frankl. Inst.* **1939**, *227*, 739–764. [CrossRef]
8. Dudley, H. The Vocoder—Electrical Re-creation of Speech. *J. Soc. Motion Pict. Eng.* **1940**, *34*, 272–278. [CrossRef]
9. Juang, B.-H.; Rabiner, L.R. *Automatic Speech Recognition—A Brief History of the Technology Development*, 2nd ed.; Elsevier: Amsterdam, The Netherlands, 2005.
10. Davis, K.H.; Biddulph, R.; Balashek, S. Automatic Recognition of Spoken Digits. *J. Acoust. Soc. Am.* **1952**, *24*, 637–642. [CrossRef]
11. Fry, D.B. Theoretical Aspects of Mechanical Speech Recognition. *J. Br. Inst. Radio Eng.* **1959**, *19*, 211–218. [CrossRef]
12. Forgie, J.W.; Forgie, C.D. Results Obtained from a Vowel Recognition Computer Program. *J. Acoust. Soc. Am.* **1959**, *31*, 1480–1489. [CrossRef]
13. Suzuki, J.; Nakata, K. Recognition of Japanese Vowels-Preliminary to the Recognition of Speech. *J. Radio Res. Lab.* **1961**, *37*, 193–212.
14. Nagata, K.; Kato, Y.; Chiba, S. Spoken Digit Recognizer for the Japanese Language. *J. Audio Eng. Soc.* **1964**, *12*, 336–342.
15. Sakai, T. The Phonetic Typewriter: Its Fundamentals and Mechanism. *Stud. Phonol.* **1961**, *1*, 140–152.
16. Kamath, U.; Liu, J.; Whitaker, J. *Deep Learning for NLP and Speech Recognition*, 1st ed.; Springer: Cham, Switzerland, 2019; pp. 369–404. [CrossRef]
17. Martin, T.B.; Nelson, A.L.; Zadell, H.J. *Speech Recognition by Feature-Abstraction Techniques*; Tech. Doc. Report No. AL TDR 64-176; Air Force Avionics Lab.: Wright-Patterson AF Base, OH, USA, 1964.
18. Vintsyuk, T.K. Speech Discrimination by Dynamic Programming. *Cybernetics* **1968**, *4*, 52–57. [CrossRef]
19. Viterbi, A. Error Bounds for Convolutional Codes and an Asymptotically Optimum Decoding Algorithm. *IEEE Trans. Inf. Theory* **1967**, *13*, 260–269. [CrossRef]
20. Itakura, F. Minimum Prediction Residual Principle Applied to Speech Recognition. *IEEE Trans. Acoust. Speech Signal Process.* **1975**, *23*, 67–72. [CrossRef]
21. Klatt, D.H. Review of the ARPA Speech Understanding Project. *J. Acoust. Soc. Am.* **1977**, *62*, 1345–1366. [CrossRef]
22. Lippmann, R.P. Review of neural networks for speech recognition. *Neural Comput.* **1989**, *1*, 1–38. [CrossRef]
23. Lowerre, B.; Reddy, R. The Harpy Speech Recognition System: Performance with Large Vocabularies. *J. Acoust. Soc. Am.* **1976**, *60*, S10–S11. [CrossRef]
24. Ferguson, J.D. *Symposium on the Application of Hidden Markov Models to Text and Speech*; Institute for Defense Analyses, Communications Research Division: Princeton, NJ, USA, 1980.
25. Wilpon, J.G.; Rabiner, L.R.; Lee, C.H.; Goldman, E.R. Automatic Recognition of Keywords in Unconstrained Speech Using Hidden Markov Models. *IEEE Trans. Acoust. Speech Signal Process.* **1990**, *38*, 1870–1878. [CrossRef]
26. Levinson, S.E.; Rabiner, L.R.; Sondhi, M.M. An Introduction to the Application of the Theory of Probabilistic Functions of a Markov Process to Automatic Speech Recognition. *Bell Syst. Tech. J.* **1983**, *62*, 1035–1074. [CrossRef]
27. Liberman, M.; Wayne, C. Human Language Technology. *AI Mag.* **2020**, *41*, 22–35. [CrossRef]
28. Young, S.J.; Evermann, G.; Gales, M.J.F.; Kershaw, D.; Moore, G.; Odell, J.J.; Ollason, D.G.; Povey, D.; Valtchev, D.; Woodland, P.C. The HTK Book. 2006. Available online: http://htk.eng.cam.ac.uk/ (accessed on 30 August 2024).
29. Graves, A.; Fernández, S.; Gomez, F.; Schmidhuber, J. Connectionist Temporal Classification: Labelling Unsegmented Sequence Data with Recurrent Neural Networks. In Proceedings of the 23rd International Conference on Machine Learning, Pittsburgh, PA, USA, 25–29 June 2006; pp. 369–376.
30. Chan, W.; Jaitly, N.; Le, Q.V.; Vinyals, O. Listen, Attend and Spell: A Neural Network for Large Vocabulary Conversational Speech Recognition. In Proceedings of the IEEE International Conference on Acoustics, Speech and Signal Processing (ICASSP), Shanghai, China, 20–25 March 2016; pp. 4960–4964. [CrossRef]
31. Zhang, Y.; Chan, W.; Jaitly, N. Very deep convolutional networks for end-to-end speech recognition. In Proceedings of the IEEE International Conference on Acoustics, Speech and Signal Processing (ICASSP), New Orleans, LA, USA, 5–9 March 2017; pp. 4845–4849.
32. Vaswani, A.; Shazeer, N.; Parmar, N.; Uszkoreit, J.; Jones, L.; Gomez, A.N.; Kaiser, Ł.; Polosukhin, I. Attention is All You Need. In Proceedings of the Advances in Neural Information Processing Systems 30 (NIPS 2017), Long Beach, CA, USA, 4–9 December 2017.
33. Schneider, S.; Baevski, A.; Collobert, R.; Auli, M. wav2vec: Unsupervised Pre-training for Speech Recognition. *arXiv* **2019**. [CrossRef]
34. Oord, A.v.d.; Li, Y.; Vinyals, O. Representation Learning with Contrastive Predictive Coding. *arXiv* **2019**. [CrossRef]

35. Baevski, A.; Zhou, Y.; Mohamed, A.; Auli, M. wav2vec 2.0: A Framework for Self-Supervised Learning of Speech Representations. In Proceedings of the Advances in Neural Information Processing Systems 33 (NeurIPS 2020), Online Conference, 6–12 December 2020; pp. 12449–12460.
36. Gulati, A.; Qin, J.; Chiu, C.-C.; Parmar, N.; Zhang, Y.; Yu, J.; Han, W.; Wang, S.; Zhang, Z.; Wu, Y.; et al. Conformer: Convolution-augmented Transformer for Speech Recognition. In Proceedings of the INTERSPEECH 2020, Shanghai, China, 25–29 October 2020; pp. 5036–5040. [CrossRef]
37. Arslan, R.S.; Barışçı, N. A Detailed Survey of Turkish Automatic Speech Recognition. *Turk. J. Electr. Eng. Comput. Sci.* **2020**, *28*, 3253–3269. [CrossRef]
38. Salor, Ö.; Pellom, B.L.; Ciloglu, T.; Hacioglu, K.; Demirekler, M. On Developing New Text and Audio Corpora and Speech Recognition Tools for the Turkish Language. In Proceedings of the 7th International Conference on Spoken Language Processing (ICSLP 2002), Denver, CO, USA, 16–20 September 2002; pp. 349–352. [CrossRef]
39. Polat, H.; Oyucu, S. Building A Speech and Text Corpus of Turkish: Large Corpus Collection with Initial Speech Recognition Results. *Symmetry* **2020**, *12*, 290. [CrossRef]
40. Artuner, H. The Design and Implementation of a Turkish Speech Phoneme Clustering System. Ph.D. Thesis, Hacettepe University, Ankara, Turkey, 1994.
41. Erzin, E. New Methods for Robust Speech Recognition. Master's Thesis, Bilkent University, Ankara, Turkey, 1995.
42. Özkan, Ö. Implementation of a Speech Recognition System for Connected Numerals. Master's Thesis, Middle East Technical University, Ankara, Turkey, 1997.
43. Uslu, E. Large Vocabulary Continuous Speech Recognition Using Hidden Markov Model. Master's Thesis, Yıldız Technical University, Istanbul, Turkey, 2007.
44. Yılmaz, C. A Large Vocabulary Speech Recognition System for Turkish. Master's Thesis, Bilkent University, Ankara, Turkey, 1999.
45. Edizkan, R. Computer Speech Recognition: Design of a Classifier in Feature Space and Subspaces. Ph.D. Thesis, Osmangazi University, Eskişehir, Turkey, 1999.
46. Şahin, S. Language Modeling for Turkish Continuous Speech Recognition. Master's Thesis, Middle East Technical University, Ankara, Turkey, 2003.
47. Dede, G. Speech Recognition with Artificial Neural Networks. Master's Thesis, Ankara Univesity, Ankara, Turkey, 2008.
48. Susman, D. Turkish Large Vocabulary Continuous Speech Recognition by Using Limited Audio Corpus. Master's Thesis, Middle East Technical University, Ankara, Turkey, 2012.
49. Tombaloğlu, B.; Erdem, H. Turkish Speech Recognition Techniques and Applications of Recurrent Units (LSTM and GRU). *Gazi Univ. J. Sci.* **2021**, *34*, 1035–1049. [CrossRef]
50. Safaya, A.; Erzin, E. Experiments on Turkish ASR with Self-Supervised Speech Representation Learning. *arXiv* **2022**. [CrossRef]
51. Mussakhojayeva, S.; Dauletbek, K.; Yeshpanov, R.; Varol, H.A. Multilingual Speech Recognition for Turkic Languages. *Information* **2023**, *14*, 74. [CrossRef]
52. Mercan, Ö.B.; Çepni, S.; Taşar, D.E.; Ozan, Ş. Performance Comparison of Pre-trained Models for Speech-to-Text in Turkish: Whisper-Small and Wav2Vec2-XLS-R-300M. *Turk. Inform. Found. Comput. Sci. Eng. J.* **2023**, *16*, 109–116. [CrossRef]
53. Chun, S.-J.; Park, J.B.; Ryu, H.; Jang, B.-S. Development and Benchmarking of a Korean Audio Speech Recognition Model for Clinician-Patient Conversations in Radiation Oncology Clinics. *Int. J. Med. Inform.* **2023**, *176*, 105112. [CrossRef]
54. Yang, H.; Zhang, M.; Tao, S.; Ma, M.; Qin, Y. Chinese ASR and NER Improvement Based on Whisper Fine-Tuning. In Proceedings of the 25th International Conference on Advanced Communication Technology (ICACT), Pyeongchang, Republic of Korea, 19–22 February 2023; pp. 213–217. [CrossRef]
55. Graham, C.; Roll, N. Evaluating OpenAI's Whisper ASR: Performance analysis across diverse accents and speaker traits. *JASA Express Lett.* **2024**, *4*, 025206. [CrossRef]
56. Wang, X.; Aitchison, L.; Rudolph, M. LoRA ensembles for large language model fine-tuning. *arXiv* **2023**. [CrossRef]
57. Arora, S.J.; Singh, R.P. Automatic Speech Recognition: A Review. *Int. J. Comput. Appl.* **2012**, *60*, 34–44. [CrossRef]
58. Dhanjal, A.S.; Singh, W. A Comprehensive Survey on Automatic Speech Recognition Using Neural Networks. *Multimed. Tools Appl.* **2024**, *83*, 23367–23412. [CrossRef]
59. Malik, M.; Malik, M.K.; Mehmood, K.; Makhdoom, I. Automatic Speech Recognition: A Survey. *Multimed. Tools Appl.* **2021**, *80*, 9411–9457. [CrossRef]
60. Wongso, W.; Lucky, H.; Suhartono, D. Pre-Trained Transformer-Based Language Models for Sundanese. *J. Big Data* **2022**, *9*, 39. [CrossRef]
61. Sutskever, I.; Vinyals, O.; Le, Q.V. Sequence to Sequence Learning with Neural Networks. In Proceedings of the 27th International Conference on Neural Information Processing Systems, Montreal, QC, Canada, 8–13 December 2014; pp. 3104–3112.
62. Bahdanau, D.; Cho, K.; Bengio, Y. Neural Machine Translation by Jointly Learning to Align and Translate. *arXiv* **2014**. [CrossRef]
63. Hendrycks, D.; Gimpel, K. Gaussian Error Linear Units (GELUs). *arXiv* **2023**. [CrossRef]
64. Salor, O.; Ciloglu, T.; Demirekler, M. METU Turkish Microphone Speech Corpus. In Proceedings of the IEEE 14th Signal Processing and Communications Applications, Antalya, Turkey, 17–19 April 2006; pp. 1–4. [CrossRef]
65. Arisoy, E.; Can, D.; Parlak, S.; Sak, H.; Saraclar, M. Turkish Broadcast News Transcription and Retrieval. *IEEE Trans. Audio Speech Lang. Process.* **2009**, *17*, 874–883. [CrossRef]

66. Ardila, R.; Branson, M.; Davis, K.; Henretty, M.; Kohler, M.; Meyer, J.; Morais, R.; Saunders, L.; Tyers, F.M.; Weber, G. Common Voice: A Massively-Multilingual Speech Corpus. *arXiv* **2020**. [CrossRef]
67. Conneau, A.; Ma, M.; Khanuja, S.; Zhang, Y.; Axelrod, V.; Dalmia, S.; Riesa, J.; Rivera, C.; Bapna, A. FLEURS: Few-shot Learning Evaluation of Universal Representations of Speech. *arXiv* **2022**. [CrossRef]
68. Oyucu, S. Development of Test Corpus with Large Vocabulary for Turkish Speech Recognition System and A New Test Procedure. *Adıyaman Univ. J. Sci.* **2022**, *9*, 156–164. [CrossRef]
69. Khan, A.; Khan, M.; Gueaieb, W.; Saddik, A.E.; De Masi, G.; Karray, F. CamoFocus: Enhancing Camouflage Object Detection with Split-Feature Focal Modulation and Context Refinement. In Proceedings of the IEEE/CVF Winter Conference on Applications of Computer Vision (WACV), Waikoloa, HI, USA, 3–8 January 2024; pp. 1423–1432. [CrossRef]
70. Khan, U.; Khan, M.; Elsaddik, A.; Gueaieb, W. DDNet: Diabetic Retinopathy Detection System Using Skip Connection-based Upgraded Feature Block. In Proceedings of the IEEE International Symposium on Medical Measurements and Applications (MeMeA), Jeju, Republic of Korea, 14–16 June 2023; pp. 1–6. [CrossRef]
71. Jurafsky, D.; Martin, J.H. *Speech and Language Processing: An Introduction to Natural Language Processing, Computational Linguistics, and Speech Recognition with Language Models*, 3rd ed.; 2024. Available online: https://web.stanford.edu/~jurafsky/slp3 (accessed on 30 August 2024).

electronics

MDPI

Article

GGTr: An Innovative Framework for Accurate and Realistic Human Motion Prediction

Biaozhang Huang [1,2] and Xinde Li [1,2,*]

1 Key Laboratory Measurement and Control of CSE, Ministry of Education, School of Automation, Southeast University, Nanjing 210096, China; bzhuang@seu.edu.cn
2 Nanjing Center for Applied Mathematics, Nanjing 211135, China
* Correspondence: xindeli@seu.edu.cn

Abstract: Human motion prediction involves forecasting future movements based on past observations, which is a complex task due to the inherent spatial-temporal dynamics of human motion. In this paper, we introduced a novel framework, GGTr, which adeptly encapsulates these patterns by integrating positional graph convolutional network (GCN) layers, gated recurrent unit (GRU) network layers, and transformer layers. The proposed model utilizes an enhanced GCN layer equipped with a positional representation to aggregate information from body joints more effectively. To address temporal dependencies, we strategically combined GRU and transformer layers, enabling the model to capture both local and global temporal dependencies across body joints. Through extensive experiments conducted on Human3.6M and CMU-MoCap datasets, we demonstrated the superior performance of our proposed model. Notably, our framework shows significant improvements in predicting long-term movements, outperforming state-of-the-art methods substantially.

Keywords: human motion prediction; graph convolutional network; gated recurrent unit; transformers

Citation: Huang, B.; Li, X. GGTr: An Innovative Framework for Accurate and Realistic Human Motion Prediction. *Electronics* **2023**, *12*, 3305. https://doi.org/10.3390/electronics12153305

Academic Editor: Grzegorz Dudek

Received: 6 July 2023
Revised: 29 July 2023
Accepted: 30 July 2023
Published: 1 August 2023

1. Introduction

Human motion prediction, the task of forecasting future human movements based on past observations, plays a critical role in various domains such as robotics, computer vision, healthcare, and sports analysis. Accurately predicting human motion is instrumental for facilitating effective human-robot collaboration [1,2], ensuring system security [3,4], analyzing human behavior and emotions [5,6], and supporting sports performance analysis [7]. However, predicting human motion presents significant challenges due to the complexity and diversity of human behaviors. First, human motion exhibits high variability and uncertainty. This is evident at the 3D skeletal level, due to the diversity in human body sizes, and at the movement level, due to individual idiosyncrasies. In scenarios with rapid changes, such as sudden reactions or motions, it is exceedingly difficult for predictive models to adapt quickly. Second, the interplay between different body parts and their coordinated movements further complicates the task. For instance, a motion initiated by one body part can propagate to other body parts in complex and often non-intuitive ways.

So, it becomes essential to capture both spatial and temporal features, as illustrated in Figure 1. Numerous research efforts have been made to address the challenges of modeling human motion. Traditional methods and machine learning methods such as hidden Markov models (HMM) [8], Gaussian processes (GP) [9], and restricted Boltzmann machine [10]. However, these methods may not fully capture the complex interdependencies and non-linear dynamics present in human motion. More recently, deep learning approaches, such as convolutional neural networks (CNNs) [11], graph convolutional networks (GCN) [12–15], temporal modules such as recurrent neural networks (RNNs) [16–21], and transformers [22–24] have been used. While existing RNN and deep learning-based models have significantly improved the prediction performance, they still have limitations. These methods often struggle to capture the dynamic and complex interactions between different body parts. The relations among body joints cannot be simply modeled by static spatial proximity; instead, they are influenced by various factors such as the individual's physical attributes, the current body state, and the motion context. Moreover, these models frequently encounter challenges in effectively capturing both local and global temporal dependencies.

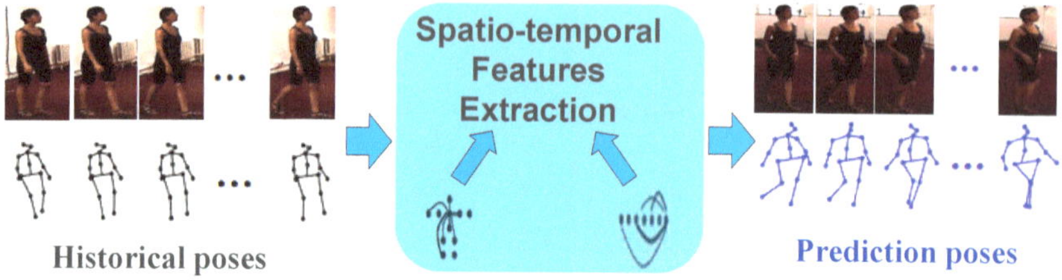

Figure 1. The process of human motion prediction. The historical sequences of human motion are subjected to feature extraction in terms of both space and time. This involves the analysis of the spatial configuration of the body, as well as the timing and sequence of these movements. The derived spatial and temporal features constitute the foundation for building a comprehensive understanding of the motion patterns.

To address these challenges, we proposed a novel approach for human motion prediction that combines positional graph convolutional network (GCN) layers, gated recurrent unit (GRU) network layers, and transformer layers, termed as GGTr. This combination allows us to better capture the complex spatial-temporal patterns in human motion data. In summary, the primary contributions of this paper include:

(1) The introduction of a novel GCN layer with positional representation, enabling better aggregation of information from adjacent body joints;
(2) The strategic combination of GRU and transformer layers to capture both local and global temporal dependencies across body joints;
(3) The conduction of extensive experiments on the Human3.6M and CMU-MoCap datasets, demonstrating the effectiveness and advantages of our proposed framework, our model shows significant improvements in predicting short-term movements. Experiments reveal that our model significantly outperforms state-of-the-art methods .

The remainder of this paper is organized as follows: Section 2 reviews related work. In Section 3, we first introduce some preliminary concepts and formalize the human motion prediction problem and the overall framework of the spatial temporal network model. Then, we discuss in detail the three model components to deal with the spatial and temporal dependencies, separately. In Section 4, experiments were conducted on two large-scale datasets, comparing the performance of the proposed method with baselines. Section 5 provides a summary and conclusion, as well as a discussion of future work.

2. Related Work

Human motion prediction is a challenging task due to the complexity and variability of human movements. This complexity arises from the intricate interplay of various factors such as the individual's physical characteristics, the environment, and the task at hand. Over the years, several approaches have been proposed to tackle this problem, each with its own strengths and limitations.

Traditional methods primarily rely on data statistical approaches or prior knowledge, such as Markov prediction models [8], Gaussian process dynamical models [9] and restricted Boltzmann machine [10], which can only tackle simple human motion patterns. Although these methods have achieved some success in certain scenarios, they still face challenges in capturing complex spatial and temporal dependencies.

Chiu et al. [25] used LSTM units to model the underlying structure of human motion hierarchically, but did not adequately utilize spatial information of human motion data. Martinez et al. [18] introduced a residual structure using GRU to model the velocity of human motion sequences, Their model focused on short-term temporal modeling, ignoring long-term dependencies and spatial structure. Jain et al. [17] combined LSTM and fully connected (FC) layers in a structural RNN model to encode high-level spatio-temporal structures in human motion sequences. Guo et al. [26] employed FC layers and GRU to model local structures and capture long-term temporal dependencies, but they did not take into account the interactions between different human body limbs. The transformer model with a self-attention mechanism has been proved to be more effective than recurrent networks in various domains [23,27,28]. It applies a multi-head attention mechanism to directly learn dependencies between each pair of input and output positions without any latency.

Graph convolutional networks (GCN) have become widely used for modeling the underlying relationships of non-Euclidean data. Kipf et al. [29] proposed a layer-wise propagation rule for nodes inspired by first-order approximation of spectral convolutions on graphs. However, this approach is limited by the characteristics of the graph. Yuan et al. [30] proposed a more flexible approach by learning node connectivity based on node neighborhood. Velickovic et al. [31] introduced self-attention to determine the neighborhood structure to be considered, providing more flexibility to the network. This approach has been applied to action recognition [32] by using a GCN to capture the temporal and spatial dependencies of human body joints via a graph defined on temporally connected kinematic trees. These techniques have been applied to human motion prediction by building the human pose as a graph and using GCN to encode the spatial connectivity of human joints. Ma et al. [33] proposed two variants of GCN to extract spatial and temporal features. They built a multi-stage structure where each stage contains an encoder and a decoder and, during training, the model is trained with intermediate supervision to learn to progressively refine the prediction. References [12,13,34] extended the graph of the human pose to multi-scale the version across the abstraction levels of the human pose. However, as these models aggregate body joint features based on an input adjacency matrix, the relation between body parts is fixed and may limit the model's ability to adapt to complex human motions.

The transformer [35] has become the dominant approach in natural language processing (NLP). The key component of the transformer is a multi-head self-attention mechanism that captures long-range dependencies. Building upon the success of the transformer in various tasks [36–38], researchers have increasingly focused on exploring its potential applications in 3D human motion prediction [22–24]. Cai et al. [22] employed a transformer-based architecture with discrete cosine transform (DCT) to capture the long-range spatial correlations and temporal dependencies in human motion dynamics. Another notable advancement is the spatio-temporal transformer (ST-Trans) mechanism proposed by Aksan et al. [23], which effectively captures the spatio-temporal dependencies of decomposed 3D human motions. However, the ST-Trans method overlooks the importance of ensuring consistency between spatial and temporal information, which is a crucial factor when dealing with time-varying data. To address this limitation, a cross-transformer approach [24] has been developed to explore effective interaction between spatial and temporal branches. This approach is designed to learn the coherence of spatial and temporal information and simultaneously enhance the model's predictive capacity. Despite these advancements, transformer-based methods may overlook local information when dealing with human motion data, warranting further investigation into this aspect.

In summary, with the development of human motion prediction in recent years, GCN/GRU/transformer-based architectures have been well explored and results have significantly improved. In this paper, we proposed a new spatial-temporal graph convolutional network framework to address the human motion prediction problem. We used graph convolutional networks with a position-wise attention mechanism to capture the spatial dependencies of the human body joints. A gated recurrent neural network with transformer layers was used to capture both local and global information of human motion sequences in the temporal dimension.

3. The Proposed Framework

Problem Fromulation. In the realm of human motion prediction, the objective is to forecast future human movements utilizing historical motion data. Specifically, these historical motion data can be expressed as a time series within a 3D skeletal structure. This structure can be denoted as $G = (V, E)$, where $V = \{v_1, v_2, \ldots, v_M\}$ represents a set of M joints in the human body, and E is a set of edges that represent the physical connections between these joints. The relationships between joints can be demonstrated by a symmetric adjacency matrix $A \in R^{M \times M}$, where the i, j-th element, A_{ij}, represents the biomechanical correlation between joints v_i and v_j. This correlation is typically gauged by the physical linkage or common motion patterns shared between two joints. Note that $A_{ij} = 0$ if there is no substantial correlation between the two respective joints. The historical motion data can be represented in a sequence $Z = (z_1, z_2, \ldots, z_\tau)$ on the 3D skeletal structure, where each $z_t \in R^{M \times 1}$ signifies the motion status of M joints at time t. With the above notations, we can formally state the problem as follows.

Given the 3D skeletal structure $G = (V, E)$ and the historical motion data $Z = (z_1, z_2, \ldots, z_\tau)$, the aim was to formulate a model f that can accept a new sequence $X = (x_1, x_2, \ldots, x_T)$ of length T as an input and predict the motion status for the subsequent T' time steps, denoted as:

$$X_{pred} = f(G; X|Z) = (x_{T+1}, \ldots, x_{T+T'}). \tag{1}$$

Moreover, during the training phase, we employed a sliding window of length $T + T'$ over the historical motion sequence Z to generate the training samples. These samples serve to train the model f.

Overview. The conceptual framework of the proposed GGTr network, illustrated in Figure 2, is primarily composed of three crucial components. The spatial graph convolutional network (GCN) layers were designed to model the spatial correlation between the human body joints graph. These layers were applied to the input representations of the gated recurrent unit (GRU), which modeled the sequential temporal relations, also referred to as local temporal dependencies. The framework also includes a transformer layer that is specifically designed to directly apprehend the long-range or global temporal dependencies within the motion sequence. The GRU and transformer layers work in tandem to capture the temporal dependencies for each joint independently, albeit from distinct perspectives. Subsequently, we delve into the spatial dependency modeling with the GCN, followed by an explanation of how the GRU layer and the transformer layer function to capture temporal dependencies, leading to a comprehensive summary of the complete framework.

3.1. Spatial Dependence Modeling

Acquiring the complex spatial dependence is a crucial problem in human motion prediction. The traditional convolutional network (CNN) can grasp local spatial features, but its application is primarily confined to Euclidean space, such as images or regular grids. However, the human body essentially forms a graph, not a two-dimensional grid. A graph is a structure composed of nodes and edges. In the context of human motion prediction, nodes can represent joints in the human body, and edges can represent connections between joints. Graphical models can effectively represent the complex relationships between human joints, which is useful for human motion prediction. This means the CNN model cannot reflect the complex topological structure of the human body and thus cannot accurately capture spatial dependence. Recently, generalizing the CNN to the graph convolutional network (GCN), which can handle arbitrary graph-structured data, has received widespread attention.

In the human motion prediction problem, if two body joints are connected or in close proximity, their movements are likely to mutually influence each other. Thus, to capture these spatial relationships, we employed the graph convolutional networks model proposed in [29,31]. This model is used to transform and propagate motion information through the graph structure. Specifically, given input motion information $X^l \in R^{M \times d^l}$ on the structure, where d^l represents the input dimension, the output $X^{l+1} \in R^{M \times d^{l+1}}$ can be computed, with d^{l+1} denoting the output dimension.

$$X^{l+1} = \sigma(\tilde{D}^{-1/2}\tilde{A}\tilde{D}^{-1/2}X^l W^l), \quad (2)$$

where $\sigma(.)$ is a non-linear activation function. In our work, we adopted ReLU $(\cdot)$, standing for REctified Linear Unit, which is advantageous for its ability to speed up the convergence of stochastic gradient descent compared to sigmoid and tanh functions. $\tilde{A} = A + I_M$ is the adjusted adjacency matrix with I_M as the M-dimensional identity matrix, and $\tilde{D}$ is the modified degree matrix, with $\tilde{D}_{ii} = \sum_j \tilde{A}_{ij}$. W^l are the parameters to be learned. For convenience, we represent the operation in Equation (2) as follows:

$$X^{l+1} = GCN_0(X^l, A). \quad (3)$$

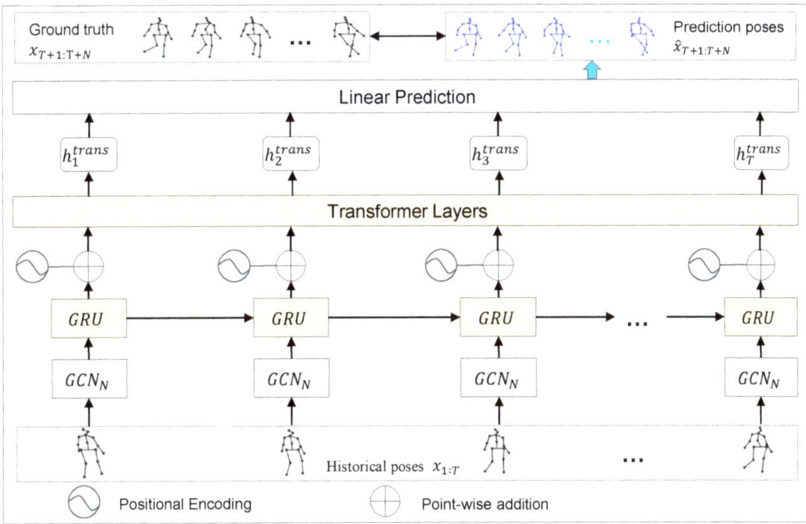

Figure 2. The whole architecture of our suggested solution for motion prediction, which employs an end-to-end framework. We encode human poses $x_{1:T}$ and feed them to GGTr. The GCN layer aids in understanding spatial relationships among body joints within the human motion network. Following the GRU is a transformer layer, designed to grasp global temporal dependencies. Ultimately, the transformer's output is harnessed to predict future motion states.

In the aforementioned formulation, the operation relies solely on the human body joints structure information, which is premised on the physical proximity between body parts. However, the interplay between body joints can be significantly more intricate. Various factors such as muscle constraints, physical capabilities, motion style, and ongoing actions can impact the motion of body parts. Therefore, the information from neighboring joints should not be aggregated equally to a given central joint when performing the aggregation in Equation (2). Recently, GaAN [39] attempted to employ the attention mechanism to model the complex relationships between graph nodes. Ideally, the aforementioned factors could be used to calculate the attention score, but these factors are not always available. Furthermore, there may be other factors influencing the relations between joints that we are not aware of. Therefore, in this paper, we proposed learning a positional representation to capture these factors for each joint. Specifically, for joints v_i, v_j, we aimed to learn two latent positional representations $h_i, h_j \in R^M$. We then modeled the pairwise relations between any body joints as:

$$\begin{aligned} e_{ij} &= a([Wh_i||Wh_j]) \\ \alpha_{ij} &= \frac{\exp(LeakyReLU(a(h_i, h_j)))}{\sum_{k=1}^{M} \exp(LeakyReLU(a(h_i, h_j)))}, \end{aligned} \tag{4}$$

where $a(.)$ is a relation score function modeled with dot product as follows:

$$a(h_i, h_j) = (Wh_i)^T Wh_j, \tag{5}$$

where W is a transformation matrix to be learned. We further employed a mask to sparsify the relation matrix α in order to reduce computational complexity:

$$mask(\alpha) = \begin{cases} \alpha_{ij}, & \text{if } \tilde{A}_{ij} > 0 \\ 0, & \text{otherwise.} \end{cases} \tag{6}$$

Subsequently, the GCN operation can be applied to the newly learned relation matrix $mask(\alpha)$:

$$X^{l+1} = \sigma(\tilde{D}_{\alpha}^{-1/2} \tilde{\alpha} \tilde{D}_{\alpha}^{-1/2} X^l W^l), \tag{7}$$

where $\tilde{\alpha} = mask(\alpha) + I_M$ and $\tilde{D}_{\alpha}$ is the degree matrix for $\tilde{\alpha}$. For simplicity, we represent the operation in Equation (7) as:

$$X^{l+1} = GCN_N(A, X^l). \tag{8}$$

Instead of the operation in (2), the operation in (8) was used to capture the spatial relations. This approach allowed us to learn a positional representation for each joint, capturing various factors that influence their relationships. By using these learned representations in combination with an attention mechanism and a sparsified relation matrix, we can effectively model complex spatial relationships between different body joints and improve the accuracy of human motion prediction.

3.2. *Temporal Dependence Modeling*

The gated recurrent unit (GRU) is a variant of a traditional RNN and can effectively capture the semantic association between long sequences and alleviate the problem of gradient vanishing or explosion. Its core structure can be divided into two parts for analysis: update gate and reset gate, illustrated in Figure 3. To capture the temporal dependency in human motion sequences, we adopted the gated recurrent unit (GRU) [40] to process the sequence information.

For each time step, we maintained a hidden representation that served as the output for the current step and influenced the information flow to the subsequent step. It is important to note that the GRU operation was applied individually to each joint in the body, and the parameters were shared for all joints. To incorporate spatial relations in human motion while processing the sequence, we applied a modified graph convolutional network (GCN) operation, as described in Equation (8), to the input representations of the GRU. Specifically, at each time step t, with input x_t and previous step's hidden representations h_{t-1}, we applied the modified GCN operation:

$$\begin{aligned} \tilde{x}_t &= GCN_N(A, x_t) \\ \tilde{h}_{t-1} &= GCN_N(A, h_{t-1}). \end{aligned} \tag{9}$$

For a body joint v_i at time step t, the history observation $x_t[i]$ contains the dynamic features for joint v_i at t-th time step. The update gate and reset gate are denoted as follows:

$$\begin{aligned} z_t &= \sigma(W_z\tilde{x}_t[i] + U_z\tilde{h}_{t-1}[i] + b_z) \\ r_t &= \sigma(W_r\tilde{x}_t[i] + U_r\tilde{h}_{t-1}[i] + b_r), \end{aligned} \tag{10}$$

where W_z, W_r, W_h, U_z, U_r, b_z, b_r are the trainable parameters.

We then calculated the candidate hidden state and the updated hidden state $h_t[i]$ as follows:

$$\begin{aligned} \tilde{h}_t[i] &= \tanh(W_h\tilde{x}_t[i] + r_t \odot U_h\tilde{h}_{t-1}[i] + b_h) \\ h_t[i] &= (1 - z_t)\tilde{h}_{t-1}[i] + z_t \odot \tilde{h}_t[i], \end{aligned} \tag{11}$$

where $\odot$ denotes the element-wise multiplication, U_h,b_h are the parameters to be learned, and $h_t[i]$ serves as extracted features of joint v_i at the next time step.

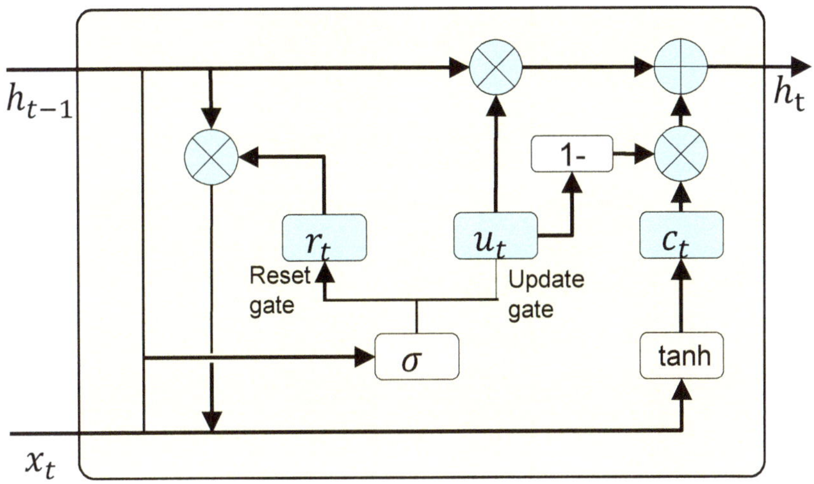

Figure 3. Architectural elements in a GRU layer.

The above are the fundamental equations and steps of GRU. By controlling the update and reset gates, GRU can dynamically update and adjust the hidden state based on different patterns in the sequence, enabling it to better capture the local temporal information. However, in the human body motion prediction problem, the temporal information may not only be sequentially dependent. Hence, it is important to capture the global temporal information for accurate human motion prediction. Thus, after processing with the GRU layer, we adopted a transformer layer [35] to capture the global dependencies following the GRU.

The transformer layer, similar to the GRU layer, was applied to each joint individually. For joint v_i, the output sequence $(h_1[i], \ldots, h_T[i])$ from GRU was taken as the input for the transformer. Figure 4 illustrates that a transformer layer consists of a multi-head attention layer, a shared feed-forward neural work layer, and normalization layers between them.

Inputs of model. The input of the model is the spatial dependency embedding sequence of each joint. Let us consider the i-th joint's spatial dependency embedding sequence $(h_1[i], h_2[i], \ldots, h_T[i])$. Although the self-attention mechanism is effective in capturing hidden dependency relationships in the sequence, it fails to maintain location information. Hence, we incorporated position encoding e_t as proposed by [35], between GRU and the transformer layer. This choice was motivated by the ability of this approach to facilitate the model's learning to attend to relative positions in a sequence. The new representations $h'_t[i]$ were computed as follows:

$$h'_t[i] = h_t[i] + e_t, \quad (12)$$

where e_t is defined as

$$e_t = \begin{cases} sin(t/10000^{2i/d_{model}}), & \text{if } i = 0, 2, 4\ldots \\ cos(t/10000^{2i/d_{model}}), & \text{otherwise.} \end{cases} \quad (13)$$

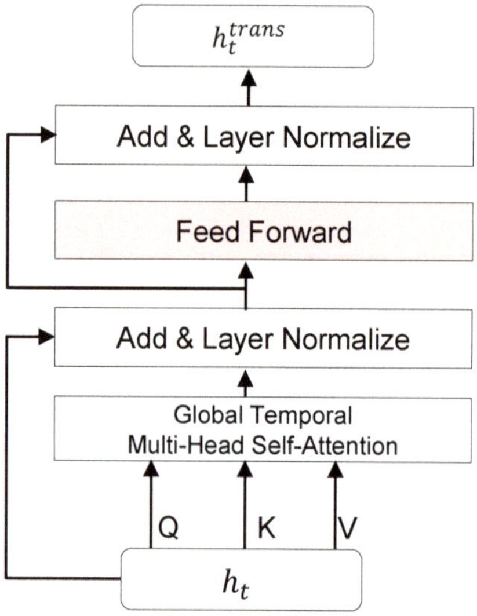

Figure 4. Architectural elements in a transformer layer.

Temporal multi-head attention. In our model, we defined a matrix $h^{v_i} \in R^{T\times d}$ by arranging $(h_1[i], h_2[i], \ldots, h_T[i])$ in a row-wise manner across the temporal axis. The multi-head attention mechanism is composed of several attention heads, which process the input in parallel and whose outputs are then combined. This concept can be represented mathematically as follows:

$$MultiHead(h^{v_i}) = Concat(head_1, \ldots, head_s)W^O. \quad (14)$$

This signifies that the output of multi-head attention is the concatenation of s single head attention blocks, each one being projected with the matrix W^O. Each single head attention block, $head_s$, can be given by:

$$\begin{aligned} head_s &= Attention(h^{v_i}) \\ &= softmax(\frac{Q_s K_s^T}{\sqrt{d_k}})V_s, \end{aligned} \quad (15)$$

where W_s^Q, W_s^K, and W_s^V denote the queries, keys, and values of the *s-th* single head attention for joint v_i, respectively. We obtained the Q_s, K_s, and V_s by a linear projection with W^Q, W^K, and W^V:

$$Q_s = h^{v_i}W_s^Q,\ K_s = h^{v_i}W_s^K,\ V_s = h^{v_i}W_s^V, \quad (16)$$

where $W_s^Q \in \mathbb{R}^{d\times d_k}$, $W_s^K \in \mathbb{R}^{d\times d_k}$, and $W_s^V \in \mathbb{R}^{d\times d_v}$ are the trainable projection matrices for the *s-th* attention head and are shared by all the joints.

Feed-forward Layer. After the multi-head attention layer, the output states are then processed by a feedforward neural network layer. This layer is identical for all joints, which includes two linear transformations and a ReLU activation function in between:

$$FFN(X) = max(0, XW_1 + b_1)W_2 + b_2, \tag{17}$$

where W_1, W_2 are the trainable parameters of the feed-forward neural network and b_1 and b_2 are bias terms.

Residual connection and normalization. As shown in Figure 4, the residual connection and normalization operators appear in each layer. The residual connection was introduced to tackle the difficulty in training deep network optimization algorithms, and normalization was applied to prevent overfitting. Given the embedded feature Z_{in}, the process of the residual connection and normalization layer is denoted as follows:

$$\begin{aligned} Z_{in}^{'} &= LayerNorm(Z_{in} + MultiHead(Z_{in})) \\ h_{out} &= LayerNorm(Z_{in}^{'} + FFN(Z_{in}^{'})), \end{aligned} \tag{18}$$

where $LayerNorm(.)$ denotes the normalization function.

Lastly, after each sub-layer in the transformer, such as the temporal multi-head attention layer and the feed-forward network layer, a layer normalization operation and a residual connection were applied. The final output of the transformer layer for joint v_i can be denoted as $h_{out}^{v_i} \in \mathbb{R}^{T \times d}$.

In summary, this approach combines both the local and global temporal information through the GRU and transformer layers, which can be highly beneficial for accurate human motion prediction. The individual sequence of movements and the overall pattern of movements are both considered, making this method a versatile and robust choice for this task.

3.3. Loss Function

To train our model, we employed an end-to-end training technique. The mean position per joint error (MPJPE) loss [41] function between the anticipated motion sequence and the ground truth motion sequence was used to analyse the difference between the predicted outcomes and the true pose, which is defined as follows:

$$L = \frac{1}{M \times T} \sum_{i=1}^{M} \sum_{t=1}^{T} ||\hat{x}_t[i] - x_t[i]||_2^2, \tag{19}$$

where M is the number of joints in human pose, T is the number of time steps in the future series, $\hat{x}_t[i]$ is the predicted joint position at the t-th time step of the i-th joint, and $x_t[i]$ is the corresponding ground truth.

We optimised the loss function using the improved Adam method (AdamW [42]), which mitigates the overfitting problem by adding a weight decay term and can significantly improve the robustness of the model.

4. Experiments

In this section, we present experiments on two large-scale human motion capture benchmark datasets (Human3.6M and CMU-MoCap) to demonstrate the effectiveness of the GGTr network for human motion prediction. We first introduced the experimental settings, including datasets, baselines, and parameter settings. Then, we conducted experiments to compare the performance of the GGTr with other baselines. Finally, we designed comprehensive ablation studies to evaluate the impact of the essential architectural components.

4.1. Datasets

Human3.6M [41] is the largest existing human motion analysis database, consisting of seven actors (S1, S5, S6, S7, S8, S9, and S11) performing 15 actions such as walking, eating, smoking, discussing, and directions. Each pose includes 32 joints, represented in the form of an exponential map. Following the data processing of [18], by converting these into 3D coordinates, eliminating redundant joints, global rotation, and translation, the resulting skeleton retains 17 joints that provide sufficient human motion details. These joints include key ones that locate major body parts (e.g., shoulders, knees, and elbows). We downsampled the frame rate to 25 fps and used S5 and S11 for testing and validation, while the remaining five actors were used for training.

CMU-MoCap (Available at http://mocap.cs.cmu.edu/ accessed on 5 July 2023) is a 3D human motion dataset, released by Carnegie Mellon University, that used 12 Vicon infrared MX-40 cameras to record the positions of 41 sensors attached to the human body, describing human motion. The dataset can be divided into six motion themes, including human interaction, interaction with environment, locomotion, physical activities and sports, situations and scenarios, and test motions. We adopted the same data preprocessing method as described in the literature [43], simplifying each human body and reducing the motion rate to 25 frames per second. Furthermore, seven actions were selected from the dataset to evaluate the model's performance. No hyperparameters were adjusted on this dataset. We used only the training and testing sets, with the splitting method consistent with common practice in the literature [43].

4.2. Implementation Details

All experiments in this paper were implemented using the PyTorch deep learning framework. The experimental environment was Ubuntu 20.04, utilizing an NVIDIA A100 GPU. During the training process, a batch size of 16 was used and the number of attention heads was set to 4. The number of GRU and transformer layers were both set to 1. The model was optimized using the AdamW optimizer. The initial learning rate was set to 0.003, with a 5% decay every 5 epochs. Training was conducted for 800 epochs, and each experiment was repeated three times to obtain an average result, ensuring a more robust evaluation of the model's performance. For the input motion prediction, a length of 25 frames (1000 ms) was considered, and the prediction generated 25 frames (1000 ms). The choice and configuration of related hyperparameters are summarized in Table 1.

Table 1. The choice and configuration of related hyperparameters.

Hyperparameter/Config	Value
Optimizer	AdamW
Base learning rate	5×10^{-3}
Weight decay	10^{-2}
Batch size	16
Warmup epochs	5
Epochs	800

4.3. Evaluation Metrics and Baselines

The evaluation metrics employed in our study were consistent with those utilized in existing algorithms [33,43]. The mean per joint position error (MPJPE) [41] was adopted as the standard measurement, which computed the average Euclidean distance (in millimeters, mm) between the predicted joint 3D coordinates and the ground truth. In addition, to further illustrate the advantages of the proposed method, a comparative analysis was conducted with several state-of-the-art approaches [15,18,22,23,33,34,43].

Res. sup. [18] is an early RNN-based method. LTD [43], MSR [34], ST-DGCN [33], and LCDC [15] utilize GCN-based methodologies. Meanwhile, LPJP [22] and STCT [23] employ transformer-based approaches. We compared the proposed method with all the above approaches on the Human3.6M dataset, and with approaches [15,18,22,34,43] on CMU-MoCap. By comparing the proposed method with these existing approaches, this study aimed to demonstrate its effectiveness and highlight its advantages in terms of accuracy and performance.

4.4. Experimental Results and Analysis

Human3.6M. Table 2 presents quantitative comparisons of our method and other approaches in predicting short-term (80 ms, 160 ms, 320 ms, 400 ms) and long-term movements (560 ms, 1000 ms) on the Human3.6M dataset. The final column provides the average performance across all tested time intervals for 15 actions.

Table 2. Prediction of 3D joint positions on Human3.6M for all actions. The best results are marked in bold.

Time(ms)	80	160	320	400	560	1000	80	160	320	400	560	1000
Action			**Walking**						**Eating**			
Res. sup. [18]	29.4	50.8	76.0	81.5	81.7	100.7	16.8	30.6	56.9	68.7	79.9	100.2
LTD [43]	12.3	23.0	39.8	46.1	54.1	59.8	8.4	16.9	33.2	40.7	53.4	77.8
ST-Trans [23]	**8.9**	**15.5**	**32.1**	**38.5**	-	-	9.4	21.1	36.4	42.3	-	-
MSR [34]	12.2	22.7	38.6	45.2	52.7	63.0	8.4	17.1	33.0	40.4	52.5	77.1
ST-DGCN [33]	10.2	19.8	34.5	40.3	48.1	56.4	7.0	15.1	**30.6**	38.1	51.1	76.0
LCDC [15]	11.1	22.4	38.8	45.2	52.7	59.8	7.0	15.5	31.7	39.2	51.9	76.2
Ours	10.3	19.5	34.9	41.8	**51.1**	**54.9**	**6.9**	**15.0**	31.6	**36.3**	**50.2**	**71.7**
Action			**Smoking**						**Discussion**			
Res. sup. [18]	23.0	42.6	70.1	82.7	94.8	137.4	32.9	61.2	90.9	96.2	121.3	161.7
LTD [43]	7.9	16.2	31.9	38.9	50.7	72.6	12.5	27.4	58.5	71.7	91.6	121.5
ST-Trans [23]	8.8	15.2	**25.1**	**24.5**	-	-	**7.9**	25.7	**39.9**	**47.5**	-	-
MSR [34]	8.0	16.3	31.3	38.2	49.5	71.6	12.0	26.8	57.1	69.7	88.6	117.6
ST-DGCN [33]	6.6	14.1	28.2	34.7	46.5	69.5	10.0	23.8	53.6	66.7	87.1	118.2
LCDC [15]	6.6	14.8	29.8	36.7	48.1	71.2	10.0	24.4	54.5	67.4	87.0	116.3
Ours	**6.4**	**14.1**	28.4	33.1	**45.3**	**67.3**	9.8	**23.2**	49.5	58.4	**83.9**	**106.5**
Action			**Directions**						**Greeting**			
Res. sup. [18]	35.4	57.3	76.3	87.7	110.1	152.5	34.5	63.4	124.6	142.5	156.1	166.5
LTD [43]	9.0	19.9	43.4	53.7	71.0	101.8	18.7	38.7	77.7	93.4	115.4	148.8
ST-Trans [23]	10.2	17.8	42.5	48.6	-	-	13.5	**26.1**	**54.0**	**73.2**	-	-
MSR [34]	8.6	19.7	43.3	53.8	71.2	100.6	16.5	37.0	77.3	93.4	116.3	147.2
ST-DGCN [33]	7.2	17.6	40.9	51.5	69.3	100.4	15.2	34.1	71.6	87.1	110.2	143.5
LCDC [15]	6.9	17.4	41.0	51.7	69.1	99.1	14.3	33.5	72.2	87.3	108.7	142.3
Ours	**6.9**	**17.0**	**39.2**	**48.4**	**66.4**	**94.6**	**13.4**	39.3	69.4	81.6	**103.3**	**137.6**
Action			**Phoning**						**Posing**			
Res. sup. [18]	38.0	69.3	115.0	126.7	141.2	131.5	36.1	69.1	130.5	157.1	194.7	240.2
LTD [43]	10.2	21.0	42.5	52.3	69.2	103.1	13.7	29.9	66.6	84.1	114.5	173.0
ST-Trans [23]	15.3	20.4	**31.4**	**38.8**	-	-	10.6	22.8	57.6	73.7	-	-
MSR [34]	10.1	20.7	41.5	51.3	68.3	104.4	12.8	29.4	67.0	85.0	116.3	174.3
ST-DGCN [33]	**8.3**	18.3	38.7	48.4	65.9	102.7	10.7	25.7	60.0	76.6	106.1	164.8
LCDC [15]	8.5	19.2	40.3	49.9	66.7	102.2	10.1	25.4	60.6	77.3	106.5	163.3
Ours	8.6	**18.4**	39.9	46.5	**63.8**	**99.1**	**9.9**	**22.6**	**57.6**	**73.5**	**103.7**	**158.4**
Action			**Purchases**						**Sitting**			
Res. sup. [18]	36.3	60.3	86.5	95.9	122.7	160.3	42.6	81.4	134.7	151.8	167.4	201.5
LTD [43]	15.6	32.8	65.7	79.3	102.0	143.5	10.6	21.9	46.3	57.9	78.3	119.7
ST-Trans [23]	17.3	32.5	**60.0**	68.3	-	-	8.5	22.9	47.8	66.8	-	-
MSR [34]	14.8	32.4	66.1	79.6	101.6	139.2	10.5	22.0	46.3	57.8	78.2	120.0
ST-DGCN [33]	12.5	28.7	60.1	73.3	95.3	133.3	8.8	19.2	42.4	53.8	74.4	116.1
LCDC [15]	12.7	29.7	62.3	75.8	97.5	137.8	8.8	19.3	42.9	54.3	74.9	117.8
Ours	**12.3**	**28.5**	61.7	**67.9**	**91.1**	**126.1**	**8.5**	**19.1**	**40.1**	**49.8**	**69.6**	**115.2**

Table 2. *Cont.*

Action	Sitting Down						Taking Photo					
Res. sup. [18]	47.3	86.0	145.8	168.9	205.3	277.6	26.1	47.6	81.4	94.7	117.0	143.2
LTD [43]	16.1	31.1	61.5	75.5	100.0	150.2	9.9	20.9	45.0	56.6	77.4	119.8
ST-Trans [23]	**9.2**	32.7	58.8	65.9	-	-	**6.8**	**16.5**	**37.9**	**48.5**	-	-
MSR [34]	16.1	31.6	62.5	76.8	102.8	155.5	9.9	21.0	44.6	56.3	77.9	121.9
ST-DGCN [33]	13.9	27.9	57.4	71.5	96.7	147.8	8.4	18.9	42.0	53.3	74.3	118.6
LCDC [15]	14.1	28.0	57.3	71.2	96.1	147.3	8.4	18.8	42.0	53.5	74.5	117.9
Ours	13.8	**26.1**	**55.3**	**65.3**	**94.2**	**141.9**	8.1	17.6	38.3	48.7	**72.8**	**110.8**
Action	**Waiting**						**Walking Dog**					
Res. sup. [18]	30.6	57.8	106.2	121.5	146.2	196.2	64.2	102.1	141.1	164.4	191.3	209.0
LTD [43]	11.4	24.0	50.1	61.5	79.4	108.1	23.4	46.2	83.5	96.0	111.9	148.9
ST-Trans [23]	9.2	20.5	59.8	62.2	-	-	22.3	67.8	103.8	122.5	-	-
MSR [34]	10.7	23.1	48.3	59.2	76.3	106.3	20.7	42.9	80.4	93.3	111.9	148.2
ST-DGCN [33]	8.9	20.1	**43.6**	54.3	72.2	103.4	18.8	39.3	73.7	86.4	104.7	139.8
LCDC [15]	8.7	20.2	44.3	55.3	73.2	105.7	19.6	41.8	77.6	90.2	109.8	147.7
Ours	**8.5**	**19.7**	44.6	**50.0**	**68.6**	**101.5**	**17.6**	**38.3**	**73.5**	**84.1**	**103.5**	**135.8**
Action	**Waiting Together**						**Average**					
Res. sup. [18]	26.8	50.1	80.2	92.2	107.6	131.1	34.7	62.0	101.1	115.5	97.6	130.5
LTD [43]	10.5	21.0	38.5	45.2	55.0	65.6	12.7	26.1	52.3	63.5	81.6	114.3
ST-Trans [23]	**7.5**	**13.7**	**27.7**	46.2	-	-	11.0	24.7	47.7	57.8	-	-
MSR [34]	10.6	20.9	37.4	43.9	52.9	65.9	12.1	25.6	51.6	62.9	81.1	114.2
ST-DGCN [33]	8.7	18.6	34.4	41.0	51.9	64.3	10.3	22.7	47.4	58.5	76.9	110.3
LCDC [15]	9.1	19.8	36.3	42.7	50.5	61.2	10.4	23.3	48.8	59.8	77.8	111.0
Ours	9.1	19.2	36.1	**39.8**	**48.4**	**57.7**	**10.0**	**21.8**	**46.8**	**55.1**	**74.4**	**105.4**

Among the comparison methods, RNN-based techniques exhibited the poorest performance, while transformer-based approaches outperformed GCN-based methods. Above all, our method emerged as the top performer. The most significant improvements in the MPJPE metric were observed with transformer-based techniques, highlighting their aptitude for modeling 3D human motion dynamics and capturing global dependencies.

Specifically, existing methods generally performed well when predicting periodic and simpler movements, such as "walking" and "eating". However, their performance dropped significantly when tasked with predicting more unpredictable and irregular movements like "directions", "posing", and "purchases". This indicates that these methods have difficulty managing the dynamic changes and local–global dependencies inherent in human motion.

On the other hand, the algorithm proposed in our study demonstrated a high prediction accuracy, even with highly complex, non-periodic, and irregular movements. Our experimental results revealed that our proposed method surpasses most baseline methods in short-term motion prediction, with even greater improvements noted in long-term prediction. Our method delivered a superior performance in the 560 ms and 1000 ms MPJPE metrics, an accomplishment attributable to GGTr's ability to fully capture spatial correlation and local–global temporal features, thereby bolstering the model's prediction accuracy.

While our predictions for movements such as "walking" , "smoking" , "greeting" and "waiting together" fell short compared to those of MSR [34], this nonetheless underscores the sophisticated nature of transformer-based approaches. Looking ahead, we are committed to further refining our model to enhance its performance.

Overall, our proposed method outperformed all the baseline models on average, proving its superior performance in motion prediction. The outstanding performance across both short-term and long-term human motion prediction highlights our model's effective capacity to capture both local and global temporal dependencies.

CMU-MoCap. To further validate the generalization of the proposed method, we compared its performance with five existing algorithms [15,18,22,34,43] on the CMU-MoCap dataset. The mean per joint position error was calculated for short-term and long-term predictions. The experimental results are shown in Table 3, which includes the actions "basketball", "basketball signal", "directing traffic", "jumping", "soccer", "walking", and "wash window", as well as the average prediction error across all actions.

Table 3. Prediction of 3D joint positions on CMU-MoCap for all actions. The best results are marked in bold.

Time(ms)	80	160	320	400	560	1000	80	160	320	400	560	1000
Action			**Basketball**						**Basketball Signal**			
Res. sup. [18]	29.5	53.1	91.2	106.0	128.7	157.4	14.6	22.1	39.1	46.6	60.0	89.9
LTD [43]	11.7	21.1	40.7	50.6	68.0	95.7	3.4	6.2	13.5	17.9	27.3	51.9
LPJP [22]	11.6	21.7	44.4	57.3	-	90.9	2.6	4.9	12.7	18.7	-	75.8
MSR [34]	10.3	18.9	37.7	47.0	62.0	86.3	3.0	5.6	12.5	16.6	25.5	50.0
LCDC [15]	9.6	17.6	35.4	44.4	60.0	**88.4**	2.6	4.7	**10.4**	13.9	21.9	46.2
Ours	**9.5**	**17.5**	**32.5**	**41.5**	**56.8**	88.4	**2.5**	**4.6**	11.5	**13.1**	**20.6**	**45.8**
Action			**Directing Traffic**						**Jumping**			
Res. sup. [18]	21.8	38.8	70.5	85.3	110.3	165.1	30.2	53.0	89.4	103.9	125.6	160.5
LTD [43]	6.8	13.4	29.6	39.1	59.6	112.8	17.1	32.1	59.8	72.5	94.3	127.2
LPJP [22]	6.2	12.7	29.1	39.6	-	149.1	12.9	27.6	73.5	92.2	-	176.6
MSR [34]	6.1	12.6	29.4	39.2	50.5	114.6	15.2	28.9	56.0	69.1	92.4	126.2
LCDC [15]	**5.0**	10.0	23.4	31.4	49.3	99.6	**12.8**	**26.1**	54.6	68.5	91.8	126.1
Ours	5.0	**9.9**	**22.4**	**30.9**	**48.6**	**93.9**	13.1	27.2	**53.6**	**67.8**	**89.8**	**116.9**
Action			**Soccer**						**Walking**			
Res. sup. [18]	26.5	47.0	81.5	96.2	117.9	139.1	14.6	22.9	36.1	40.9	51.1	69.5
LTD [43]	13.6	24.3	44.4	54.3	73.1	111.6	6.7	11.1	18.1	21.0	25.2	32.4
LPJP [22]	**9.2**	**18.4**	39.2	49.5	-	93.9	6.7	10.7	21.7	27.5	-	37.4
MSR [34]	10.9	19.4	37.4	47.0	65.3	101.9	6.4	10.3	16.9	20.1	25.5	36.8
LCDC [15]	10.3	19.0	36.8	45.7	62.3	96.9	6.3	10.4	16.1	18.6	23.3	33.6
Ours	9.8	19.0	**35.3**	**44.6**	**59.7**	**92.7**	**5.8**	**10.2**	**15.4**	**17.3**	**22.9**	**33.2**
Action			**Wash Window**						**Average**			
Res. sup. [18]	19.3	31.8	56.1	66.0	83.6	125.9	22.4	38.4	66.2	77.8	96.7	129.6
LTD [43]	5.9	11.3	24.1	31.0	43.4	66.9	9.3	17.1	32.9	40.9	55.9	85.5
LPJP [22]	5.4	11.3	29.2	39.6	-	79.1	7.8	15.3	35.7	46.3	-	100.4
MSR [34]	5.4	10.9	24.5	31.8	45.1	70.2	8.2	15.2	30.5	38.7	52.3	83.7
LCDC [15]	**4.8**	**9.5**	22.0	29.0	42.5	68.9	7.3	**13.9**	28.4	35.9	50.1	80.0
Ours	4.8	9.5	**20.3**	**28.0**	**41.3**	**67.4**	**7.2**	14.0	**27.3**	**34.7**	**48.5**	**76.9**

Through quantitative evaluation, we clearly observe that our method effectively handles various types of actions and consistently achieves a superior performance across all of them. These empirical findings reinforce the superiority of our approach in human motion prediction, both for short-term and long-term predictions. The consistent and significant performance improvement over state-of-the-art methods on the dataset demonstrates the robustness of our method.

Notably, as can be seen from Tables 2 and 3, our model performed well on the Human3.6m and CMU-MoCap datasets for prediction tasks up to 320 ms, and even better for tasks above 320 ms. This intriguing performance pivot at 320 ms may represent a transition point where prognostic difficulty shifts from short to long-term. We believe this is due to our model's capability to capture local and global time dependencies across body joints through a strategic combination of GRU and transformer layers, effectively handling this transition. Furthermore, this phenomenon could be tied to the inherent complexity of human movement, especially when the prediction time exceeds 320 ms. This complexity poses a challenge for models that rely on short-term prognosis. However, our model, thanks to its specific structure and training procedure, seems to cope with this challenge more effectively. In future work, we plan to delve deeper into this "prognostic barrier" at 320 ms, aiming to better understand its underlying causes and how we can further improve our model's performance at this critical transition point. This understanding will potentially enable us to optimize the dynamics of 3D joint position prediction.

4.5. Qualitative Comparison

To enhance our intuitive understanding and facilitate the evaluation of our model, we provided a visualization of the motion prediction results. Figure 5 illustrates three examples of predicted poses using our proposed method, alongside three other baseline methods. The visualization results for the "phoning", "discussion", and "purchases" actions of the Human3.6M dataset are presented in Figure 5. The first row in each subplot displays the ground truth pose sequences (in black), followed by the predicted poses (in blue). In other words, each row presents the prediction results from one model.

(c)

Figure 5. Qualitative analysis of the Human3.6M dataset: comparing phoning, discussion, and purchases scenarios. (**a**) Phoning; (**b**) Discussion; (**c**) Purchases.

The visualization results indicate that our model is capable of adequately capturing spatial dependencies and local–global temporal dependencies. It is noticeable that the predictions generated by our method show higher similarity to the actual sequences and better continuity between frames. For instance, in the case of subtler movements such as "phoning", our model successfully captures the long-distance temporal dependencies concealed within the movement sequence, yielding superior long-term predictions. Moreover, in the "purchases" motion visualization, the movements between hands are more coordinated. This illustrates our model's proficiency in forecasting highly complicated irregular movements and complex periodic motions.

4.6. Ablation Study

To critically assess the contribution of each component in our model, we performed a set of ablation studies on the Human3.6M dataset. All architecture parameters were kept constant to ensure a fair comparison of each module's impact. These experiments focused on assessing the impact of the graph convolutional network (GCN_N), gated recurrent units (GRU), and transformer layers (Tr) on the model's performance. The experimental results are presented in Table 4. The optimal performance was achieved by integrating these three components.

Table 4. The influence of the GCN_N, GRU, and transformer layers (Tr) on the Human3.6M dataset, on average, is notable. These three components of our model significantly contribute to its overall accuracy. The best results are marked in bold.

			Human3.6M,MPJPE (mm)					
GCN_N	GRU	Tr	80	160	320	400	560	1000
	√	√	10.3	23.2	48.1	57.0	75.7	107.4
√		√	10.2	22.7	47.5	56.2	75.3	107.0
√	√		10.2	23.5	47.7	57.8	77.2	111.0
√	√	√	**10.0**	**21.8**	**46.8**	**55.1**	**74.4**	**105.4**

GCN_N: We used the original graph convolution module in place of the proposed module. As shown in the first and third rows of Table 4, when this module is replaced, prediction performance decreases. This result clearly indicates that there is critical spatially relevant information hidden in the adjacent pose. When this information is ignored, it is difficult for the model to capture time evolution trends, resulting in degraded performance.

GRU and transformer layers(Tr): The GRU unit, designed to capture local temporal dependence, shows a remarkable performance, enhancing the accuracy of short-term predictions. The transformer layer exhibits exceptional ability in handling global temporal dependence, which improves the accuracy of long-term predictions. We removed the transformer layer directly from the proposed method. It can be seen that the long-term prediction performance of the model was significantly reduced, and the short-term prediction performance was also slightly reduced.

5. Conclusions

In this paper, we have proposed a novel framework for human motion prediction that leverages the power of position-wise enhanced graph convolutional networks, gated recurrent unit networks, and transformer layers. By strategically combining these networks, our model effectively captures spatial information across body joints and temporally aligns these dependencies, both locally and globally. The proposed framework has shown significant improvements in predicting long-term movements, surpassing existing state-of-the-art methods by a substantial margin. Experiments on the Human3.6M and CMU-MoCap datasets provide evidence supporting the effectiveness of our proposed model. The efficacy of our approach accentuates the potential of integrating advanced neural network architectures for improved understanding and prediction of complex human motion dynamics. Future work will explore the integration of more sophisticated attention mechanisms and deep learning architectures to further enhance prediction accuracy and efficiency.

Author Contributions: Conceptualization, B.H.; methodology, B.H.; software, B.H.; validation, B.H.; formal analysis, B.H.; investigation, B.H.; resources, B.H.; data curation, B.H.; writing—original draft preparation, B.H.; writing—review and editing, B.H.; visualization, B.H.; supervision, X.L.; project administration, X.L.; funding acquisition, X.L. All authors have read and agreed to the published version of the manuscript.

Funding: This work was supported in part by the National Natural Science Foundation of China under grants 62233003 and 62073072, the Key Projects of the Key R&D Program of Jiangsu Province under grants BE2020006 and BE2020006-1, and Shenzhen Natural Science Foundation under grants JCYJ20210324132202005 and JCYJ20220818101206014.

Institutional Review Board Statement: Not applicable.

Informed Consent Statement: Not applicable.

Data Availability Statement: The datasets generated and/or analyzed during the current study are publicly available. The Human3.6M dataset can be accessed through the reference in [41]. The CMU-MoCap dataset is publicly available and can be accessed online at http://mocap.cs.cmu.edu/ accessed on 5 July 2023. The use of these datasets is governed by their respective usage policies.

Conflicts of Interest: The authors declare no conflict of interest.

Abbreviations

The following abbreviations are used in this manuscript:

GGTr	Graph Convolutional, Gated Recurrent Unit, and Transformer layers
GCN	Graph convolutional networks
GRU	Gated recurrent unit
CNNs	Convolutional neural networks
RNN	Recurrent neural networks
GNNs	Graph neural networks

References

1. Koppula, H.S.; Saxena, A. Anticipating human activities using object affordances for reactive robotic response. *IEEE Trans. Pattern Anal. Mach. Intell.* **2015**, *38*, 14–29.
2. Gui, L.Y.; Zhang, K.; Wang, Y.X.; Liang, X.; Moura, J.M.; Veloso, M. Teaching robots to predict human motion. In Proceedings of the 2018 IEEE/RSJ International Conference on Intelligent Robots and Systems (IROS), Madrid, Spain, 1–5 October 2018; pp. 562–567.
3. Li, H.; Li, X.; Zhang, Z.; Hu, C.; Dunkin, F.; Ge, S.S. ESUAV-NI: Endogenous Security Framework for UAV Perception System Based on Neural Immunity. *IEEE Trans. Ind. Inform.* **2023**. [CrossRef]
4. Choi, S.H.; Park, K.B.; Roh, D.H.; Lee, J.Y.; Mohammed, M.; Ghasemi, Y.; Jeong, H. An integrated mixed reality system for safety-aware human-robot collaboration using deep learning and digital twin generation. *Robot. Comput.-Integr. Manuf.* **2022**, *73*, 102258. [CrossRef]
5. Dong, Y.; Li, X.; Dezert, J.; Zhou, R.; Zhu, C.; Wei, L.; Ge, S.S. Evidential reasoning with hesitant fuzzy belief structures for human activity recognition. *IEEE Trans. Fuzzy Syst.* **2021**, *29*, 3607–3619.
6. Sheng, W.; Li, X. Multi-task learning for gait-based identity recognition and emotion recognition using attention enhanced temporal graph convolutional network. *Pattern Recognit.* **2021**, *114*, 107868.
7. Kong, Y.; Wei, Z.; Huang, S. Automatic analysis of complex athlete techniques in broadcast taekwondo video. *Multimed. Tools Appl.* **2018**, *77*, 13643–13660. [CrossRef]
8. Lehrmann, A.M.; Gehler, P.V.; Nowozin, S. Efficient nonlinear Markov models for human motion. In Proceedings of the Conference on Computer Vision and Pattern Recognition, Columbus, OH, USA, 23–28 June 2014.
9. Wang, J.M.; Fleet, D.J.; Hertzmann, A. Gaussian Process Dynamical Models for Human Motion. *IEEE Trans. Pattern Anal. Mach. Intell.* **2007**, *30*, 283–298.
10. Taylor, G.W.; Hinton, G.E.; Roweis, S. Modeling human motion using binary latent variables. In Proceedings of the Advances in Neural Information Processing Systems 19 (NIPS 2006), Cambridge, MA, USA, 4–7 December 2006; Volume 19.
11. Li, C.; Zhang, Z.; Lee, W.S.; Lee, G.H. Convolutional sequence to sequence model for human dynamics. In Proceedings of the IEEE Conference on Computer Vision and Pattern Recognition, Salt Lake City, UT, USA, 18–23 June 2018; pp. 2275–2284.
12. Li, M.; Chen, S.; Chen, X.; Zhang, Y.; Wang, Y.; Tian, Q. Symbiotic Graph Neural Networks for 3D Skeleton-Based Human Action Recognition and Motion Prediction. *IEEE Trans. Pattern Anal. Mach. Intell.* **2021**, *44*, 3316–3333. [CrossRef]
13. Li, M.; Chen, S.; Zhao, Y.; Zhang, Y.; Wang, Y.; Tian, Q. Dynamic multiscale graph neural networks for 3d skeleton based human motion prediction. In Proceedings of the IEEE/CVF Conference on Computer Vision and Pattern Recognition, Seattle, WA, USA, 13–19 June 2020; pp. 214–223.
14. Zhong, C.; Hu, L.; Zhang, Z.; Ye, Y.; Xia, S. Spatio-Temporal Gating-Adjacency GCN For Human Motion Prediction. In Proceedings of the Conference on Computer Vision and Pattern Recognition, New Orleans, LA, USA, 18–24 June 2022.
15. Fu, J.; Yang, F.; Dang, Y.; Liu, X.; Yin, J. Learning Constrained Dynamic Correlations in Spatiotemporal Graphs for Motion Prediction. *IEEE Trans. Neural Netw. Learn. Syst.* **2023**. [CrossRef]
16. Fragkiadaki, K.; Levine, S.; Felsen, P.; Malik, J. Recurrent network models for human dynamics. In Proceedings of the 2015 IEEE International Conference on Computer Vision (ICCV), Santiago, Chile, 7–13 December 2015; pp. 4346–4354.
17. Jain, A.; Zamir, A.R.; Savarese, S.; Saxena, A. Structural-rnn: Deep learning on spatio-temporal graphs. In Proceedings of the 2016 IEEE Conference on Computer Vision and Pattern Recognition (CVPR), Las Vegas, NV, USA, 27–30 June 2016; pp. 5308–5317.
18. Martinez, J.; Black, M.J.; Romero, J. On human motion prediction using recurrent neural networks. In Proceedings of the IEEE Conference on Computer Vision and Pattern Recognition, Honolulu, HI, USA, 21–26 July 2017; pp. 2891–2900.

19. Liu, Z.; Wu, S.; Jin, S.; Liu, Q.; Lu, S.; Zimmermann, R.; Cheng, L. Towards natural and accurate future motion prediction of humans and animals. In Proceedings of the Conference on Computer Vision and Pattern Recognition, Long Beach, CA, USA, 15–20 June 2019.
20. Shu, X.; Zhang, L.; Qi, G.J.; Liu, W.; Tang, J. Spatiotemporal co-attention recurrent neural networks for human-skeleton motion prediction. *IEEE Trans. Pattern Anal. Mach. Intell.* **2021**, *44*, 3300–3315.
21. Liu, Z.; Wu, S.; Jin, S.; Ji, S.; Liu, Q.; Lu, S.; Cheng, L. Investigating pose representations and motion contexts modeling for 3D motion prediction. *IEEE Trans. Pattern Anal. Mach. Intell.* **2022**, *45*, 681–697. [CrossRef]
22. Cai, Y.; Huang, L.; Wang, Y.; Cham, T.J.; Cai, J.; Yuan, J.; Liu, J.; Yang, X.; Zhu, Y.; Shen, X.; et al. Learning progressive joint propagation for human motion prediction. In Proceedings of the European Conference on Computer Vision, Glasgow, UK, 23–28 August 2020; pp. 226–242.
23. Aksan, E.; Kaufmann, M.; Cao, P.; Hilliges, O. A spatio-temporal transformer for 3d human motion prediction. In Proceedings of the 2021 International Conference on 3D Vision (3DV), London, UK, 1–3 December 2021; pp. 565–574.
24. Yu, H.; Fan, X.; Hou, Y.; Pei, W.; Ge, H.; Yang, X.; Zhou, D.; Zhang, Q.; Zhang, M. Towards Realistic 3D Human Motion Prediction with A Spatio-temporal Cross-transformer Approach. *IEEE Trans. Circuits Syst. Video Technol.* **2023**. [CrossRef]
25. Chiu, H.K.; Adeli, E.; Wang, B.; Huang, D.A.; Niebles, J.C. Action-agnostic human pose forecasting. In Proceedings of the 2019 IEEE Winter Conference on Applications of Computer Vision (WACV), Waikoloa Village, HI, USA, 7–11 January 2019; pp. 1423–1432.
26. Guo, X.; Choi, J. Human motion prediction via learning local structure representations and temporal dependencies. In Proceedings of the AAAI Conference on Artificial Intelligence, Honolulu, HI, USA, 27 January–1 February 2019; Volume 33, pp. 2580–2587.
27. Zhou, L.; Zhou, Y.; Corso, J.J.; Socher, R.; Xiong, C. End-to-end dense video captioning with masked transformer. In Proceedings of the IEEE Conference on Computer Vision and Pattern Recognition, Salt Lake City, UT, USA, 18–23 June 2018; pp. 8739–8748.
28. Liu, P.J.; Saleh, M.; Pot, E.; Goodrich, B.; Sepassi, R.; Kaiser, L.; Shazeer, N. Generating wikipedia by summarizing long sequences. *arXiv* **2018**, arXiv:1801.10198.
29. Kipf, T.N.; Welling, M. Semi-supervised classification with graph convolutional networks. *arXiv* **2016**, arXiv:1609.02907.
30. Yuan, J.; Cao, M.; Cheng, H.; Yu, H.; Xie, J.; Wang, C. A unified structure learning framework for graph attention networks. *Neurocomputing* **2022**, *495*, 194–204. [CrossRef]
31. Velickovic, P.; Cucurull, G.; Casanova, A.; Romero, A.; Lio, P.; Bengio, Y. Graph attention networks. *Stat* **2017**, *1050*, 10–48550.
32. Yan, S.; Xiong, Y.; Lin, D. Spatial temporal graph convolutional networks for skeleton-based action recognition. In Proceedings of the AAAI Conference on Artificial Intelligence, New Orleans, LA, USA, 2–7 February 2018; Volume 32.
33. Ma, T.; Nie, Y.; Long, C.; Zhang, Q.; Li, G. Progressively Generating Better Initial Guesses Towards Next Stages for High-Quality Human Motion Prediction. In Proceedings of the Conference on Computer Vision and Pattern Recognition, New Orleans, LA, USA, 18–24 June 2022.
34. Dang, L.; Nie, Y.; Long, C.; Zhang, Q.; Li, G. MSR-GCN: Multi-Scale Residual Graph Convolution Networks for Human Motion Prediction. In Proceedings of the International Conference on Computer Vision, New Orleans, LA, USA, 18–24 June 2021.
35. Vaswani, A.; Shazeer, N.; Parmar, N.; Uszkoreit, J.; Jones, L.; Gomez, A.N.; Kaiser, Ł.; Polosukhin, I. Attention is all you need. In Proceedings of the Advances in Neural Information Processing Systems 30 (NIPS 2017), Long Beach, CA, USA, 4–9 December 2017 ; Volume 30.
36. Carion, N.; Massa, F.; Synnaeve, G.; Usunier, N.; Kirillov, A.; Zagoruyko, S. End-to-end object detection with transformers. In Proceedings of the Computer Vision–ECCV 2020: 16th European Conference, Glasgow, UK, 23–28 August 2020; pp. 213–229.
37. Dosovitskiy, A.; Beyer, L.; Kolesnikov, A.; Weissenborn, D.; Zhai, X.; Unterthiner, T.; Dehghani, M.; Minderer, M.; Heigold, G.; Gelly, S.; et al. An image is worth 16x16 words: Transformers for image recognition at scale. *arXiv* **2020**, arXiv:2010.11929.
38. Zhu, X.; Su, W.; Lu, L.; Li, B.; Wang, X.; Dai, J. Deformable detr: Deformable transformers for end-to-end object detection. *arXiv* **2020**, arXiv:2010.04159.
39. Zhang, J.; Shi, X.; Xie, J.; Ma, H.; King, I.; Yeung, D.Y. GaAN: Gated Attention Networks for Learning on Large and Spatiotemporal Graphs. In Proceedings of the 34th Conference on Uncertainty in Artificial Intelligence 2018, UAI 2018, Monterey, CA, USA, 6–10 August 2018.
40. Cho, K.; Van Merriënboer, B.; Gulcehre, C.; Bahdanau, D.; Bougares, F.; Schwenk, H.; Bengio, Y. Learning phrase representations using RNN encoder-decoder for statistical machine translation. *arXiv* **2014**, arXiv:1406.1078.
41. Ionescu, C.; Papava, D.; Olaru, V.; Sminchisescu, C. Human3. 6m: Large scale datasets and predictive methods for 3d human sensing in natural environments. *IEEE Trans. Pattern Anal. Mach. Intell.* **2013**, *36*, 1325–1339. [CrossRef]
42. Loshchilov, I.; Hutter, F. Decoupled weight decay regularization. *arXiv* **2017**, arXiv:1711.05101.
43. Mao, W.; Liu, M.; Salzmann, M.; Li, H. Learning trajectory dependencies for human motion prediction. In Proceedings of the IEEE International Conference on Computer Vision, Seoul, Republic of Korea, 27 October–2 November 2019; pp. 4317–4326.

electronics

Article

ArRASA: Channel Optimization for Deep Learning-Based Arabic NLU Chatbot Framework

Meshrif Alruily

Faculty of Computer and Information Sciences, Jouf University, Sakaka 72388, Saudi Arabia; mfalruily@ju.edu.sa

Abstract: Since the introduction of deep learning-based chatbots for knowledge services, many research and development efforts have been undertaken in a variety of fields. The global market for chatbots has grown dramatically as a result of strong demand. Nevertheless, open-domain chatbots' limited functional scalability poses a challenge to their implementation in industries. Much work has been performed on creating chatbots for languages such as English, Chinese, etc. Still, there is a need to develop chatbots for other languages such as Arabic, Persian, etc., as they are widely used on the Internet today. In this paper, we introduce, ArRASA as a channel optimization strategy based on a deep-learning platform to create a chatbot that understands Arabic. ArRASA is a closed-domain chatbot that can be used in any Arabic industry. The proposed system consists of four major parts. These parts include tokenization of text, featurization, intent categorization and entity extraction. The performance of ArRASA is evaluated using traditional assessment metrics, i.e., accuracy and F1 score for the intent classification and entity extraction tasks in the Arabic language. The proposed framework archives promising results by securing 96%, 94% and 94%, 95% accuracy and an F1 score for intent classification and entity extraction, respectively.

Keywords: Arabic; natural language understanding; deep learning; chatbot

Citation: Alruily, M. ArRASA: Channel Optimization for Deep Learning-Based Arabic NLU Chatbot Framework. *Electronics* **2022**, *11*, 3745. https://doi.org/10.3390/electronics11223745

Academic Editors: Grzegorz Dudek and Rui Pedro Lopes

Received: 8 September 2022
Accepted: 7 November 2022
Published: 15 November 2022

1. Introduction

The Arabic language is among the five most commonly used online languages. It is used for conversion among large communities around the world. Technological innovation has a significant impact on people's lives. In the field of computer science, a great deal has been accomplished in recent years. Artificial intelligence (AI) has produced remarkable and important achievements [1]. As AI interacts with various scientific fields, it has an increased in importance in recent years. Many aspects of artificial intelligence are covered, including natural language processing (NLP). A human language is a natural language (English, Arabic, or Spanish). In AI, machine learning and chatbots, intent classification is classifying someone's intent by analyzing their language. Intent classification is a kind of NLP that focuses on categorizing text into different categories to interpret text better.

Intents are generic characteristics that link a user's text to a bot action (prediction workflow). For example, the whole sentence "What is the weather today?" will map to the 'weather inquiry' intent, not just a portion of it. [2]. In the last decade, intent classification and entity extraction have been widely used to develop chatbots for various languages. Since Arabic is the fourth-largest language used on the Internet, intent classification for Arabic is necessary. Very little work has been performed on Arabic intent classification and entity extraction. Moreover, there are a few articles on the development of chatbots for the Arabic language.

Machine learning and natural language processing are used in intent classification to automatically match specific sentences and words with a suitable intent [3]. For example, a machine learning model could discover that words, such as buy and acquire, are often linked with the urge to buy. On the other hand, intent classifiers must be trained using text samples, often referred to as training data. Tags such as Interested, Need Information,

Unsubscribe, Wrong Person, Email Bounce, Autoreply and others may be useful when going through customer emails.

NLP is a subfield of AI that uses natural language to allow human–computer interaction and communication. NLP has spawned a slew of new applications. A chatbot is one of the most intriguing natural language artificial intelligence applications [4]. A chatbot is software that uses natural language to conduct a human–computer interaction through auditory or textual means. As a result, it functions as a virtual assistant that uses artificial intelligence to mimic conversational abilities and human-like behavior [5]. It also contains embedded information that aids in identifying and comprehending the phrase and the generation of the right answer. Many research articles have been published in this area due to the importance of sentiment analysis. However, this research has concentrated on English and other Indo-European languages. In morphologically rich languages such as Arabic, there has been very little research on sentiment analysis [6]. Despite this, many academics have focused on sentiment analysis in Arabic due to the growing number of Arabic internet users and the exponential development of Arabic online content in the past decade. Pipelines can be used to streamline a workflow for machine learning. Pre-processing, extraction of features, categorization and post-processing are all possible steps in the pipeline. Many other necessary phases in this pipeline may be added according to the complexity of applications. By optimization, we intend to modify the model for optimum performance. Any learning model's effectiveness depends on choosing the parameters that produce the greatest outcomes. The concept of optimization can be compared to a search algorithm that explores a range of parameters and picks out the best among them.

Because Arabic is such a complicated language, developing Arabic chatbots has posed a significant challenge to the academic community. Only a few works have tried to create Arabic chatbots so far. ArabChat [7] is one such project, as follows: a rule-based chatbot capable of pattern matching and delivering appropriate responses to user inquiries. BOTTA [8], another project, is a retrieval-based model that supports the Egyptian dialect. Ollobot is a rule-based chatbot that provides health monitoring and assistance in the medical sector [9]. However, because of its restricted functional scalability, an open-domain chatbot cannot be successfully used in every business. Furthermore, since most chatbot frameworks are written in English, building an efficient and multi-objective chatbot for Arabic is necessary. This research proposes an ArRASA, a pipeline optimization approach based on a deep learning-based open-source chatbot system that understands Arabic, to solve this issue.

The proposed approach consists of the following steps: Tokenization, feature extraction, specific intent classification and suitable entity extraction are the four phases of this closed-domain chatbot. A closed-domain chatbot, also known as a domain-specific chatbot, focuses on a certain range of issues and provides limited replies based on the business issue. For instance, a food delivery chatbot can only let users place, monitor, or cancel an order. Such straight-shooting discussion is kind of bumping into an acquaintance as follows: you expect people to be likely to inquire about your work and maybe comment on the environment. You have prepared answers to every topic, and the idea is just to satisfy the enquiries. While an open-domain chatbot is required to grasp any matter and provide appropriate answers. The proposed model can be scaled by adding more intents and entities. Open-domain chatbots are less effective in the industry, so the proposed study focuses on developing closed-domain chatbots. Moreover, a handsome amount of work is performed using traditional machine and deep learning approaches, while the proposed study uses transformers-based techniques for the development of a more effective and reliable chatbot.

This paper discusses ArRASA, a pipeline optimization approach based on a deep learning-based open-source chatbot system that understands Arabic. To cope with this topic, first, we discuss the Arabic language and its different perspectives and challenges, as it has some special characteristics and rules to deal with a problem. We discuss the related approaches in the literature review section. The proposed methodology discusses the complete operations of the ArRASA. The proposed model can be scaled by adding more intents and entities. In terms of Arabic language understanding, an optimization experiment is carried out at each step. The prime contributions of the proposed solution can be summarized as follows:

- ArRASA is a channel optimization strategy proposed based on a deep-learning platform to create a chatbot that understands Arabic;
- ArRASA is a novel approach for a closed-domain chatbot using RASA (an open-source conversational AI platform) that can be used in any Arabic industry;
- Tokenization, feature extraction, specific intent classification and suitable entity extraction are the four phases of the proposed approach;
- The performance of ArRASA is evaluated using traditional assessment metrics, i.e., accuracy and F1 score for the intent classification and entity extraction tasks in the Arabic language;
- The performance is also compared with the existing approaches regarding accuracy and F1 score.

The remainder of the paper is organized as follows: Section 2 discusses the related work and Arabic language, and its challenges are elaborated in Section 3. The proposed solution is developed in Section 4, while the system structure is discussed in Section 5. The performance evaluation is presented in Sections 6 and 7 concludes the paper.

2. Related Work

BOTTA [8] is the first Arabic dialect chatbot developed for Egyptian Arabic to work as a conversational agent to mimic user-friendly chats. Various components of the BOTTA chatbot are defined, and it presents various solutions. Researchers working on Arabic chatbot technology can access the BOTTA database files for free and with public access.

Shawar et al. [10] show how machine-learning techniques were used to create an Arabic chatbot that accepts user feedback in Arabic and responds with Qur'anic quotes. A device that learned conversational patterns from a corpus of transcribed conversations was used to create various chatbots that spoke English, French and Afrikaans. Because the Qur'an is not a copy of a dialogue, the learning method has been altered to accommodate the Qur'an's format in terms of sooras and ayyas.

Bashir et al. [11] propose a method for using named entity recognition and text categorization using deep learning methods in the Arabic area of home automation. To do this, we provide an NLU module that can be further combined with an ASR, a conversation manager and a natural language generator module to create a fully functional dialogue system. The process of gathering and annotating the data, constructing the intent classifier and entity extractor models, and ultimately the assessment of these techniques against various benchmarks are all included in the study.

AlHumoud et al. [12] summarize published Arabic chatbot studies to recognize information gaps and illustrate areas that need more investigation and research. This research found a scarcity of Arabic chatbots and that all available works are retrieval-based. The experiments are divided into the following two classes, depending on the method of chatbot communication interaction: text and voice conversational chatbots. The study was presented and assessed according to the deployment method, the duration and breadth of the presentations, and the model used for the chatbot dataset. According to the study, all the assessed chatbots used a retrieval-based dataset model.

Nabiha [13] is a chatbot that uses the Saudi Arabic dialect to converse with King Saud University Information Technology (IT) students. As a consequence, Nabiha will be the first Saudi chatbot to communicate in the Saudi dialect. Nabiha is accessible on several platforms, including Android, Twitter and the Web, to make it simpler to use. Students may contact Nabiha by downloading an app, tweeting her, or visiting her website. According to the students in the IT department who tested Nabiha, the results were acceptable, given the general challenges of the Arabic language and the Saudi dialect.

The study in [14] is the first Arabic end-to-end generative model for task-oriented DS (AraConv). It makes use of various parameters for the multilingual transformer model mT5. We also provide the Arabic-TOD discourse dataset, which was utilized to train and evaluate the AraConv model. Compared to research employing identical monolingual conditions, the findings obtained are fair. We propose joint training, in which the model is jointly trained on Arabic conversation data with data from one or two high-resource languages such as English and Chinese, to minimize issues related to a short training dataset and enhance the AraConv model's outcomes.

Many authors worked on the development of Arabic chatbots, but most of them worked on the development of open-domain chatbots. Open-domain chatbots are less effective in the industry, so the proposed study focuses on developing closed-domain chatbots. Moreover, a handsome amount of work is performed using traditional machine and deep learning approaches, while the proposed study uses transformer-based techniques for the development of a more effective and reliable chatbot. The previous studies focused on the development of chatbots, but few worked on optimizing the proposed techniques. The proposed technique also worked on optimizing the proposed architecture for enhancing the accuracy and efficiency of the proposed Arabic chatbot; Table 1 presents the comparison of previous techniques.

Table 1. Comparison of previous techniques.

Ref.	Domain	Technique	Data	Accuracy
[8]	Open	CNN & RNN	3173 Arabic Questions	94%
[10]	Islamic Hadith	SVM	Islamic hadith	87%
[11]	Open	LSTMs and CNNs	AQMAR	92%
[12]	Open	CNN & SVM	TALAA AFAQ Data	82%
[13]	Open	Hybrid Learning	600 FAQ Pages	85%
[14]	Open	AraConv	Arabic-TOD	68%

Rasa is a platform for building AI-powered, quality chatbots in the industry. It is used by developers all around the world to build chatbots and contextual assistants. ArRASA is a channel optimization strategy based on a deep-learning platform to create a chatbot that understands Arabic. ArRASA is a closed-domain chatbot that can be used in any Arabic industry. As we proposed an optimized Arabic language chatbot using RASA, so we named it ArRASA.

3. Arabic Language

With about 300 million people speaking Arabic, it is one of the world's most commonly spoken languages. It is also widely spoken as the primary language in the Central African Republic of Chad, a non-Arab nation, and a minority language in Afghanistan and Israel (where Arabic and Hebrew are both official languages). Iran and Nigeria are among those countries [15]. Arabic, along with Chinese, English, French, Russian and Spanish, became one of the six official languages of the United Nations in 1974. In India, Indonesia, Pakistan and Tanzania, about one billion Muslims study Arabic as a foreign or second language for liturgical and scholastic reasons. Several Muslim and Arab populations in the United States use Arabic in their everyday contacts and for religious reasons.

Challenges of Arabic Language

Dialectal Variation: Arabic has various dialects, all of which are very distinct from one another, as follows: the official written and reading language is Modern Standard Arabic (MSA), and many dialects are spoken versions of the language [15]. Unlike the MSA, which has an official standard orthography and a plethora of resources, Arabic dialects lack such norms and resources. In terms of phonology, morphology and vocabulary, dialects differ from MSA and each other. Dialects are not recognized as languages in the Arab world and are not taught in schools. Dialectal Arabic, on the other hand, is widely used in online chats. This is why we believe it is more fitting to concentrate on dialectal Arabic in the sense of a chatbot.

Orthographic Ambiguity and Inconsistency: Arabic orthography uses optional diacritical marks to represent short vowels and consonantal doubling, which are seldom used in the text. As a consequence, there is a lot of uncertainty. Furthermore, Arabic writers often misspell various difficult letters, including the Alif-Hamza forms and Ta-Marbuta [16]. Regarding Arabic dialects, orthography is compounded by the lack of standard orthographies [17].

Geomorphological Richness of Arabic: Gender, number, person, voice, aspect and other characteristics are all inflected in Arabic words, as well as taking a variety of connected clitics [8]. This is especially challenging in the context of a chatbot system. Due to the gender-specific nature of verbs, adjectives and pronouns, the chatbot must answer in the following two ways: for male and female users. The ArRASA solves the geomorphological richness of Arabic issue by using the data about gender, number, person, etc., in the dataset. Moreover, the proposed model has various advantages, i.e., is easy to integrate because it is developed using the open-source RASA platform and supports single and multiple intents.

4. Proposed Solution

As we know, the number of services and products is growing rapidly around the globe. Due to this, the number of queries to the producers is also increasing. To solve this problem, companies hire individuals to serve as customer support for their products and services. However, this procedure of responding to consumers' questions is expensive for the company and quite slow for the users. There must be an effective and accessible approach to addressing this issue. Various researchers presented automated chatbots that give responses to customer queries instead of humans in various languages. Researchers presented different Arabic chatbots to work on the Arabic language. These chatbots have their own limitations. We propose a framework for optimizing Arabic chatbots by using the RASA framework, which is one of the current leading open-source platforms for chatbot development. The reason behind using the RASA is that it has not been used for Arabic chatbots in the past. ArRASA is a channel optimization method that uses a deep-learning model to develop an Arabic chatbot. ArRASA is a closed-domain chatbot that may be utilized in any Arabic industry.

4.1. Natural Language Understanding

Natural language processing (NLP) is concerned with how machines interpret language and promote "natural" back-and-forth contact between humans and computers. On the other hand, natural language comprehension is concerned with a machine's capacity to comprehend human language [17]. NLU is the process of rearranging unstructured data so that computers can "understand" and interpret it. For example, Machine Translation, Automatic Ticket Routing and Questioning Answer are established based on the concept of NLU. Natural language understanding (NLU), which translates natural language speech into a machine-readable format, is the primary technology used by chatbots. Figure 1 depicts the NLUs design, and the NLUs preprocessing phase is split into two parts. Tokenization is the initial step, in which a corpus is divided into tokens, which are grammatically intangible language units. The second stage is featurization, which involves extracting the properties of each token. Following the preprocessing step, the purpose is classified to properly comprehend the user's request, and an object is extracted to give a suitable answer [18]. As a result, a user-friendly chatbot framework can be created. Intent classification is the technique of determining a user's intent based on a user's statement. Entities are preset collections of items that make sense, such as names, organizations, time expressions, numbers and other groups of objects. Various sets of entities are needed to be collected for each chatbot. Intents and entities are used to understand what a user wants and how to generate the correct answer to the user's query. The RASA NLU can be used in chatbots and AI assistants for language understanding, emphasizing intent categorization and entity extraction. RASA NLU can interpret data using these two features. We formed a training dataset to recognize the intent and extract the entity using the RASA NLU pipeline. Rasa is a platform for building AI-powered, quality chatbots in the industry. Developers use it all around the world to build chatbots and contextual assistants. As described in Section 5, the training set contains a variety of intents and entities, and there may be no entity or multiple entities in any sentence.

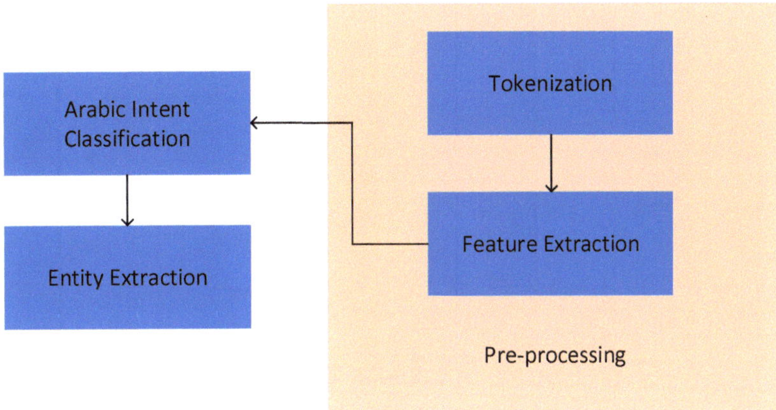

Figure 1. Structure of Arabic NLU.

4.2. Pre-Training Setup

We utilize the masked language modeling (MLM) task to accomplish the first pre-training objective, which involves whole-word masking and replacing 15% of the N input tokens. The [MASK] token is used 80 percent of the time, a random token 10% of the time and the original token 10% to replace those tokens. By forcing the computer to anticipate the whole word rather than only parts of it as whole word masking raises the pre-training challenge. The next sentence prediction (NSP) task, which allows the model to identify the relationship between two phrases and is helpful for a range of language comprehension tasks such as question answering and machine translation, is one that we often employ. We mask a particular percentage of words or phrases in MLM, and the system is intended to guess such masked words based on other words in the text. Since the representation of the masked term is learned based on the words that appear on both sides of the masked term. Moreover, The MLM systems are bidirectional in structure. As MLM is the process of masking words in a series with a masked token and training the model to populate that mask with a suitable token. As a result, the model will concentrate on both the right and left contexts. So, using the MLM for the proposed model enables the proposed model to understand the context of terms both at the beginning and at the end of a phrase.

4.3. DIET (Dual Intent and Entity Transformer)

DIET is a multi-task transformer that conducts intent classification and entity recognition at the same time. It allows to plug-and-play pre-trained embeddings such as BERT, GloVe, ConveRT and others [19]. No one collection of embeddings consistently performs well across various datasets in the tests. As a result, a modular architecture is particularly essential.

DIET is a software development process that incorporates a modular design. In terms of accuracy and performance, it is comparable to large-scale, pre-trained language models. It is 6X quicker to train than the present state of the art. On language comprehension benchmarks such as GLUE [20] and SuperGLUE [21], large-scale pre-trained language models have demonstrated promising results, with significant gains over previous pre-training techniques such as GloVe [22] and supervised approaches. These embeddings are well suited to generalize across tasks since they were trained on large-scale natural language text corpora.

Input phrases are interpreted as a series of tokens, either words or sub-words, based on the featurization pipeline. We add a special classification token for the Arabic language at the end of each phrase. Each input token is characterized using sparse and/or dense characteristics. At the token level, one-hot encodings of character n-grams ($n \leq 5$) and multi-hot encodings of character n-grams ($n \leq 5$) are scarce. Because character n-grams contain much redundant information, we use dropout for these sparse features to prevent overfitting. Figure 2 presents the proposed optimized pipeline architecture for the Arabic chatbot.

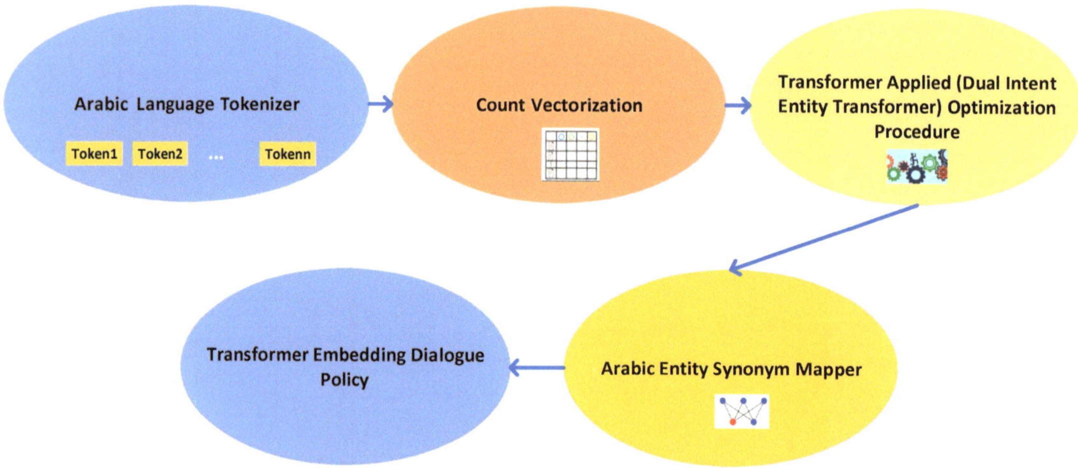

Figure 2. Proposed optimized pipeline architecture for Arabic chatbot.

A two-layer transformer with relative position attention is utilized for encoding context throughout the whole phrase. The input dimension of the transformer design must be the same as the transformer layers. The concatenated features are sent through another fully connected layer with shared weights across all sequence stages to match the dimension of the transformer layers, which is set to 256 for the proposed model.

5. System Architecture

Although the overall architecture of the proposed framework is identical to that of the DIET baseline model (DIET-Base), numerous tests were conducted to enhance intent classification and entity extraction performance. The ideal number of epochs was determined through a performance experiment. The ideal number of epochs was chosen as 100. The structure of the proposed framework is illustrated in Figure 3.

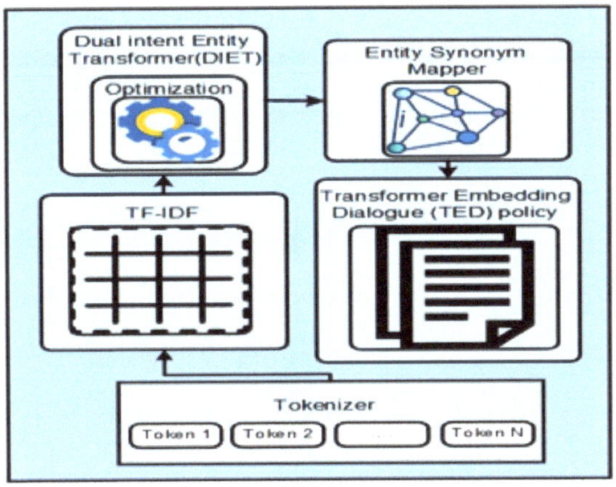

Figure 3. Proposed architecture.

The tokenizer extracts tokens from the data, and these tokens are sent to the proposed transformer layer through feed-forward layers of the LSTM model. The transformer layer provides a sequence (a) of entity labels, which is utilized as input data for the conditional random field (CRF) technique, which generates the sequence ($Xentity$) of entity labels. The loss of an entity can be computed by the negative value of the log-likelihood of CRF, as shown in Equation (1).

$$Entity = \text{CRF}(a, Xentity) \quad (1)$$

This mechanism reduces the weight sparsity from 0.85 to 0.75, and the number of transformer layers is raised from two to four. For parameter optimization, the number of embedding dimensions of the model increases from 25 to 35, and the hidden layer size increases from 256 to 512. The characteristics of the proposed architecture are listed in Table 2. There are now four total transformer layers, up from the two before.

Table 2. Parameter comparison.

Parameter	DIET-Base	Proposed-DIET
The Number of Transformer Layer	2	3
Masked Language Model	Yes	Yes
Transformer Size	256	512
Drop Rate	0.25	0.25
Embedding Dimension	20	35
Hidden Layer Size	256,128	512,128

6. Experiments and Results

There are various steps involves in the process of intent classification. These steps are given below as follows:

6.1. Data Gathering

The initial phase in the NLP life cycle is data collection. This step aims to find and collect relevant data about the subject. It is indeed among the most crucial stages in the life cycle of NLP [23]. The output's efficiency will be determined by the quantity and quality of the data collected. The more data there is, the more precise the prediction will be. The dataset used in the study was created using different datasets. Those datasets include the dataset proposed by Bashir et al. [14]. We have used these datasets and some scraped data from Arabic websites and newspapers to create our data for the proposed framework. Datasets were created for the studies in this article based on typical activities that apply to a broad range of industrial sectors. The data collection includes seven categories for intent categorization. Greeting (greet), closure (goodbye), emotions (happy, sad), food (food-related menu), departmental contact details (dept. contacts), division of labor works (Pers work) and calculator are examples of these categories (Calc). The dataset's distribution is shown in Figure 4.

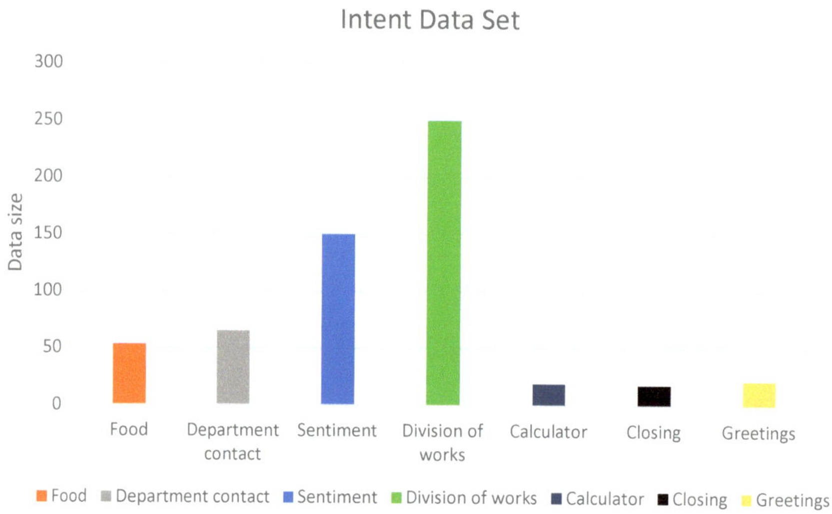

Figure 4. Dataset distribution.

A total of 2540 datasets containing the following seven entities were created for the entity extraction experiment. These include department (dept), date (date), work (work), place (place), company (company), name (name), number (num), time (time) and no entity. The division of these is illustrated in Table 3.

Table 3. Entity extraction data

Entity	Count
Date	120
Time	32
Name	73
Company	12
Work	720
Department	223
Number	37
No_Entity	1824

6.2. Data Preprocessing

When there is not enough data, oversampling can be used. By making rare samples better, it seeks to balance the dataset. Various new rare samples are produced using techniques such as repetition, bootstrapping, or SMOTE (synthetic minority over-sampling technique). We applied the SMOTE technique using the Python standard library "imblearn". SMOTE initially selects a point at random from the rare class and calculates its k-nearest neighbors. Between the selected point and its neighbors, the synthesized points are placed. We need to prepare the data after it has been collected in order to move further. Data preparation refers to the process of organizing and preparing data for use in the machine learning process. In this step, unwanted phrases, words, whitespaces and other unnecessary data are removed from the gathered data [23]. It is the technique for refining and turning raw data into the form used for ML/DL models. It is the procedure of cleaning the data, determining the variables to utilize and changing the data into a suitable format for analysis in the processing phase. It is among the most crucial steps in the entire procedure. We preprocess the data to convert it into a form so that it can be used for the deep learning models.

6.2.1. Tokenization

Tokenization is the most critical phase in data preprocessing, where all the words from the text are gathered and the number of times each word appears is counted. Five tokenizers were used for this purpose. These tokenizers include Takseem, Tf-idf, WhiteSpace, Arcab and ConveRT. With the help of these tokenizers, we determine how many times a single word appears in the text. In a dataset, we count words and create tokens for distinct words that occur. Each word is given a unique number when tokens are created. The token includes one-of-a-kind feature values that are used to create feature vectors. A tokenization library called tkseem has many methods for tokenizing and preprocessing Arabic text. This library is widely used for the tokenization of Arabic text. Arcab is a data-driven, unsupervised method for tokenizing subwords in Arabic phrases. There is no pre-tokenization phase where terms are extracted depending on the whitespaces; instead, it considers the training corpus as a sequence of raw Unicode characters. This allows the technique to be used for any string of characters, making it language-neutral. Transformer-backed dual-encoder networks serve as the foundation for ConveRT (conversational representations from transformers), a compact model of neural response selection for dialogue that has proven to perform at the cutting edge on various response selection tasks as well as in transfer learning for intent classification tasks. The performance of various tokenizers is listed in Table 4.

Table 4. Tokenization performance of tokenizers.

Task	WhiteSpace		Arcab		ConveRT	
	Train	Test	Train	Test	Train	Test
Entity Extraction	0.86	0.75	0.972	0.954	0.842	0.763
Intent Classification	1.00	0.962	1.00	0.978	1.00	0.973

6.2.2. Stop Word Removal

Stop words are unnecessary words, i.e., مع, لاجل, لذا, that exist in phrases but have no significance or clues about their contents. Examples of such words are so, for and with. Articles, conjunctions, pronouns (i.e., هم, هي, هو), prepositions (i.e., حول, الى,في, من), demonstratives and interrogatives (i.e., لمن, متى, اين) are further instances of these unimportant words. Once the dataset has been transformed into unique tokens, the next step is to delete every unnecessary word with no significance, e.g., whitespaces, commas, full stops, colons, semicolons and punctuation marks. Stop word elimination is the name given to the method of eliminating unnecessary words. Table 5 presents some stop words used in the study.

Table 5. Few stop words used in the study.

	Arabic Word	English Meaning
Prepositions	في	in
	على	on
	إلى	to
Pronouns	انا	I
	نحن	we
Adverbs	تحت	below
	فوق	above
	الآن	now
	منذ	since
Question	ماذا	what
	متى	when
Articles	إذا	if
	ثم	then
	عدا	except

6.2.3. Featurization

Methods for feature selection are used in machine learning techniques. An attribute of a system or process that has been built from the initial input variables is represented by a feature. Due to the enormous magnitude of the data, it is challenging to train effective classifiers before deleting the undesirable characteristics. A real-world classification challenge may be better understood by reducing the number of characteristics that are redundant or unnecessary. Feature selection aids in data comprehension, lessens the impact of dimensionality, reduces processing needs and enhances prediction performance. To increase prediction accuracy, feature selection selects a subset of features. Featurization is the conversion of words into meaningful numbers (or vectors) that the deep learning algorithm can use for its training. For this purpose, we use the features of the count vector featurizer, lexical syntactic featurizer and Tf-idf featurizer. For feature extraction, the TF-IDF technique uses word statistical data. This solely evaluates the expressions for terms that are the same throughout the texts, such as ASCLL, despite considering that synonyms may replace them.

The performance of used featurizers is compared for analysis purposes. The count vectorizer outperforms all three featurizers for both tasks, i.e., intent classification and entity extraction. The performance of these featurizers is listed in Table 6.

Table 6. Performance comparison of featurizers.

Task	Count Vector		Lexical Syntactic		Tf-Idf Featurizer	
	Train	Test	Train	Test	Train	Test
Entity Extraction	0.983	0.963	0.972	0.944	0.952	0.923
Intent Classification	1.00	0.976	1.00	0.972	1.00	0.973

The first phase of the proposed model was trained on 100 epochs to evaluate intent classification and entity extraction performance. The accuracy of the trained transformer-based model over 100 epochs is illustrated in Figure 5 below.

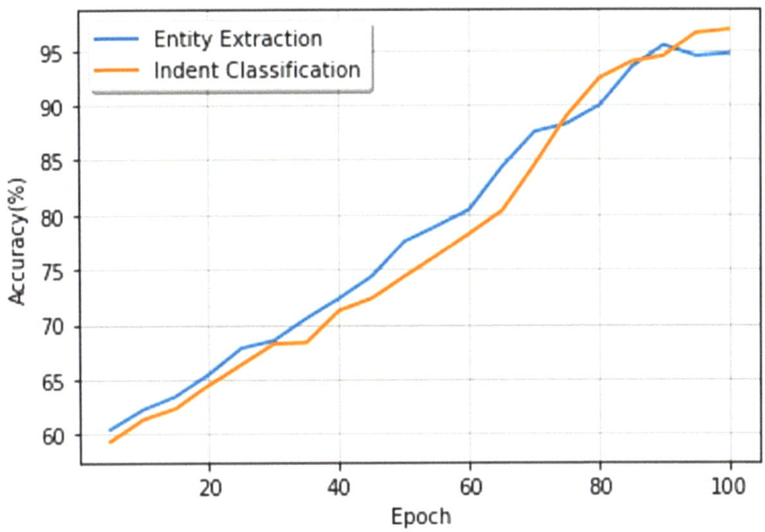

Figure 5. Accuracy of the proposed model.

As shown in the figure above, the proposed model achieves 97% accuracy for intent classification and 95% for entity extraction tasks. The performance of the model was also analyzed with the F1 score metric. The F1 score of the proposed model on both tasks.

As shown in Figure 6, the proposed model gains an F1 score of 95% for entity extraction and 96% for intent classification. This research compared the suggested intent classifier to existing intent classifiers in terms of intent classification and entity extraction. A performance assessment experiment was conducted to compute the DIET-base classifiers, keyword classifiers and fallback classifiers. According to the performance evaluation results, the proposed model's F1 score was 17.8%, 0.2% and 0.3% in intent classification from a given number of sentences. For entity extraction, the value of the F1 score was 3.1, 2.3 and 2.9% higher than the traditional DIET-base, keyword and fallback classifier. The results comparison of the proposed model for intent classification with other models is illustrated in Figure 7.

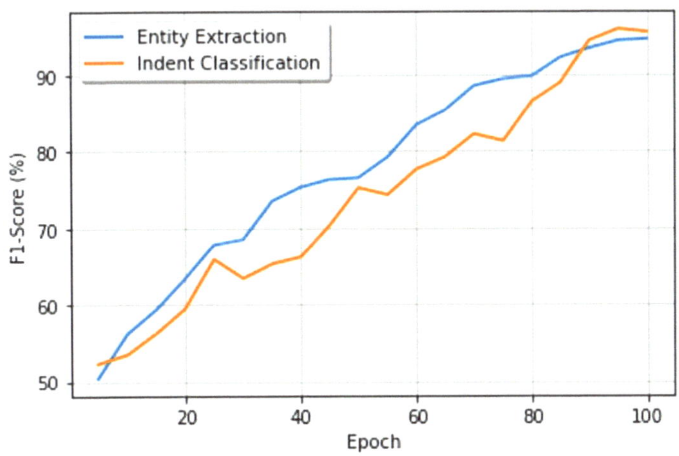

Figure 6. F1 score of the proposed model.

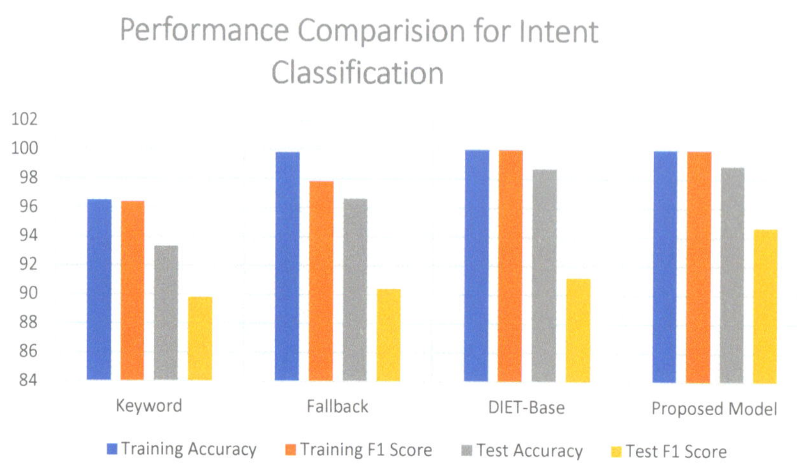

Figure 7. Performance comparison for intent classification.

Confusion matrices are a widely used metric when attempting to solve classification issues. Both binary and multiclass classification tasks can be performed with it. The confusion matrix for the entity extraction task is illustrated in Table 7.

Table 7. Confusion matrix for entity extraction.

	Date	Time	Name	Company	Work	Number	Department	No_Entity
Date	70	0	0	0	0	0	2	0
Time	0	15	0	0	0	1	0	0
Name	0	0	31	3	0	0	2	0
Company	2	0	0	8	0	1	0	0
Work	0	1	0	1	524	0	13	21
Number	0	0	2	1	0	19	0	0
Department	0	0	0	0	1	0	104	1
No_Entity	0	2	23	3	0	0	3	782

The confusion matrix for the indent classification tasks is also calculated in the evaluation phase of the study. Table 8 presents the indent classification confusion matrix.

Table 8. Confusion matrix for indent classification.

	Food	Department	Sentiment	Div. of Works	Calulator	Closing	Greetings
Food	18	1	0	0	0	0	3
Department	0	34	0	3	0	0	0
Sentiment	0	0	81	5	0	0	3
Div. of Works	1	0	0	127	3	0	1
Calulator	0	0	0	0	7		0
Closing	0	0	1	0	0	9	0
Greetings	0	0	0	0	1	0	12

Furthermore, the suggested model's entity extractor was evaluated with existing entity extraction models. A performance evaluation occurs for a conditional random field (CRF) and DIET-Base. The F1 scores of the suggested model were 1.4, 0.9 and 0.3% higher in intent classification and 4.2, 3.1 and 2.6% higher in the entity extraction, as per the performance evaluation findings. The performance of the entity extractor of the proposed model is illustrated in Figure 8. The main reason for the high accuracy and performance of the proposed model is the use of Dual Intent and Entity Transformer (DIET) for the Arabic language. The previous studies used different techniques for developing Arabic NLUs, but Rasa provides that DIET is a multi-task transformer framework that simultaneously performs intent categorization and entity recognition. It allows us to plug-and-play a variety of pre-trained embeddings. Moreover, in terms of accuracy and stability, it is comparable to large-scale, pre-trained language models.

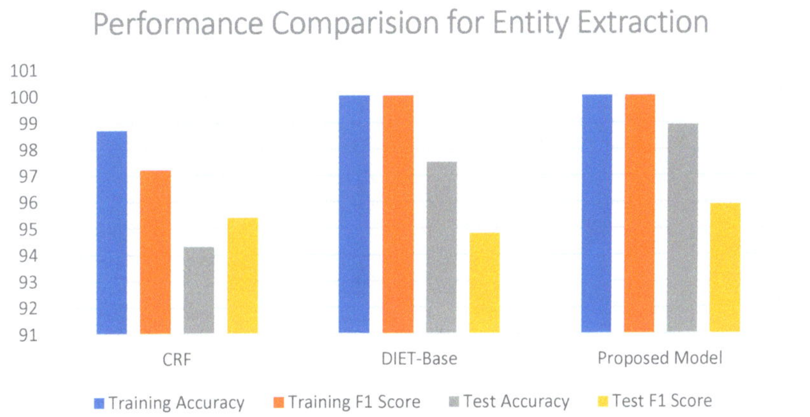

Figure 8. Performance of proposed model for entity extraction.

The comparison is performed to check the effectiveness of the proposed system. Some recent models for Arabic NLUs are studied for this purpose, and a comparison has been made on the basis of accuracy and F1 score. Table 9 presents the comparison of the proposed system with previous studies. I have compared the performance of the proposed RASA-based Arabic chatbot with some existing studies, i.e., Faud et al. [17] and Bashir et al. [14] According to the statistics obtained, the proposed scheme outperforms both existing approaches in terms of accuracy and F1 score.

Table 9. Comparison with previous studies.

Model	Intent Classification		Entity Extraction	
	Train	Test	Train	Test
	Accuracy	F1	Accuracy	F1
Fuad et al. [17]	0.90	0.80	0.92	0.86
Bashir et al. [14]	0.92	0.85	0.93	0.91
DIET-Base	0.86	0.75	0.972	0.954
ArRASA	1.00	0.962	1.00	0.978

We have performed a comparison of the proposed dataset with another dataset proposed by Fuad [17], as shown in Figure 9. The proposed model achieved an efficient accuracy level on the dataset provided by Fuad [17]. Figure 9 presents the comparison of accuracy and F1 score on both datasets.

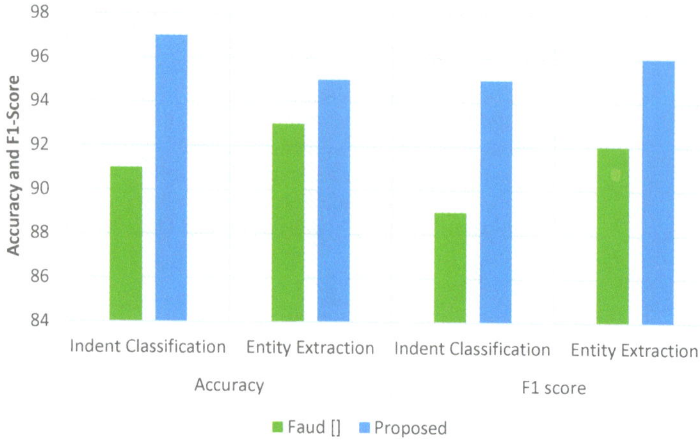

Figure 9. Comparison of accuracy and F1 score with an existing approach.

7. Conclusions

This article presents ArRASA, a deep learning-based channel optimization framework for an open-source Arabic chatbot platform to interact with users remotely. ArRASA is a closed domain chatbot that can be used in nearly any Arabic industry. There are four phases, i.e., tokenization, feature extraction, suitable intent classification, and proper entity extraction, used in the proposed model and these are also tuned to interpret the Arabic language. The Taqseem tokenizer, specific for the Arabic language and a few others, was used for tokenization, while the count vector featurizer was utilized for featurization. This study created the DIET-based Arabic model (ArRASA) for the intent classification and proper entity extraction phases by tweaking and optimizing the DIET-Base model's parameters. The accuracy of the proposed system for intent classification is 96%, while it achieved 94% accuracy for the entity extraction task. The proposed system gained a 95% F1 score for intent classification and 94% for entity extraction.

Funding: This research received no external funding.

Conflicts of Interest: The authors declare that they have no conflict of interest to report regarding the present study.

References

1. Rickli, J.M. *The Economic, Security and Military Implications of Artificial Intelligence for the Arab Gulf Countries;* Emirates Diplomatic Academy: Abu Dhabi, United Arab Emirates, 2018; pp. 1–13.
2. Hahm, Y.; Kim, J.; An, S.; Lee, M.; Choi, K.S. Chatbot Who Wants to Learn the Knowledge: KB-Agent. In Proceedings of the 17th International Semantic Web Conference (ISWC 2018), NLIWod4, Monterey, CA, USA, 8–12 October 2018. 4p.
3. Aleem, S.; Huda, N.u.; Amin, R.; Khalid, S.; Alshamrani, S.S.; Alshehri, A. Machine Learning Algorithms for Depression: Diagnosis, Insights, and Research Directions. *Electronics* **2022**, *11*, 1111. [CrossRef]
4. Sarddar, D.; Dey, R.K.; Bose, R.; Roy, S. Topic modeling as a tool to gauge political sentiments from twitter feeds. *Int. J. Nat. Comput. Res.* **2020**, *9*, 14–35. [CrossRef]
5. Wolf, T.; Debut, L.; Sanh, V.; Chaumond, J.; Delangue, C.; Moi, A.; Cistac, P.; Rault, T.; Louf, R.; Funtowicz, M.; et al. Transformers: State-of-the-art natural language processing. In Proceedings of the 2020 Conference on Empirical Methods in Natural Language Processing: System Demonstrations, Online, 3 June 2020; pp. 38–45.
6. Iqbal, A.; Amin, R.; Iqbal, J.; Alroobaea, R.; Binmahfoudh, A.; Hussain, M. Sentiment Analysis of Consumer Reviews Using Deep Learning. *Sustainability* **2022**, *14*, 10844. [CrossRef]
7. Hijjawi, M.; Bandar, Z.; Crockett, K.; Mclean, D. ArabChat: An arabic conversational agent. In Proceedings of the 2014 6th International Conference on Computer Science and Information Technology (CSIT), Piscataway, NJ, USA, 26–27 March 2014; IEEE: Piscataway, NJ, USA; pp. 227–237.
8. Ali, D.A.; Habash, N. Botta: An arabic dialect chatbot. In Proceedings of the COLING 2016, the 26th International Conference on Computational Linguistics: System Demonstrations, Osaka, Japan, 11–16 December 2016; pp. 208–212.

9. Fadhil, A. OlloBot-towards a text-based arabic health conversational agent: Evaluation and results. In Proceedings of the International Conference on Recent Advances in Natural Language Processing (RANLP 2019), Varna, Bulgaria, 2–4 September 2019; pp. 295–303.
10. Shawar, A.; Atwell, E.S. An Arabic chatbot giving answers from the Qur'an. In Proceedings of the TALN04: XI Conference sur le Traitement Automatique des Langues Naturelles, Fez, Morocco, 19–22 April 2004; ATALA: Monza, Italy, 2004; Volume 2, pp. 197–202.
11. Bashir, A.M.; Hassan, A.; Rosman, B.; Duma, D.; Ahmed, M. Implementation of a neural natural language understanding component for Arabic dialogue systems. *Procedia Comput. Sci.* **2018**, *142*, 222–229. [CrossRef]
12. AlHumoud, S.; al Wazrah, A.; Aldamegh, W. Arabic chatbots: A survey. *Int. J. Adv. Comput. Sci. Appl.* **2018**, *9*, 535–541. [CrossRef]
13. Al-Ghadhban, D.; Al-Twairesh, N. Nabiha: An Arabic dialect chatbot. *Int. J. Adv. Comput. Sci. Appl.* **2020**, *11*, 1–8. [CrossRef]
14. Fuad, A.; Al-Yahya, M. AraConv: Developing an Arabic Task-Oriented Dialogue System Using Multi-Lingual Transformer Model mT5. *Appl. Sci.* **2022**, *12*, 1881. [CrossRef]
15. Wilie, B.; Vincentio, K.; Winata, G.I.; Cahyawijaya, S.; Li, X.; Lim, Z.Y.; Soleman, S.; Mahendra, R.; Fung, P.; Bahar, S. Indonlu: Benchmark and resources for evaluating indonesian natural language understanding. *arXiv* **2020**, arXiv:2009.05387.
16. Bunk, T.; Varshneya, D.; Vlasov, V.; Nichol, A. Diet: Lightweight language understanding for dialogue systems. *arXiv* **2020**, arXiv:2004.09936.
17. Wang, A.; Singh, A.; Michael, J.; Hill, F.; Levy, O.; Bowman, S. GLUE: A multi-task benchmark and analysis platform for natural language understanding. *arXiv* **2020**, arXiv:1804.07461.
18. Habash, N.Y. Introduction to Arabic Natural Language Processing. In *Synthesis Lectures on Human Language Technologies*; Springer: Cham, Switzerland, 2010; Volume 3, pp. 1–187.
19. Al-Ayyoub, M.; Khamaiseh, A.A.; Jararweh, Y.; Al-Kabi, M.N. A comprehensive survey of arabic sentiment analysis. *Inf. Process. Manag.* **2019**, *56*, 320–342. [CrossRef]
20. Habash, N.; Eryani, F.; Khalifa, S.; Rambow, O.; Abdulrahim, D.; Erdmann, A.; Faraj, R.; Zaghouani, W.; Bouamor, H.; Zalmout, N.; et al. Unified guidelines and resources for Arabic dialect orthography. In Proceedings of the Eleventh International Conference on Language Resources and Evaluation (LREC 2018), Miyazaki, Japan, 7–12 May 2018.
21. Wang, A.; Pruksachatkun, Y.; Nangia, N.; Singh, A.; Michael, J.; Hill, F.; Levy, O.; Bowman, S. SuperGLUE: A multi-task benchmark and analysis platform for natural language understanding. *Adv. Neural Inf. Process. Syst.* **2019**, *32*, 3261–3275.
22. Pennington, J.; Socher, R.; Manning, C.D. Glove: Global vectors for word representation. In Proceedings of the 2014 Conference on Empirical Methods in Natural Language Processing (EMNLP), Doha, Qatar, 25–29 October 2014; pp. 1532–1543.
23. Zelaya, C.V.G. Towards explaining the effects of data preprocessing on machine learning. In Proceedings of the 2019 IEEE 35th international conference on data engineering (ICDE), Macao, China, 8–12 April 2019; IEEE: Piscataway, NJ, USA, 2019; pp. 2086–2090.

electronics

MDPI

Article

Research on Log Anomaly Detection Based on Sentence-BERT

Caiping Hu [1,*], Xuekui Sun [2], Hua Dai [2], Hangchuan Zhang [1] and Haiqiang Liu [1]

1 Department of Computer Engineering, Jinling Institute of Technology, Nanjing 211169, China; 19850303315@163.com (H.Z.); 00000005207@jit.edu.cn (H.L.)
2 School of Computer Science, Nanjing University of Posts and Telecommunications, Nanjing 210023, China; kasonsun@foxmail.com (X.S.); daihua@njupt.edu.cn (H.D.)
* Correspondence: hucp@jit.edu.cn

Abstract: Log anomaly detection is crucial for computer systems. By analyzing and processing the logs generated by a system, abnormal events or potential problems in the system can be identified, which is helpful for its stability and reliability. At present, due to the expansion of the scale and complexity of software systems, the amount of log data grows enormously, and traditional detection methods have been unable to detect system anomalies in time. Therefore, it is important to design log anomaly detection methods with high accuracy and strong generalization. In this paper, we propose the log anomaly detection method LogADSBERT, which is based on Sentence-BERT. This method adopts the Sentence-BERT model to extract the semantic behavior characteristics of log events and implements anomaly detection through the bidirectional recurrent neural network, Bi-LSTM. Experiments on the open log data set show that the accuracy of LogADSBERT is better than that of the existing log anomaly detection methods. Moreover, LogADSBERT is robust even under the scenario of new log event injections.

Keywords: anomaly detection; log; deep learning; Sentence-BERT; semantic feature

Citation: Hu, C.; Sun, X.; Dai, H.; Zhang, H.; Liu, H. Research on Log Anomaly Detection Based on Sentence-BERT. *Electronics* **2023**, *12*, 3580. https://doi.org/10.3390/electronics12173580

Academic Editor: Grzegorz Dudek

Received: 23 July 2023
Revised: 17 August 2023
Accepted: 22 August 2023
Published: 24 August 2023

1. Introduction

Logs usually contain information about the operational status of a system, including operation records, fault information, security time, etc., which can provide a comprehensive view of the system's operational status [1]. Logs are time-series in nature; the information in the logs is recorded by time, which allows us to analyze it in order to gain insight into the operation of the system. Logs can provide a historical view—they collect all information about the application, and there are a lot of helpful insights that can be gleaned from an application's history record, including information about potential problems and benchmarks for determining when a process becomes an exception. Logs can monitor the behavior of a system, and in contrast to other data sources, they can go deeper into the system and track the actual behavior of the system as it runs. Log records contain information and trends during system operation. Analyzing and mining the log data can help detect and diagnose system anomalies.

With the expansion of software systems' scale, complexity, and application scope, the number of logs generated shows exponential growth, making it difficult for the traditional log anomaly detection methods based on rules and statistics. In order to adapt to the development of software systems, researchers have shifted their research focus to deep learning-based solutions, and, currently, log anomaly detection based on deep learning has become a hot spot in the field of anomaly detection [2]. Compared to the traditional methods based on rules and statistics, an anomaly detection method based on deep learning requires no human intervention and can quickly and accurately identify abnormal behaviors in logs. Moreover, traditional log anomaly detection methods are constrained by the limitations of algorithms and capacity, whereas a log anomaly detection method based on deep learning can process a large amount of data in parallel. It can efficiently solve the problems of repeated sampling and information extraction. In addition, deep learning models can extract useful information from dozens of data metrics, which can better capture the details of the log data that reflect the anomalies of the system. This is because log data are usually in plain text format, and natural language processing is a specialized field for processing and analyzing text data. For example, chatbots [3] based on machine translation have become popular in recent years. Most of the log anomaly detection methods based on deep learning that have emerged so far are associated with natural language processing (NLP). NLP is used to extract the semantic features in log files, such as vocabulary, phrases, sentences, and grammatical structures. These features are useful for pattern recognition and classification in log anomaly detection, and the models built in this way can better process and analyze the log data, as well as predict abnormal behaviors and events.

In this paper, we propose the log anomaly detection method LogADSBERT. It uses the Sentence-BERT model [4] to extract the semantic features of log events and realizes the final anomaly detection using the recurrent neural network model Bi-LSTM [5]. LogADSBERT consists of two stages: the model training and the anomaly detection. In the model training stage, the log parser parses the original logs into log events and log triples. The log events are used as the corpus to train the Sentence-BERT model, and the log triples are used to construct a sliding window sequence of log event semantic vectors to train the Bi-LSTM neural network classification model, Bi-LSTM-ADM. In the anomaly detection stage, Bi-LSTM-ADM is used to detect anomalies in the log data. LogADSBERT can achieve anomaly detection with high accuracy and robustness.

The contributions of this paper can be summarized as follows:

1. We construct a log event semantic feature extraction model, T-SBERT, based on the Sentence-BERT model, which can convert log events into log event semantic feature representations. The Bidirectional Long Short-Term Memory Recurrent Neural Network model (Bi-LSTM) with an attention mechanism is adopted to generate an anomaly detection model.
2. We propose a log event semantic feature matching algorithm and an anomaly detection algorithm. The log event semantic matching dictionary is established, and the log anomaly detection method LogADSBERT, based on Sentence-BERT, is constructed. It is, to the best of our knowledge, the first to extract log event semantic features using the Sentence-BERT model.
3. In the scenario of new log event injection, LogADSBERT can ensure high accuracy and strong robustness of anomaly detection. Experiment results demonstrate the effectiveness of the proposed method.

This paper is structured as follows: Section 2 discusses the related work; Section 3 presents the preliminary knowledge of this paper; Section 4 presents the definitions related to the proposed method; Section 5 presents the framework of our anomaly detection method; Section 6 describes the experiments used to evaluate the effectiveness of the proposed method; and finally, the conclusion is provided in Section 7.

2. Related Work

The traditional log anomaly detection methods are based on rules and statistics [6–8] and generally need to analyze normal and abnormal behavior patterns using mathematical counting methods. They usually define a set of features, design response rules for each feature, and combine these rules into a complete system. In the testing stage, the newly generated logs are compared with the existing rules to determine the existence of anomalies. For example, Prewett et al. [7] proposed the log file analysis tool Logsurfer, which achieves anomaly detection by defining rules for the expected behavior of the system and then matching them using regular expressions. At the same time, Logsurfer can also update its rule set at runtime. Rouilard et al. [8] proposed the SEC simple temporal correlator to create feature rule sets by analyzing log sequences, which reduces the false alarm rate but is less automated and incurs higher labor costs. Due to the expansion and update of the scale of log data, the traditional log anomaly detection methods based on rules and statistics are usually not effective in detecting complex and or unknow anomalies. Thus, researchers in the field have shifted their research direction to the area of machine learning and deep learning.

Traditional machine learning log anomaly detection includes supervised and unsupervised machine learning methods. Supervised machine learning methods include Support Vector Classifier (SVM) [9,10], Linear Regression (LR) [11,12], Decision Tree (DT) [13], K-Neighborhood Algorithm (KNN) [14], etc. These are based on the log frequency statistics vector to record the frequency of occurrence of each log event within the log sequence, and they use the frequency statistics vector as input and dichotomous labels as the classification result. Unsupervised machine learning methods include Principal Component Analysis (PCA) [15] and clustering-based methods such as Isolated Forest (IF) [16], Invariant Mining (IM) [17], and Log Clustering (LC) [18]. These use unlabeled data for training, and unsupervised log anomaly detection can be achieved.

The deep learning-based log anomaly detection methods [19–21] usually have three steps: First, a log parser is used to split the system log data into two parts, the log event and the parameter. The log event describes the system or process behavior, and the parameter element records state information such as the timestamp and the process identifier. Second, the behavior sequence of the system or process is constructed using the timestamp and log event of the log record. Third, anomaly detection is performed based on the behavioral sequences. Researchers have been developing log anomaly detection methods based on recurrent neural networks. For example, Du et al. [19] trained LSTM based on log keys and parameters to obtain a log key anomaly detection model and a parameter value anomaly detection model. They combined two models to achieve anomaly detection. However, the log key is the index of the log event, which is not combined with the semantic features in the real sense. Log key-based detection requires knowledge of the size of the collection of log events before the detection, which may fail when the log events are updated or added. Meng et al. [20] proposed a template2vec-based method, LogAnomaly, that used the Bi-LSTM model with an attention mechanism to combine log event features and word features within the event to obtain the log event semantic feature space vector. When the log event is updated, the semantic feature vector of the log event is computed first, and then the existing log event is replaced by selecting the closest log event with the Euclidean distance. However, the performance drops sharply when more log events are added. Brown et al. [21] also proposed an LSTM-based approach for routine detection that incorporates multiple implementations of attention mechanisms into the LSTM model to extract log features and achieve eventual anomaly detection. Although the experiments show a high accuracy rate for this method on the LANL cyber security datasets, the experimental datasets are relatively limited, and high accuracy cannot be achieved on several publicly available and commonly used datasets. This method only focuses on discovering relationships hidden in system logs and the effectiveness of multiple attention mechanisms in log anomaly detection, which causes limitations in practical application scenarios. In addition, the BERT model and its derivative models, which have recently become popular in the field of natural language processing, have been used in the field of log anomaly detection. For example, Chen et al. [22] produced semantic log vectors by utilizing a pre-trained language BERT model and used the linear classification to detect anomalies. This method uses a single BERT implementation, which may lose semantic information in sequence feature extraction processing. Zhang et al. [23] adopted the SBERT model to extract the semantic representation of log events, which considers the semantic and word order relationship of each word in log events. They designed a GRU model for anomaly detection; however, as the content of exception log is diverse, including sequence pattern, frequency, correlation, etc., GRU can only capture one-way sequence information. Guo et al. [24] learned the patterns of normal log sequences using two novel, self-supervised training tasks: the masked log message prediction and volume of hypersphere minimization. Nevertheless, this work does not identify and train the semantic information of abnormal logs.

Currently, the log anomaly detection methods based on rules and statistics can no longer meet the rapid development of software systems, and machine learning-based log anomaly detection suffers from weak feature extraction ability, poor adaptability, large labor cost, and low accuracy rate compared to deep learning. Therefore, current log anomaly detection research focuses on the deep learning-based methods. However, the existing log anomaly detection methods based on deep learning still do not fully utilize the semantic information existing in the log data, as well as some other feature information such as frequency statistics, location embedding, etc. As a result, the accuracy rate of the methods does not reach the required standard, and the robustness of these methods to the addition of new logs needs to be further improved.

3. Preliminary Knowledge

3.1. Log Parser

System log data as semi-structured data are difficult to input directly into model training and detection, so processing semi-structured log data into structured log data is the first step of data processing and is crucial for subsequent anomaly detection. A system log data includes variable and constant parts. When generating a log, it is actually a process of combining constants and variables. The variable is the log parameters, which change dynamically depending on the type of log generated. The constants are usually fixed and unchanged log events that are the system log in the parameter part of the use of wildcard replacement to get the standard event. LogParser does exactly the opposite of the log generation process; the log parser must generate logs reverse-parsed into log events and parameters in order to better complete the anomaly detection—there are many open-source log parsers to choose from. Currently, log parsers [25–29] can be divided into two main groups: log parsers based on clustering and log parsers based on heuristic structures.

3.2. Self-Attention Mechanism

A self-attention approach was designed by Google in 2017 [30], which was an implementation of the original attention mechanism proposed in 2014 [31]. Early attention mechanisms need to use other neural networks to extract relevant features, compute intermediate states, and finally give different attention to each intermediate state through the attention mechanism. Now, the self-attention mechanism does not need to use other neural networks to extract sequence features. It directly uses the self-attention mechanism to learn sequence features, which solves the problem of other neural networks not being able to perform in parallel and long short-term dependence.

3.3. Sentence-BERT Model

The Sentence-BERT model [3] is a derivative of the pre-training model BERT that sheds the decoder of the Transformer model so that the construction of BERT is the encoder part of the Transformer. BERT has proved to be effective in a variety of NLP tasks, and with pre-training and fine-tuning, it can obtain better results. Sentence-BERT comes from a similar background. It was constructed based on the Siamese Network and Triplet Network [32]; it performs better in clustering and semantic-based retrieval tasks and can quickly and efficiently realize sentence semantic similarity computation and obtain sentence vector representations, etc. In this paper, the pre-training Sentence-BERT uses the log data for training and fine-tuning so that it can obtain better vector representations.

3.4. Bi-LSTM Neural Network Model

Long Short-Term Memory (LSTM) [33] is a common recurrent neural network model that has a much longer memory. It solves the gradient vanishing and long-distance dependence problems that recurrent neural networks are prone to. It has been proved in recent years that LSTM shows good performance in several natural language processing tasks. The Bi-LSTM model [5] is used in the research methodology of this paper, which employs a bidirectional LSTM model. It is a combination of forward LSTM as well as reverse LSTM, where the hidden output of the current layer is obtained by splicing the processed results of the forward inputs with the processed outputs of the reverse inputs. Bi-LSTM captures backward and forwards temporal correlation and can maximize the use of historical and future information through bi-directional propagation to achieve better performance.

4. Definitions of LogADSBERT

Assuming that the system log set is $L = \{l_1, l_2, \ldots, l_n\}$. After parsing the log set L using LogParser, we obtain a set of the log events $T = \{t_1, t_2, \ldots, t_m\}$ and a set of the log triples $P = \{p_1, p_2, \ldots, p_n\}$.

Definition 1 (Log Event (LE)). *A log event is a structured text information obtained by removing the variable parameter from the system logs l_i using the log parser, which is denoted as $t_i \in T$.*

Definition 2 (Log Triple (LT)). *A log triple is a structured log information obtained by parsing the system logs through the log parser, which is denoted as p_i = (id, t, ts), where id is the process ID, t is the log event, and ts is the timestamp of the log generation.*

Definition 3 (Log Event Semantic Vector (LE-SV)). *Taking the log events of T as the input of the T-SBERT model, the output is the log event semantic vector set $V = \{v_1, v_2, \ldots, v_m\}$.*

Definition 4 (Log Event Semantic Dictionary (LE-SD)). *The log event semantic dictionary is denoted as D, and D is initialized as the mapping set $t_i \rightarrow v_j$, that is $D = \{ t_i \rightarrow v_j | t_i \in T, v_j \in V \}$. When a new type of log appears, the log event semantic vector of the new log is obtained by the log event semantic matching algorithm based on the T-SBERT model, and the new mapping $t_i \rightarrow v_j$ is added to the log event semantic dictionary.*

Definition 5 (Log Event Semantic Vector Sliding Window (LE-SV-SW)). *Assuming that h is the size of a sliding window, $T_i = \{e_1, e_2, \ldots, e_q\}$ is the sequence of the log event, and $T_i \subseteq T$ is the sequence of the log event, the semantic matching algorithm of the log event based on the T-SBERT model converts the log event sequence T_i into the log event semantic vector sequence S_i = $<v_{e_1}, v_{e_2}, \ldots, v_{e_q}>$. Given $v_{e_{j+1}} \in S_i$, the corresponding sliding window is denoted as $W(S_i, v_{e_j})$ which is generated according to the following rules.*

1. *If $(h \le j < q)$, then $W(S_i, v_{e_j}) = <v_{e_{j-h+1}}, v_{e_{j-h+2}}, \ldots, v_{e_j}>$;*
2. *Else, $W(S_i, v_{e_j}) = \varnothing$.*

In addition, for the log event semantic vector sequence S_i that meets the first requirements, the window set of S_i is $W_{s_i} = \{W(S_i, v_{e_j}) | v_{e_j} \in S_i \wedge j \in [h,q)\}$, and the number of items in W_{s_i} is q-h. The corresponding log event semantic vector set is $V_{e_{j+1}} = \{v_{e_{j+1}} | v_{e_{j+1}} \in S_i \wedge j \in [h,q)\}$.

Definition 6 (Log Sequence Anomaly Detection (LSAD)). *Assuming that the log event sequence is $T_i = \{e_1, e_2, \ldots, e_q\}$, the log event semantic vector window set is $W_{s_i} = \{W(S_i, v_{e_j}) \mid v_{e_j} \in S_i \wedge j \in [h, q)\}$, and the corresponding set of log event semantic vector $v_{e_{j+1}}$ is $V_{e_{j+1}} = \{v_{e_{j+1}} \mid v_{e_{j+1}} \in S_i \wedge j \in [h,q)\}$, the result vector set predicted by the Bi-LSTM-ADM with inputting W_{s_i} is $R_{e_{j+1}} = \{r_{e_{j+1}} \mid j \in [h,q)\}$. Given the threshold ξ, the log sequence anomaly detection is performed as follows.*

1. *For each $v_{e_{j+1}} \in V_{e_{j+1}}$ and $\forall\, r_{e_{j+1}} \in R_{e_{j+1}}$, if the similarity between $v_{e_{j+1}}$ and $r_{e_{j+1}}$ is greater than the threshold ξ, it can be determined that the log event sequence T_i is normal;*
2. *Otherwise, the log event sequence T_i is abnormal.*

5. Algorithms of LogADSBERT

The proposed LogADSBERT consists of two stages: the model training and the anomaly detection. The specific implementation process of these two stages is described as follows.

Model training stage: The log parser parses the logs into a set of log events and a set of log triples. The set of log events is used as training data for Sentence-BERT and is trained to generate the T-SBERT log event vector generation model based on the *TSBERTTrain* algorithm (Algorithm 1). While the log triples are ordered according to the time stamp *ts* and transformed into a sequence of log event semantic vectors using the log event semantic matching algorithm based on T-SBERT model (Algorithm 2), they are converted into sequences of log event semantic vectors, then the sliding window mechanism is utilized and sliding window training data are constructed based on the log event semantic vector sequences. The Bi-LSTM model is trained to generate the Bi-LSTM-ADM model using the BILSTMADMTrain algorithm (Algorithm 3).

Anomaly detection stage: The logs to be detected are first transformed into a set of log triples using the log parser, then the log event semantic matching algorithm is used to obtain a log event semantic vector sequence. Finally, the log event semantic vector sequence is used to complete the log anomaly detection by the *LogADSBERTDetect* algorithm (Algorithm 4).

The framework of the proposed log anomaly detection method LogADSBERT is shown in Figure 1.

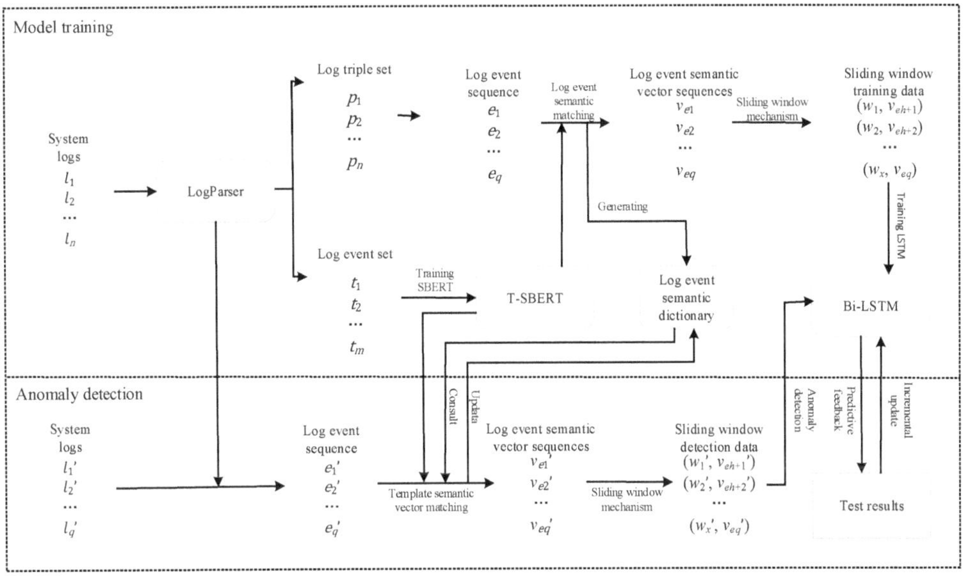

Figure 1. The framework of the LogADSBERT anomaly detection method.

5.1. Sentence-BERT Training Algorithm

In the model training stage, the Sentence BERT model is trained to convert log events into log event semantic vectors, and then the Bi-LSTM model is trained.

TSBERTTrain(T): The log event semantic vector generation model T-SBERT is generated based on the Sentence-BERT model using the log event dataset T. First, the text corpus (TC) is initialized to be empty, the log event set T is preprocessed to obtain the text corpus, and TC is fed into the Sentence-BERT model to generate the T-SBERT model. The specific process of T-SBERT model generation is shown in Algorithm 1. The log event semantic dictionary D is initialized to be empty and is used to store the mapping relationship between log events and log event semantic vectors.

Algorithm 1: TSBERTTrain(T)

```
Input: Log event set T
Output: Log event semantic vector generation model T-SBERT
Initialize the text corpus TC = ∅;
Initialize log event semantic dictionary D = ∅;
Initialize the Sentence-BERT model instance;
FOR t_i ∈ T DO
  Split t_i into word lists WL;
  FOR EACH word IN WL DO
    word = lowerCase(word);
    IF word is a stop-words or no semantic identifiers THEN
      Remove word from WL;
    END IF
  END FOR
  Add the corresponding WL of the processed sentence to the corpus;
  Add the corpus to the TC;
END FOR
Train Sentence-BERT model to get T-SBERT using text library TC;
RETURN T-SBERT;
```

5.2. Log Event Semantic Matching Algorithm

Before the Bi-LSTM model training and anomaly detection, each log event in a sequence of log events needs to be converted into a log event semantic vector.

LESVMatch (t_i, T-SBERT): Log Event Semantic Vector Matching Algorithm based on T-SBERT implements the process of transforming log events to log event topics in the training and detection stage. For log event t_i, the log event semantic dictionary D is first queried to see if there exists a mapping relationship for $t_i \rightarrow v_j$. If there is no mapping relation for $t_i \rightarrow v_j$, then t_i is processed with the log event processing described in Algorithm 1 and inputted into the log event semantic vector model, and the corresponding log event semantic vector $v_j{}'$ is obtained and returned. At the same time, the new mapping relationship for $t_i{}' \rightarrow v_j{}'$ is added to the log event semantic dictionary D. If there exists a mapping for $t_i \rightarrow v_j$, then the corresponding log event semantic vector v_j is returned. The specific algorithm of log event semantic vector matching is shown in Algorithm 2.

Algorithm 2: LESVMatch(t_i, T-SBERT)

```
Input: Log Event t_i, Log event semantic vector model T-SBERT
Output: Log event semantic vector v_j
IF k_i IN D THEN
    RETURN D(k_i);
END IF;
Split k_i into the word list WL;
FOR EACH word IN WL DO
    lowerCase(word);
    IF word is a stop-words or no semantic identifiers THEN
      Remove word from WL;
    END IF
END FOR
Add the corresponding WL of the processed sentence to the corpus;
v_j = T-SBERT (corpus);
The mapping {t_i → v_j} is added to the log event semantic dictionary D;
RETURN v_j;
```

5.3. Bi-LSTM Training Algorithm

After the T-SBERT training is completed, the Bi-LSTM also needs to be trained for learning the normal log behavior patterns.

BILSTMADMTrain(S, h): The log event prediction model training algorithm uses the sliding window training pairs generated from the sequence of log event semantic vectors (Definition 5) to train the Bi-LSTM model to obtain the log event prediction model Bi-LSTM-ADM. The initial sliding window length is h. The log event sequence $T_i = \{e_1, e_2, \ldots, e_q\}$ will be converted into the log event semantic vector sequence $S_i = <v_{e_1}, v_{e_2}, \ldots, v_{e_q}>$ by Algorithm 2. Sliding with the size of the sliding window h to construct the training data pair (*TDP*), the sliding window is denoted as $W(S_i, v_{e_j})$. The training data pair *TDP* constructed by $v_{e_{j+1}}$ is denoted as $(w_i, v_{e_{j+1}})$, and the training data pair *TDP* is stored in the list to form the training data pair list (*TDPL*). The Bi-LSTM model is trained with *TDPL* to obtain the log event prediction model Bi-LSTM-ADM, which is then used for log event prediction for further anomaly detection. The specific process of Bi-LSTM training to generate Bi-LSTM-ADM is shown in Algorithm 3.

Algorithm 3: BILSTMADMTrain (S, h)

Input: Sliding window length h, Log event semantic vector sequence set $S = \{<v_{e_1,1}, v_{e_1,2}, \ldots, v_{e_1,q_1}>, <v_{e_2,1}, v_{e_2,2}, \ldots, v_{e_2,q_2}>, \ldots, <v_{e_f,1}, v_{e_f,2}, \ldots, v_{e_f,q_f}>\}$
Output: Log prediction model Bi-LSTM-ADM

Initialize the $TPDL = \varnothing$;
Initialize the Bi-LSTM model;
FOR $S_i \in S \wedge i \in [1, f]$ **DO**
  FOR $j = h, h+1, \ldots, q-1$ **DO**
    According to Definition 5 to generate the log event semantic vector sliding window $W(S_i, v_{e_j})$;
    IF $W(S_i, v_{e_j}) = \varnothing$ **THEN**
      CONTINUE;
    END IF
    Generate the $TDP = (w_i, v_{e_{j+1}})$ and add the *TDPL*;
  END FOR
END FOR
Using *TPDL* as training datasets to train Bi-LSTM to generate Bi-LSTM-ADM;
RETURN Bi-LSTM-ADM;

5.4. Anomaly Detection Algorithm

In the anomaly detection stage, the log will be detected using the T-SBERT model, log event semantic matching algorithm, and Bi-LSTM-ADM model.

LogADSBERTDetect(S_i, h, ξ, Bi-LSTM-ADM): In the anomaly detection implementation algorithm, for the sequence of log events $T_i = \{e_1, e_2, \ldots, e_q\}$ to be detected, the sliding windows set of log event semantic vectors W_{S_i} is generated using Algorithms 1 and 2. The set consisting of semantic vectors of log events corresponding to W_{S_i} is denoted as $V_{e_{j+1}}$. The prediction set of result vectors obtained from the input of W_{S_i} to the Bi-LSTM-ADM is $R_{e_{j+1}} = \{r_{e_{j+1}} \mid j \in [h, q)\}$. Given the threshold ξ, the sequence anomaly determination method is as follows: for $\forall v_{e_{j+1}} \in V_{e_{j+1}}$ and $r_{e_{j+1}} \in R_{e_{j+1}}$, if the similarity between $v_{e_{j+1}}$ and $r_{e_{j+1}}$ is greater than ξ, then it is determined that there is no anomaly in T_i; otherwise, there is an anomaly in T_i. The specific process of log anomaly detection algorithm implementation is shown in Algorithm 4.

Algorithm 4: LogADSBERTDetect (S_i, h, ξ, Bi-LSTM-ADM)

Input: Sequence of log event semantic vectors $S_i = \langle v_{e_1}, v_{e_2}, \ldots, v_{e_q} \rangle$, Sliding window size h, Threshold value ξ, Bi-LSTM-ADM model
Output: TRUE-normal/FALSE-abnormal

FOR $j = h, h+1, \ldots, q-1$ **DO**
  Generate the event semantic vector sliding window $W(S_i, v_{e_j})$ and add the value $v_{e_{j+1}}$ into $V_{e_{j+1}}$;
  IF $W(S_i, v_{e_j}) = \varnothing$ **THEN**
    CONTINUE;
  END IF
  Input $W(S_i, v_{e_j})$ into Bi-LSTM-ADM to obtain the prediction vector $r_{e_{j+1}}$;
  Add $r_{e_{j+1}}$ to the set of prediction result vectors $R_{e_{j+1}}$;
  IF $Similarity(v_{e_{j+1}}, r_{e_{j+1}}) < \xi$ **THEN**
    RETURN FALSE;
  END IF
END FOR
RETURN TRUE;

6. Evaluation

In this section, we evaluate the proposed LogADSBERT by conducting experiments on the real log datasets. We implement the LogADSBERT together with the existing log anomaly detection methods based on deep learning, such as DeepLog [19] and LogAnomaly [20].

6.1. Experimental Setting

6.1.1. Evaluation Metrics

The evaluation metrics for this experiment are the false positive, false negative, precision, recall, and F1-Score.

1. False positive: the number of normal log sequences marked as abnormal, which are denoted as FP.
2. False negative: the number of abnormal log sequences marked as normal, which are denoted as FN.
3. Precision: the proportion of log sequences with real anomalies that are correctly marked out; the computation of precision is shown in Equation (1).

$$\text{Precision} = \frac{\text{TP}}{\text{TP} + \text{FP}} \tag{1}$$

4. Recall: the proportion of log sequences with real anomalies that are successfully marked; the computation of recall is shown in Equation (2).

$$\text{Recall} = \frac{\text{TP}}{\text{TP} + \text{FN}} \tag{2}$$

5. F1-Score: the reconciliation average of the detection result accuracy and detection result completeness, which is denoted as F1-Score; the calculation of F1-Score is shown in Equation (3).

$$\text{F1-Score} = \frac{2 \times \text{Precision} \times \text{Recall}}{\text{Precision} + \text{Recall}} \tag{3}$$

6.1.2. Environment and Hyperparameters

The operating system of the experimental equipment is Windows 10 64-bit, the memory size is 32 GB, the CPU is AMD Ryzen 5 3600 4.2 Ghz six cores and twelve threads, and the GPU is Nvidia GTX 1660S. The IDE is PyCharm 2021 with python 3.6. The Sentence-BERT model, Bi-LSTM model, and Self-Attention mechanism were constructed based on the framework of Pytorch 1.4. The experimental comparison method is DeepLog, LogAnomaly.

The experimental parameters were set according to the characteristics of the log data, the structure of the model, and the final experimental results. We tried a variety of different parameter combinations and found that the following parameters can achieve the best detection results. Table 1 shows the specific hyperparameter Settings.

Table 1. Experimental hyperparameters.

Hyperparameters	Value
Learning rate	0.001
Batch size	2048
Epoch	300
l (Neural network layers)	2
α (Hide layer cell size)	64
h (Sliding window size)	10

6.1.3. Experimental Datasets

The log datasets used in this experiment come from Hadoop Distributed File System (HDFS) [34] and OpenStack [35]. The HDFS log dataset comes from more than 200 of Amazon's EC2 nodes and contains 11,175,629 log entries. The OpenStack log datasets platform project contains 1,335,318 log entries. We selected some of the data that have been processed by domain experts for our experiments. The duplicate logs were removed from the log dataset. The log data needed to be further parsed and processed before it could be used for our experiments. We used the open-source log parser LogParser to parse logs. According to relevant research in the field, the unsupervised or semi-supervised learning methods can avoid data imbalance and data noise to a certain extent using normal log data as training data, and they can improve the accuracy and efficiency of detection. Therefore, we chose normal logs as the training data. The specific information of the log sequence is shown in Table 2.

Table 2. Setup of log datasets.

Log Datasets	Number of Sessions			Number of Log Events
	Training Data	Normal	Abnormal	
HDFS	7333	14,296	4251	46
OpenStack	514	4904	425	40

6.2. Result

1. Precision, Recall, and F1-Score

Figure 2 shows the precision, recall, and F1-Score of LogADSBERT on the HDFS dataset. It indicates that LogADSBERT is better than DeepLoog and LogAnomaly in all performance metrics. In the F1-Score, LogADSBERT improves by 7.0% and 4.3% compared to DeepLog and LogAnomaly, respectively. There are improvements in both precision and recall for LogADSBERT. Specifically, LogADSBERT improves 8.8% and 5.1% more than DeepLog in precision and recall, respectively. Moreover, LogADSBERT improves 5.5% and 3.0% more than LogAnomaly in precision and recall, respectively.

Figure 3 illustrates the precision, recall, and F1-score of the three methods on the OpenStack dataset. The performance of LogADSBERT compared to DeepLog and LogAnomaly on the OpenStack dataset is more pronounced than on the HDFS dataset. There is already a more pronounced gap between LogADSBERT and the better-performing method, LogAnomaly, in terms of precision and F1-Score, with a difference of 7.1% and 7.0%, respectively. In addition, LogADSBERT achieves 100% in terms of recall performance, whereas the other methods achieve more than 90%.

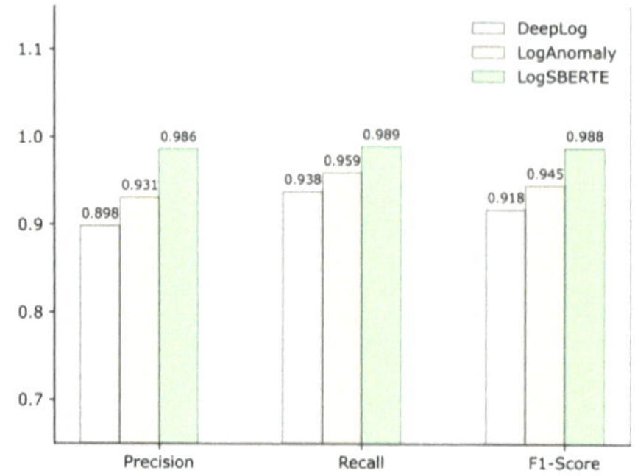

Figure 2. Accuracy on HDFS.

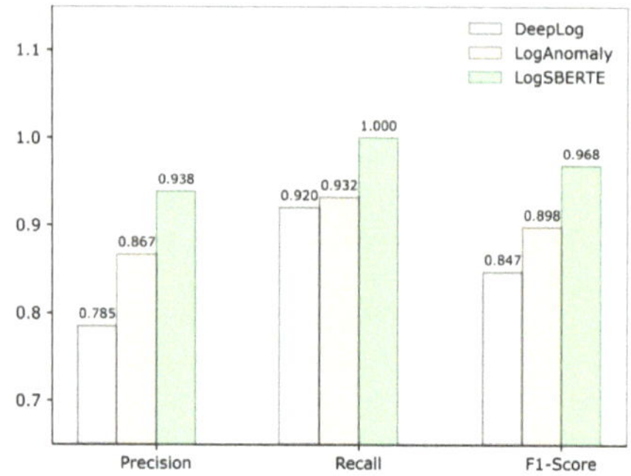

Figure 3. Accuracy on OpenStack.

According to the above analysis, LogADSBERT is superior to DeepLog and LogAnomaly in precision, recall and F1-Score. The reason is that LogADSBERT based on the Sentence-BERT model can capture more important log semantic features, and Bi-LSTM with an attention mechanism can enhance the extraction of the logs' semantic features to improve the accuracy of the anomaly detection.

2. Statistics of FP and FN

Tables 3 and 4 show the number of FP and FN of LogADSBERT, DeepLog, and LogAnomaly on the data set HDFS and OpenStack, respectively.

Table 3. Statistics on the number of FP and FN on the HDFS dataset.

Evaluation Metrics	DeepLog	LogAnomaly	LogADSBERT
False positive (FP)	451	303	59
False negative (FN)	265	174	47

Table 4. Statistics of the number of FP and FN on the OpenStack dataset.

Evaluation Metrics	DeepLog	LogAnomaly	LogADSBERT
False positive (FP)	107	61	28
False negative (FN)	34	29	0

Table 3 shows the number of FP and FN of the three methods on the HDFS dataset. The FP and FN of DeepLog and LogAnomaly are both significantly higher than those of LogADSBERT. Compared to the worst-performing method DeepLog, the FP and FN of

LogADSBERT are reduced by 244 and 127, respectively, which means that LogADSBERT makes an 80.5% and 80.0% improvement in the FP and FN, respectively.

Table 4 shows the number of FP and FN of the three methods on the OpenStack dataset. The result is similar to that shown in Table 3. The number of FP and FN in LogADSBERT is obviously less than that of DeepLog and LogAnomaly. It indicates that LogADSBERT outperforms DeepLog and LogAnomaly in the FP and FN metrics on the OpenStack dataset.

3. Effects of different parameters on LogADSBERT

The experiments on the effect of different parameters on the precision, recall, and F1-Score of LogADSBERT needed to be carried out using a control variable. For simplicity, the more commonly used HDFS dataset was adopted in the experiment. The results of the experiment are shown in Figures 4–7.

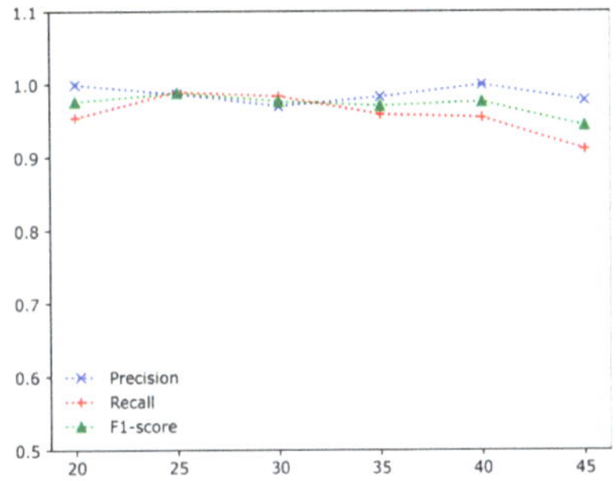

Figure 4. Number of log events: *t*.

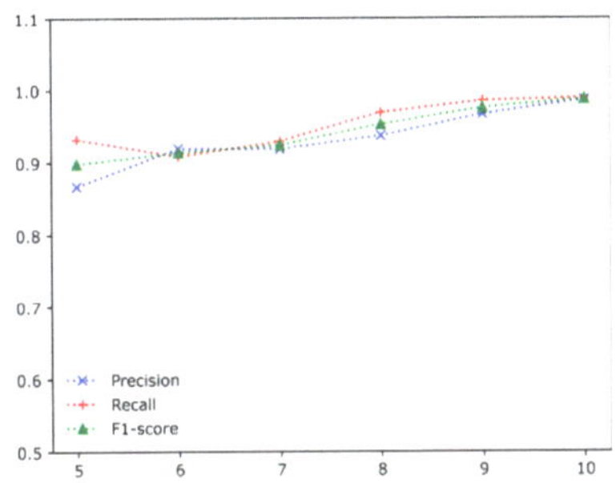

Figure 5. Sliding window size: *h*.

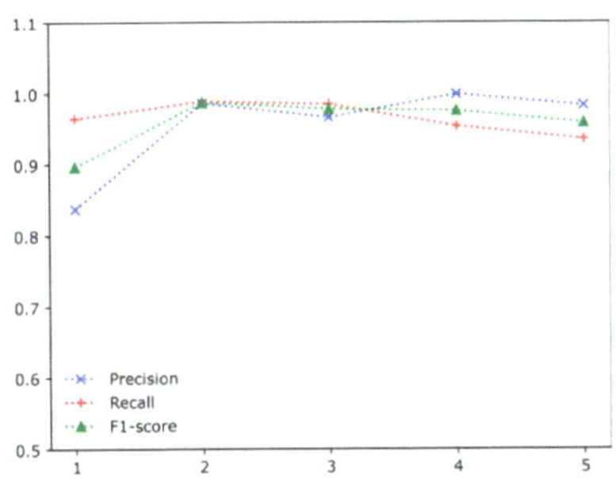

Figure 6. Number of neural network layers: *l*.

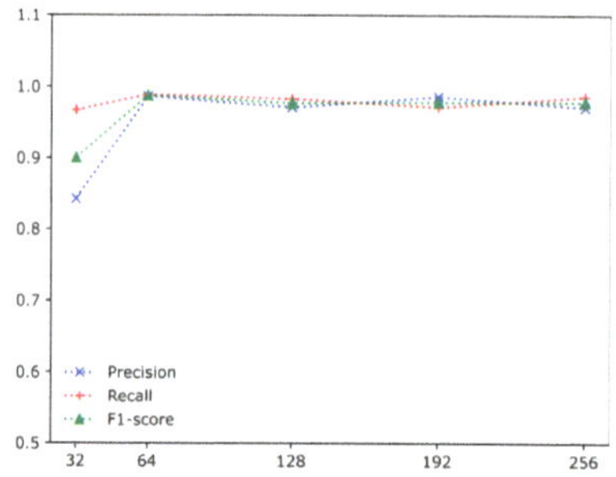

Figure 7. Hide layer unit size: α.

Figure 4 shows the effect of t on the three performance metrics of LogADSBERT. When t = 40, the performance of LogADSBERT is optimal, and when t = 45, the performance of the method decreases, but overall, the effect is not significant. Figure 5 shows the effect of the sliding window size h on the three performance metrics of LogADSBERT, where the accuracy of LogADSBERT is gradually improved as h increases. As shown in Figures 6 and 7, the effects of the number of neural network layers l and the hidden layer unit size α on the LogADSBERT's precision, recall, and F1-Score all reach the highest rate at l = 2 and α = 64. In summary, under the conditions of different hyperparameters of the number of log events t, sliding window size h, the number of neural network layers l, and the size of the hidden layer unit α, LogADSBERT can ensure the stability of the overall performance and obtain a high accuracy, which means that LogADSBERT is robust. In this way, it can cope with the various uncertainties and complex factors that need to be faced in the actual network system application scenario to achieve accurate and stable anomaly detection.

4. Performance comparison of new log event injection

In order to further validate the robustness and effectiveness of LogADSBERT, we conducted experiments involving the addition of new log events on the HDFS dataset. We once again used precision, recall, and F1-Score as the performance metrics, and the comparison methods employed DeepLog and LogAnomaly. The set of log events in the training stage covers the system log datasets and contains 13 log events, and the number of newly added log events was 33. DeepLog does not provide a solution for newly added log events, and here, it was set to mark the log sequence as abnormal when the newly added log events were detected. The results of the experiments are shown in Table 5.

Table 5. Experimental results of new log event injection.

Evaluation Metrics	DeepLog	LogAnomaly	LogADSBERT
Precision	0.409	0.552	0.937
Recall	0.976	0.932	0.928
F1-Score	0.577	0.694	0.932

Table 5 shows that for LogADSBERT, two of the evaluation metrics, precision and F1-Score, were significantly better than for the other two methods. In particular, the F1-Score reached 93.2%, which is 23.8% higher than LogAnomaly. Since LogADSBERT is based on the semantic features of log events for log anomaly detection, the new log events will be matched by a T-SBERT-based log event semantic matching algorithm to obtain the most similar log event semantic representations, so it can vastly reduce the impact of new log events on the anomaly detection results. Additionally, in the experiments, DeepLog was set to detect all log sequences of the new log events as abnormal log sequences, which would certainly lead to a significantly better DeepLog detection rate compared with the other methods, but this setting made the number of FP too high and, consequently, both the precision and F1-Score were much lower than for the other methods. The solution strategy of LogAnomaly for new log events is to replace the log events by calculating the Euclidean distance with the already determined log events; however, this method does not represent the new log events well, and when the number of new log events is too large, the overall performance decreases rapidly. In summary, LogADSBERT, a log anomaly detection method based on Sentence-BERT, maintains strong robustness in the scenario of adding new log events.

7. Conclusions

In this paper, to solve the existing problems of log anomaly detection methods based on deep learning, we proposed a Sentence-BERT-based log anomaly detection method, LogADSBERT. The proposed anomaly detection model trained by inputting the log event corpus not only extracts the log event information containing semantic features, but also obtains the most relevant log event semantic information based on the log event semantic matching algorithm for the newly added log events. The proposed method shows improved accuracy compared to the existing anomaly detection methods, and it also shows robustness when new log events are added.

With the rapid development of software systems, log anomaly detection needs to be updated and iterated to meet new requests. In the future, the following aspects should be focused on: (1) optimizing the preprocessing of log data to improve the efficiency of anomaly detection; and (2) realizing multimodal log anomaly detection, where log anomaly detection integrates multiple types of log data to conduct joint analysis and processing to improve the accuracy and robustness of anomaly detection.

Author Contributions: Conceptualization, C.H. and H.D.; methodology, C.H. and X.S.; software, C.H. and X.S.; validation, H.D., H.Z. and C.H.; formal analysis, X.S. and H.D.; investigation, H.Z.; resources, X.S. and C.H.; data curation, H.L.; writing—original draft preparation, C.H., H.Z. and X.S.; writing—review and editing, C.H. and H.D.; visualization, X.S.; supervision, H.D. and C.H.; project administration, C.H. and H.D.; funding acquisition, C.H. All authors have read and agreed to the published version of the manuscript.

Funding: This research was funded by Jinling Institute of Technology High-level Talent Research Start-up Project (JIT-RCYJ-202102), Key R&D Plan Project of Jiangsu Province (BE2022077), Jinling Institute of Technology Science and Education Integration Project (2022KJRH18), and Jiangsu Province College Student Innovation Training Program Project (202313573080Y, 202313573081Y).

Data Availability Statement: This research employed publicly available datasets for its experimental studies.

Conflicts of Interest: The authors declare no conflict of interest.

References

1. Lam, H.; Russell, D.; Tang, D.; Munzner, T. Session viewer: Visual exploratory analysis of web session logs. In Proceedings of the2007 IEEE Symposium on Visual Analytics Science and Technology, Sacramento, CA, USA, 30 October–1 November 2007; IEEE: Piscataway, NJ, USA, 2007; pp. 147–154.
2. Yadav, R.B.; Kumar, P.S.; Dhavale, S.V. A survey on log anomaly detection using deep learning. In Proceedings of the 2020 8th International Conference on Reliability, Infocom Technologies and Optimization (Trends and Future Directions) (ICRITO), Noida, India, 4–5 June 2020; IEEE: Piscataway, NJ, USA, 2020; pp. 1215–1220.
3. Anastasiou, D.; Ruge, A.; Ion, R.; Segărceanu, S.; Suciu, G.; Pedretti, O.; Gratz, P.; Afkari, H. A machine translation-powered chatbot for public administration. In Proceedings of the 23rd Annual Conference of the European Association for Machine Translation, Ghent, Belgium, 1–3 June 2022; pp. 327–328.
4. Reimers, N.; Gurevych, I. Sentence-BERT: Sentence Embeddings using Siamese BERT-Networks. In Proceedings of the 2019 Conference on Empirical Methods in Natural Language Processing and the 9th International Joint Conference on Natural Language Processing (EMNLP-IJCNLP), Hong Kong, China, 3–7 November 2019; pp. 3982–3992.
5. Jang, B.; Kim, M.; Harerimana, G.; Kang, S.U.; Kim, J.W. Bi-LSTM model to increase accuracy in text classification: Combining Word2vec CNN and attention mechanism. *Appl. Sci.* **2020**, *10*, 5841. [CrossRef]

6. Roy, S.; König, A.C.; Dvorkin, I.; Kumar, M. Perfaugur: Robust diagnostics for performance anomalies in cloud services. In Proceedings of the 2015 IEEE 31st International Conference on Data Engineering, Seoul, Republic of Korea, 13–17 April 2015; IEEE: Piscataway, NJ, USA, 2015; pp. 1167–1178.
7. Prewett, J.E. Analyzing cluster log files using logsurfer. In Proceedings of the 4th Annual Conference on Linux Clusters, St. Petersburg, Russia, 2–4 June 2003; Citeseer: State College, PA, USA, 2003; pp. 1–12.
8. Rouillard, J.P. Real-time Log File Analysis Using the Simple Event Correlator (SEC). *LISA* **2004**, *4*, 133–150.
9. Liang, Y.; Zhang, Y.; Xiong, H.; Sahoo, R. Failure prediction in ibm bluegene/l event logs. In Proceedings of the Seventh IEEE International Conference on Data Mining (ICDM 2007), Omaha, NE, USA, 28–31 October 2007; IEEE: Piscataway, NJ, USA, 2007; pp. 583–588.
10. Wang, Y.; Wong, J.; Miner, A. Anomaly intrusion detection using one class SVM. In *Proceedings of the Fifth Annual IEEE SMC Information Assurance Workshop, West Point, NY, USA, 10–11 June 2004*; IEEE: Piscataway, NJ, USA, 2004; pp. 358–364.
11. Breier, J.; Branišová, J. Anomaly detection from log files using data mining techniques. In *Information Science and Applications*; Springer: Berlin/Heidelberg, Germany, 2015; pp. 449–457.
12. He, P.; Zhu, J.; He, S.; Li, J.; Lyu, M.R. Towards automated log parsing for large-scale log data analysis. *IEEE Trans. Dependable Secur. Comput.* **2017**, *15*, 931–944. [CrossRef]
13. Chen, M.; Zheng, A.X.; Lloyd, J.; Jordan, M.I.; Brewer, E. Failure diagnosis using decision trees. In Proceedings of the International Conference on Autonomic Computing, New York, NY, USA, 17–19 May 2004; IEEE: Piscataway, NJ, USA, 2004; pp. 36–43.
14. Ying, S.; Wang, B.; Wang, L.; Li, Q.; Zhao, Y.; Shang, J.; Huang, H.; Cheng, G.; Yang, Z.; Geng, J. An improved KNN-based efficient log anomaly detection method with automatically labeled samples. *ACM Trans. Knowl. Discov. Data (TKDD)* **2021**, *15*, 1–22. [CrossRef]
15. Xu, W.; Huang, L.; Fox, A.; Patterson, D.; Jordan, M.I. Detecting large-scale system problems by mining console logs. In Proceedings of the ACM SIGOPS 22nd Symposium on Operating Systems Principles, Big Sky, MT, USA, 11–14 October 2009; pp. 117–132.
16. Xu, D.; Wang, Y.; Meng, Y.; Zhang, Z. An improved data anomaly detection method based on isolation forest. In Proceedings of the 2017 10th International Symposium on Computational Intelligence and Design (ISCID), Hangzhou, China, 9–10 December 2017; IEEE: Piscataway, NJ, USA, 2017; Volume 2, pp. 287–291.
17. Lou, J.G.; Fu, Q.; Yang, S.; Xu, Y.; Li, J. Mining Invariants from Console Logs for System Problem Detection. In Proceedings of the USENIX Annual Technical Conference, Virtual, 14–16 July 2010; pp. 1–14.
18. Vaarandi, R.; Pihelgas, M. Logcluster-a data clustering and pattern mining algorithm for event logs. In Proceedings of the 2015 11th International Conference on Network and Service Management (CNSM), Barcelona, Spain, 9–13 November 2015; IEEE: Piscataway, NJ, USA, 2015; pp. 1–7.
19. Du, M.; Li, F.; Zheng, G.; Srikumar, V. Deeplog: Anomaly detection and diagnosis from system logs through deep learning. In Proceedings of the 2017 ACM SIGSAC Conference on Computer and Communications Security, Dallas, TX, USA, 30 October–3 November 2017; pp. 1285–1298.
20. Meng, W.; Liu, Y.; Zhu, Y.; Zhang, S.; Pei, D.; Liu, Y.; Chen, Y.; Zhang, R.; Tao, S.; Sun, P.; et al. LogAnomaly: Unsupervised detection of sequential and quantitative anomalies in unstructured logs. *IJCAI* **2019**, *19*, 4739–4745.
21. Brown, A.; Tuor, A.; Hutchinson, B.; Nichols, N. Recurrent neural network attention mechanisms for interpretable system log anomaly detection. In Proceedings of the First Workshop on Machine Learning for Computing Systems, Tempe, AZ, USA, 12 June 2018; pp. 1–8.
22. Chen, S.; Liao, H. Bert-log: Anomaly detection for system logs based on pre-trained language model. *Appl. Artif. Intell.* **2022**, *36*, 2145642. [CrossRef]
23. Zhang, M.; Chen, J.; Liu, J.; Wang, J.; Shi, R.; Sheng, H. LogST: Log semi-supervised anomaly detection based on sentence-BERT. In Proceedings of the 2022 7th International Conference on Signal and Image Processing (ICSIP), Suzhou, China, 20–22 July 2022; IEEE: Piscataway, NJ, USA, 2022; pp. 356–361.
24. Guo, H.; Yuan, S.; Wu, X. Logbert: Log anomaly detection via bert. In Proceedings of the 2021 International Joint Conference on Neural Networks (IJCNN), Shenzhen, China, 18–22 July 2021; IEEE: Piscataway, NJ, USA, 2021; pp. 1–8.
25. Mizutani, M. Incremental mining of system log format. In Proceedings of the 2013 IEEE International Conference on Services Computing, Santa Clara, CA, USA, 28 June–3 July 2013; IEEE: Piscataway, NJ, USA, 2013; pp. 595–602.
26. Shima, K. Length matters: Clustering system log messages using length of words. *arXiv* **2016**, arXiv:1611.03213.
27. Hamooni, H.; Debnath, B.; Xu, J.; Zhang, H.; Jiang, G.; Mueen, A. Logmine: Fast pattern recognition for log analytics. In Proceedings of the 25th ACM International on Conference on Information and Knowledge Management, Indianapolis, IN, USA, 24–28 October 2016; pp. 1573–1582.
28. He, P.; Zhu, J.; Zheng, Z.; Lyu, M.R. Drain: An online log parsing approach with fixed depth tree. In Proceedings of the 2017 IEEE International Conference on Web Services (ICWS), Honolulu, HI, USA, 25–30 June 2017; IEEE: Piscataway, NJ, USA, 2017; pp. 33–40.
29. Makanju, A.; Zincir-Heywood, A.N.; Milios, E.E. A lightweight algorithm for message type extraction in system application logs. *IEEE Trans. Knowl. Data Eng.* **2011**, *24*, 1921–1936. [CrossRef]

30. Vaswani, A.; Shazeer, N.; Parmar, N.; Uszkoreit, J.; Jones, L.; Gomez, A.N.; Kaiser, Ł.; Polosukhin, I. Attention is all you need. In Proceedings of the 31st International Conference on Neural Information Processing Systems, Long Beach, CA, USA, 4–9 December 2017; Curran Associates Inc.: New York, NY, USA; pp. 6000–6010.
31. Bahdanau, D.; Cho, K.; Bengio, Y. Neural machine translation by jointly learning to align and translate. *arXiv* **2014**, arXiv:1409.0473.
32. Hoffer, E.; Ailon, N. Deep metric learning using triplet network. In Proceedings of the Similarity-Based Pattern Recognition: Third International Workshop, SIMBAD 2015, Copenhagen, Denmark, 12–14 October 2015; Springer International Publishing: Berlin/Heidelberg, Germany, 2015; pp. 84–92.
33. Hochreiter, S.; Schmidhuber, J. Long short-term memory. *Neural Comput.* **1997**, *9*, 1735–1780. [CrossRef] [PubMed]
34. Shvachko, K.; Kuang, H.; Radia, S.; Chansler, R. The hadoop distributed file system. In Proceedings of the 2010 IEEE 26th Symposium on Mass Storage Systems and Technologies (MSST), Lake Tahoe, NV, USA, 3–7 May 2010; IEEE: Piscataway, NJ, USA, 2010; pp. 1–10.
35. Sefraoui, O.; Aissaoui, M.; Eleuldj, M. OpenStack: Toward an open-source solution for cloud computing. *Int. J. Comput. Appl.* **2012**, *55*, 38–42. [CrossRef]

electronics

Article

Picture Fuzzy Soft Matrices and Application of Their Distance Measures to Supervised Learning: Picture Fuzzy Soft k-Nearest Neighbor (PFS-kNN)

Samet Memiş

Department of Marine Engineering, Faculty of Maritime Studies, Bandırma Onyedi Eylül University, Balıkesir 10200, Türkiye; samettmemis@gmail.com

Abstract: This paper redefines picture fuzzy soft matrices (*pfs*-matrices) because of some of their inconsistencies resulting from Cuong's definition of picture fuzzy sets. Then, it introduces several distance measures of *pfs*-matrices. Afterward, this paper proposes a new kNN-based classifier, namely the Picture Fuzzy Soft k-Nearest Neighbor (PFS-kNN) classifier. The proposed classifier utilizes the Minkowski's metric of *pfs*-matrices to find the k-nearest neighbor. Thereafter, it performs an experimental study utilizing four UCI medical datasets and compares to the suggested approach using the state-of-the-art kNN-based classifiers. To evaluate the performance of the classification, it conducts ten iterations of five-fold cross-validation on all the classifiers. The findings indicate that PFS-kNN surpasses the state-of-the-art kNN-based algorithms in 72 out of 128 performance results based on accuracy, precision, recall, and F1-score. More specifically, the proposed method achieves higher accuracy and F1-score results compared to the other classifiers. Simulation results show that *pfs*-matrices and PFS-kNN are capable of modeling uncertainty and real-world problems. Finally, the applications of *pfs*-matrices to supervised learning are discussed for further research.

Keywords: soft sets; picture fuzzy sets; picture fuzzy soft matrices; distance measures; machine learning; k-nearest neighbor (kNN)

MSC: 03E72; 15B15; 62H30; 68T05

Citation: Memiş, S. Picture Fuzzy Soft Matrices and Application of Their Distance Measures to Supervised Learning: Picture Fuzzy Soft k-Nearest Neighbor (PFS-kNN). *Electronics* **2023**, *12*, 4129. https://doi.org/10.3390/electronics12194129

Academic Editor: Grzegorz Dudek

Received: 12 August 2023
Revised: 25 September 2023
Accepted: 29 September 2023
Published: 3 October 2023

1. Introduction

In daily life events, we frequently come across many intricate challenges that are full of uncertainties. Such uncertainties may be impossible to model using traditional mathematical approaches. As a result, state-of-the-art mathematical techniques are needed to model such uncertainties. To avoid ambiguities, Zadeh created the idea of fuzzy sets (f-sets) [1]. f-sets are common mathematical tools used in numerous domains, ranging from computer science [2,3] to pure mathematics [4–9]. Figure 1 shows some hybrid extensions of f-sets.

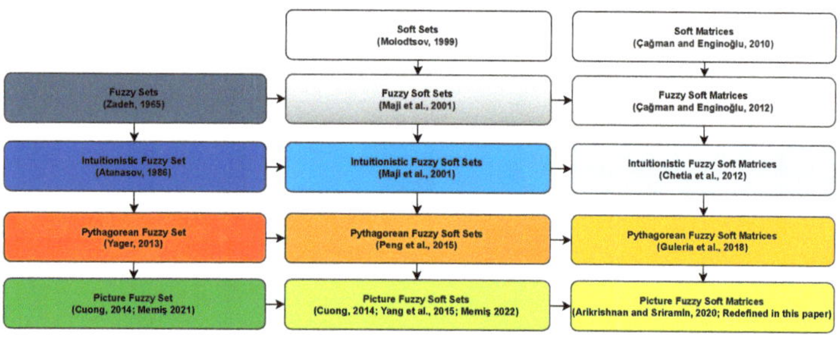

Figure 1. Some hybrid versions and extensions of fuzzy and soft sets [1,7,9–22].

An f-set has entries indicated by $\mu(x)$, i.e., a membership degree for x. Because $\mu(x) + \nu(x) = 1$, the non-membership degree $\nu(x)$ is calculated by subtracting the $\mu(x)$ from 1. However, if $\mu(x) + \nu(x) < 1$, it is not as simple, and there is additional uncertainty. As an extension of f-sets, intuitionistic fuzzy sets (*if*-sets) [10] have been proposed to model this form of uncertainty. An *if*-set has entries indicated by $\mu(x)$ and $\nu(x)$, namely membership and non-membership degrees, respectively, such that $0 \leq \mu(x) + \nu(x) \leq 1$ (Figure 2). In contrast to fuzzy sets, the idea of intuitionistic fuzzy sets can depict problems where $0 \leq \mu(x) + \nu(x) < 1$. In addition, the indeterminacy degree is determined as $1 - (\mu(x) + \nu(x))$.

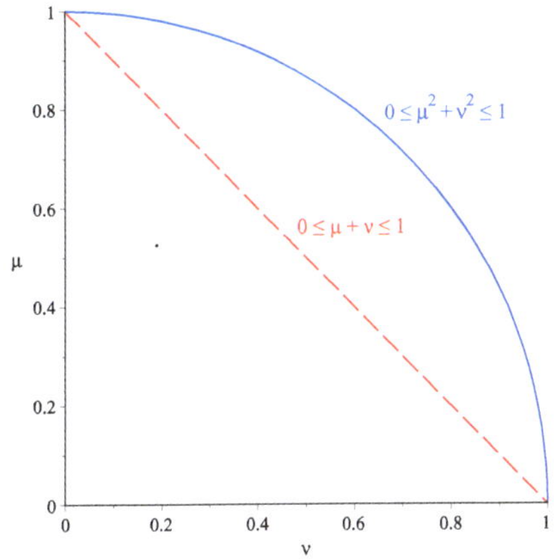

Figure 2. Comparison of space of intuitionistic and Pythagorean fuzzy membership.

Although f-sets and *if*-sets may overcome many difficulties and uncertainties [23], far more are encountered in practice. Consider the voting process for a presidential election. During this procedure, the electorate's decisions can be divided into three categories: yes, no, and abstention. To represent such a process, Cuong proposed the notion of picture fuzzy sets (*pf*-sets) [16]. A *pf*-set has elements with the degrees of membership, non-membership, and neutral membership denoted by $\mu(x)$, $\nu(x)$, and $\eta(x)$, respectively. The refusal to vote or non-participation in voting leads to the indeterminacy described above. Furthermore, $1 - (\mu(x) + \eta(x) + \nu(x))$ reflects the degree of indeterminacy in *pf*-sets because $\mu(x) + \eta(x) + \nu(x) \leq 1$ in Cuong's definition. Even though *pf*-sets model the aforementioned difficulties, the definitions and operations put forward by Cuong have conceptual errors. Memiş [21] revised the idea of *pf*-sets and associated operations to maintain consistency, where $\mu(x) + \eta(x) + \nu(x) \leq 2$.

Conversely, *pf*-sets are unable to model the problems comprising parameters and alternatives (objects) with a picture fuzzy membership (*pf*-membership) degree. In other words, *pfs*-sets [16,18,24] can represent problems with alternatives (objects) using *pf*-membership (Figure 3), with the expert voting on whether to accept, reject, or abstain from the alternatives.

Recently, various studies have been conducted on *pf*-sets and *pfs*-sets. The idea of a rough picture set has been introduced, and several of its topological features, including the lower and upper rough picture fuzzy approximation operators, have also been investigated [25]. The creation of clustering algorithms that can explore latent knowledge from a large number of datasets is an emerging research field in *pf*-sets. The distance and similarity measure is one of the most crucial tools in clustering that establishes the level of association between two objects. Therefore, generalized picture distance measure has been defined, and it has been applied to picture fuzzy clustering [26]. In addition to distance measure, picture fuzzy similarity has also been studied [27,28]. A technique for solving decision-making issues utilizing the generalized *pfs*-sets and an adjustable weighted soft discernibility matrix has been presented, and threshold functions have been defined [29].

A weighted soft discernibility matrix in the generalized *pfs*-sets has been employed to offer an illustrative example to demonstrate the superiority of the suggested approach therein. Matrix representations of mathematical concepts, such as *pfs*-sets are crucial in the context of computerizing [30,31]. Thus, Arikrishnan and Sriram [20] define picture fuzzy soft matrices and investigate their algebraic structures. Because the related study is based on Cuong's [16] study, there are some theoretical inconsistencies. Moreover, Arikrishnan and Sriram have only focused on the algebraic structures. The study of Sahu et al. [32] aims to analyze students' characteristics, such as career, memory, interest, knowledge, environment, and attitude, in order to predict the most suitable career path. This will enable students to explore and excel in their chosen field comfortably. A hybridized distance measure has been proposed, using picture fuzzy numbers to evaluate students, subjects, and students' characteristics for career selection. However, related studies only rely on fictitious problem data. A research study that integrates *pfs*-sets with Quality Function Deployment (QFD) to propose a Multiple Criteria Group Decision-Making (MCGDM) method has been discussed [33]. In this approach, the preferences of the decision-makers are collected in linguistic terms and transformed into Picture Fuzzy Numbers (PFNs). The study applies the proposed MCGDM method to rank social networking sites, specifically evaluating Facebook, Whatsapp, Instagram, and Twitter, providing valuable insights into their comparative performance. The study of Lu et al. [34] has introduced the concept of generalized *pfs*-sets by combining an image fuzzy soft set with a fuzzy parameter set. They discuss five main operations for generalized *pfs*-sets: subset, equality, union, intersection, and complement.

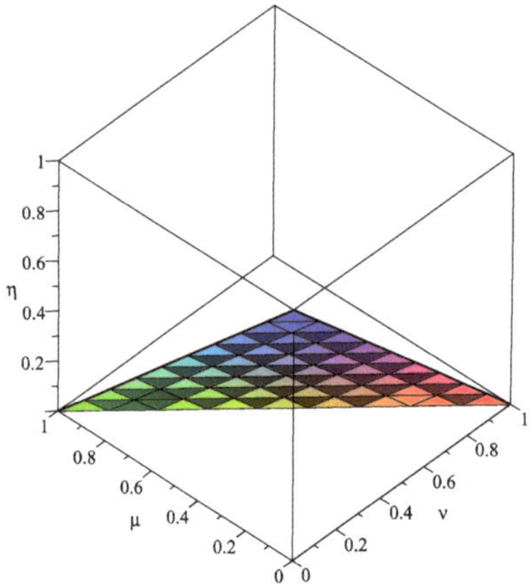

Figure 3. Space of picture fuzzy membership.

Suppose the problem has picture fuzzy uncertainty and a large number of data. In that case, *pfs*-sets cannot operate efficiently with a large number of data. Therefore, processing data through the computer is compulsory, and the matrix versions of the *pfs*-sets are needed. The concept of picture fuzzy soft matrices (*pfs*-matrices) was propounded in 2020 [20]; however, in the aforementioned study, only the algebraic structures of the concept have been investigated. To this end, this paper redefines the concept of *pfs*-matrices, defines the distance measures of the *pfs*-matrices, and applies them to supervised learning to manifest their modeling ability. The major contributions of this paper are as follows:

- *pfs*-matrices are redefined, and some of their basic properties are investigated.
- Distance measures of *pfs*-matrices are introduced.
- Picture fuzzy soft k-nearest neighbor (PFS-kNN) based on distance measure of *pfs*-matrices is proposed.
- An application of PFS-kNN to medical diagnosis is provided.

In Section 2 of the paper, definitions of *pf*-sets and *pfs*-sets are provided. In Section 3, the motivations of the redefining of *pfs*-matrices are detailed. In Section 4, the idea of *pfs*-matrices is redefined, and their properties are further examined. In Section 5, distance measures of *pfs*-matrices are introduced, and their basic properties are researched. In Section 6, a PFS-*k*NN classifier is proposed. In Section 7, the proposed classifier is applied to medical diagnosis and compared with the well-known *k*NN-based classifiers. Finally, we discuss *pfs*-matrices and PFS-*k*NN and provide conclusive remarks for further research.

2. Preliminaries

In this section, we present the concepts of *pf*-sets and *pfs*-sets by considering the notations used across this study. Across this paper, let E and U denote the parameter and alternative sets, respectively.

Definition 1 ([16,21])**.** *Let f be a function such that $f : E \to [0,1] \times [0,1] \times [0,1]$. Then, the graphic*

$$\{(x, f(x)) : x \in E\} = \{(x, \mu(x), \eta(x), \nu(x)) : x \in E\}$$

is called a picture fuzzy set (pf-set) over E. Here, a pf-set is denoted by $\left\{ \left(\left\langle \begin{smallmatrix} \mu(x) \\ \eta(x) \\ \nu(x) \end{smallmatrix} \right\rangle x \right) : x \in E \right\}$ *instead of* $\{(x, \mu(x), \eta(x), \nu(x)) : x \in E\}$.

Moreover, for all $x \in E$, $\mu(x) + \nu(x) \leq 1$ and $\mu(x) + \eta(x) + \nu(x) \leq 2$. Furthermore, μ, η, and ν are the membership, neutral membership, and non-membership functions, respectively, and the indeterminacy degree of the element $x \in E$ is defined by $\pi(x) = 1 - (\mu(x) + \nu(x))$.

In the present paper, the set of all the *pf*-sets over E is symbolized by $PF(E)$ and $f \in PF(E)$.

Remark 1. *In $PF(E)$, the notations graph(f) and f are interchangeable since they have generated each other uniquely. Thus, we prefer the notation f to graph(f) for brevity, provided that it results in no confusion.*

Definition 2 ([16,22])**.** *Let α be a function such that $\alpha : E \to PF(U)$. Then, the graphic*

$$\{(x, \alpha((x, \mu(x), \eta(x), \nu(x)))) : x \in E\}$$

is called a picture fuzzy soft set (pfs-set) parameterized via E over U (or briefly over U).

Throughout this paper, the set of all the *pfs*-sets over U is symbolized by $PFS_E(U)$.

Remark 2. *In $PFS_E(U)$, the notations graph(α) and α are interchangeable since they have generated each other uniquely. Thus, we prefer the notation α to graph(α) for brevity, provided that it results in no confusion.*

Example 1. *Let $E = \{x_1, x_2, x_3, x_4\}$ and $U = \{u_1, u_2, u_3, u_4, u_5\}$. Then,*

$$\alpha = \left\{ \left(x_1, \left\{ \left\langle \begin{smallmatrix} 0.8 \\ 0.1 \\ 0.1 \end{smallmatrix} \right\rangle u_1, \left\langle \begin{smallmatrix} 0.1 \\ 0.2 \\ 0.7 \end{smallmatrix} \right\rangle u_3, \left\langle \begin{smallmatrix} 1 \\ 0 \\ 0 \end{smallmatrix} \right\rangle u_5 \right\} \right), \left(x_2, \left\{ \left\langle \begin{smallmatrix} 0.6 \\ 0.4 \\ 0 \end{smallmatrix} \right\rangle u_2, \left\langle \begin{smallmatrix} 0 \\ 0.5 \\ 0.5 \end{smallmatrix} \right\rangle u_4 \right\} \right), \left(x_3, \left\{ \left\langle \begin{smallmatrix} 0.7 \\ 0 \\ 0.2 \end{smallmatrix} \right\rangle u_3 \right\} \right), \right.$$
$$\left. \left(x_4, \left\{ \left\langle \begin{smallmatrix} 0.1 \\ 0.3 \\ 0.2 \end{smallmatrix} \right\rangle u_2, \left\langle \begin{smallmatrix} 0.4 \\ 0.2 \\ 0.4 \end{smallmatrix} \right\rangle u_5 \right\} \right) \right\}$$

is a pfs-set over U.

3. Motivations of the Redefining of *pfs*-Matrices

This section discusses the definition, fundamental operations, and counter-examples to Arikrishnan and Sriram's definition [20], based on Cuong's definition [16], considering the notations employed throughout the rest of the study.

Definition 3 ([16]). *Let* $\kappa : E \to [0,1] \times [0,1] \times [0,1]$. *Then, the graphic*

$$\{(x, \kappa(x)) : x \in E\} = \left\{ \left(\left\langle \begin{smallmatrix} \mu(x) \\ \eta(x) \\ \nu(x) \end{smallmatrix} \right\rangle x \right) : x \in E \right\}$$

is called a picture fuzzy set (pf-set) over E such that $\mu(x) + \eta(x) + \nu(x) \leq 1$.

In this section, the set of all the *pf*-sets over E according to Cuong's definition is denoted by $PF_C(E)$ and $\kappa \in PF_C(E)$.

Definition 4 ([16]). *Let* $\kappa_1, \kappa_2 \in PF_C(E)$. *For all* $x \in E$, *if* $\mu_1(x) \leq \mu_2(x)$, $\eta_1(x) \leq \eta_2(x)$, *and* $\nu_1(x) \geq \nu_2(x)$, *then* κ_1 *is called a subset of* κ_2 *and is denoted by* $\kappa_1 \tilde{\subseteq} \kappa_2$.

Definition 5 ([16]). *Let* $\kappa_1, \kappa_2 \in PF_C(E)$. *If* $\kappa_1 \tilde{\subseteq} \kappa_2$ *and* $\kappa_2 \tilde{\subseteq} \kappa_1$, *then* κ_1 *and* κ_2 *are called equal pf-sets and are denoted by* $\kappa_1 = \kappa_2$.

Definition 6 ([16]). *Let* $\kappa_1, \kappa_2, \kappa_3 \in PF_C(E)$. *For all* $x \in E$, *if* $\mu_3(x) = \max\{\mu_1(x), \mu_2(x)\}$, $\eta_3(x) = \min\{\eta_1(x), \eta_2(x)\}$, *and* $\nu_3(x) = \min\{\nu_1(x), \nu_2(x)\}$, *then* κ_3 *is called union of* κ_1 *and* κ_2 *and is denoted by* $\kappa_3 = \kappa_1 \tilde{\cup} \kappa_2$.

Definition 7 ([16]). *Let* $\kappa_1, \kappa_2, \kappa_3 \in PF_C(E)$. *For all* $x \in E$, *if* $\mu_3(x) = \min\{\mu_1(x), \mu_2(x)\}$, $\eta_3(x) = \min\{\eta_1(x), \eta_2(x)\}$, *and* $\nu_3(x) = \max\{\nu_1(x), \nu_2(x)\}$, *then* κ_3 *is called intersection of* κ_1 *and* κ_2 *and is denoted by* $\kappa_3 = \kappa_1 \tilde{\cap} \kappa_2$.

Definition 8 ([16]). *Let* $\kappa_1, \kappa_2 \in PF_C(E)$. *For all* $x \in E$, *if* $\mu_2(x) = \nu_1(x)$, $\eta_2(x) = \eta_1(x)$, *and* $\nu_2(x) = \mu_1(x)$, *then* κ_2 *is called complement of* κ_1 *and is denoted by* $\kappa_2 = \kappa_1^{\tilde{c}}$.

To hold the conditions "Empty *pf*-set over E is a subset of all the *pf*-set over E" and "All *pf*-sets over E are the subset of universal *pf*-set over E", the definition and operations of *pf*-sets in [16] must be as follows [21]:

Definition 9 ([21]). *Let* $\kappa \in PF_C(E)$. *For all* $x \in E$, *if* $\mu(x) = 0$, $\eta(x) = 0$, *and* $\nu(x) = 1$, *then* κ *is called empty pf-set and is denoted by* $\left\langle \begin{smallmatrix} 0 \\ 0 \\ 1 \end{smallmatrix} \right\rangle E_C$ *or* 0_{E_C}.

Definition 10 ([21]). *Let* $\kappa \in PF_C(E)$. *For all* $x \in E$, *if* $\mu(x) = 1$, $\eta(x) = 1$, *and* $\nu(x) = 0$, *then* κ *is called universal pf-set and is denoted by* $\left\langle \begin{smallmatrix} 1 \\ 1 \\ 0 \end{smallmatrix} \right\rangle E_C$ *or* 1_{E_C}.

Cuong's definitions have led to the inconsistencies in Examples 2 and 3 [21]:

Example 2 ([21]). *There is a contradiction in Definition 10 since* $1 + 1 + 0 \not\leq 1$, *i.e.,* $1_{E_C} \notin PF_C(E)$. *Moreover, even if* $1_{E_C} \in PF_C(E)$, $(1_{E_C})^{\tilde{c}} \neq 0_{E_C}$.

Example 3 ([21]). *Let* $\kappa \in PF_C(E)$ *such that* $\kappa = \left\{ \left\langle \begin{smallmatrix} 0.1 \\ 0.2 \\ 0.3 \end{smallmatrix} \right\rangle x \right\}$. *Then,* $\kappa \tilde{\cup} 0_E \neq \kappa$ *and* $\kappa \tilde{\cup} 1_{E_C} \neq 1_{E_C}$.

Therefore, Memiş [21] has provided the definition and operations of *pf*-sets in [16] to overcome the aforementioned inconsistencies.

Definition 11 ([16,18]). *$A \subseteq E$. The set*

$$\left\{\left(x, F_A\left(\left(\left\langle\begin{smallmatrix}\mu(x)\\ \eta(x)\\ \nu(x)\end{smallmatrix}\right\rangle x\right)\right)\right) : x \in A \subseteq E\right\}$$

is called a pfs-set over U, where F_A is a mapping given by $F : A \to PF_C(U)$.

In this section, the set of all the *pfs*-sets over U according to Cuong's definition is denoted by $PFS_C(U)$ and $F_A \in PFS_C(U)$.

Cuong [16] defined *pfs*-sets based on his own definition and operations of *pf*-sets. As a result, the inconsistencies mentioned earlier also apply to his concept of *pfs*-sets. Additionally, Yang et al. [18] claimed to have introduced the concept of *pf*-sets, even though Cuong had already defined it in [16]. Thus, the concept of *pfs*-sets has also similar inconsistencies therein. Hence, *pfs*-sets were redefined to deal with inconsistencies mentioned above [22].

Furthermore, the concept of *pfs*-matrices has similar inconsistencies therein, since Arikrishnan and Sriram [20] have introduced the *pfs*-matrices according to Cuong's definition [16] and defined their union, intersection, and complement.

Definition 12 ([20]). *Let $F_A \in PFS_C(U)$. Then, $[a_{ij}]$ is called pfs-matrix of F_A and defined by*

$$[a_{ij}] := \begin{bmatrix} a_{11} & a_{12} & a_{13} & \cdots & a_{1n} & \cdots \\ a_{21} & a_{22} & a_{23} & \cdots & a_{2n} & \cdots \\ \vdots & \vdots & \vdots & \ddots & \vdots & \vdots \\ a_{m1} & a_{m2} & a_{m3} & \cdots & a_{mn} & \cdots \\ \vdots & \vdots & \vdots & \ddots & \vdots & \ddots \end{bmatrix}$$

such that for $i \in \{1, 2, \cdots\}$ and $j \in \{1, 2, \cdots\}$,

$$a_{ij} := F_A\left(\left\langle\begin{smallmatrix}\mu(x_j)\\ \eta(x_j)\\ \nu(x_j)\end{smallmatrix}\right\rangle x_j\right)(u_i)$$

Here, if $|U| = m$ and $|E| = n$, then $[a_{ij}]$ has order $m \times n$.

In the present study, the membership, neutral membership, and non-membership degrees of $[a_{ij}]$, i.e., μ_{ij}, η_{ij}, and ν_{ij}, will be denoted by μ^a_{ij}, η^a_{ij}, and ν^a_{ij}, respectively, as long as they do not cause any confusion. Moreover, the set of all the *pfs*-matrices over U according to Arikrishnan and Sriram's definition is denoted by $PFS_{AS}[U]$ and $F_A \in PFS_{AS}[U]$.

It must be noted that the following definitions from [20] expressed the notations employed throughout the present paper. Definitions of inclusion and equality in the *pfs*-matrices space is provided according to Arikrishnan and Sriram's definitions.

Definition 13. *Let $[a_{ij}], [b_{ij}] \in PFS_{AS}[U]$. For all i and j, if $\mu^a_{ij} \leq \mu^b_{ij}$, $\eta^a_{ij} \leq \eta^b_{ij}$, and $\nu^a_{ij} \geq \nu^b_{ij}$, then $[a_{ij}]$ is called a submatrix of $[b_{ij}]$ and is denoted by $[a_{ij}] \tilde{\subseteq} [b_{ij}]$.*

Definition 14. *Let $[a_{ij}], [b_{ij}] \in PFS_{AS}[U]$. For all i and j, if $\mu^a_{ij} = \mu^b_{ij}$, $\eta^a_{ij} = \eta^b_{ij}$, and $\nu^a_{ij} = \nu^b_{ij}$, then $[a_{ij}]$ and $[b_{ij}]$ are called equal pfs-matrices and denoted by $[a_{ij}] = [b_{ij}]$.*

Definition 15 ([20]). *Let $[a_{ij}], [b_{ij}], [c_{ij}] \in PFS_{AS}[U]$. For all i and j, if $\mu^c_{ij} = \max\{\mu^a_{ij}, \mu^b_{ij}\}$, $\eta^c_{ij} = \min\{\eta^a_{ij}, \eta^b_{ij}\}$, and $\nu^c_{ij} = \min\{\nu^a_{ij}, \nu^b_{ij}\}$, then $[c_{ij}]$ is called union of $[a_{ij}]$ and $[b_{ij}]$ and denoted by $[a_{ij}] \tilde{\cup} [b_{ij}]$.*

Definition 16 ([20])**.** *Let $[a_{ij}], [b_{ij}], [c_{ij}] \in PFS_{AS}[U]$. For all i and j, if $\mu^c_{ij} = \min\{\mu^a_{ij}, \mu^b_{ij}\}$, $\eta^c_{ij} = \min\{\eta^a_{ij}, \eta^b_{ij}\}$, and $\nu^c_{ij} = \max\{\nu^a_{ij}, \nu^b_{ij}\}$, then $[c_{ij}]$ is called intersection of $[a_{ij}]$ and $[b_{ij}]$ and denoted by $[a_{ij}]\tilde{\cap}[b_{ij}]$.*

Definition 17 ([20])**.** *Let $[a_{ij}], [b_{ij}] \in PFS_{AS}[U]$. For all i and j, if $\mu^b_{ij} = \nu^a_{ij}$, $\eta^b_{ij} = \eta^a_{ij}$, and $\nu^b_{ij} = \mu^a_{ij}$, then $[b_{ij}]$ is complement of $[a_{ij}]$ and denoted by $[a_{ij}]^{\tilde{c}}$.*

According to Arikrishnan and Sriram's definitions, the definitions of empty and universal *pfs*-matrices must be defined as in Definitions 18 and 19, respectively, to hold the conditions "Empty *pfs*-matrices over U is a submatrix of all the *pfs*-matrices over U" and "All *pfs*-matrices over U are the submatix of universal *pfs*-matrix over U".

Definition 18. *Let $[a_{ij}] \in PFS_{AS}[U]$. For all i and j, if $\mu_{ij} = 0$, $\eta_{ij} = 0$, and $\nu_{ij} = 1$, then $[a_{ij}]$ is empty pfs-matrix and is denoted by $\left[\left\langle\begin{smallmatrix}0\\0\\1\end{smallmatrix}\right\rangle\right]$.*

Definition 19. *Let $[a_{ij}] \in PFS_{AS}[U]$. For all i and j, if $\mu_{ij} = 1$, $\eta_{ij} = 1$, and $\nu_{ij} = 0$, then $[a_{ij}]$ is universal pfs-matrix and is denoted by $\left[\left\langle\begin{smallmatrix}1\\1\\0\end{smallmatrix}\right\rangle\right]$.*

Arikrishnan and Sriram's definitions have resulted in the inconsistencies in Examples 4 and 5:

Example 4. *There is a contradiction in Definition 19 since $1 + 1 + 0 \not\leq 1$, namely, $\left[\left\langle\begin{smallmatrix}1\\1\\0\end{smallmatrix}\right\rangle\right] \notin PFS_{AS}[U]$. Moreover, even if $\left[\left\langle\begin{smallmatrix}1\\1\\0\end{smallmatrix}\right\rangle\right] \in PFS_{AS}[U]$, $\left[\left\langle\begin{smallmatrix}1\\1\\0\end{smallmatrix}\right\rangle\right]^{\tilde{c}} = \left[\left\langle\begin{smallmatrix}0\\1\\1\end{smallmatrix}\right\rangle\right] \neq \left[\left\langle\begin{smallmatrix}0\\0\\1\end{smallmatrix}\right\rangle\right]$.*

Example 5. *Let $[a_{ij}] \in PFS_{AS}[U]$ such that $[a_{ij}] = \begin{bmatrix} \left\langle\begin{smallmatrix}0.4\\0.3\\0.1\end{smallmatrix}\right\rangle & \left\langle\begin{smallmatrix}0.2\\0.4\\0.3\end{smallmatrix}\right\rangle \\ \left\langle\begin{smallmatrix}0.7\\0.1\\0.1\end{smallmatrix}\right\rangle & \left\langle\begin{smallmatrix}0.1\\0.5\\0.2\end{smallmatrix}\right\rangle \end{bmatrix}$. Then,*

$$[a_{ij}]\tilde{\cup}\left[\left\langle\begin{smallmatrix}0\\0\\1\end{smallmatrix}\right\rangle\right] = \begin{bmatrix} \left\langle\begin{smallmatrix}0.4\\0\\0.1\end{smallmatrix}\right\rangle & \left\langle\begin{smallmatrix}0.2\\0\\0.3\end{smallmatrix}\right\rangle \\ \left\langle\begin{smallmatrix}0.7\\0\\0.1\end{smallmatrix}\right\rangle & \left\langle\begin{smallmatrix}0.1\\0\\0.2\end{smallmatrix}\right\rangle \end{bmatrix} \neq \begin{bmatrix} \left\langle\begin{smallmatrix}0.4\\0.3\\0.1\end{smallmatrix}\right\rangle & \left\langle\begin{smallmatrix}0.2\\0.4\\0.3\end{smallmatrix}\right\rangle \\ \left\langle\begin{smallmatrix}0.7\\0.1\\0.1\end{smallmatrix}\right\rangle & \left\langle\begin{smallmatrix}0.1\\0.5\\0.2\end{smallmatrix}\right\rangle \end{bmatrix} = [a_{ij}]$$

and

$$[a_{ij}]\tilde{\cup}\left[\left\langle\begin{smallmatrix}1\\1\\0\end{smallmatrix}\right\rangle\right] = \begin{bmatrix} \left\langle\begin{smallmatrix}1\\0.3\\0\end{smallmatrix}\right\rangle & \left\langle\begin{smallmatrix}1\\0.4\\0\end{smallmatrix}\right\rangle \\ \left\langle\begin{smallmatrix}1\\0.1\\0\end{smallmatrix}\right\rangle & \left\langle\begin{smallmatrix}1\\0.5\\0\end{smallmatrix}\right\rangle \end{bmatrix} \neq \left[\left\langle\begin{smallmatrix}1\\1\\0\end{smallmatrix}\right\rangle\right].$$

Consequently, since the aforesaid definitions and operations of *pfs*-matrices and how they operate are inconsistent, this concept and its operations must be redefined.

4. Picture Fuzzy Soft Matrices (*pfs*-Matrices)

Cuong [16] and Yang et al. [18] have introduced the concept of *pfs*-sets to address the need for more general mathematical modeling of specific issues involving additional uncertainties. In addition, Yang et al. [18] have proposed an adjustable soft discernibility approach based on *pfs*-sets and applied it to a decision-making problem. Memiş [22] has redefined the concept of *pfs*-sets and applied it to a project selection problem. The applications described in the aforementioned studies demonstrate the successful use of *pfs*-sets in addressing various issues with the uncertainties modeled by membership, non-membership, and neutral degrees, namely picture fuzzy uncertainties. These results suggest that researching the idea of *pfs*-sets is worthwhile. However, it is important to note that these ideas have drawbacks, such as complexity and lengthy computation times. Therefore, it is crucial to understand their matrix representations, i.e., *pfs*-matrices, and ensure their theoretical consistency in the context of computerizing the aforementioned problems. For instance, for utilizing *pfs*-sets in machine learning, *pfs*-matrices, which are matrix representation of *pfs*-sets, and their consistent theoretical definition and operations are needed.

Thus, in the present section, we make consistent the idea of *pfs*-matrices and present some of its fundamental properties. Since some of the propositions in this section have elementary proof, only the propositions with the complex proof are demonstrated.

Definition 20. *Let $\alpha \in PFS_E(U)$ (See Definition 2). Then, $[a_{ij}]$ is called pfs-matrix of α and defined by*

$$[a_{ij}] := \begin{bmatrix} a_{11} & a_{12} & a_{13} & \cdots & a_{1n} & \cdots \\ a_{21} & a_{22} & a_{23} & \cdots & a_{2n} & \cdots \\ \vdots & \vdots & \vdots & \ddots & \vdots & \vdots \\ a_{m1} & a_{m2} & a_{m3} & \cdots & a_{mn} & \cdots \\ \vdots & \vdots & \vdots & \ddots & \vdots & \ddots \end{bmatrix}$$

such that for $i \in \{1,2,\cdots\}$ and $j \in \{1,2,\cdots\}$,

$$a_{ij} := \alpha\left(\left\langle\begin{smallmatrix}\mu(x_j)\\ \eta(x_j)\\ \nu(x_j)\end{smallmatrix}\right\rangle x_j\right)(u_i)$$

Here, if $|U| = m$ and $|E| = n$, then $[a_{ij}]$ has order $m \times n$.

In the present study, the membership, neutral membership, and non-membership degrees of $[a_{ij}]$, i.e., μ_{ij}, η_{ij}, and ν_{ij}, will be denoted by μ^a_{ij}, η^a_{ij}, and ν^a_{ij}, respectively, as long as they do not cause any confusion. Moreover, the set of all the *pfs*-matrices parameterized via E over U (briefly over U) is denoted by $PFS_E[U]$ and $[a_{ij}], [b_{ij}], [c_{ij}] \in PFS_E[U]$.

Example 6. *The pfs-matrix of α given in Example 1 is as follows:*

$$[a_{ij}] = \begin{bmatrix} \left\langle\begin{smallmatrix}0.8\\0.1\\0.1\end{smallmatrix}\right\rangle & \left\langle\begin{smallmatrix}0\\1\\1\end{smallmatrix}\right\rangle & \left\langle\begin{smallmatrix}0\\1\\1\end{smallmatrix}\right\rangle & \left\langle\begin{smallmatrix}0\\1\\1\end{smallmatrix}\right\rangle \\ \left\langle\begin{smallmatrix}0\\0\\1\end{smallmatrix}\right\rangle & \left\langle\begin{smallmatrix}0.6\\0.4\\0\end{smallmatrix}\right\rangle & \left\langle\begin{smallmatrix}0\\1\\1\end{smallmatrix}\right\rangle & \left\langle\begin{smallmatrix}0.1\\0.3\\0.2\end{smallmatrix}\right\rangle \\ \left\langle\begin{smallmatrix}0.1\\0.2\\0.7\end{smallmatrix}\right\rangle & \left\langle\begin{smallmatrix}0\\1\\1\end{smallmatrix}\right\rangle & \left\langle\begin{smallmatrix}0.7\\0\\0.2\end{smallmatrix}\right\rangle & \left\langle\begin{smallmatrix}0\\0\\1\end{smallmatrix}\right\rangle \\ \left\langle\begin{smallmatrix}0\\0\\1\end{smallmatrix}\right\rangle & \left\langle\begin{smallmatrix}0\\1\\1\end{smallmatrix}\right\rangle & \left\langle\begin{smallmatrix}0\\1\\1\end{smallmatrix}\right\rangle & \left\langle\begin{smallmatrix}0\\1\\1\end{smallmatrix}\right\rangle \\ \left\langle\begin{smallmatrix}1\\0\\0\end{smallmatrix}\right\rangle & \left\langle\begin{smallmatrix}0\\0.5\\0.5\end{smallmatrix}\right\rangle & \left\langle\begin{smallmatrix}0\\1\\1\end{smallmatrix}\right\rangle & \left\langle\begin{smallmatrix}0.4\\0.2\\0.4\end{smallmatrix}\right\rangle \end{bmatrix}$$

Definition 21. *Let $[a_{ij}] \in PFS_E[U]$. For all i and j, if $\mu_{ij} = \lambda$, $\eta_{ij} = \varepsilon$, and $\nu_{ij} = \omega$, then $[a_{ij}]$ is $(\lambda, \varepsilon, \omega)$-pfs-matrix and denoted by $\left[\left\langle\begin{smallmatrix}\lambda\\ \varepsilon\\ \omega\end{smallmatrix}\right\rangle\right]$. Moreover, $\left[\left\langle\begin{smallmatrix}0\\1\\1\end{smallmatrix}\right\rangle\right]$ is empty pfs-matrix and $\left[\left\langle\begin{smallmatrix}1\\0\\0\end{smallmatrix}\right\rangle\right]$ is universal pfs-matrix.*

Definition 22. *Let $[a_{ij}], [b_{ij}], [c_{ij}] \in PFS_E[U]$, $I_E := \{j : x_j \in E\}$, and $R \subseteq I_E$. For all i and j, if*

$$\mu_{ij}^{c} = \begin{cases} \mu_{ij}^{a}, & j \in R \\ \mu_{ij}^{b}, & j \in I_E \setminus R \end{cases}, \eta_{ij}^{c} = \begin{cases} \eta_{ij}^{a}, & j \in R \\ \eta_{ij}^{b}, & j \in I_E \setminus R \end{cases}, \text{and } \nu_{ij}^{c} = \begin{cases} \nu_{ij}^{a}, & j \in R \\ \nu_{ij}^{b}, & j \in I_E \setminus R \end{cases}$$

then $[c_{ij}]$ is called Rb-restriction of $[a_{ij}]$ and is denoted by $[(a_{Rb})_{ij}]$. Briefly, if $[b_{ij}] = \left[\left\langle\begin{smallmatrix}0\\1\\1\end{smallmatrix}\right\rangle\right]$, then $[(a_R)_{ij}]$ can be used instead of $[(a_{Rb})_{ij}]$. It is clear that

$$(a_R)_{ij} = \begin{cases} \left\langle\begin{smallmatrix}\mu_{ij}^{a}\\ \eta_{ij}^{a}\\ \nu_{ij}^{a}\end{smallmatrix}\right\rangle, & j \in R \\ \left\langle\begin{smallmatrix}0\\1\\1\end{smallmatrix}\right\rangle, & j \in I_E \setminus R \end{cases}$$

Definition 23. *Let $[a_{ij}], [b_{ij}] \in PFS_E[U]$. For all i and j, if $\mu_{ij}^{a} \leq \mu_{ij}^{b}$, $\eta_{ij}^{a} \geq \eta_{ij}^{b}$, and $\nu_{ij}^{a} \geq \nu_{ij}^{b}$, then $[a_{ij}]$ is called a submatrix of $[b_{ij}]$ and denoted by $[a_{ij}]\tilde{\subseteq}[b_{ij}]$.*

Definition 24. *Let $[a_{ij}], [b_{ij}] \in PFS_E[U]$. For all i and j, if $\mu_{ij}^{a} = \mu_{ij}^{b}$, $\eta_{ij}^{a} = \eta_{ij}^{b}$, and $\nu_{ij}^{a} = \nu_{ij}^{b}$, then $[a_{ij}]$ and $[b_{ij}]$ are called equal pfs-matrices and denoted by $[a_{ij}] = [b_{ij}]$.*

Proposition 1. *Let $[a_{ij}], [b_{ij}], [c_{ij}] \in PFS_E[U]$. Then,*

i. $[a_{ij}]\tilde{\subseteq}\left[\left\langle\begin{smallmatrix}1\\0\\0\end{smallmatrix}\right\rangle\right]$

ii. $\left[\left\langle\begin{smallmatrix}0\\1\\1\end{smallmatrix}\right\rangle\right]\tilde{\subseteq}[a_{ij}]$

iii. $[a_{ij}]\tilde{\subseteq}[a_{ij}]$

iv. $([a_{ij}]\tilde{\subseteq}[b_{ij}] \wedge [b_{ij}]\tilde{\subseteq}[a_{ij}]) \Leftrightarrow [a_{ij}] = [b_{ij}]$

v. $([a_{ij}]\tilde{\subseteq}[b_{ij}] \wedge [b_{ij}]\tilde{\subseteq}[c_{ij}]) \Rightarrow [a_{ij}]\tilde{\subseteq}[c_{ij}]$

vi. $([a_{ij}] = [b_{ij}] \wedge [b_{ij}] = [c_{ij}]) \Rightarrow [a_{ij}] = [c_{ij}]$

Proof. The proofs of *i-vi* are straightforward. □

Remark 3. *From Proposition 1, it is straightforward that the inclusion relation herein is a partial ordering relation in $PFS_E[U]$.*

Definition 25. *Let $[a_{ij}], [b_{ij}] \in PFS_E[U]$. If $[a_{ij}]\tilde{\subseteq}[b_{ij}]$ and $[a_{ij}] \neq [b_{ij}]$, then $[a_{ij}]$ is called a proper submatrix of $[b_{ij}]$ and denoted by $[a_{ij}]\tilde{\subsetneq}[b_{ij}]$.*

Definition 26. *Let $[a_{ij}], [b_{ij}], [c_{ij}] \in PFS_E[U]$. For all i and j, if $\mu_{ij}^{c} = \max\{\mu_{ij}^{a}, \mu_{ij}^{b}\}$, $\eta_{ij}^{c} = \min\{\eta_{ij}^{a}, \eta_{ij}^{b}\}$, and $\nu_{ij}^{c} = \min\{\nu_{ij}^{a}, \nu_{ij}^{b}\}$, then $[c_{ij}]$ is called union of $[a_{ij}]$ and $[b_{ij}]$ and denoted by $[a_{ij}]\tilde{\cup}[b_{ij}]$.*

Definition 27. *Let $[a_{ij}], [b_{ij}], [c_{ij}] \in PFS_E[U]$. For all i and j, if $\mu_{ij}^{c} = \min\{\mu_{ij}^{a}, \mu_{ij}^{b}\}$, $\eta_{ij}^{c} = \max\{\eta_{ij}^{a}, \eta_{ij}^{b}\}$, and $\nu_{ij}^{c} = \max\{\nu_{ij}^{a}, \nu_{ij}^{b}\}$, then $[c_{ij}]$ is called intersection of $[a_{ij}]$ and $[b_{ij}]$ and denoted by $[a_{ij}]\tilde{\cap}[b_{ij}]$.*

Example 7. *Assume that two pfs-matrices* $[a_{ij}]$ *and* $[b_{ij}]$ *are as follows:*

$$[a_{ij}] = \begin{bmatrix} \left\langle\begin{smallmatrix}0.2\\0.3\\0.5\end{smallmatrix}\right\rangle & \left\langle\begin{smallmatrix}0\\1\\1\end{smallmatrix}\right\rangle & \left\langle\begin{smallmatrix}1\\0\\0\end{smallmatrix}\right\rangle \\ \left\langle\begin{smallmatrix}0.1\\0.5\\0.2\end{smallmatrix}\right\rangle & \left\langle\begin{smallmatrix}0.6\\0.4\\0\end{smallmatrix}\right\rangle & \left\langle\begin{smallmatrix}0.9\\0\\0.1\end{smallmatrix}\right\rangle \\ \left\langle\begin{smallmatrix}1\\0\\0\end{smallmatrix}\right\rangle & \left\langle\begin{smallmatrix}0.8\\0\\0\end{smallmatrix}\right\rangle & \left\langle\begin{smallmatrix}0.5\\0.1\\0.2\end{smallmatrix}\right\rangle \end{bmatrix} \quad \text{and} \quad [b_{ij}] = \begin{bmatrix} \left\langle\begin{smallmatrix}0.6\\0.2\\0.1\end{smallmatrix}\right\rangle & \left\langle\begin{smallmatrix}0.7\\0.2\\0\end{smallmatrix}\right\rangle & \left\langle\begin{smallmatrix}0.5\\0.4\\0.1\end{smallmatrix}\right\rangle \\ \left\langle\begin{smallmatrix}0\\1\\1\end{smallmatrix}\right\rangle & \left\langle\begin{smallmatrix}1\\0\\0\end{smallmatrix}\right\rangle & \left\langle\begin{smallmatrix}0.1\\0.8\\0.1\end{smallmatrix}\right\rangle \\ \left\langle\begin{smallmatrix}0.4\\0.3\\0.3\end{smallmatrix}\right\rangle & \left\langle\begin{smallmatrix}0.1\\0.3\\0.2\end{smallmatrix}\right\rangle & \left\langle\begin{smallmatrix}1\\0\\0\end{smallmatrix}\right\rangle \end{bmatrix}$$

Then,

$$[a_{ij}]\tilde{\cup}[b_{ij}] = \begin{bmatrix} \left\langle\begin{smallmatrix}0.6\\0.2\\0.1\end{smallmatrix}\right\rangle & \left\langle\begin{smallmatrix}0.7\\0.2\\0\end{smallmatrix}\right\rangle & \left\langle\begin{smallmatrix}1\\0\\0\end{smallmatrix}\right\rangle \\ \left\langle\begin{smallmatrix}0.1\\0.5\\0.2\end{smallmatrix}\right\rangle & \left\langle\begin{smallmatrix}1\\0\\0\end{smallmatrix}\right\rangle & \left\langle\begin{smallmatrix}0.9\\0\\0.1\end{smallmatrix}\right\rangle \\ \left\langle\begin{smallmatrix}1\\0\\0\end{smallmatrix}\right\rangle & \left\langle\begin{smallmatrix}0.6\\0\\0\end{smallmatrix}\right\rangle & \left\langle\begin{smallmatrix}1\\0\\0\end{smallmatrix}\right\rangle \end{bmatrix} \quad \text{and} \quad [a_{ij}]\tilde{\cap}[b_{ij}] = \begin{bmatrix} \left\langle\begin{smallmatrix}0.2\\0.3\\0.5\end{smallmatrix}\right\rangle & \left\langle\begin{smallmatrix}0\\1\\1\end{smallmatrix}\right\rangle & \left\langle\begin{smallmatrix}0.5\\0.4\\0.1\end{smallmatrix}\right\rangle \\ \left\langle\begin{smallmatrix}0\\1\\1\end{smallmatrix}\right\rangle & \left\langle\begin{smallmatrix}0.6\\0.4\\0\end{smallmatrix}\right\rangle & \left\langle\begin{smallmatrix}0.1\\0.8\\0.1\end{smallmatrix}\right\rangle \\ \left\langle\begin{smallmatrix}0.4\\0.3\\0.3\end{smallmatrix}\right\rangle & \left\langle\begin{smallmatrix}0.1\\0.3\\0.2\end{smallmatrix}\right\rangle & \left\langle\begin{smallmatrix}0.5\\0.1\\0.2\end{smallmatrix}\right\rangle \end{bmatrix}$$

Proposition 2. *Let* $[a_{ij}], [b_{ij}], [c_{ij}] \in PFS_E[U]$. *Then,*

i. $[a_{ij}]\tilde{\cup}[a_{ij}] = [a_{ij}]$ *and* $[a_{ij}]\tilde{\cap}[a_{ij}] = [a_{ij}]$

ii. $[a_{ij}]\tilde{\cup}\left[\left\langle\begin{smallmatrix}0\\1\\1\end{smallmatrix}\right\rangle\right] = [a_{ij}]$ *and* $[a_{ij}]\tilde{\cap}\left[\left\langle\begin{smallmatrix}0\\1\\1\end{smallmatrix}\right\rangle\right] = \left[\left\langle\begin{smallmatrix}0\\1\\1\end{smallmatrix}\right\rangle\right]$

iii. $[a_{ij}]\tilde{\cup}\left[\left\langle\begin{smallmatrix}1\\0\\0\end{smallmatrix}\right\rangle\right] = \left[\left\langle\begin{smallmatrix}1\\0\\0\end{smallmatrix}\right\rangle\right]$ *and* $[a_{ij}]\tilde{\cap}\left[\left\langle\begin{smallmatrix}1\\0\\0\end{smallmatrix}\right\rangle\right] = [a_{ij}]$

iv. $[a_{ij}]\tilde{\cup}[b_{ij}] = [b_{ij}]\tilde{\cup}[a_{ij}]$ *and* $[a_{ij}]\tilde{\cap}[b_{ij}] = [b_{ij}]\tilde{\cap}[a_{ij}]$

v. $([a_{ij}]\tilde{\cup}[b_{ij}])\tilde{\cup}[c_{ij}] = [a_{ij}]\tilde{\cup}([b_{ij}]\tilde{\cup}[c_{ij}])$ *and* $([a_{ij}]\tilde{\cap}[b_{ij}])\tilde{\cap}[c_{ij}] = [a_{ij}]\tilde{\cap}([b_{ij}]\tilde{\cap}[c_{ij}])$

vi. $[a_{ij}]\tilde{\cup}([b_{ij}]\tilde{\cap}[c_{ij}]) = ([a_{ij}]\tilde{\cup}[b_{ij}])\tilde{\cap}([a_{ij}]\tilde{\cup}[c_{ij}])$ *and*
$[a_{ij}]\tilde{\cap}([b_{ij}]\tilde{\cup}[c_{ij}]) = ([a_{ij}]\tilde{\cap}[b_{ij}])\tilde{\cup}([a_{ij}]\tilde{\cap}[c_{ij}])$

Proof. *vi.* Let $[a_{ij}], [b_{ij}], [c_{ij}] \in PFS_E[U]$. Then,

$$\begin{aligned} [a_{ij}]\tilde{\cup}([b_{ij}]\tilde{\cap}[c_{ij}]) &= [a_{ij}]\tilde{\cup}\left[\left\langle\begin{matrix}\min\{\mu^b_{ij}, \mu^c_{ij}\}\\ \max\{\eta^b_{ij}, \eta^c_{ij}\}\\ \max\{\nu^b_{ij}, \nu^c_{ij}\}\end{matrix}\right\rangle\right] \\ &= \left[\left\langle\begin{matrix}\max\{\mu^a_{ij}, \min\{\mu^b_{ij}, \mu^c_{ij}\}\}\\ \min\{\eta^a_{ij}, \max\{\eta^b_{ij}, \eta^c_{ij}\}\}\\ \min\{\nu^a_{ij}, \max\{\nu^b_{ij}, \nu^c_{ij}\}\}\end{matrix}\right\rangle\right] \\ &= \left[\left\langle\begin{matrix}\min\{\max\{\mu^a_{ij}, \mu^b_{ij}\}, \max\{\mu^a_{ij}, \mu^c_{ij}\}\}\\ \max\{\min\{\eta^a_{ij}, \eta^b_{ij}\}, \min\{\eta^a_{ij}, \eta^c_{ij}\}\}\\ \max\{\min\{\nu^a_{ij}, \nu^b_{ij}\}, \min\{\nu^a_{ij}, \nu^c_{ij}\}\}\end{matrix}\right\rangle\right] \\ &= \left[\left\langle\begin{matrix}\max\{\mu^a_{ij}, \mu^b_{ij}\}\\ \min\{\eta^a_{ij}, \eta^b_{ij}\}\\ \min\{\nu^a_{ij}, \nu^b_{ij}\}\end{matrix}\right\rangle\right]\tilde{\cap}\left[\left\langle\begin{matrix}\max\{\mu^a_{ij}, \mu^c_{ij}\}\\ \min\{\eta^a_{ij}, \eta^c_{ij}\}\\ \min\{\nu^a_{ij}, \nu^c_{ij}\}\end{matrix}\right\rangle\right] \\ &= ([a_{ij}]\tilde{\cup}[b_{ij}])\tilde{\cap}([a_{ij}]\tilde{\cup}[c_{ij}]) \end{aligned}$$

The proof of $[a_{ij}]\tilde{\cap}([b_{ij}]\tilde{\cup}[c_{ij}]) = ([a_{ij}]\tilde{\cap}[b_{ij}])\tilde{\cup}([a_{ij}]\tilde{\cap}[c_{ij}])$ is similar to the aforementioned proof. In addition, the proofs of *i-v* are straightforward. □

Definition 28. *Let* $[a_{ij}], [b_{ij}], [c_{ij}] \in PFS_E[U]$. *For all i and j, if* $\mu_{ij}^c = \min\{\mu_{ij}^a, \nu_{ij}^b\}$, $\eta_{ij}^c = \max\{\eta_{ij}^a, 1-\eta_{ij}^b\}$, *and* $\nu_{ij}^c = \max\{\nu_{ij}^a, \mu_{ij}^b\}$, *then* $[c_{ij}]$ *is called difference between* $[a_{ij}]$ *and* $[b_{ij}]$ *and denoted by* $[a_{ij}]\tilde{\setminus}[b_{ij}]$.

Proposition 3. *Let* $[a_{ij}] \in PFS_E[U]$. *Then,*

i. $[a_{ij}]\tilde{\setminus}\left[\left\langle\begin{smallmatrix}0\\1\\1\end{smallmatrix}\right\rangle\right] = [a_{ij}]$

ii. $[a_{ij}]\tilde{\setminus}\left[\left\langle\begin{smallmatrix}1\\0\\0\end{smallmatrix}\right\rangle\right] = \left[\left\langle\begin{smallmatrix}0\\1\\1\end{smallmatrix}\right\rangle\right]$

Proof. The proofs of *i* and *ii* are straightforward. □

Remark 4. *It must be emphasized that the difference operation herein is non-commutative and non-associative.*

Definition 29. *Let* $[a_{ij}], [b_{ij}] \in PFS_E[U]$. *For all i and j, if* $\mu_{ij}^b = \nu_{ij}^a$, $\eta_{ij}^b = 1-\eta_{ij}^a$, *and* $\nu_{ij}^b = \mu_{ij}^a$, *then* $[b_{ij}]$ *is complement of* $[a_{ij}]$ *and denoted by* $[a_{ij}]^{\tilde{c}}$ *or* $[a_{ij}^{\tilde{c}}]$. *It is clear that* $[a_{ij}]^{\tilde{c}} = \left[\left\langle\begin{smallmatrix}1\\0\\0\end{smallmatrix}\right\rangle\right]\tilde{\setminus}[a_{ij}]$.

Proposition 4. *Let* $[a_{ij}], [b_{ij}] \in PFS_E[U]$. *Then,*

i. $\left([a_{ij}]^{\tilde{c}}\right)^{\tilde{c}} = [a_{ij}]$

ii. $\left[\left\langle\begin{smallmatrix}0\\1\\1\end{smallmatrix}\right\rangle\right]^{\tilde{c}} = \left[\left\langle\begin{smallmatrix}1\\0\\0\end{smallmatrix}\right\rangle\right]$

iii. $[a_{ij}]\tilde{\setminus}[b_{ij}] = [a_{ij}]\tilde{\cap}[b_{ij}]^{\tilde{c}}$

iv. $[a_{ij}]\tilde{\subseteq}[b_{ij}] \Rightarrow [b_{ij}]^{\tilde{c}}\tilde{\subseteq}[a_{ij}]^{\tilde{c}}$

Proof. The proofs of *i-iv* are straightforward. □

Proposition 5. *Let* $[a_{ij}], [b_{ij}] \in PFS_E[U]$. *Then, the following De Morgan's laws are valid.*

i. $\left([a_{ij}]\tilde{\cup}[b_{ij}]\right)^{\tilde{c}} = [a_{ij}]^{\tilde{c}}\tilde{\cap}[b_{ij}]^{\tilde{c}}$

ii. $\left([a_{ij}]\tilde{\cap}[b_{ij}]\right)^{\tilde{c}} = [a_{ij}]^{\tilde{c}}\tilde{\cup}[b_{ij}]^{\tilde{c}}$

Proof. *i.* Let $[a_{ij}], [b_{ij}] \in PFS_E[U]$. Then,

$$
\begin{aligned}
\left([a_{ij}]\tilde{\cup}[b_{ij}]\right)^{\tilde{c}} &= \left[\left\langle\begin{matrix}\max\{\mu_{ij}^a, \mu_{ij}^b\}\\ \min\{\eta_{ij}^a, \eta_{ij}^b\}\\ \min\{\nu_{ij}^a, \nu_{ij}^b\}\end{matrix}\right\rangle\right]^{\tilde{c}} \\
&= \left[\left\langle\begin{matrix}\min\{\nu_{ij}^a, \nu_{ij}^b\}\\ 1-\min\{\eta_{ij}^a, \eta_{ij}^b\}\\ \max\{\mu_{ij}^a, \mu_{ij}^b\}\end{matrix}\right\rangle\right] \\
&= \left[\left\langle\begin{matrix}\min\{\nu_{ij}^a, \nu_{ij}^b\}\\ \max\{1-\eta_{ij}^a, 1-\eta_{ij}^b\}\\ \max\{\mu_{ij}^a, \mu_{ij}^b\}\end{matrix}\right\rangle\right] \\
&= \left[\left\langle\begin{matrix}\nu_{ij}^a\\ 1-\eta_{ij}^a\\ \mu_{ij}^a\end{matrix}\right\rangle\right]\tilde{\cap}\left[\left\langle\begin{matrix}\nu_{ij}^b\\ 1-\eta_{ij}^b\\ \mu_{ij}^b\end{matrix}\right\rangle\right] \\
&= [a_{ij}]^{\tilde{c}}\tilde{\cap}[b_{ij}]^{\tilde{c}}
\end{aligned}
$$

The proof of *ii* is similar to the aforementioned proof. □

Definition 30. *Let $[a_{ij}], [b_{ij}], [c_{ij}] \in PFS_E[U]$. For all i and j, if*

$$\mu^c_{ij} = \max\Big\{\min\{\mu^a_{ij}, \nu^b_{ij}\}, \min\{\mu^b_{ij}, \nu^a_{ij}\}\Big\}$$

$$\eta^c_{ij} = \min\Big\{\max\{\eta^a_{ij}, 1-\eta^b_{ij}\}, \max\{\eta^b_{ij}, 1-\eta^a_{ij}\}\Big\}$$

and

$$\nu^c_{ij} = \min\Big\{\max\{\nu^a_{ij}, \mu^b_{ij}\}, \max\{\nu^b_{ij}, \mu^a_{ij}\}\Big\}$$

then $[c_{ij}]$ is called symmetric difference between $[a_{ij}]$ and $[b_{ij}]$ and denoted $[a_{ij}]\tilde{\triangle}[b_{ij}]$.

Proposition 6. *Let $[a_{ij}], [b_{ij}] \in PFS_E[U]$. Then,*

i. $[a_{ij}]\tilde{\triangle}\left[\left\langle\begin{smallmatrix}0\\1\\1\end{smallmatrix}\right\rangle\right] = [a_{ij}]$

ii. $[a_{ij}]\tilde{\triangle}\left[\left\langle\begin{smallmatrix}1\\0\\0\end{smallmatrix}\right\rangle\right] = [a_{ij}]^{\tilde{c}}$

iii. $[a_{ij}]\tilde{\triangle}[b_{ij}] = [b_{ij}]\tilde{\triangle}[a_{ij}]$

iv. $[a_{ij}]\tilde{\triangle}[b_{ij}] = \Big([a_{ij}]\tilde{\setminus}[b_{ij}]\Big)\tilde{\cup}\Big([b_{ij}]\tilde{\setminus}[a_{ij}]\Big)$

Proof. *iv*. Let $[a_{ij}], [b_{ij}] \in PFS_E[U]$. Then,

$$\begin{aligned}
[a_{ij}]\tilde{\triangle}[b_{ij}] &= \left[\left\langle\begin{matrix}\max\Big\{\min\Big\{\mu^a_{ij}, \nu^b_{ij}\Big\}, \min\Big\{\mu^b_{ij}, \nu^a_{ij}\Big\}\Big\}\\ \min\Big\{\max\Big\{\eta^a_{ij}, 1-\eta^b_{ij}\Big\}, \max\Big\{\eta^b_{ij}, 1-\eta^a_{ij}\Big\}\Big\}\\ \min\Big\{\max\Big\{\nu^a_{ij}, \mu^b_{ij}\Big\}, \max\Big\{\nu^b_{ij}, \mu^a_{ij}\Big\}\Big\}\end{matrix}\right\rangle\right] \\
&= \left[\left\langle\begin{matrix}\min\Big\{\mu^a_{ij}, \nu^b_{ij}\Big\}\\ \max\Big\{\eta^a_{ij}, 1-\eta^b_{ij}\Big\}\\ \max\Big\{\nu^a_{ij}, \mu^b_{ij}\Big\}\end{matrix}\right\rangle\right]\tilde{\cup}\left[\left\langle\begin{matrix}\min\Big\{\mu^b_{ij}, \nu^a_{ij}\Big\}\\ \max\Big\{\eta^b_{ij}, 1-\eta^a_{ij}\Big\}\\ \max\Big\{\nu^a_{ij}, \nu^c_{ij}\Big\}\end{matrix}\right\rangle\right] \\
&= \Big([a_{ij}]\tilde{\setminus}[b_{ij}]\Big)\tilde{\cup}\Big([b_{ij}]\tilde{\setminus}[a_{ij}]\Big)
\end{aligned}$$

The proofs of *i-iii* are similar to the proof mentioned above. □

Remark 5. *It must be emphasized that the symmetric difference operation herein is non-associative.*

5. Distance Measures of *pfs*-Matrices

This section, firstly, defines the concept of metrics over $PFS_E[U]$. One of the significant goals herein is to contribute to *pf*-sets and soft sets theoretically. The other goal is to improve the modeling skill of *pfs*-matrices for classification problems in machine learning owing to the aforementioned theoretical contribution. Throughout this study, let $I_n = \{1, 2, \dots, n\}$.

Definition 31. *Let $d : PFS_E[U] \times PFS_E[U] \to \mathbb{R}$ be a function. Then, d is a metric over $PFS_E[U]$ for all $[a_{ij}], [b_{ij}], [c_{ij}] \in PFS_E[U]$ if d satisfies the following properties,*

i. $d([a_{ij}], [b_{ij}]) = 0 \Leftrightarrow [a_{ij}] = [b_{ij}]$

ii. $d([a_{ij}], [b_{ij}]) = d([b_{ij}], [a_{ij}])$

iii. $d([a_{ij}], [b_{ij}]) \leq d([a_{ij}], [c_{ij}]) + d([c_{ij}], [b_{ij}])$

Secondly, Minkowski, Euclidean, and Hamming metrics over $PFS_E[U]$ are propounded. Thereafter, their three properties are investigated.

Proposition 7. *The function $d_M^p : PFS_E[U] \times PFS_E[U] \to \mathbb{R}$ defined by*

$$d_M^p([a_{ij}],[b_{ij}]) := \left(\frac{1}{3}\sum_{i=1}^{m}\sum_{j=1}^{n}\left(\left|\mu_{ij}^a - \mu_{ij}^b\right|^p + \left|\eta_{ij}^a - \eta_{ij}^b\right|^p + \left|\nu_{ij}^a - \nu_{ij}^b\right|^p + \left|\pi_{ij}^a - \pi_{ij}^b\right|^p\right)\right)^{\frac{1}{p}}$$

such that $p \in \mathbb{N}^+$ is Minkowski metric over $PFS_E[U]$. Its normalized version, namely normalized Minkowski metric, is defined as follows:

$$\hat{d}_M^p([a_{ij}],[b_{ij}]) := \left(\frac{1}{3mn}\sum_{i=1}^{m}\sum_{j=1}^{n}\left(\left|\mu_{ij}^a - \mu_{ij}^b\right|^p + \left|\eta_{ij}^a - \eta_{ij}^b\right|^p + \left|\nu_{ij}^a - \nu_{ij}^b\right|^p + \left|\pi_{ij}^a - \pi_{ij}^b\right|^p\right)\right)^{\frac{1}{p}}$$

such that $p \in \mathbb{N}^+$.

Specifically, d_M^1 and d_M^2 are Hamming and Euclidean metrics and represented by d_H and d_E, respectively. Moreover, $\hat{d}_M^1$ and $\hat{d}_M^2$ are normalized Hamming and Euclidean metrics and are represented by $\hat{d}_H$ and $\hat{d}_E$, respectively.

Proof. Let $[a_{ij}],[b_{ij}],[c_{ij}] \in PFS_E[U]$ and $p \in \mathbb{N}^+$. Satisfying of d_M^p the conditions *i* and *ii* is straightforward from Definition 31. Then,

$$\begin{aligned}
iii.\ d_M^p([a_{ij}],[b_{ij}]) &= \left(\frac{1}{3}\sum_{i=1}^{m}\sum_{j=1}^{n}\left(\left|\mu_{ij}^a - \mu_{ij}^b\right|^p + \left|\eta_{ij}^a - \eta_{ij}^b\right|^p + \left|\nu_{ij}^a - \nu_{ij}^b\right|^p + \left|\pi_{ij}^a - \pi_{ij}^b\right|^p\right)\right)^{\frac{1}{p}} \\
&= \left(\frac{1}{3}\sum_{i=1}^{m}\sum_{j=1}^{n}\left(\left|\mu_{ij}^a - \mu_{ij}^c + \mu_{ij}^c - \mu_{ij}^b\right|^p + \left|\eta_{ij}^a - \eta_{ij}^c + \eta_{ij}^c - \eta_{ij}^b\right|^p\right.\right. \\
&\quad \left.\left. + \left|\nu_{ij}^a - \nu_{ij}^c + \nu_{ij}^c - \nu_{ij}^b\right|^p + \left|\pi_{ij}^a - \pi_{ij}^c + \pi_{ij}^c - \pi_{ij}^b\right|^p\right)\right)^{\frac{1}{p}} \\
&\leq \left(\frac{1}{3}\sum_{i=1}^{m}\sum_{j=1}^{n}\left(\left|\mu_{ij}^a - \mu_{ij}^c\right|^p + \left|\mu_{ij}^c - \mu_{ij}^b\right|^p + \left|\eta_{ij}^a - \eta_{ij}^c\right|^p + \left|\eta_{ij}^c - \eta_{ij}^b\right|^p\right.\right. \\
&\quad \left.\left. + \left|\nu_{ij}^a - \nu_{ij}^c\right| + \left|\nu_{ij}^c - \nu_{ij}^b\right|^p + \left|\pi_{ij}^a - \pi_{ij}^c\right|^p + \left|\pi_{ij}^c - \pi_{ij}^b\right|^p\right)\right)^{\frac{1}{p}} \\
&\leq \left(\frac{1}{3}\sum_{i=1}^{m}\sum_{j=1}^{n}\left(\left|\mu_{ij}^a - \mu_{ij}^c\right|^p + \left|\eta_{ij}^a - \eta_{ij}^c\right|^p + \left|\nu_{ij}^a - \nu_{ij}^c\right|^p + \left|\pi_{ij}^a - \pi_{ij}^c\right|^p\right)\right)^{\frac{1}{p}} \\
&\quad + \left(\frac{1}{3}\sum_{i=1}^{m}\sum_{j=1}^{n}\left(\left|\mu_{ij}^c - \mu_{ij}^b\right|^p + \left|\eta_{ij}^c - \eta_{ij}^b\right|^p + \left|\nu_{ij}^c - \nu_{ij}^b\right|^p + \left|\pi_{ij}^c - \pi_{ij}^b\right|^p\right)\right)^{\frac{1}{p}} \\
&= d_M^p([a_{ij}],[c_{ij}]) + d_M^p([c_{ij}],[b_{ij}])
\end{aligned}$$

Moreover, $0 \leq |\mu_{ij}^a - \mu_{ij}^b| \leq 1$, $0 \leq |\eta_{ij}^a - \eta_{ij}^b| \leq 1$, $0 \leq |\nu_{ij}^a - \nu_{ij}^b| \leq 1$, and $0 \leq |\pi_{ij}^a - \pi_{ij}^b| \leq 1$ because $0 \leq \mu_{ij}^a, \mu_{ij}^b, \eta_{ij}^a, \eta_{ij}^b, \nu_{ij}^a, \nu_{ij}^b, \pi_{ij}^a, \pi_{ij}^b \leq 1$, for all $i \in I_m$ and $j \in I_n$. Hence,

$$\begin{aligned}
0 &\leq |\mu_{ij}^a - \mu_{ij}^b|^p + |\eta_{ij}^a - \eta_{ij}^b|^p + |\nu_{ij}^a - \nu_{ij}^b|^p + |\pi_{ij}^a - \pi_{ij}^b|^p \\
&\leq |\mu_{ij}^a - \mu_{ij}^b| + |\eta_{ij}^a - \eta_{ij}^b| + |\nu_{ij}^a - \nu_{ij}^b| + |\pi_{ij}^a - \pi_{ij}^b| \\
&\leq |\mu_{ij}^a| + |\mu_{ij}^b| + |\eta_{ij}^a - \eta_{ij}^b| + |\nu_{ij}^a| + |\nu_{ij}^b| + |\pi_{ij}^a| + |\pi_{ij}^b|
\end{aligned}$$

$$
\begin{aligned}
&= \mu^a_{ij} + \mu^b_{ij} + |\eta^a_{ij} - \eta^b_{ij}| + \nu^a_{ij} + \nu^b_{ij} + \pi^a_{ij} + \pi^b_{ij} \\
&= \mu^a_{ij} + \mu^b_{ij} + |\eta^a_{ij} - \eta^b_{ij}| + \nu^a_{ij} + \nu^b_{ij} + (1 - \mu^a_{ij} - \nu^a_{ij}) + (1 - \mu^b_{ij} - \nu^b_{ij}) \\
&= 2 + |\eta^a_{ij} - \eta^b_{ij}| \\
&\leq 3
\end{aligned}
$$

Then,

$$
\begin{aligned}
\left(\frac{1}{3mn}\sum_{i=1}^{m}\sum_{j=1}^{n} 0\right)^{\frac{1}{p}} \leq \hat{d}^p_M([a_{ij}],[b_{ij}]) &\leq \left(\frac{1}{3mn}\sum_{i=1}^{m}\sum_{j=1}^{n} 3\right)^{\frac{1}{p}} \\
0 \leq \hat{d}^p_M([a_{ij}],[b_{ij}]) &\leq \left(\frac{1}{3mn}3mn\right)^{\frac{1}{p}} \\
0 \leq \hat{d}^p_M([a_{ij}],[b_{ij}]) &\leq 1
\end{aligned}
$$

□

Proposition 8. *Let* $\left[\left\langle\begin{smallmatrix}0\\1\\1\end{smallmatrix}\right\rangle\right]_{m\times n}, \left[\left\langle\begin{smallmatrix}1\\0\\0\end{smallmatrix}\right\rangle\right]_{m\times n} \in PFS_E[U]$ *and* $p \in \mathbb{N}^+$. *Then,*

$$
d^p_M\left(\left[\left\langle\begin{smallmatrix}0\\1\\1\end{smallmatrix}\right\rangle\right], \left[\left\langle\begin{smallmatrix}1\\0\\0\end{smallmatrix}\right\rangle\right]\right) = \sqrt[p]{mn} \quad and \quad \hat{d}^p_M\left(\left[\left\langle\begin{smallmatrix}0\\1\\1\end{smallmatrix}\right\rangle\right], \left[\left\langle\begin{smallmatrix}1\\0\\0\end{smallmatrix}\right\rangle\right]\right) = 1
$$

Proof. The proof is straightforward. □

Proposition 9. *Let* $[a_{ij}]_{m\times n}, [b_{ij}]_{m\times n} \in PFS_E[U]$ *and* $p \in \mathbb{N}^+$. *Then,* $d^p_M([a_{ij}],[b_{ij}]) \leq \sqrt[p]{mn}$.

Proof. The proof is straightforward. □

Proposition 10. *Let* $[a_{ij}]_{m\times n}, [b_{ij}]_{m\times n}, [c_{ij}]_{m\times n} \in PFS_E[U]$ *and* $p \in \mathbb{N}^+$. *Then,*

i. $[a_{ij}]\tilde{\subseteq}[b_{ij}]\tilde{\subseteq}[c_{ij}] \Rightarrow \left(d^p_M([a_{ij}],[b_{ij}]) \leq d^p_M([a_{ij}],[c_{ij}]) \wedge d^p_M([b_{ij}],[c_{ij}]) \leq d^p_M([a_{ij}],[c_{ij}])\right)$

ii. $[a_{ij}]\tilde{\subseteq}[b_{ij}]\tilde{\subseteq}[c_{ij}] \Rightarrow \left(\hat{d}^p_M([a_{ij}],[b_{ij}]) \leq \hat{d}^p_M([a_{ij}],[c_{ij}]) \wedge \hat{d}^p_M([b_{ij}],[c_{ij}]) \leq \hat{d}^p_M([a_{ij}],[c_{ij}])\right)$

Proof. The proofs of *i* and *ii* are straightforward. □

6. Picture Fuzzy Soft *k*-Nearest Neighbor Classifier: PFS-*k*NN

In this section, firstly, the basic expressions and notations to be required for the suggested PFS-*k*NN based on *pfs*-matrices are provided. Throughout the paper, let $D = [d_{ij}]_{m\times(n+1)}$ represent a data matrix. The last column of D consists of class labels of the data. Here, m and n are the numbers of samples and attributes in D, respectively. Moreover, let $(D_{train})_{m_1\times n}$, $C_{m_1\times 1}$, and $(D_{test})_{m_2\times n}$ derived from attained D denote a training matrix, class matrix of the training matrix, and the testing matrix, respectively, such that $m_1 + m_2 = m$. Moreover, let $U_{k\times 1}$ be a matrix comprising of unique class labels of $C_{m_1\times 1}$. Further, let $D_{i-train}$ and D_{i-test} represent ith rows of D_{train} and D_{test}, respectively. In a similar manner, $D_{train-j}$ and D_{test-j} represent jth rows of D_{train} and D_{test}, respectively. Furthermore, let $T'_{m_2\times 1}$ stand for the predicted classes of the testing queries.

Definition 32. *Let $u \in \mathbb{R}^n$. Then, the vector $\hat{u} \in \mathbb{R}^n$ such that $j \in I_n$ defined by*

$$\hat{u}_j := \begin{cases} \frac{u_j - \min\limits_{k\in I_n}\{u_k\}}{\max\limits_{k\in I_n}\{u_k\} - \min\limits_{k\in I_n}\{u_k\}}, & \max\limits_{k\in I_n}\{u_k\} \neq \min\limits_{k\in I_n}\{u_k\} \\ 1, & \max\limits_{k\in I_n}\{u_k\} = \min\limits_{k\in I_n}\{u_k\} \end{cases}$$

is called normalized u, i.e., normalizing vector of u.

Definition 33. *Consider the training matrix $(D_{train})_{m_1 \times n}$ attained from $D = [d_{ij}]_{m\times(n+1)}$, $i \in I_{m_1}$, and $j \in I_n$. Then, the matrix defined by*

$$\tilde{d}_{ij-train} := \begin{cases} \frac{d_{ij-train} - \min\limits_{k\in I_m}\{d_{kj}\}}{\max\limits_{k\in I_m}\{d_{kj}\} - \min\limits_{k\in I_m}\{d_{kj}\}}, & \max\limits_{k\in I_m}\{d_{kj}\} \neq \min\limits_{k\in I_m}\{d_{kj}\} \\ 1, & \max\limits_{k\in I_m}\{d_{kj}\} = \min\limits_{k\in I_m}\{d_{kj}\} \end{cases}$$

is called feature-fuzzification matrix of D_{train}, namely column normalized matrix of D_{train}, and it is denoted by $\tilde{D}_{train} = [\tilde{d}_{ij-train}]_{m_1\times n}$.

Definition 34. *Consider the testing matrix $(D_{test})_{m_2 \times n}$ attained from $D = [d_{ij}]_{m\times(n+1)}$, $i \in I_{m_2}$, and $j \in I_n$. Then, the matrix defined by*

$$\tilde{d}_{ij-test} := \begin{cases} \frac{d_{ij-test} - \min\limits_{k\in I_m}\{d_{kj}\}}{\max\limits_{k\in I_m}\{d_{kj}\} - \min\limits_{k\in I_m}\{d_{kj}\}}, & \max\limits_{k\in I_m}\{d_{kj}\} \neq \min\limits_{k\in I_m}\{d_{kj}\} \\ 1, & \max\limits_{k\in I_m}\{d_{kj}\} = \min\limits_{k\in I_m}\{d_{kj}\} \end{cases}$$

is called feature-fuzzification matrix of D_{test}, namely column normalized matrix of D_{test}, and it is denoted by $\tilde{D}_{test} = [\tilde{d}_{ij-test}]_{m_1\times n}$.

Definition 35. *Let $\tilde{D}_{train} = [\tilde{d}_{ij-train}]_{m_1\times n}$ be a feature-fuzzification matrix of $(D_{train})_{m_1\times n}$. Then, the matrix*

$$\tilde{\tilde{D}}^{\lambda}_{train} = [\tilde{\tilde{d}}^{\lambda}_{train-ij}] = \left[\left\langle \begin{matrix} \mu^{\tilde{\tilde{D}}^{\lambda}}_{ij-train} \\ \eta^{\tilde{\tilde{D}}^{\lambda}}_{ij-train} \\ \nu^{\tilde{\tilde{D}}^{\lambda}}_{ij-train} \end{matrix} \right\rangle\right]_{m_1\times n}$$

is called feature picture fuzzification of $\tilde{D}_{train}$ and is defined by

$$\mu^{\tilde{\tilde{D}}^{\lambda}}_{ij-train} := 1 - (1 - \tilde{d}_{ij-train})^{\lambda}, \quad \eta^{\tilde{\tilde{D}}^{\lambda}}_{ij-train} := \frac{\tilde{d}_{ij-train}}{\lambda}, \quad and \quad \nu^{\tilde{\tilde{D}}^{\lambda}}_{ij-train} := (1 - \tilde{d}_{ij-train})^{\lambda(\lambda+1)}$$

such that $i \in I_{m_1}$, $j \in I_n$, and $\lambda \in [0, \infty)$.

Definition 36. *Let $\tilde{D}_{test} = [\tilde{d}_{ij-test}]_{m_2\times n}$ be a feature-fuzzification matrix of $(D_{test})_{m_2\times n}$. Then, the matrix*

$$\tilde{\tilde{D}}^{\lambda}_{test} = [\tilde{\tilde{d}}^{\lambda}_{test-ij}] = \left[\left\langle \begin{matrix} \mu^{\tilde{\tilde{D}}^{\lambda}}_{ij-test} \\ \eta^{\tilde{\tilde{D}}^{\lambda}}_{ij-test} \\ \nu^{\tilde{\tilde{D}}^{\lambda}}_{ij-test} \end{matrix} \right\rangle\right]_{m_2\times n}$$

is called feature picture fuzzification of $\tilde{D}_{test}$ and is defined by

$$\mu^{\tilde{\tilde{D}}^{\lambda}}_{ij-test} := 1 - (1 - \tilde{d}_{ij-test})^{\lambda}, \quad \eta^{\tilde{\tilde{D}}^{\lambda}}_{ij-test} := \frac{\tilde{d}_{ij-test}}{\lambda}, \quad and \quad \nu^{\tilde{\tilde{D}}^{\lambda}}_{ij-test} := (1 - \tilde{d}_{ij-test})^{\lambda(\lambda+1)}$$

such that $i \in I_{m_2}$, $j \in I_n$, and $\lambda \in [0, \infty)$.

Definition 37. *Let* $(\tilde{D}_{train})_{m_1\times n}$ *be a feature-fuzzification matrix of* $(D_{train})_{m_1\times n}$ *and* $\tilde{\tilde{D}}^{\lambda}_{train} = [\tilde{\tilde{d}}^{\lambda}_{train-ij}] = \left[\left\langle \begin{matrix}\mu^{\tilde{\tilde{D}}^{\lambda}}_{ij-train}\\ \eta^{\tilde{\tilde{D}}^{\lambda}}_{ij-train}\\ \nu^{\tilde{\tilde{D}}^{\lambda}}_{ij-train}\end{matrix}\right\rangle\right]_{m_1\times n}$ *be the picture fuzzification of* $\tilde{D}_{train}$. *Then, the pfs-matrix* $\left[b_{ij}^{\tilde{\tilde{D}}^{\lambda}_{k-train}}\right]_{1\times n}$ *is the training pfs-matrix attained by* k^{th} *row of* $\tilde{\tilde{D}}^{\lambda}_{train}$ *and is defined by* $b_{1j}^{\tilde{\tilde{D}}^{\lambda}_{k-train}} := \left\langle \begin{matrix}\mu^{\tilde{\tilde{D}}^{\lambda}}_{kj-train}\\ \eta^{\tilde{\tilde{D}}^{\lambda}}_{kj-train}\\ \nu^{\tilde{\tilde{D}}^{\lambda}}_{kj-train}\end{matrix}\right\rangle$ *such that* $k \in I_{m_1}$ *and* $j \in I_n$.

Definition 38. *Let* $(\tilde{D}_{test})_{m_2\times n}$ *be a a feature-fuzzification matrix of* $(D_{test})_{m_2\times n}$ *and* $\tilde{\tilde{D}}^{\lambda}_{test} = [\tilde{\tilde{d}}^{\lambda}_{test-ij}] = \left[\left\langle \begin{matrix}\mu^{\tilde{\tilde{D}}^{\lambda}}_{ij-test}\\ \eta^{\tilde{\tilde{D}}^{\lambda}}_{ij-test}\\ \nu^{\tilde{\tilde{D}}^{\lambda}}_{ij-test}\end{matrix}\right\rangle\right]_{m_2\times n}$ *be the picture fuzzification of* $\tilde{D}_{test}$. *Then, the pfs-matrix* $\left[a_{ij}^{\tilde{\tilde{D}}^{\lambda}_{k-test}}\right]_{1\times n}$ *is called the testing pfs-matrix attained by* k^{th} *row of* $\tilde{\tilde{D}}^{\lambda}_{test}$ *and is defined by* $a_{1j}^{\tilde{\tilde{D}}^{\lambda}_{k-test}} := \left\langle \begin{matrix}\mu^{\tilde{\tilde{D}}^{\lambda}}_{kj-test}\\ \eta^{\tilde{\tilde{D}}^{\lambda}}_{kj-test}\\ \nu^{\tilde{\tilde{D}}^{\lambda}}_{kj-test}\end{matrix}\right\rangle$ *such that* $k \in I_{m_1}$ *and* $j \in I_n$.

Secondly, a new classifier named PFS-*k*NN employing the Minkowski metric of *pfs*-matrices is suggested (Algorithm 1). Pseudocode of the proposed PFS-*k*NN is presented in Algorithm 1. In Line 1, it obtains feature fuzzification of testing and training matrices required for feature picture fuzzification. In Line 2, the feature picture fuzzification of testing and training matrices utilizing their feature fuzzification versions. The aim herein is to make the data ready in a way that can be used in the distance calculation of *pfs*-matrices. In Lines 3–4, the *i*th testing *pfs*-matrix is constructed by extracting *i*th sample from the feature picture fuzzification of the testing matrix. Similarly, in Lines 5–6, the *j*th training *pfs*-matrix is constructed by extracting *j*th sample from the feature picture fuzzification of the training matrix. In Line 7, the distance between the *i*th test sample and the *j*th training sample is calculated utilizing the Minkowski metric over the *pfs*-matrices in accordance with Proposition 7, and Dm_{j1} is attained. In Line 9, *k*-nearest neighbor according to the matrix of picture fuzzy soft distances, namely Dm_{j1}, is determined. In Line 10, the most repetitive class label (predicted class label) of the determined *k*-nearest neighbor is obtained. In Line 11, the predicted class label, particularly diagnosis label in medical diagnosis, is assigned to the test sample. In Line 12–13, finally, the predicted label (class) matrix is created for the test queries.

Algorithm 1 PFS-*k*NN's pseudocode

Input: $(D_{train})_{m_1\times n}$, $C_{m_1\times 1}$, $(D_{test})_{m_2\times n}$, k, λ, and p
Output: $T'_{m_2\times 1}$
PFS-*k*NN(D_{train}, C, D_{test}, k, λ, p)
1: Calculate feature fuzzification of D_{test} and D_{train}, i.e., $\tilde{D}_{test}$ and $\tilde{D}_{train}$ ▷ See Definition 33 and 34
2: Calculate feature picture fuzzification of $\tilde{D}_{test}$ and $\tilde{D}_{train}$, i.e., $\tilde{\tilde{D}}^{\lambda}_{test}$ and $\tilde{\tilde{D}}^{\lambda}_{train}$ ▷ See Definition 35 and 36
3: **for** i from 1 to m_2 **do**
4: Calculate the testing *pfs*-matrix $\left[a_{ij}^{\tilde{\tilde{D}}^{\lambda}_{i-test}}\right]_{1\times n}$ employing $\tilde{\tilde{D}}^{\lambda}_{i-test}$
5: **for** j from 1 to m_1 **do**
6: Calculate the training *pfs*-matrix $\left[b_{ij}^{\tilde{\tilde{D}}^{\lambda 2}_{j-train}}\right]_{1\times n}$ employing $\tilde{\tilde{D}}^{\lambda}_{j-train}$
7: $Dm_{j1} \leftarrow d^p_M\left(\left[a_{ij}^{\tilde{\tilde{D}}^{\lambda 2}_{k-test}}\right], \left[b_{ij}^{\tilde{\tilde{D}}^{\lambda 2}_{k-train}}\right]\right)$ ▷ See Proposition 7
8: **end for**
9: Find k-nearest neighbor using $[Dm_{j1}]$
10: Find the most repetitive class label in the considered k-nearest neighbor
11: $t'_{k1} \leftarrow$ most repetitive class label (predicted class label)
12: **end for**
13: **return** $T'_{m_2\times 1}$

7. Application of PFS-*k*NN to Medical Diagnosis

In this section, firstly, details of the datasets used in simulation and the setting of the compared classifiers are provided according to the methodology presented in Figure 4. Afterward, the performance metrics for classification problems are introduced. Finally, simulation results for several medical datasets in UC Irvine Machine Learning Repository (UCI-MLR) [35] are presented, and the discussion of the results are provided.

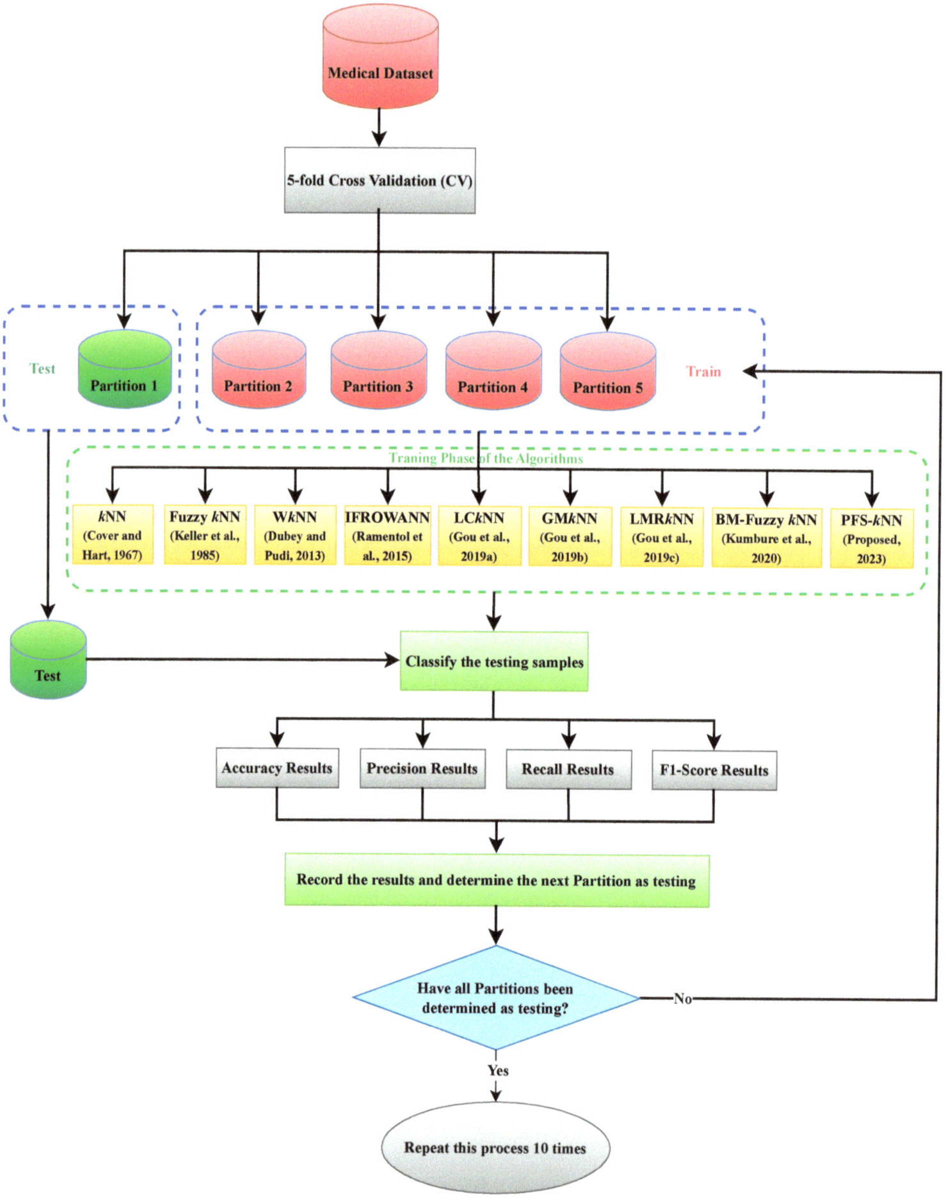

Figure 4. Simulation methodology of the present study via *k*NN-based classifiers [36–43].

7.1. Medical Datasets

One of the major motivations of this paper is the applicability of PFS-kNN in medical diagnosis. Therefore, the well-known and commonly used four medical diagnosis datasets in UCI-MLR [35] were chosen. This subsection offers descriptions of the following medical datasets employed in the simulation, provided in Table 1: "Breast Tissue", "Parkinsons[sic]", "Breast Cancer Wisconsin", and "Indian Liver".

Breast Tissue [35]: This dataset measured impedance frequencies: 15.625, 31.25, 62.5, 125, 250, 500, and 1000 KHz. The aforesaid frequencies were used to test the impedance of freshly removed breast tissue. The impedance spectrum is formed by these data plotted in the (actual, imaginary) plane, from which the features of the breast tissue are calculated. The dataset can be used to predict the categorization of either the original six classes or four classes by combining the mastopathy, fibro-adenoma, and glandular types whose distinction is unnecessary (they cannot be differentiated accurately).

Parkinsons[sic] [35]: The dataset consists of a range of biological voice measurements from 31 patients, 23 of whom have Parkinson's disease. Each column in the dataset stands for a separate vocal measure, and each row corresponds to one of these people's 195 voice recordings ("name" column). The major purpose of the data is to differentiate between healthy and Parkinson's disease patients by utilizing the "status" column, which is set to 0 for healthy and 1 for Parkinson's disease patients.

Breast Cancer Wisconsin (Diagnostic) [35]: This dataset uses a digitized picture of a fine needle aspirate (FNA) of a breast mass to construct characteristics. They describe the characteristics of the cell nuclei shown in the photograph. The separation plane mentioned above was created using the Multisurface approach-Tree (MSM-T), a classification approach that constructs a decision tree using linear programming [44]. To locate relevant features, an exhaustive search in the space of 1–4 features and 1–3 separation planes was utilized. The exact linear program used to obtain the separation plane in 3-dimensional space is described in [45].

Indian Liver Patient (ILPD) [35]: This data collection contains 416 records for liver patients and 167 for non-liver patients. The dataset was gathered in the northeastern state of Andhra Pradesh, India. The selector is a class label categorizing people (liver sick or not). This data collection has 441 male and 142 female patients records. Any patient over the age of 89 is labeled as "90".

Table 1. Properties of several medical datasets in UCI.

No.	Name	Instance Number	Attribute Number	Class Number	Imbalance
1	Breast Tissue	106	9	6	✓
2	Parkinsons[sic]	195	22	2	✓
3	Breast Cancer Wisconsin	569	30	2	✓
4	Indian Liver	583	10	2	✓

7.2. Quality Metrics for Classification Performance

In this subsection, the mathematical expressions of the quality metrics for binary and multi classification [46], i.e., Accuracy, Precision, Sensitivity (or Recall), and F1-Score, are presented to make a comparison of the considered classifiers. Assume that $D_{test} = \{y_1, y_2, \ldots, y_n\}$ is n queries to be classified, $T = \{t_1, t_2, \ldots, t_n\}$ is their ground truth class sets, $T' = \{t'_1, t'_2, \ldots, t'_n\}$ is their prediction class sets, and l is their number of the class. The quality metrics for binary classification are as follows:

$$\text{Accuracy}(T, T') := \frac{TP + TN}{TP + TN + FP + FN}$$

$$\text{Precision}(T, T') := \frac{TP}{TP + FP}$$

$$\text{Recall}(T,T') := \frac{TP}{TP+FN}$$

$$\text{F1-Score}(T,T') := \frac{2TP}{2TP+FP+FN}$$

where true positive (TP), true negative (TN), false positive (FP), and false negative (FN) are defined as follows:

$$TP := \left|\left\{y_j | 1 \in T_j \wedge 1 \in T'_j, 1 \le j \le l\right\}\right|$$

$$TN := \left|\left\{y_j | 0 \notin T_j \wedge 0 \notin T'_j, 1 \le j \le l\right\}\right|$$

$$FP := \left|\left\{y_j | 0 \notin T_j \wedge 1 \in T'_j, 1 \le j \le l\right\}\right|$$

$$FN := \left|\left\{y_j | 1 \in T_j \wedge 0 \notin T'_j, 1 \le j \le l\right\}\right|$$

such that $|.|$ stands for the cardinality of a set.

The performance metrics for multi classification are as follows:

$$\text{Accuracy}(T,T') := \frac{1}{l}\sum_{i=1}^{l}\frac{TP_i+TN_i}{TP_i+TN_i+FP_i+FN_i}$$

$$\text{Precision}(T,T') := \frac{1}{l}\sum_{i=1}^{l}\frac{TP_i}{TP_i+FP_i}$$

$$\text{Recall}(T,T') := \frac{1}{l}\sum_{i=1}^{l}\frac{TP_i}{TP_i+FN_i}$$

$$\text{F1-Score}(T,T') := \frac{1}{l}\sum_{i=1}^{l}\frac{2TP_i}{2TP_i+FP_i+FN_i}$$

where ith true positive (TP_i), ith true negative (TN_i), ith false positive (FP_i), and ith false negative (FN_i) for the class i are defined as follows:

$$TP_i := \left|\left\{x_j | i \in T_j \wedge i \in T'_j, 1 \le k \le l\right\}\right|$$

$$TN_i := \left|\left\{x_j | i \notin T_j \wedge i \notin T'_j, 1 \le k \le l\right\}\right|$$

$$FP_i := \left|\left\{x_j | i \notin T_j \wedge i \in T'_j, 1 \le k \le l\right\}\right|$$

$$FN_i := \left|\left\{x_j | i \in T_j \wedge i \notin T'_j, 1 \le k \le l\right\}\right|$$

such that $|.|$ stands for the cardinality of a set.

7.3. Diagnosis Results for Medical Diagnosis

In this subsection, the comparison of PFS-*k*NN with the well-known and state-of-the-art *k*NN-based classifiers (Table 2), i.e., *k*NN [36], Fuzzy *k*NN [37], W*k*NN [38], IFROWANN [39], LC*k*NN [40], GM*k*NN [41], LMR*k*NN [42], and BM-Fuzzy *k*NN [43], is performed by employing a computer with I(R)Core(TM) I5-4200H CPU@2.80GHz and 8 GB RAM and MATLAB R2021b software. Random 10 runs rely on the five-fold cross-validation (CV) [47,48], generating the classifiers' performance results in which each CV, of which four parts are selected for training and the other for testing (for more details about CV, see [47]), randomly split the considered dataset into five parts. Table 3 presents the average Accuracy, Precision, Recall, and F1-Score results of PFS-*k*NN, *k*NN, Fuzzy *k*NN, W*k*NN, IFROWANN, LC*k*NN, GM*k*NN, LMR*k*NN, and BM-Fuzzy *k*NN for the datasets.

Table 2. Details of the *k*NN-based classifier.

Ref.	Year	Classifier	Number of Nearest Neigbors		Employed-Concept				Distance	Inverse Distance	Class Distribution Impact	Class Imbalance Impact
			Fixed	Adaptive	Crisp	Fuzzy Set	*fr*-Set	*pfs*-Matrix				
[36]	1967	*k*NN	✓		✓				✓			
[37]	1985	Fuzzy *k*NN	✓			✓				✓		
[38]	2013	W*k*NN	✓		✓					✓	✓	
[39]	2015	IFROWANN		✓			✓		✓			✓
[40]	2019	LC*k*NN	✓		✓				✓			
[41]	2019	GM*k*NN	✓						✓		✓	
[42]	2019	LMR*k*NN	✓						✓		✓	
[43]	2020	BM-Fuzzy *k*NN	✓			✓				✓		
Proposed	2023	PFS-*k*NN	✓					✓	✓			

Table 3. Diagnosis performance results of the *k*NN-based classifiers.

Medical Datasets	Classifiers	Accuracy	Precision	Recall	F1-Score
Breast Tissue	*k*NN	86.59	61.12	57.98	62.94
	Fuzzy *k*NN	85.34	59.32	54.39	59.18
	W*k*NN	86.72	61.24	58.59	62.87
	IFROWANN	85.65	64.38	56.02	67.18
	LC*k*NN	75.37	20.07	23.89	40.15
	GM*k*NN	88.45	**66.72**	**63.55**	66.45
	LMR*k*NN	84.09	54.66	51.62	58.62
	BM-Fuzzy *k*NN	85.57	60.82	57.79	62.09
	PFS-*k*NN	**88.51**	65.34	60.84	**67.95**
Parkinsons[sic]	*k*NN	85.03	74.57	62.16	66.53
	Fuzzy *k*NN	84.92	73.14	64.49	67.23
	W*k*NN	84.92	73.14	64.49	67.23
	IFROWANN	68.26	44.18	**100**	61.08
	LC*k*NN	68.05	42.07	68.80	51.38
	GM*k*NN	83.85	68.53	68.96	67.31
	LMR*k*NN	68.97	42.33	70.82	52.64
	BM-Fuzzy *k*NN	78.10	55.91	63.20	58.42
	PFS-*k*NN	**91.18**	**89.38**	73.51	**79.80**
Breast Cancer	*k*NN	92.90	**92.92**	87.79	90.18
	Fuzzy *k*NN	92.46	92.29	87.18	89.57
	W*k*NN	92.46	92.29	87.18	89.57
	IFROWANN	78.07	63.25	**99.53**	77.27
	LC*k*NN	79.03	67.13	87.98	75.98
	GM*k*NN	93.09	91.60	89.91	90.64
	LMR*k*NN	86.82	81.50	83.85	82.54
	BM-Fuzzy *k*NN	91.95	91.00	87.27	88.97
	PFS-*k*NN	**93.59**	90.18	93.17	**91.56**
Indian Liver	*k*NN	66.55	75.08	79.55	77.22
	Fuzzy *k*NN	65.97	76.15	76.20	76.12
	W*k*NN	65.97	76.15	76.20	76.12
	IFROWANN	30.21	**100**	2.19	4.24
	LC*k*NN	67.07	75.40	**79.96**	77.58
	GM*k*NN	67.36	77.72	76.16	76.87
	LMR*k*NN	60.93	77.33	64.04	69.97
	BM-Fuzzy *k*NN	65.73	75.88	76.28	76.01
	PFS-*k*NN	**67.46**	75.57	77.98	**77.69**

Accuracy, Precision, Recall, and F1-Score results are offered in percentage. The best results are shown in bold.

Based on the results obtained from Accuracy, it is evident that PFS-*k*NN surpasses all other *k*NN-based classifiers that were compared. This is similarly observed when it comes to F1-Score results. However, it should be noted that the proposed approach has lower Precision and Recall results when compared to the other classifiers. Nevertheless, the results are still close to the highest score in general.

These simulation results manifest that *pfs*-matrices and PFS-*k*NN can model uncertainty and real-world problems, such as medical diagnosis and machine learning. It is important to note that applying these models can significantly impact the accuracy of such issues, leading to more reliable and effective solutions. Therefore, using PFS-*k*NN and *pfs*-matrices is recommended when dealing with similar problems.

In this study, we evaluated the Accuracy performance values of various algorithms on four medical datasets. To obtain a comprehensive understanding of the algorithms' performance, we ran each algorithm 50 times (10 times five-fold cross-validation) and plotted the results as box plots in Figure 5.

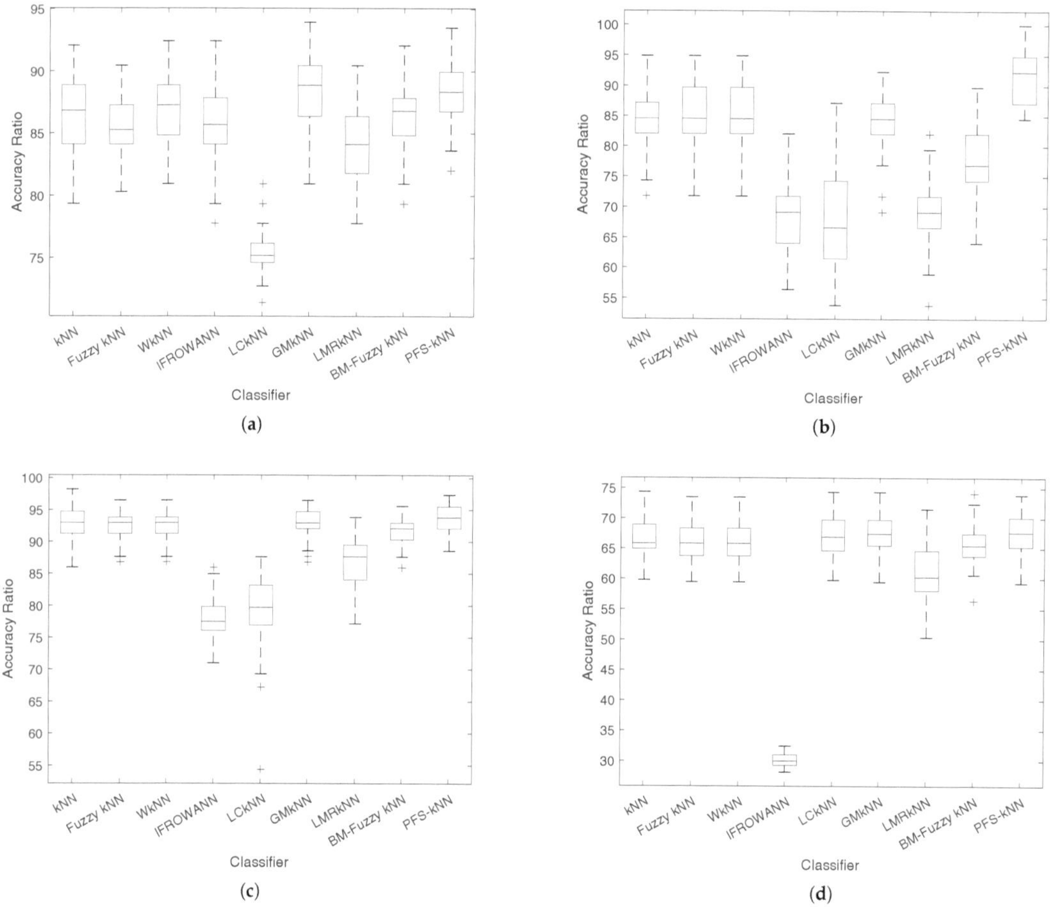

Figure 5. Box plot of Accuracy results of 50 runs for the classifiers: (**a**) Breast Tissue, (**b**) Parkinson's, (**c**) Breast Cancer, (**d**) Indian Liver.

From the visual results in Figure 5a–d, we can observe that PFS-*k*NN outperforms the other algorithms, with the highest performance value and a performance value distribution that is close to normal distribution. This indicates that PFS-*k*NN is a reliable algorithm for these medical datasets.

Similarly, in Figure 5b, we see that PFS-*k*NN produces the highest performance results, with the 50 performance values almost following a normal distribution. Moreover, the distance between quartiles is relatively low, suggesting that PFS-*k*NN is consistent in performance.

Overall, the box plots in Figure 5 demonstrate that PFS-*k*NN is a superior algorithm compared to the others evaluated in this study, and it is a promising option for medical data analysis.

8. Discussion on PFS-*k*NN in Medical Diagnosis and Supervised Learning

This section discusses the significance of the proposed PFS-*k*NN classifier's performance on medical diagnosis datasets herein.

Accuracy and F1-Score Dominance:The achievement of PFS-*k*NN outperforming all other *k*NN-based classifiers in terms of Accuracy and F1-Score is remarkable. Accuracy measures the overall correctness of the classifier's predictions, while the F1-Score considers both precision and recall. These metrics are crucial in medical diagnosis, where accurately identifying and classifying medical conditions can be a life-or-death matter. The superior performance of PFS-*k*NN in these areas indicates its potential as a valuable tool for enhancing the accuracy and effectiveness of medical diagnoses.

Precision and Recall Trade-Off: While PFS-*k*NN performs well in terms of Accuracy and F1-Score, it is observed to have slightly lower Precision and Recall compared to other classifiers. Precision measures the ratio of correctly predicted positive cases to all predicted positive cases, while Recall measures the ratio of correctly predicted positive cases to all actual positive cases. In medical diagnosis, Precision is vital for minimizing false positive errors, and Recall is crucial for reducing false negatives. The slightly lower Precision and Recall values suggest that PFS-*k*NN might be more cautious when making positive predictions, possibly to reduce false positive errors. However, the results are still close to the highest scores overall, indicating a reasonable balance between these metrics.

Modeling Uncertainty and Real-World Problems: Addressing the concept of *pfs*-matrices and their role in modeling uncertainty in practical scenarios, such as medical diagnosis, is significant. Medical diagnosis frequently deals with intricate and uncertain data, and the capability of PFS-*k*NN to model uncertainty is a valuable advantage. This indicates that the classifier is flexible and resilient in handling various demanding datasets, making it suitable for real-world applications where data are inherently uncertain and noisy.

Impact on Accuracy and Reliability: The practical importance of using PFS-*k*NN and *pfs*-matrices in areas, such as medical diagnosis mentioned in the previous section indicates that they can notably affect accuracy. By enhancing accuracy in medical diagnosis, they can provide more dependable and efficient solutions, decrease misdiagnosis rates, and improve patient outcomes. This emphasizes the potential of PFS-*k*NN to make a valuable contribution to the healthcare industry, where precision and accuracy are crucial.

Recommendation for Similar Problems: The suggestion to utilize PFS-*k*NN and *pfs*-matrices as a conclusion highlights the belief in the effectiveness of this approach. This indicates that the advantages demonstrated in the research are not restricted to the dataset employed for assessment but can also apply to other medical diagnosis scenarios or related fields.

In brief, the performance of the proposed PFS-*k*NN classifier on medical diagnosis datasets, assessed using Minkowski metrics over *pfs*-matrices, demonstrates its potential to enhance the accuracy and dependability of medical diagnoses. While there are some trade-offs in Precision and Recall, the overall superiority in Accuracy and F1-Score, coupled with its capability to model uncertainty, positions PFS-*k*NN as a promising tool for improving healthcare and addressing real-world challenges in supervised learning.

9. Conclusions

This paper redefined the idea of *pfs*-matrices, and their fundamental properties were examined extensively. Afterward, distance measures of *pfs*-matrices were introduced. Then, PFS-*k*NN, via the aforementioned distance measures, was suggested and applied to medical diagnosis. The results manifested that the concept of *pfs*-matrices and the proposed PFS-*k*NN approach can model uncertainty and real-world problems such as medical diagnosis.

The current study, which focuses on soft sets, has significantly contributed to the literature in both theoretical and practical aspects. This study has introduced three crucial additions that redefine the mathematics underlying *pfs*-matrices and proposed new distance measures between *pfs*-matrices and PFS-*k*NN. By doing so, this paper has expanded the understanding of this field and enhanced its applicability in real-world problems. In addition, this research has gained prominence in the literature due to its innovative contributions, which have opened up new avenues for further exploration and research in the field.

In future works, there is potential for further investigation into the algebraic and topological structures of *pfs*-matrices and the exploration of new distance and similarity measures. While *pfs*-matrices have proven effective in addressing specific problems, it is essential to acknowledge their limitations when dealing with picture fuzzy parameters. To overcome this issue, research can be conducted on several related concepts, such as intuitionistic fuzzy parameterized intuitionistic fuzzy soft matrices (*ifpifs*-matrices) [49,50], aggregation operators of *pfs*-matrices [51,52], picture fuzzy parameterized picture fuzzy soft sets (*pfppfs*-sets) [53], and picture fuzzy parameterized picture fuzzy soft matrices (*pfppfs*-matrices). Additionally, interval-valued intuitionistic fuzzy parameterized interval-valued intuitionistic fuzzy soft sets (*d*-sets) [4] and interval-valued intuitionistic fuzzy parameterized interval-valued intuitionistic fuzzy soft matrices (*d*-matrices) [5] are other related concepts that may be worth exploring. We can better understand their potential applications and limitations by studying and applying these concepts to different real-world problems. For instance, different real-world problems, such as trend prediction of component stock [54], remote sensing image fusion [55], and Landsat image fusion [56] can be investigated, and the applications of *pfs*-matrices to them can be focused.

Funding: This research received no external funding.

Data Availability Statement: The datasets employed and analyzed during the present study are available from the UCI-MLR.

Conflicts of Interest: The author declares no conflict of interest.

References

1. Zadeh, L.A. Fuzzy Sets. *Inf. Control* **1965**, *8*, 338–353. [CrossRef]
2. Memiş, S.; Enginoğlu, S.; Erkan, U. Numerical Data Classification via Distance-Based Similarity Measures of Fuzzy Parameterized Fuzzy Soft Matrices. *IEEE Access* **2021**, *9*, 88583–88601. [CrossRef]
3. Memiş, S.; Enginoğlu, S.; Erkan, U. Fuzzy Parameterized Fuzzy Soft *k*-Nearest Neighbor Classifier. *Neuroomputing* **2022**, *500*, 351–378. [CrossRef]
4. Aydın, T.; Enginoğlu, S. Interval-Valued Intuitionistic Fuzzy Parameterized Interval-Valued Intuitionistic Fuzzy Soft Sets and Their Application in Decision-Making. *J. Ambient. Intell. Humaniz. Comput.* **2021**, *12*, 1541–1558. [CrossRef]
5. Aydın, T.; Enginoğlu, S. Interval-Valued Intuitionistic Fuzzy Parameterized Interval-Valued Intuitionistic Fuzzy Soft Matrices and Their Application to Performance-Based Value Assignment to Noise-Removal Filters. *Comput. Appl. Math.* **2022**, *41*, 192. [CrossRef]
6. Mushrif, M.M.; Senqupta, S.; Ray, A.K. Texture Classification Using a Novel, Soft-Set Theory Based Classification Algorithm. In Proceedings of the 7th Asian Conference on Computer Vision, Hyderabad, India, 13–16 January 2006; pp. 246–254.
7. Çağman, N.; Enginoğlu, S. Soft Matrix Theory and Its Decision Making. *Comput. Math. Appl.* **2010**, *59*, 3308–3314. [CrossRef]
8. Zimmermann, H.J., *Fuzzy Set Theory and Its Applications*; Springer Science+Business Media: New York, NY, USA, 2011.
9. Çağman, N.; Enginoğlu, S. Fuzzy Soft Matrix Theory and Its Application in Decision Making. *Iran. J. Fuzzy Syst.* **2012**, *9*, 109–119.
10. Atanassov, K.T. Intuitionistic Fuzzy Sets. *Fuzzy Sets Syst.* **1986**, *20*, 87–96. [CrossRef]
11. Molodtsov, D. Soft Set Theory-First Results. *Comput. Math. Appl.* **1999**, *37*, 19–31. [CrossRef]

12. Maji, P.K.; Biswas, R.; Roy, A.R. Fuzzy Soft Sets. *J. Fuzzy Math.* **2001**, *9*, 589–602.
13. Maji, P.K.; Biswas, R.; Roy, A.R. Intuitionistic Fuzzy Soft Sets. *J. Fuzzy Math.* **2001**, *9*, 677–692.
14. Chetia, B.; Das, P.K. Some Results of Intuitionistic Fuzzy Soft Matrix Theory. *Adv. Appl. Sci. Res.* **2012**, *3*, 412–423.
15. Yager, R.R. Pythagorean Fuzzy Subsets. In Proceedings of the 2013 Joint IFSA World Congress and NAFIPS Annual Meeting (IFSA/NAFIPS) Conference, Edmonton, AB, Canada, 25–29 May 2021; pp. 57–61.
16. Cuong, B.C. Picture Fuzzy Sets. *J. Comput. Sci. Cybern.* **2014**, *30*, 409–420.
17. Peng, X.; Yang, Y.; Song, J.; Jiang, Y. Pythagorean Fuzzy Soft Set and Its Application. *Comput. Eng.* **2015**, *41*, 224–229.
18. Yang, Y.; Liang, C.; Ji, S.; Liu, T. Adjustable Soft Discernibility Matrix Based on Picture Fuzzy Soft Sets and Its Applications in Decision Making. *J. Intell. Fuzzy Syst.* **2015**, *29*, 1711–1722. [CrossRef]
19. Guleria, A.; Bajaj, R.K. On Pythagorean Fuzzy Soft Matrices, Operations and Their Applications in Decision Making and Medical Diagnosis. *Soft Comput.* **2018**, *23*, 7889–7900. [CrossRef]
20. Arikrishnan, A.; Sriram, S. Algebraic Operations on Picture Fuzzy Soft Matrices. *Adv. Math. Sci. J.* **2020**, *9*, 6349–6358. [CrossRef]
21. Memiş, S. A Study on Picture Fuzzy Sets. In Proceedings of the 7th IFS and Contemporary Mathematics Conference, Mersin, Turkey, 25–29 May 2021; pp. 125–132.
22. Memiş, S. Another View on Picture Fuzzy Soft Sets and Their Product Operations with Soft Decision-Making. *J. New Theory* **2022**, *2022*, 1–13. [CrossRef]
23. Atanassov, K.T., *On Intuitionistic Fuzzy Sets Theory*; Springer: Berlin/Heidelberg, Germany, 2012.
24. Naeem, K.; Memiş, S. Picture Fuzzy Soft σ-Algebra and Picture Fuzzy Soft Measure and Their Applications to Multi-Criteria Decision-Making. *Granul. Comput.* **2023**, *8*, 397–410. [CrossRef]
25. Thao, N.X.; Dinh, N.V. Rough Picture Fuzzy Set and Picture Fuzzy Topologies. *J. Comput. Sci. Cybern.* **2015**, *31*, 245–253. [CrossRef]
26. Sezgin, A. A New Approach to Semigroup Theory I: Soft Union Semigroups, Ideals and Bi-Ideals. *Algebra Lett.* **2016**, *2016*, 3.
27. Jin, J.; Garg, H.; You, T. Generalized Picture Fuzzy Distance and Similarity Measures on the Complete Lattice and Their Applications. *Expert Syst. Appl.* **2023**, *220*, 119710. [CrossRef]
28. Wang, T.; Wu, X.; Garg, H.; Liu, Q.; Chen, G. A Prospect Theory-Based MABAC Algorithm with Novel Similarity Measures and Interactional Operations for Picture Fuzzy Sets and Its Applications. *Eng. Appl. Artif. Intell.* **2023**, *126*, 106787. [CrossRef]
29. Khan, M.J.; Kumam, P.; Liu, P.; Kumam, W.; Rehman, H. An Adjustable Weighted Soft Discernibility Matrix Based on Generalized Picture Fuzzy Soft Set and Its Applications in Decision Making. *J. Intell. Fuzzy Syst.* **2020**, *38*, 2103–2118. [CrossRef]
30. Memiş, S.; Enginoğlu, S.; Erkan, U. A Classification Method in Machine Learning Based on Soft Decision-Making via Fuzzy Parameterized Fuzzy Soft Matrices. *Soft Comput.* **2022**, *26*, 1165–1180. [CrossRef]
31. Memiş, S.; Enginoğlu, S.; Erkan, U. A New Classification Method Using Soft Decision-Making Based on An Aggregation Operator of Fuzzy Parameterized Fuzzy Soft Matrices. *Turk. J. Electr. Eng. Comput. Sci.* **2022**, *30*, 871–890. [CrossRef]
32. Sahu, R.; Dash, S.R.; Das, S. Career Selection of Students Using Hybridized Distance Measure Based on Picture Fuzzy Set and Rough Set Theory. *Decis. Mak. Appl. Manag. Eng.* **2021**, *4*, 104–126. [CrossRef]
33. Singh, A.; Kumar, S. Picture Fuzzy Set and Quality Function Deployment Approach Based Novel Framework for Multi-Criteria Group Decision Making Method. *Eng. Appl. Artif. Intell.* **2021**, *104*, 104395. [CrossRef]
34. Lu, H.; Khalil, A.M.; Alharbi, W.; El-Gayar, M.A. A New Type of Generalized Picture Fuzzy Soft Set and Its Application in Decision Making. *J. Intell. Fuzzy Syst.* **2021**, *40*, 12459–12475. [CrossRef]
35. Dua, D.; Graff, C. UCI Machine Learning Repository. 2019. Available online: https://archive.ics.uci.edu/ (accessed on 30 May 2023).
36. Cover, T.M.; Hart, P.E. Nearest Neighbor Pattern Classification. *IEEE Trans. Inf. Theory* **1967**, *13*, 21–27. [CrossRef]
37. Keller, J.M.; Gray, M.R.; Givens, J.A. A Fuzzy K-Nearest Neighbor Algorithm. *IEEE Trans. Syst. Man Cybern.* **1985**, *15*, 580–585. [CrossRef]
38. Dubey, H.; Pudi, V. Class Based Weighted *k*-Nearest Neighbor over Imbalance Dataset. In Proceedings of the 17th Pacific-Asia Conference on Advances in Knowledge Discovery and Data Mining, Gold Coast, Australia, 14–17 April 2013; pp. 305–316.
39. Ramentol, E.; Vluymans, S.; Verbiest, N.; Caballero, Y.; Bello, R.; Cornelis, C.; Herrera, F. IFROWANN: Imbalanced Fuzzy-Rough Ordered Weighted Average Nearest Neighbor Classification. *IEEE Trans. Fuzzy Syst.* **2015**, *23*, 1622–1636. [CrossRef]
40. Gou, J.; Qiu, W.; Yi, Z.; Shen, X.; Zhan, Y.; Ou, W. Locality Constrained Representation-Based K-Nearest Neighbor Classification. *Knowl.-Based Syst.* **2019**, *167*, 38–52. [CrossRef]
41. Gou, J.; Ma, H.; Ou, W.; Zheng, S.; Rao, Y.; Yang, H. A Generalized Mean Distance-Based k-Nearest Neighbor Classifier. *Expert Syst. Appl.* **2019**, *115*, 356–372. [CrossRef]
42. Gou, J.; Qiu, W.; Yi, Z.; Xu, Y.; Mao, Q.; Zhan, Y. A Local Mean Representation-Based k-Nearest Neighbor Classifier. *ACM Trans. Intell. Syst. Technol.* **2019**, *10*, 29:1–29:25. [CrossRef]
43. Kumbure, M.M.; Luukka, P.; Collan, M. A New Fuzzy k-Nearest Neighbor Classifier Based on the Bonferroni mean. *Pattern Recognit. Lett.* **2020**, *140*, 172–178. [CrossRef]
44. Bennett, K.P. *Decision Tree Construction Via Linear Programming*; Technical Report; University of Wisconsin-Madison Department of Computer Sciences: Madison, WI, USA, 1992.
45. Bennett, K.P.; Mangasarian, O.L. Robust Linear Programming Discrimination of Two Linearly Inseparable Sets. *Optim. Methods Softw.* **2006**, *1*, 23–34. [CrossRef]

46. Fawcett, T. An Introduction to ROC Analysis. *Pattern Recognit. Lett.* **2006**, *27*, 861–874. [CrossRef]
47. Stone, M. Cross-Validatory Choice and Assessment of Statistical Predictions. *J. R. Stat. Soc. Ser. B (Methodol.)* **1974**, *36*, 111–147. [CrossRef]
48. Erkan, U. A Precise and Stable Machine Learning Algorithm: Eigenvalue Classification (EigenClass). *Neural Comput. Appl.* **2021**, *33*, 5381–5392. [CrossRef]
49. Enginoğlu, S.; Arslan, B. Intuitionistic Fuzzy Parameterized Intuitionistic Fuzzy Soft Matrices and Their Application in Decision-Making. *Comput. Appl. Math.* **2020**, *39*, 325. [CrossRef]
50. Memiş, S.; Arslan, B.; Aydın, T.; Enginoğlu, S.; Camcı, Ç. Distance and Similarity Measures of Intuitionistic Fuzzy Parameterized Intuitionistic Fuzzy Soft Matrices and Their Applications to Data Classification in Supervised Learning. *Axioms* **2023**, *12*, 463. [CrossRef]
51. Dhumras, H.; Bajaj, R.K. Modified EDAS Method for MCDM in Robotic Agrifarming with Picture Fuzzy Soft Dombi Aggregation Operators. *Soft Comput.* **2023**, *27*, 5077–5098. [CrossRef]
52. Mahmood, T.; Ali, Z.; Naeem, M. Aggregation Operators and CRITIC-VIKOR Method for Confidence Complex q-Rung Orthopair Normal Fuzzy Information and Their Applications. *CAAI Trans. Intell. Technol.* **2023**, *8*, 40–63. [CrossRef]
53. Memiş, S. Picture Fuzzy Parameterized Picture Fuzzy Soft Sets and Their Application in a Performance-Based Value Assignment Problem to Salt-and-Pepper Noise Removal Filters. *Int. J. Fuzzy Syst.* **2023**, *2023*, 1–15.
54. Li, P.; Gu, H.; Yin, L.; Li, B. Research on Trend Prediction of Component Stock in Fuzzy Time Series Based on Deep Forest. *CAAI Trans. Intell. Technol.* **2022**, *7*, 617–626. [CrossRef]
55. Singh, D.; Kaur, M.; Singh, H. Remote Sensing Image Fusion Using Fuzzy Logic and Gyrator Transform. *Remote. Sens. Lett.* **2018**, *9*, 5077–5098. [CrossRef]
56. Singh, D.; Garg, D.; Pannu, H.S. Efficient Landsat Image Fusion Using Fuzzy and Stationary Discrete Wavelet Transform. *Imaging Sci. J.* **2017**, *65*, 108–114. [CrossRef]

electronics

MDPI

Article

Meteorological Variables Forecasting System Using Machine Learning and Open-Source Software

Jenny Aracely Segovia *, Jonathan Fernando Toaquiza *, Jacqueline Rosario Llanos * and David Raimundo Rivas

Department of Electrical and Electronic Engineering, Universidad de las Fuerzas Armadas (ESPE), Sangolquí 171103, Ecuador

* Correspondence: jasegovia4@espe.edu.ec (J.A.S.); tcjonathan@espe.edu.ec (J.F.T.); jdllanos1@espe.edu.ec (J.R.L.)

Abstract: The techniques for forecasting meteorological variables are highly studied since prior knowledge of them allows for the efficient management of renewable energies, and also for other applications of science such as agriculture, health, engineering, energy, etc. In this research, the design, implementation, and comparison of forecasting models for meteorological variables have been performed using different Machine Learning techniques as part of Python open-source software. The techniques implemented include multiple linear regression, polynomial regression, random forest, decision tree, XGBoost, and multilayer perceptron neural network (MLP). To identify the best technique, the mean square error (RMSE), mean absolute percentage error (MAPE), mean absolute error (MAE), and coefficient of determination (R^2) are used as evaluation metrics. The most efficient techniques depend on the variable to be forecasting, however, it is noted that for most of them, random forest and XGBoost techniques present better performance. For temperature, the best performing technique was Random Forest with an R^2 of 0.8631, MAE of 0.4728 °C, MAPE of 2.73%, and RMSE of 0.6621 °C; for relative humidity, was Random Forest with an R^2 of 0.8583, MAE of 2.1380RH, MAPE of 2.50% and RMSE of 2.9003 RH; for solar radiation, was Random Forest with an R^2 of 0.7333, MAE of 65.8105 W/m^2, and RMSE of 105.9141 W/m^2; and for wind speed, was Random Forest with an R^2 of 0.3660, MAE of 0.1097 m/s, and RMSE of 0.2136 m/s.

Keywords: machine learning; forecasting models; meteorological variables; Python

Citation: Segovia, J.A.; Toaquiza, J.F.; Llanos, J.R.; Rivas, D.R. Meteorological Variables Forecasting System Using Machine Learning and Open-Source Software. *Electronics* **2023**, *12*, 1007. https://doi.org/10.3390/electronics12041007

Academic Editor: Grzegorz Dudek

Received: 4 January 2023
Revised: 4 February 2023
Accepted: 6 February 2023
Published: 17 February 2023

1. Introduction

Since the 17th century, meteorological variables have been of great interest throughout history, with the creation of the first instruments for measuring meteorological variables aiming to accurately predict the weather. For this purpose, mathematical and statistical methods and computer programs are used, most of which are of a non-linear nature [1]. Nowadays, climatic conditions change under various influences. For example, atmospheric pollution is increasing, so climate change is occurring and threatening the planet [2], which is why the measurement of meteorological variables has grown in importance as the information provided by the meteorological stations is important for monitoring climate change [3].

Climate is defined by the grouping of meteorological phenomena that are related to each other; although each of them is studied separately, it must be taken into account that a change in one produces a variation in the others [4]. The actual weather is characterised by the wind, temperature, and humidity variables forced by radiative fluxes and surface latent and sensible heat fluxes. The local climate usually denotes the mean state of the atmosphere over a 20–30-year period for a given location and day (or season) of the year. For this reason, meteorological variables are usually modeled by means of computational, numerical, and statistical techniques, most of which are nonlinear [5]. Forecasting certain climatic variables is a great challenge due to the variable behavior of the climate, which makes it impossible to optimally manage renewable energies and obtain a greater benefit from them.

There are multiple scientific studies of modeling and prediction in order to forecast future conditions of phenomena in various fields; among the most prominent are ARIMA, Chaos Theory, and Neural Networks [6]. Forecasting models have evolved in recent decades, from smart systems with formal rules and logical theories, to the emergence of artificial intelligence techniques that allow us to propose alternatives in the treatment of information [7].

Currently, forecasting models have a high impact and are used for several applications, such as management of energy units for renewable resources microgrids [8,9], load estimation methods for isolated communities that do not receive energy or only receive it for a limited time each day [10,11], the operation of energy systems [12,13], in agriculture to predict the water consumption of plants and plan the irrigation sheet [14], in agriculture 4.0 for the prediction of variables that affect the quality of crops, for micronutrient analysis and prediction of soil chemical parameters [15], optimization of agricultural procedures and increasing productivity in the field, forecasting of SPI and Meteorological Drought Based on the Artificial Neural Network and M5P Model Tree [16], and in controllers based on forecasting models and predictive controllers. They are also used in the health field to predict the solar radiation index and to obtain a correct assessment in people with skin cancer [17], therefore, all the applications mentioned above need forecasting models that have the lowest error rate for their effective operation.

Having a forecasting model system is costly because computer packages are used in which licensing costs can be significant. On the other hand, free software is an option to reduce costs. This research proposes a system based on free software (Python), which is currently used at industrial level for its reliability, for example in applications such as the following: Advanced Time Series: Application of Neural Networks for Time Series Forecasting [18], Machine Learning in Python: main developments and technological trends in data science, Machine Learning and artificial intelligence [19], Development of an smart tool focused on artificial vision and neural networks for weed recognition in rice plantations, using Python programming language [20], etc.

In this research, different prediction techniques were evaluated and compared—among them, multiple linear regression, polynomial regression, random forest, decision tree, XGBoost, and multilayer perceptron neural network—in order to identify the best performing strategy, using evaluation metrics such as the root mean square error (RMSE) and the coefficient of determination (R^2). The variables to be predicted are temperature, relative humidity, solar radiation, and wind speed, from data taken from the weather station located in Ecuador, Tungurahua province, Baños. The predicted variables will be the inputs for a smart irrigation system and used for an energy management system of a microgrid based on predictive control, therefore, models with high approximation to online measurements are required.

The contributions of this work are as follows: (i) To design, validate, and compare different machine learning techniques, and with them select the best technique that adapts to climate variables for agriculture and energy applications, (ii) To develop a forecast system for climate variables of low cost based in free software (Python), (iii) To generate forecasting models that can be replicated for other types of variables applied to smart control systems based on forecasting models.

2. Design of Forecasting Models for Meteorological Variables

This section describes the prediction techniques used and their design. In this research, the following meteorological variables are studied and predicted: temperature, relative humidity, wind speed, and solar radiation.

The techniques designed, evaluated, and compared are the following: multiple linear regression, polynomial regression, random forest, decision tree, XGBoost, and neural network—multilayer perceptron. To obtain the forecast of meteorological variables, the design methodology shown in Figure 1 is implemented.

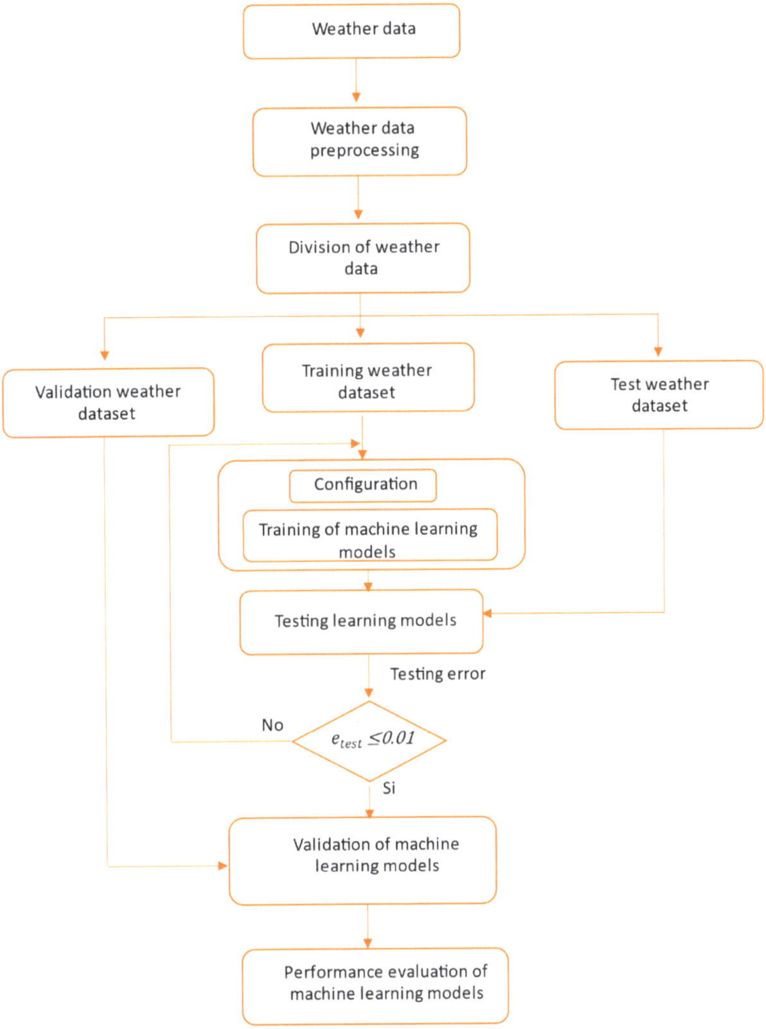

Figure 1. Flowchart of the methodology used to obtain forecasting models for meteorological variables.

2.1. Obtaining the Database

For the implementation of the forecasting models, information was obtained from the page of the Tungurahua hydrometeorological network, where there are several meteorological stations, including the Baños family park, located in Ecuador, Tungurahua province, Baños, coordinates $X = 9,845,439$, $Y = 791,471$ that counts the parameters of precipitation (mm), temperature (°C), relative humidity (%), wind speed (m/s), wind direction (°), solar radiation (W/m^2), and evapotranspiration (mm). For the design of the models, only the values of temperature, solar radiation, relative humidity, and wind speed were taken, since after a previous analysis of correlation between meteorological variables, the variables with lower correlation with the variable to be predicted are discarded. It is important to note that the values of temperature, solar radiation (net solar radiation at surface), and relative humidity were measured at a distance of 2 m, while the wind speed was measured at 10 m.

2.2. Data Preprocessing

From the database obtained, 1 year of information was available (from 23 July 2021 to 15 June 2022), which was preprocessed to take data every 5 min for each variable (temperature, relative humidity, wind speed, and solar radiation). To make a forecast, it is important to verify that there are no missing data in the measurements or to implement a data filling method; in this case, a Python algorithm was implemented, which calculates the average of the existing list of data and automatically fills in the missing data.

2.3. Dataset Division

To verify that the models work correctly, the available database is divided into three groups: training set, test set, and validation set. As its name indicates, the first one will be used to train the forecasting models, the second one will be used to evaluate the test set, and the third one to validate each of the implemented models [17,21].

After data preprocessing, a total of 93,780 data were obtained for each variable, where 80% of the database (75,024 data) is used to train the models, 20% (18,756 data) to test the models, and 2 days (576 data) were used for the validation of the models.

2.4. Design of the Forecasting Models

2.4.1. Multiple Linear Regression

It is a technique that allows modeling the relationship between a continuous variable and one or more independent variables by adjusting a linear equation. It is called simple linear regression when there is one independent variable, and if there is more than one, it is called multiple linear regression. In this context, the modeled variables are called dependent or response variables (y); and the independent variables are called regressors, predictors, or features (X) [22]. Multiple linear regression is defined by Equation (1)

$$y = a + b_1 X_1 + b_2 X_2 + \cdots + b_n X_n \quad (1)$$

where: $X_1, X_2, \ldots X_n$: are the predictor or independent variables, $b_1, b_2, \ldots b_n$: coefficients of the predictor variables, a : constant of the relationship between the dependent and independent variable, and y : predicted or dependent variable.

After performing different heuristic tests and using sensitivity analysis for this forecasting technique, it is deduced that the best parameters for tuning are those described in Table 1.

Table 1. Tuning parameters for the multiple linear regression techniques.

Multiple Linear Regression	
Predicted Variable	**Inputs Variables**
Temperature	Solar radiation, relative humidity, wind speed
Solar radiation	Temperature, relative humidity, wind speed
Wind speed	Temperature, solar radiation, relative humidity
Relative Humidity	Temperature, solar radiation, wind speed

2.4.2. Polynomial Regression

A linear regression with polynomial attributes that uses the relationship between the dependent (y) and independent (X) variables to find the best way to draw a line through the data points. This technique is used when the data are more complex than a simple straight line [23], and is defined by Equation (2).

$$y = a + b_1 X_i + b_2 X_i{}^2 + b_3 X_i{}^3 + \ldots + b_n X_i{}^n \quad (2)$$

where: $X_1, X_2, \ldots X_n$: are the predictor or independent variables, $b_1, b_2, \ldots b_n$: coefficients of the predictor variables, a : constant of the relationship between the dependent and independent variable, and y : predicted or dependent variable.

After performing different heuristic tests and using sensitivity analysis for this forecasting technique, it is deduced that the best parameters for tuning are those described in Table 2.

Table 2. Tuning parameters for polynomial regression technique.

Polynomial Regression		
Predicted Variable	**Inputs Variables**	**Degree of the Polynomial**
Temperature	Solar radiation, relative humidity, wind speed	4
Solar radiation	Temperature, relative humidity, wind speed	5
Wind speed	Temperature, solar radiation, relative humidity	6
Relative Humidity	Temperature, solar radiation, wind speed	4

2.4.3. Decision Tree

Values by learning decision rules derived from features and can be used for classification, regression, and multi-output tasks. Decision trees work by dividing the feature space into several simple rectangular regions, divided by parallel divisions of axes. To obtain a prediction, the mean or mode of the responses of the training observations, within the partition to which the new observation belongs, is used [23]. This is defined by Equation (3).

$$G_i = 1 - \sum_{k=1}^{m} (P_{i,k})^2 \tag{3}$$

where: $P_{i,k}$: is the radio of class k instances among the training instances in the ith node, m : number of class labels, and G_i (Gini impurity): represents the measure for constructing decision trees.

After performing different heuristic tests and using sensitivity analysis for this forecast technique, it is deduced that the best parameters for tuning are those described in Table 3.

Table 3. Tuning parameters for the decision tree technique.

Decision Tree			
Predicted Variable	**Inputs Variables**	**Max_Depth**	**Min_Samples_Leaf**
Temperature	Solar radiation, relative humidity, wind speed	10	18
Solar radiation	Temperature, relative humidity, wind speed	10	7
Wind speed	Temperature, solar radiation, relative humidity	19	6
Relative Humidity	Temperature, solar radiation, wind speed	9	16

2.4.4. Random Forest

A supervised learning algorithm that uses an ensemble learning method for regression that combines predictions from several machine learning algorithms (decision trees) to make a more accurate prediction than a single model [23]. Figure 2 shows that the random forest algorithm is composed of a collection of decision trees, and each tree in the set is composed of a sample of data extracted from a training set (DATASET); for a regression task, the individual decision trees are averaged (Average) until the predicted value (Prediction) is obtained.

In general, deep decision trees tend to overfit, while random forests avoid this by generating random subsets of features and using those subsets to build smaller trees. The generalization error for random forests is based on the strength of the individual constructed trees and their correlation [24].

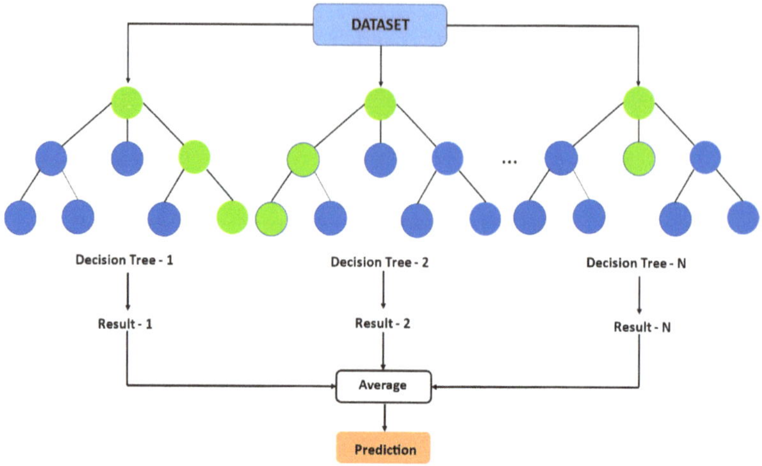

Figure 2. Algorithm for making predictions using random forest.

This technique has several parameters that can be configured, such as the following:

N° estimators: the number of trees in the forest. Max leaf nodes: the maximum number of leaf nodes, this hyperparameter sets a condition for splitting the tree nodes and thus restricts the growth of the tree. If after splitting there are more terminal nodes than the specified number, the splitting stops and the tree does not continue to grow, which helps to avoid overfitting. And Max features: the maximum number of features that are evaluated for splitting at each node, increasing max_features generally improves model performance, since each node now has a greater number of options to consider [23].

After performing different heuristic tests and using sensitivity analysis for this forecast technique, it is deduced that the best parameters for tuning are those described in Table 4.

Table 4. Tuning parameters for the random forest technique.

Random Forest				
Predicted Variable	**Inputs Variables**	**N° Estimators**	**Max Leaf Nodes**	**Max Features**
Temperature	Solar radiation, relative humidity, wind speed	100	3000	0.1
Solar radiation	Temperature, relative humidity, wind speed	100	3000	0.1
Wind speed	Temperature, solar radiation, relative humidity	100	2000	0.3
Relative Humidity	Temperature, solar radiation, wind speed	100	2000	0.2

2.4.5. Extreme Gradient Boosting (XGboost)

The XGBoost algorithm is a scalable tree-boosting system that can be used for both classification and regression tasks. It performs a second-order Taylor expansion on the loss function and can automatically use multiple threads of the central processing unit (CPU) for parallel computing. In addition, XGBoost uses a variety of methods to avoid overfitting [25].

Figure 3 shows the XGBoost algorithm; decision trees are created sequentially (Decision Tree-1, Decision Tree-2, Decision Tree-N) and weights play an important role in XGBoost. Weights are assigned to all independent variables, which are then entered into the decision tree that predicts the outcomes (Result-1, Result-2, Result-N). The weights of variables incorrectly predicted by the tree are increased and these variables are then fed into the second decision tree (Residual error). These individual predictors are then grouped (Average) to give a strong and more accurate model (Prediction).

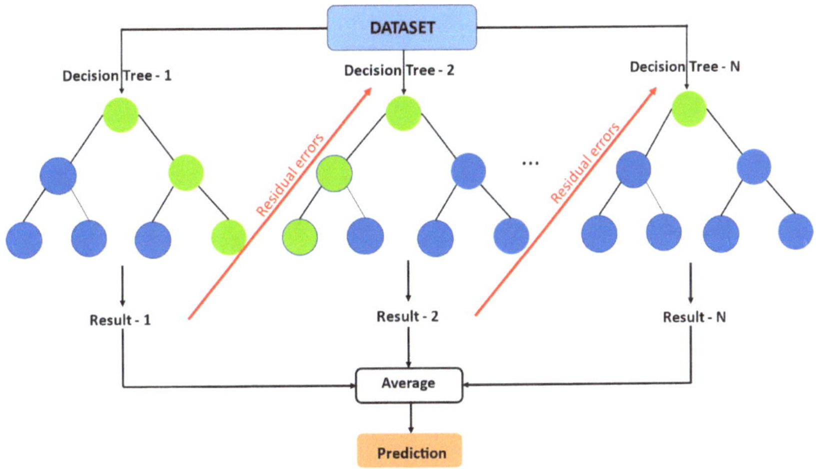

Figure 3. Structure of an XGBoost algorithm for regression.

After performing different heuristic tests and using sensitivity analysis for this forecast technique, it is deduced that the best parameters for its tuning are those described in Table 5.

Table 5. Tuning parameters for the XGboost technique.

	XGBoost		
Predicted Variable	**Inputs Variables**	**Max Depth**	**N° Estimators**
Temperature	Solar radiation, relative humidity, wind speed	2	100
Solar radiation	Temperature, relative humidity, wind speed	2	20
Wind speed	Temperature, solar radiation, relative humidity	5	19
Relative Humidity	Temperature, solar radiation, wind speed	7	19

2.4.6. Neural Network—Multilayer Perceptron

It is an effective and widely used model for modeling many real situations. The multilayer perceptron is a hierarchical structure consisting of several layers of fully interconnected neurons, which input neurons are outputs of the previous layer. Figure 4 shows the structure of a multilayer perceptron neural network; the input layer is made up of r units (where r is the number of external inputs) that merely distribute the input signals to the next layer; the hidden layer is made up of neurons that have no physical contact with the outside; the number of hidden layers is variable (u); and the output layer is made up of l neurons (where l is the number of external outputs) whose outputs constitute the vector of external outputs of the multilayer perceptron [26].

The training of the neural network consists of calculating the linear combination from a set of input variables, with a bias term, applying an activation function, generally the threshold or sign function, giving rise to the network output. Thus, the weights of the network are adjusted by the method of supervised learning by error correction (backpropagation), in such a way that the expected output is compared with the value of the output variable to be obtained, the difference being the error or residual. Each neuron behaves independently of the others: each neuron receives a set of input values (an input vector), calculates the scalar product of this vector and the vector of weights, adds its own bias, applies an activation function to the result, and returns the final result obtained [26].

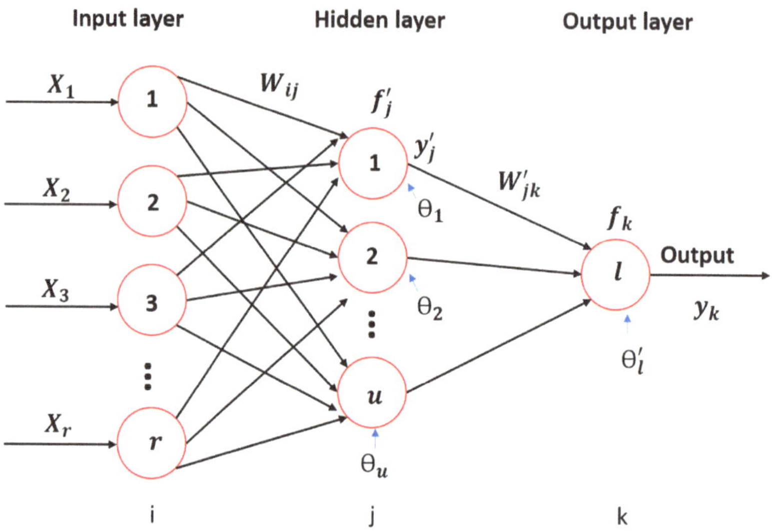

Figure 4. Structure of a multilayer perceptron neural network.

In general, all weights and biases will be different. The output of the multilayer perceptron neural network is defined by Equation (4). Where: y_k is the output, f_k activation function of output layer, θ'_k bias of the output layer, W_{ij} hidden layer weights, y'_j output of the hidden layer, f'_j activation function of the hidden layer, X_i neuron inputs, W'_{jk} output layer weights, θ_j bias of hidden layer, r is the number of inputs for the neuron j from the hidden layer, and u is the number of inputs for the neuron k from the output layer [27].

$$
\begin{aligned}
y'_j &= f'_j\left(\sum_{i=1}^{r} X_i W_{ij} - \theta_j\right) \\
y_k &= f_k\left(\sum_{j=1}^{u} y'_j W'_{jk} - \theta'_k\right)
\end{aligned}
\tag{4}
$$

For this research, backpropagation was used as a training technique. After performing different heuristic tests and using sensitivity analysis for this forecasting technique, it is deduced that the best parameters for its tuning are those described in Table 6.

Table 6. Tuning parameters for the multilayer perceptron neural network technique.

Neural Network—Multilayer Perceptron						
Predicted Variable	**Inputs Variables**	**Input Layer Neurons**	**N° Epoch**	**Batch Size**	**Hidden Layer Neurons**	**Activation Function**
Temperature	Solar radiation, relative humidity, wind speed	3	5000	128	32	Hidden: ReLU Out: Sigmoid
Solar radiation	Temperature, relative humidity, wind speed	3	5000	128	32	Hidden: ReLU Out: Sigmoid
Wind speed	Temperature, solar radiation, relative humidity	3	3000	128	32	Hidden: ReLU Out: Sigmoid
Relative Humidity	Temperature, solar radiation, wind speed	3	5000	128	32	Hidden: ReLU Out: Sigmoid

3. Results

3.1. Indicators for Assessing the Performance of Weather Forecasting Models

To measure the performance of the forecast techniques for each of the variables described above, two types of metrics were used: to evaluate the forecast accuracy, the mean square error RMSE is used, which allows comparing their results and defining the technique with the lowest error, and therefore, the best method for each variable to be predicted. In addition, to determine if the implemented models perform well in their training and to define their predictive ability, the coefficient of determination is R^2.

3.1.1. Coefficient of Determination (R^2)

R^2 or coefficient of determination can be in the range of $[-\infty, 1]$ it is used to determine the ability of a model to predict future results. The best possible result is 1, and occurs when the prediction coincides with the values of the target variable, while the closer to zero, the less well-fitted the model is and, therefore, the less reliable it is. R^2 can take negative values because the prediction can be arbitrarily bad [28]. It is defined as Equation (5), described by 1 minus the sum of total squares divided by the sum of squares of the residuals.

$$R^2 = 1 - \frac{\sum (y_c - \hat{y}_c)^2}{\sum (y_c - \overline{y})^2} \tag{5}$$

where: y_c: are the values taken by the target variable, $\hat{y}_c$: are the values of the prediction, and $\overline{y}$: is the mean value of the values taken by the target variable.

3.1.2. Mean Square Error (RMSE)

The root mean square error, also known as root mean square deviation, measures the amount of error between two sets of data. That is, it compares the predicted value with the observed or known value [28]. It is given by Equation (6):

$$\text{RMSE} = \sqrt{\frac{1}{o} \sum_{c=1}^{o} (y_c - \hat{y}_c)^2} \tag{6}$$

where: y_c: are the values taken by the target variable, $\hat{y}_c$: are the values of the prediction, and o: is the sample size.

3.1.3. Mean Absolute Percentage Error (MAPE)

Mean absolute percentage error is an evaluation metric for regression problems; the idea of this metric is to be sensitive to relative errors. MAPE is the mean of all absolute percentage errors between the predicted and actual values [29]. It is given by Equation (7):

$$\text{MAPE} = \frac{1}{o} \sum_{c=1}^{o} \left| \frac{y_c - \hat{y}_c}{y_c} \right| * 100\% \tag{7}$$

where y_c: are the values taken by the target variable, $\hat{y}_c$: are the values of the prediction, and o: is the sample size.

Equation (7) helps to understand one of the important caveats when using MAPE, since to calculate this metric, you need to divide the difference by the actual value. This means that if you have actual values close to 0 or at 0, the MAPE score will receive a division error by 0 or will be extremely high. Therefore, it is recommended not to use MAPE when it has real values close to 0 [30].

3.1.4. Mean Absolute Error (MAE)

Mean absolute error is a common metric to use for measuring the error of regression predictions. The mean absolute error of a model is the mean of the absolute values of the individual prediction errors on over all instances in the test set. Each prediction error is the difference between the true value and the predicted value for the instance [16,31]. It is given by Equation (8):

$$\text{MAE} = \frac{1}{o}\sum_{c=1}^{o} | \, y_c - \hat{y}_c | \tag{8}$$

where: y_c: are the values taken by the target variable, $\hat{y}_c$: are the values of the prediction, and o: is the sample size.

3.2. Case Study

For the implementation of the forecast techniques for meteorological variables (temperature, wind speed, solar radiation, and relative humidity), the Python programming language was used. Information was obtained from the Parque de la Familia Baños meteorological station, located in Ecuador, Tungurahua province, Baños, coordinates $X = 9{,}845{,}439$, $Y = 791{,}471$. From the database obtained, 1 year of information was available (from 23 July 2021 to 15 June 2022) with a sampling time of 5 min having a total of 93,780 data for each variable, where 80% of the database (75,024 data) is used to test the models, 20% (18,756 data) to test the models, and 2 days (576 data) were used for validation. To obtain the values of the evaluation metrics (RMSE, MAE, MAPE y R^2) the validation data corresponding to the days 10 June 2022 and 11 June 2022 were used.

The forecast techniques implemented for all variables are the following: multiple linear regression, polynomial regression, decision tree, random forest, XGboost, and multilayer perceptron neural network.

To identify which of the models is more efficient, evaluation metrics such as root mean square error (RMSE), mean absolute percentage error (MAPE), and mean absolute error (MAE) are used over the entire validation range, while to evaluate whether the forecasting algorithms fit correctly, the R^2 metric is used. It is important to note that these metrics evaluate different aspects; the RMSE, MAPE, and MAE evaluate the forecasting error, while R^2 allows to analyze how well a regression model fits the real data.

3.2.1. Temperature Forecasting

Table 7 shows the results of the evaluation metrics: root mean square error (RMSE), mean absolute percentage error (MAPE), mean absolute error (MAE), and coefficient of determination (R^2) for each of the techniques used for temperature forecasting. The calculation of the root mean square error, mean absolute percentage error, and mean absolute error was obtained by averaging the errors of the validation data (576 data), while the calculation of the coefficient of determination (R^2) used the data from the training set and the test set (93,780 data).

Table 7. Evaluation metrics for temperature forecasting.

Technique	Coefficient of Determination (R^2)	Mean Absolute Error (MAE) [°C]	Mean Absolute Percentage Error (MAPE) [%]	Mean Square Error (RMSE) [°C]
Multiple linear regression	0.8244	0.6597	3.71	0.8453
Polynomial regression	0.8406	0.6097	3.51	0.8146
Decision tree	0.8593	0.5097	2.95	0.7333
Random forest	0.8631	0.4728	2.73	0.6621
XGboost	0.8599	0.5335	3.09	0.7565
Multilayer perceptron	0.8226	0.9124	5.51	1.2498

Table 7 shows that R^2 obtained from the implemented algorithms converge to appropriate values, i.e., there is a correct approximation between the real temperature and the predicted temperature, thus guaranteeing the good performance of the algorithm, which allows a comparison of the performance in terms of forecast error. Comparison of the root mean square errors (RMSE), mean absolute percentage errors (MAPE), and mean absolute errors (MAE), and analysis of the coefficient of determination R^2 of the different techniques implemented show that the best performing technique for forecasting the temperature variable is Random Forest, with an R^2 of 0.8631, MAE of 0.4728 °C, MAPE of 2.73%, and RMSE of 0.6621 °C. This is followed by XGBoost, with an R^2 of 0.8599, MAE of 0.5335 °C, MAPE of 3.09%, and RMSE of 0.7565 °C.

Figure 5 shows the real (red) and prediction (blue) profiles using the different Machine Learning techniques to predict the temperature variable: (a) Multiple linear regression technique, (b) Polynomial regression technique, (c) Decision tree technique, (d) Random Forest technique, (e) XGboost technique, (f) Multilayer perceptron neural network technique. Figure 5c,d, validate that the best performance corresponds to the Decision tree and Random forest techniques.

3.2.2. Relative Humidity Forecasting

Table 8 shows the results of the evaluation metrics: root mean square error (RMSE), mean absolute percentage error (MAPE), mean absolute error (MAE), and coefficient of determination (R^2) for each of the techniques used for relative humidity forecasting. The calculation of the root mean square error, mean absolute percentage error, and mean absolute error was obtained by averaging the errors of the validation data (576 data), while the calculation of the coefficient of determination (R^2) used the data from the training set and the test set (93,780 data).

Table 8. Evaluation metrics for relative humidity forecasting.

Technique	Coefficient of Determination (R^2)	Mean Absolute Error (MAE) [RH]	Mean Absolute Percentage Error (MAPE) [%]	Mean Square Error (RMSE) [RH]
Multiple linear regression	0.7815	3.0900	3.56	3.7475
Polynomial regression	0.8420	2.2816	2.68	3.0163
Decision tree	0.8547	2.2685	2.65	3.2083
Random forest	0.8583	2.1380	2.50	2.9003
XGboost	0.8597	2.2907	2.67	3.1444
Multilayer perceptron	0.8013	4.6055	5.64	5.5759

Table 8 shows that R^2 obtained from the implemented algorithms converge to appropriate values, i.e., there is a correct approximation between the real relative humidity and the predicted relative humidity, thus guaranteeing the good performance of the algorithm, which allows a comparison of the performance in terms of forecast error. Comparison of the root mean square errors (RMSE), mean absolute percentage errors (MAPE), and mean absolute errors (MAE), and analysis of the coefficient of determination R^2 of the different techniques implemented show that the best performing techniques for forecasting the relative humidity variable are Random Forest, with an R^2 of 0.8583, MAE of 2.1380 RH, MAPE of 2.50%, and RMSE of 2.9003 RH; and XGBoost, with an R^2 of 0.8597, MAE of 2.2907 RH, MAPE of 2.67%, and RMSE of 3.1444 RH.

Figure 6 shows the real (red) and prediction (blue) profiles using the different Machine Learning techniques to predict the relative humidity variable: (a) Multiple linear regression technique, (b) Polynomial regression technique, (c) Decision tree technique, (d) Random forest technique, (e) XGboost technique, (f) Multilayer perceptron neural network technique. Figure 6d and Figure 6c validate that the best performance corresponds to the Random forest and Decision tree techniques.

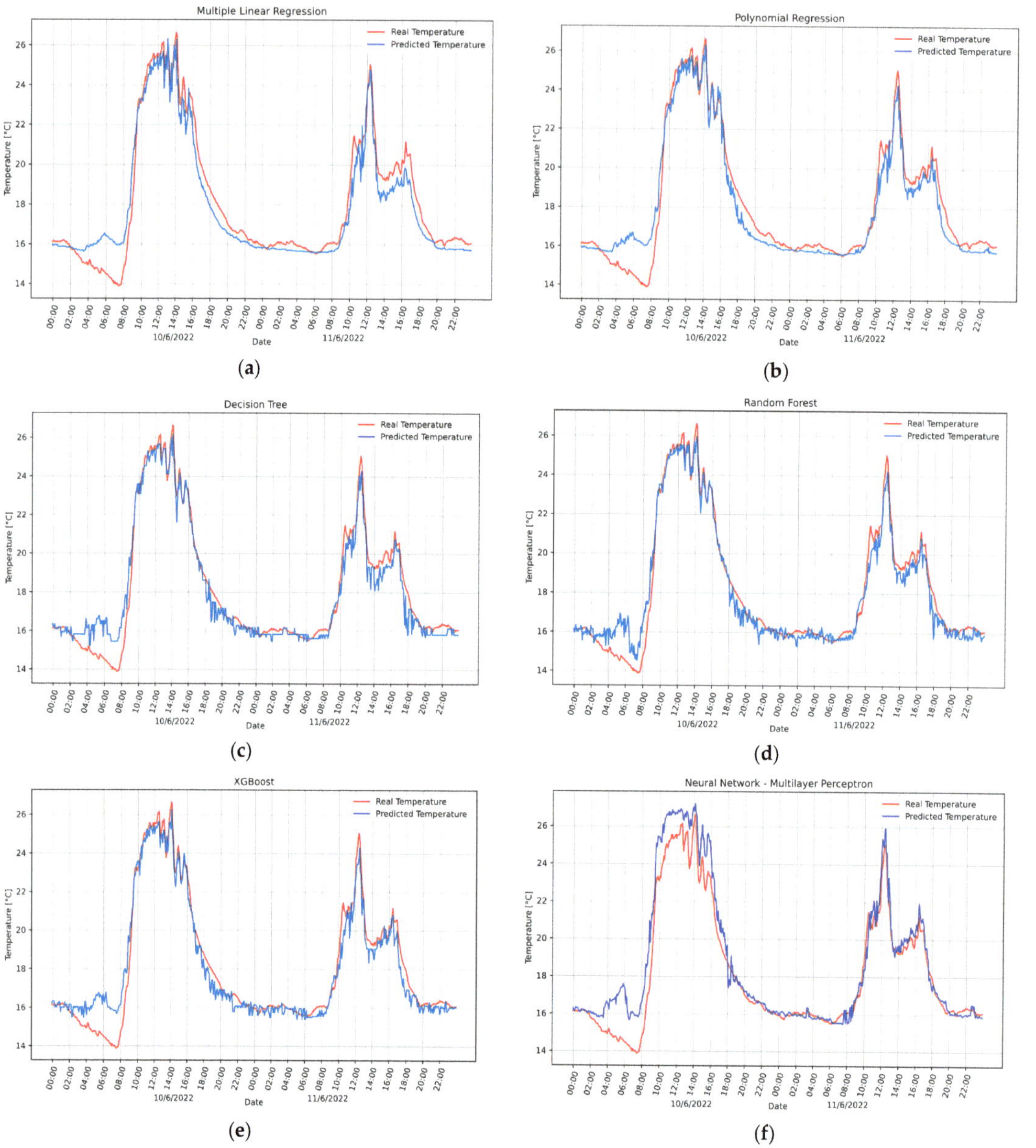

Figure 5. Temperature forecast techniques: (**a**) Multiple linear regression, (**b**) Polynomial regression, (**c**) Decision tree, (**d**) Random forest, (**e**) XGboost, (**f**) Multilayer perceptron neural network.

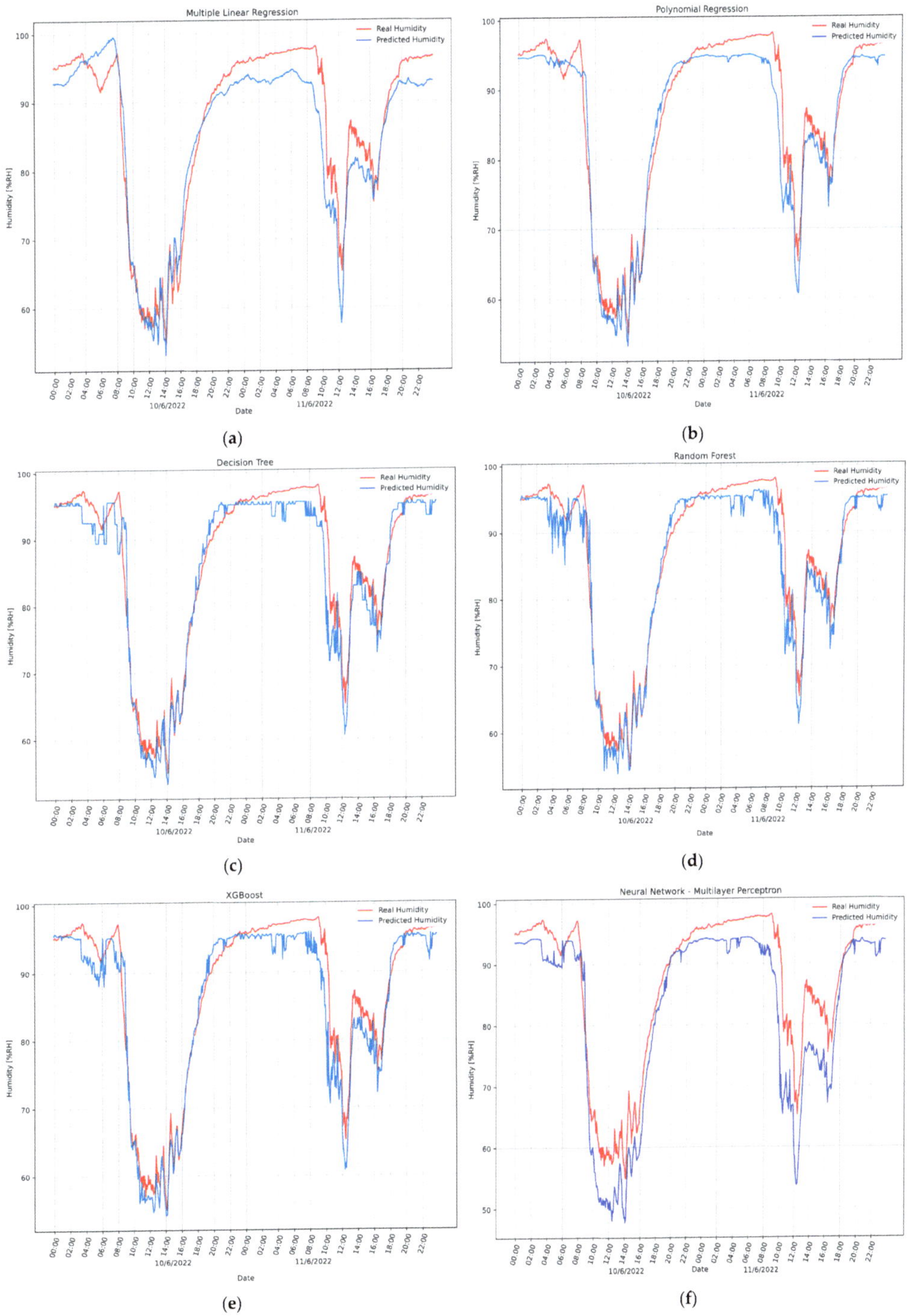

Figure 6. Techniques for relative humidity forecasting: (**a**) Multiple linear regression, (**b**) Polynomial regression, (**c**) Decision tree, (**d**) Random forest, (**e**) XGboost, (**f**) Multilayer perceptron neural network.

3.2.3. Solar Radiation Forecasting

Table 9 shows the results of the evaluation metrics: root mean square error (RMSE), mean absolute error (MAE), and coefficient of determination (R^2) for each of the techniques used for solar radiation forecasting. The calculation of the root mean square error, and mean absolute error was obtained by averaging the errors of the validation data (576 data), while the calculation of the coefficient of determination (R^2) used the data from the training set and the test set (93,780 data).

Table 9. Evaluation metrics for solar radiation forecasting.

Technique	Coefficient of Determination (R^2)	Mean Absolute Error (MAE) [W/m^2]	Mean Square Error (RMSE) [W/m^2]
Multiple linear regression	0.6689	106.9741	164.7435
Polynomial regression	0.7394	76.6667	129.1836
Decision tree	0.7253	75.8177	127.3530
Random forest	0.7333	65.8105	105.9141
XGboost	0.7075	87.6137	145.0170
Multilayer perceptron	0.7423	88.5897	140.0681

Table 9 shows that R^2 obtained from the implemented algorithms converge to appropriate values, i.e., there is a correct approximation between the real solar radiation and the predicted solar radiation, thus guaranteeing the good performance of the algorithm, which allows a comparison of the performance in terms of forecast error. Comparison of the root mean square errors (RMSE), and mean absolute errors (MAE), and analysis of the coefficient of determination R^2 of the different techniques implemented show that the best performing techniques for forecasting the solar radiation variable are Random Forest with an R^2 of 0.7333, MAE of 65.8105 W/m^2, and RMSE of 105.9141 W/m^2; and Decision Tree with an R^2 of 0.7253, MAE of 75.8177 W/m^2, and RMSE of 127.3530 W/m^2.

Figure 7 shows the real (red) and prediction (blue) profiles using the different Machine Learning techniques to predict the variable solar radiation: (a) Multiple linear regression technique, (b) Polynomial regression technique, (c) Decision tree technique, (d) Random forest technique, (e) XGboost technique, (f) Multilayer perceptron neural network technique. Figure 7d validates that the best performance corresponds to the Random forest technique.

3.2.4. Wind Speed Forecasting

Table 10 shows the results of the evaluation metrics: root mean square error (RMSE), mean absolute error (MAE), and coefficient of determination (R^2) for each of the techniques used for wind speed forecasting. The calculation of the root mean square error and mean absolute error was obtained by averaging the errors of the validation data (576 data), while the calculation of the coefficient of determination (R^2) used the data from the training set and the test set (93,780 data).

Table 10 shows that R^2 obtained from the implemented algorithms converge to appropriate values, i.e., there is an acceptable approximation between the real wind speed and the predicted wind speed, thus guaranteeing the good performance of the algorithm, which allows a comparison of the performance in terms of forecast error. Comparison of the root mean square errors (RMSE) and mean absolute errors (MAE) and analysis of the coefficient of determination R^2 of the different techniques implemented show that the best performing techniques for forecasting the wind speed variable are Random Forest with an R^2 of 0.3660, MAE of 0.1097 m/s, and RMSE of 0.2136 m/s; and XGBoost with an R^2 of 0.3866, MAE of 0.1439 m/s, and RMSE of 0.3131 m/s. It should be taken into account that due to the high variability of wind speed, the implemented techniques have a lower coefficient of determination compared to the other variables; however, forecasts with acceptable errors were obtained. In this case, the value of the mean absolute percentage errors (MAPE) is not taken into account because it is used only when it is known that the quantity to be predicted remains well above 0.

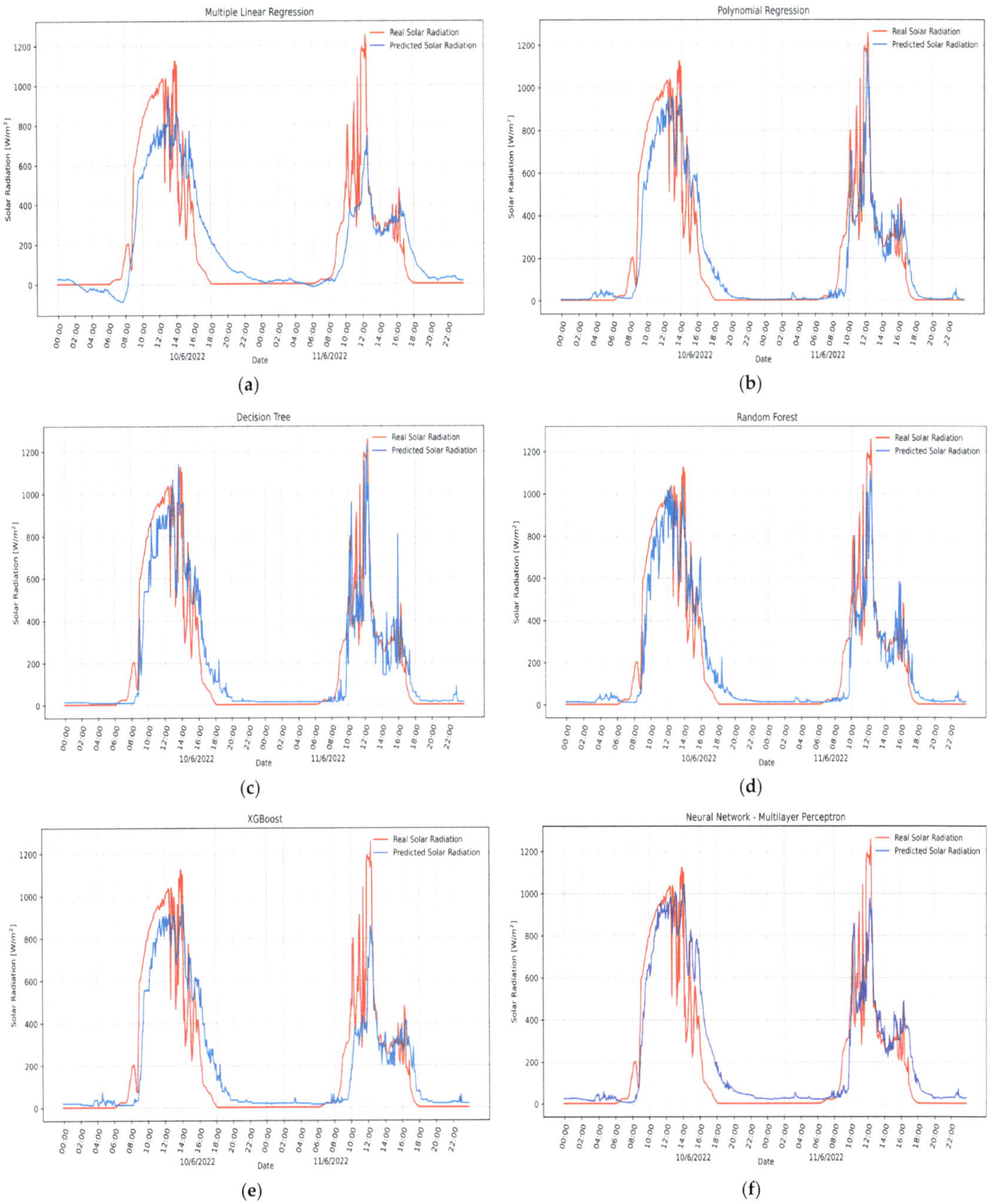

Figure 7. Solar radiation forecast techniques: (**a**) Multiple linear regression, (**b**) Polynomial regression, (**c**) Decision tree, (**d**) Random forest, (**e**) XGboost, (**f**) Multilayer perceptron neural network.

Table 10. Evaluation metrics for wind speed forecasting.

Technique	Coefficient of Determination (R^2)	Mean Absolute Error (MAE) [m/s]	Mean Square Error (RMSE) [m/s]
Multiple linear regression	0.3428	0.1614	0.3354
Polynomial regression	0.3770	0.1428	0.3159
Decision tree	0.2142	0.1256	0.2705
Random forest	0.3660	0.1097	0.2136
XGboost	0.3866	0.1439	0.3131
Multilayer perceptron	0.3270	0.1654	0.3616

Figure 8 shows the real (red) and prediction (blue) profiles using the different Machine Learning techniques to predict the wind speed variable: (a) Multiple linear regression technique, (b) Polynomial regression technique, (c) Decision tree technique, (d) Random forest technique, (e) XGboost technique, (f) Multilayer perceptron neural network technique. Figure 8d validates that the best performance corresponds to the Random forest technique.

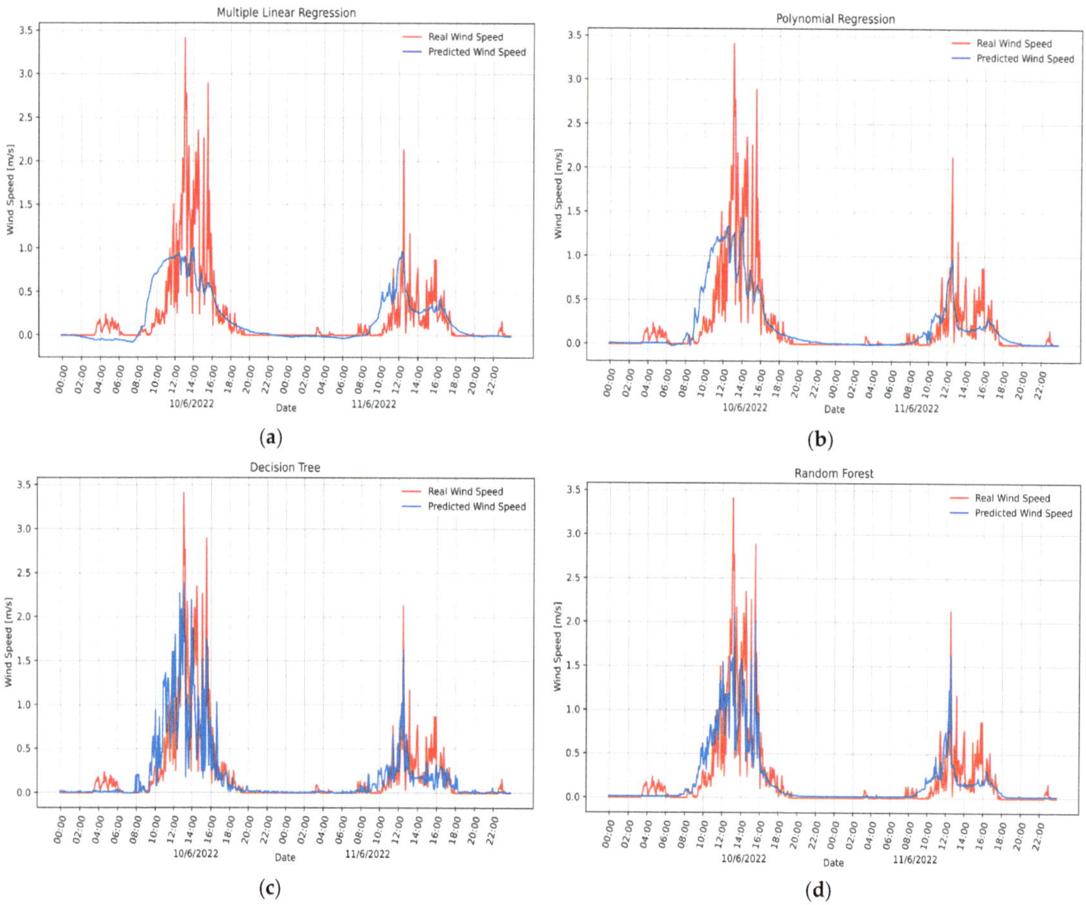

Figure 8. *Cont.*

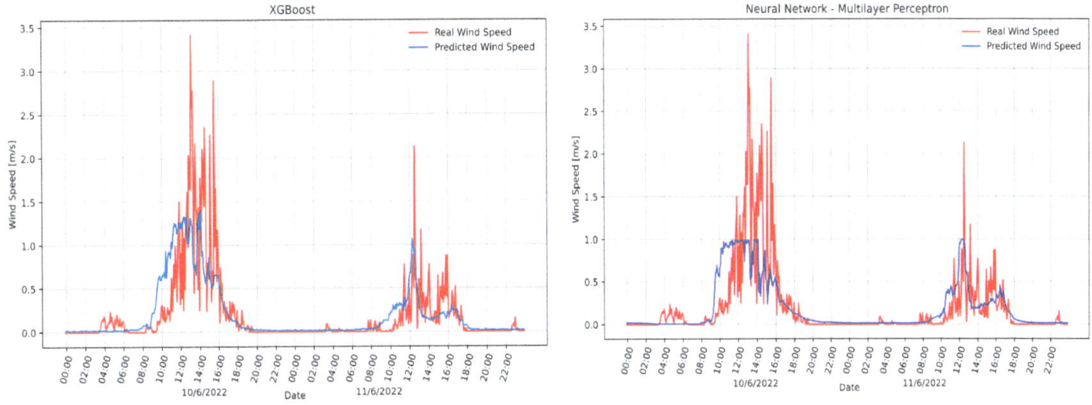

(e) (f)

Figure 8. Techniques for wind speed forecast: (**a**) Multiple linear regression, (**b**) Polynomial regression, (**c**) Decision tree, (**d**) Random forest, (**e**) XGboost, (**f**) Multilayer perceptron neural network.

4. Conclusions

For the forecasting of meteorological variables in this research, information obtained from the Parque de la Familia Baños meteorological station located in Ecuador was used and the following prediction techniques were tested: multiple linear regression, polynomial regression, decision tree, random forest, XGBoost, and multilayer perceptron neural network. For forecasting the temperature variable, a better result is obtained by using Random Forest with an R^2 of 0.8631, MAE of 0.4728 °C, MAPE of 2.73%, and RMSE of 0.6621 °C. In addition, XGBoost also performed well with an R^2 of 0.8599, MAE of 0.5335 °C, MAPE of 3.09%, and RMSE of 0.7565 °C. For forecasting the relative humidity variable, a better result is obtained by using Random Forest with an R^2 of 0.8583, MAE of 2.1380 RH, MAPE of 2.50%, and RMSE of 2.9003 RH. In addition, XGBoost also performed well with an R^2 of 0.8597, MAE of 2.2907 RH, MAPE of 2.67%, and RMSE of 3.1444 RH. For forecasting the solar radiation variable, a better result is obtained by using Random Forest with an R^2 of 0.7333, MAE of 65.8105 W/m^2, and RMSE of 105.9141 W/m^2. In addition, Decision Tree also performed well with an R^2 of 0.7253, MAE of 75.8177 W/m^2, and RMSE of 127.3530 W/m^2. For forecasting the wind speed variable, a better result is obtained by using Random Forest, with an R^2 of 0.3660, MAE of 0.1097 m/s, and RMSE of 0.2136 m/s. In addition, XGBoost also performed well, with an R^2 of 0.3866, MAE of 0.1439 m/s, and RMSE of 0.3131 m/s.

It can be observed that wind speed has the highest variability compared to the other predicted variables, therefore, the results of the techniques implemented show that the coefficient of determination R^2 of this variable has a lower value. This is due to the type of signal we are trying to predict; however, acceptable predictions were obtained.

The prediction of meteorological variables (temperature, solar radiation, wind speed, and relative humidity) will allow future projects to be implemented in the study area, such as intelligent agriculture to support food problems in that area and the implementation of a microgrid based on renewable resources where prediction models will support the planning and operation of the microgrid in real time, allowing clean energy to this locality, contributing to the reduction in the use of fossil resources, which is the goal that different countries have set as part of their policies.

Author Contributions: Conceptualization, J.A.S., J.F.T., J.R.L. and D.R.R.; methodology, J.A.S., J.F.T., J.R.L. and D.R.R.; software J.A.S. and J.F.T.; validation, J.A.S. and J.F.T.; formal analysis, J.A.S., J.F.T., J.R.L. and D.R.R.; investigation, J.A.S., J.F.T. and J.R.L.; resources, J.A.S. and J.F.T.; data curation, J.A.S. and J.F.T.; writing—original draft preparation, J.A.S., J.F.T., J.R.L. and D.R.R..; writing—review and editing, J.A.S., J.F.T., J.R.L. and D.R.R.; visualization, J.A.S., J.F.T., J.R.L. and D.R.R.; supervision, J.R.L. and D.R.R.; project administration, J.R.L.; funding acquisition, J.R.L. All authors have read and agreed to the published version of the manuscript.

Funding: This research received no external funding.

Data Availability Statement: Not applicable.

Acknowledgments: This work was supported in part by the Universidad de las Fuerzas Armadas ESPE through the Project "Optimal energy management systems for hybrid generation systems", under Project 2023-pis-03. In addition, the authors would like to thank to the project EE-GNP-0043-2021-ESPE, REDTPI4.0-CYTED, Conv-2022-05-UNACH, "SISMO-ROSAS"–UPS.

Conflicts of Interest: The authors declare no conflict of interest.

References

1. Ayala, M.F. *Analisis de la Dinamica Caoticapara la Series Temporales de Variables Meteorologicas en la Estacion Climatica de Chone*; Universidad de las Fuerzas Armadas ESPE: Sangolquí, Ecuador, 2017; Available online: http://repositorio.espe.edu.ec/handle/21000/13629 (accessed on 24 November 2022).
2. Erdil, A.; Arcaklioglu, E. The prediction of meteorological variables using artificial neural network. *Neural Comput. Appl.* **2013**, *22*, 1677–1683. [CrossRef]
3. Ruiz-Ayala, D.C.; Vides-Herrera, C.A.; Pardo-García, A. Monitoreo de variables meteorológicas a través de un sistema inalámbrico de adquisición de datos. *Rev. Investig. Desarro. Innov.* **2018**, *8*, 333–341. [CrossRef]
4. Inzunza, J.C. Meteorologia Descriptiva. *Univ. Concepción Dep. Geofísica* **2015**, 1–34. Available online: http://www2.udec.cl/~jinzunza/meteo/cap1.pdf (accessed on 24 November 2022).
5. Millán, H.; Kalauzi, A.; Cukic, M.; Biondi, R. Nonlinear dynamics of meteorological variables: Multifractality and chaotic invariants in daily records from Pastaza, Ecuador. *Theor. Appl. Climatol.* **2010**, *102*, 75–85. [CrossRef]
6. Acurio, W.; Pilco, V. *Técnicas Estadísticas para la Modelación y Predicción de la Temperatura y Velocidad del Viento en la Provincia de Chimborazo*; Escuela Superior Politénica de Chimborazo: Riobamba, Ecuador, 2019. Available online: http://dspace.espoch.edu.ec/handle/123456789/10955 (accessed on 28 November 2022).
7. Tong, H. *Non-Linear Time Series: A Dynamical System Approach*; Oxford University Press: Oxford, UK, 1990.
8. Palma-Behnke, R.; Benavides, C.; Aranda, E.; Llanos, J.; Sáez, D. Energy management system for a renewable based microgrid with a demand side management mechanism. In Proceedings of the IEEE Symposium on Computational Intelligence Applications in Smart Grid 2011, Paris, France, 11–15 April 2011; pp. 1–8. [CrossRef]
9. Rodríguez, M.; Salazar, A.; Arcos-Aviles, D.; Llanos, J.; Martínez, W.; Motoasca, E. A Brief Approach of Microgrids Implementation in Ecuador: A Review. In *Lecture Notes in Electrical Engineering*; Springer: Cham, Switzerland, 2021; Volume 762, pp. 149–163. [CrossRef]
10. Llanos, J.; Morales, R.; Núñez, A.; Sáez, D.; Lacalle, M.; Marín, L.G.; Hernández, R.; Lanas, F. Load estimation for microgrid planning based on a self-organizing map methodology. *Appl. Soft Comput.* **2017**, *53*, 323–335. [CrossRef]
11. Caquilpan, V.; Saez, D.; Hernandez, R.; Llanos, J.; Roje, T.; Nunez, A. Load estimation based on self-organizing maps and Bayesian networks for microgrids design in rural zones. In Proceedings of the 2017 IEEE PES Innovative Smart Grid Technologies Conference—Latin America (ISGT Latin America), Quito, Ecuador, 20–22 September 2017; pp. 1–6. [CrossRef]
12. Palma-Behnke, R.; Benavides, C.; Lanas, F.; Severino, B.; Reyes, L.; Llanos, J.; Saez, D. A microgrid energy management system based on the rolling horizon strategy. *IEEE Trans. Smart Grid* **2013**, *4*, 996–1006. [CrossRef]
13. Rey, J.M.; Vera, G.A.; Acevedo-Rueda, P.; Solano, J.; Mantilla, M.A.; Llanos, J.; Sáez, D. A Review of Microgrids in Latin America: Laboratories and Test Systems. *IEEE Lat. Am. Trans.* **2022**, *20*, 1000–1011. [CrossRef]
14. Javier, G.; Quevedo-Nolasco, A.; Castro-Popoca, M.; Arteaga-Ramírez, R.; Vázquez-Peña, M.A.; Zamora-Morales, B.P.; Aguado-Rodríguez, G.J.; Quevedo-Nolasco, A.; Castro-Popoca, M.; Arteaga-Ramírez, R.; et al. Predicción de Variables Meteorológicas por Medio de Modelos Arima. *Agrociencia* **2016**, *50*, 1–13.
15. Gulhane, V.A.; Rode, S.V.; Pande, C.B. Correlation Analysis of Soil Nutrients and Prediction Model Through ISO Cluster Unsupervised Classification with Multispectral Data. *Springer Link* **2022**, *82*, 2165–2184. [CrossRef]
16. Pande, C.B.; Al-Ansari, N.; Kushwaha, N.L.; Srivastava, A.; Noor, R.; Kumar, M.; Moharir, K.N.; Elbeltagi, A. Forecasting of SPI and Meteorological Drought Based on the Artificial Neural Network and M5P Model Tree. *Land* **2022**, *11*, 2040. [CrossRef]
17. Mora Cunllo, V.E. Diseño e Implementación de un Modelo Software Basado en Técnicas de Inteligencia Artificial, para Predecir el índice de Radiación Solar en Riobamba-Ecuador. 2015. Available online: http://repositorio.espe.edu.ec/bitstream/21000/12216/1/T-ESPEL-MAS-0027.pdf (accessed on 24 November 2022).

18. Universitario, S.; Estad, E.N.; Aplicada, S.; Fern, R.A.; Javier, F.; Morales, A. *Series Temporales Avanzadas: Aplicación de Redes Neuronales para el Pronóstico de Series de Tiempo*; Universidad de Granada: Granada, Spain, 2021.
19. Raschka, S.; Patterson, J.; Nolet, C. Machine learning in python: Main developments and technology trends in data science, machine learning, and artificial intelligence. *Information* **2020**, *11*, 193. [CrossRef]
20. Carlos, J.; Rodriguez, M. Desarrollo de una Herramienta Inteligente Centrada en Visión Plantaciones de Arroz, Usando Lenguaje de Programación Python. Ph.D. Thesis, Universidad de Guayaquil, Guayaquil, Ecuador, 2022.
21. Ben Bouallègue, Z.; Cooper, F.; Chantry, M.; Düben, P.; Bechtold, P.; Sandu, I. Statistical modelling of 2m temperature and 10m wind speed forecast errors. *Mon. Weather. Rev.* **2022**. Available online: https://journals.ametsoc.org/view/journals/mwre/aop/MWR-D-22-0107.1/MWR-D-22-0107.1.xml (accessed on 18 January 2023). [CrossRef]
22. Montero Granados, R. *Modelos de Regresión Lineal Múltiple*; Technical Report; Documentos de Trabajo en Economía Aplicada; Universidad de Granada: Granada, Spain, 2006.
23. Aurélien, G. *Hands-on Machine Learning with Scikit-Learn & Tensorflow*; O'Reilly Media, Inc.: Sebastopol, CA, USA, 2017.
24. Elbeltagi, A.; Kumar, M.; Kushwaha, N.L.; Pande, C.B.; Ditthakit, P.; Vishwakarma, D.K.; Subeesh, A. Drought indicator analysis and forecasting using data driven models: Case study in Jaisalmer, India. *Stoch. Environ. Res. Risk Assess.* **2022**, *37*, 113–131. [CrossRef]
25. Luckner, M.; Topolski, B.; Mazurek, M. Application of XGBoost Algorithm. *Data Anal.* **2017**, *10244*, 661–671. [CrossRef]
26. Menacho Chiok, C.H. Modelos de regresión lineal con redes neuronales. *An. Científicos* **2014**, *75*, 253. [CrossRef]
27. Popescu, M.C.; Balas, V.E.; Perescu-Popescu, L.; Mastorakis, N. Multilayer perceptron and neural networks. *WSEAS Trans. Circuits Syst.* **2009**, *8*, 579–588.
28. Soto-Bravo, F.; González-Lutz, M.I. Analysis of statistical methods to evaluate the performance of simulation models in horticultural crops. *Agron. Mesoam.* **2019**, *30*, 517–534. [CrossRef]
29. Gopi, A.; Sharma, P.; Sudhakar, K.; Ngui, W.K.; Kirpichnikova, I.; Cuce, E. Weather Impact on Solar Farm Performance: A Comparative Analysis of Machine Learning Techniques. *Sustainability* **2023**, *15*, 439. [CrossRef]
30. de Myttenaere, A.; Golden, B.; Le Grand, B.; Rossi, F. Mean Absolute Percentage Error for regression models. *Neurocomputing* **2016**, *192*, 38–48. [CrossRef]
31. Chai, T.; Draxler, R.R. Root mean square error (RMSE) or mean absolute error (MAE)? -Arguments against avoiding RMSE in the literature. *Geosci. Model Dev.* **2014**, *7*, 1247–1250. [CrossRef]

electronics

MDPI

Review

Bias Mitigation via Synthetic Data Generation: A Review

Mohamed Ashik Shahul Hameed, Asifa Mehmood Qureshi and Abhishek Kaushik *

Dundalk Institute of Technology, A91 K584 Dundalk, Ireland
* Correspondence: abhishek.kaushik@dkit.ie

Abstract: Artificial intelligence (AI) is widely used in healthcare applications to perform various tasks. Although these models have great potential to improve the healthcare system, they have also raised significant ethical concerns, including biases that increase the risk of health disparities in medical applications. The under-representation of a specific group can lead to bias in the datasets that are being replicated in the AI models. These disadvantaged groups are disproportionately affected by bias because they may have less accurate algorithmic forecasts or underestimate the need for treatment. One solution to eliminate bias is to use synthetic samples or artificially generated data to balance datasets. Therefore, the purpose of this study is to review and evaluate how synthetic data can be generated and used to mitigate biases, specifically focusing on the medical domain. We explored high-quality peer-reviewed articles that were focused on synthetic data generation to eliminate bias. These studies were selected based on our defined inclusion criteria and exclusion criteria and the quality of the content. The findings reveal that generated synthetic data can help improve accuracy, precision, and fairness. However, the effectiveness of synthetic data is closely dependent on the quality of the data generation process and the initial datasets used. The study also highlights the need for continuous improvement in synthetic data generation techniques and the importance of evaluation metrics for fairness in AI models.

Keywords: synthetic data; artificial data; bias; fairness; AI; data generation

1. Introduction

Bias in AI models can be defined as systematic errors that affect the algorithm and unfairly favor certain outcomes over others [1]. These biases can originate from various sources, such as using imbalanced or underrepresented datasets to train the models, the algorithms themselves, and the ways AI models are being deployed by humans. In healthcare, these biases can lead to significant consequences of disparities in treatment outcomes for specific racial, gender, or demographic groups, resulting in unequal treatment that may lead to life-threatening incidences. They have a direct impact on patient medical outcomes. Biased models can lead to misdiagnosis, inappropriate treatment plans, and unequal access to medical resources [2]. For instance, a used model to estimate breast cancer density is trained on data that are under-inclusive of African-American women and will generate recommendations that are not well-suited for that population [3]. Moreover, Kiyasseh et al. [4] deployed a surgical AI model to assess the skill level of robotic surgeries in completing different surgical activities. However, it was found that the model exhibited an underskilling or overskilling bias. Underskilling occurs when an AI model incorrectly predicts that a certain surgical skill is of a lower grade than it actually is, hence reducing surgical performance. In contrast, overskilling occurred when the AI model incorrectly improved surgical performance by estimating that a certain skill would be a higher caliber than it was.

Therefore, the broad aim behind ensuring fairness, accuracy, and equality through bias mitigation in AI models within the medical domain is to create fair and equal outcomes for a diverse set of populations.

Citation: Shahul Hameed, M.A.; Qureshi, A.M.; Kaushik, A. Bias Mitigation via Synthetic Data Generation: A Review. *Electronics* **2024**, *13*, 3909. https://doi.org/10.3390/electronics13193909

Academic Editor: Grzegorz Dudek

Received: 29 August 2024
Revised: 23 September 2024
Accepted: 24 September 2024
Published: 2 October 2024

There are several techniques to eliminate biases from datasets. These techniques include the collection of diverse and representative data [5], handling at the algorithmic level [6], pre-processing of datasets and post-processing of the model output to reduce bias [7], and synthetic data generation [8].

Generating data is one of the several strategies to mitigate bias. It can be defined as artificial data that mimics the statistical properties and patterns of real-world information [9]. While other techniques tend to reduce or process the datasets to ensure fairness, which may result in information loss, synthetic data generation helps to preserve the data distribution and add statistically similar data samples to reduce bias. In healthcare settings, synthetic data can be utilized as a substitute for real patient data while avoiding privacy issues, which allows for the simulation and sharing of sensitive patient data. There exist multiple methods, including Generative Adversarial Networks (GANs), Variational Auto-Encoders (VAEs), the Synthetic Minority Over-sampling Technique (SMOTE), Bayesian networks, and statistical sampling methods, to generate synthetic data. These methods have been used vastly to generate new artificial datasets that capture the structure and distribution of actual datasets. These synthetic datasets can help to tackle situations where there is bias or no additional data to work with while trying to improve the fairness and accuracy of AI algorithms [4]. Using synthetic data in healthcare is also a solution to patient data privacy. Moreover, synthetic data allows you to create big, diverse datasets to train models.

This article reviews research studies that are focused on bias mitigation via synthetic data generation techniques.

Motivation

AI systems can produce biased results that both reflect and amplify human prejudices within a community, including historical and contemporary social injustice. Bias may exist in the algorithm, the original training set, or the predictions the algorithm makes. It can be passed on through racial, religious, and gender stereotypes [10]. Synthetic data can be a viable solution to preserve patient data privacy and mitigate bias in the data. Synthetic data methodologies tend to capture the structure and distributions found in real datasets while minimizing bias and protecting individually identifiable [11]. Moreover, synthetic data allows us to create big, diverse datasets to train AI models. Therefore, this paper explores the literature to highlight the application of synthetic data generation to mitigate bias. The study provides a comprehensive review of the methods and techniques used to generate synthetic data. Also, the limitations of these models are discussed. The hypothesis and formulated research questions are as follows:

Hypothesis: *Synthetic data can be used to mitigate bias in medical data effectively, resulting in unbiased, accurate, and equitable healthcare datasets.*

RQ1. What are the most common methods or techniques to generate synthetic data to handle biases in the dataset?

RQ2. What are the limitations of the existing techniques used for synthetic data generation?

The rest of the article is structured as follows:

Section 2 explains the search methodology. Section 3 gives an overview of the bias mitigation techniques. Section 4 discusses the hypothesis and research questions. Section 5 concludes the discussion.

2. Search Methodology

Figure 1 shows the detailed search methodology used to conduct this review. Several major databases, including Google Scholar, IEEE Xplore, Pubmed, ScienceDirect, and ACM Digital Library, were explored. Google Scholar was used for its broad and inclusive nature. It covers many topics and has many articles from interdisciplinary fields, so it is a great resource for literature reviews. PubMed was chosen for its focus on biomedical and life science literature. Since the focus is on AI applications in healthcare, PubMed has high-quality reviews and survey papers to obtain peer-reviewed medical research articles on the impact and implementation of AI in clinical settings. The ACM Digital Library was included for its focus on computing and information technology research. It is great for finding research on algorithm development, computational methods, and technical advancements in synthetic data generation and bias mitigation in AI. IEEE Xplore was chosen for its large collection of technology research and application implementation papers, especially in AI, ML, and synthetic data. It has technical papers and theory conference articles on the latest AI technologies and their applications in healthcare.

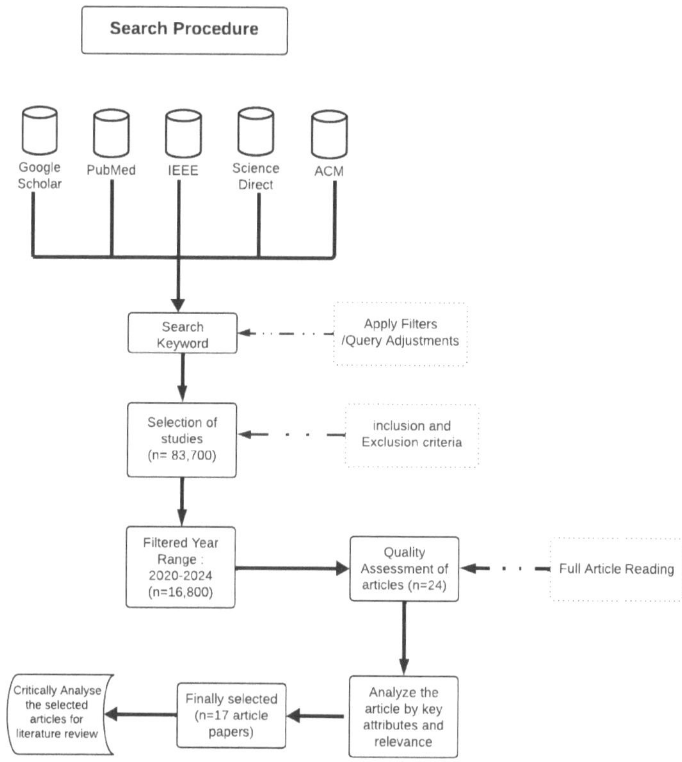

Figure 1. Search methodology workflow.

The selections are based on the scope, relevance, and credibility of the databases and article papers in the fields of AI, Machine Learning (ML), synthetic data, and healthcare. A search query was formulated to find research articles on bias in AI, ML, Deep Learning (DL), and synthetic data generation in healthcare:

"((Bias) AND (Artificial Intelligence OR Machine Learning OR Deep Learning) AND (Synthetic Data) AND (text OR tabular dataset))"

Slight adjustments were made to the query to refine the results further. These adjustments included using synonyms of these terms, including fairness, biases, data bias, artificial data, generated data, and medical data.

To obtain the most relevant and recent studies, inclusion and exclusion criteria were devised as follows:

2.1. Inclusion Criteria

- Research articles that are focused on bias and bias handling in AI models using synthetic data generation were included.

- Research articles published between 2020 and 2024 were included to review the relevant, latest techniques.
- Research studies that were published in conferences, journals, book chapters, or proceedings were included.
- Research articles only written in the English language were selected.

2.2. Exclusion Criteria

- Research articles that did not align with our research questions were excluded.
- Non-peer-reviewed articles were not considered.

About 83,700 papers were found in this first search using the Google Scholar database platform. By applying inclusion and exclusion criteria and restricting the year of publication between 2020 and 2024, the total was dropped to about 16,800 papers. The dynamic of scientific studies in this field from 2020 to 2023 was approximately recorded as 13,200, 17,400, 21,500, and 28,000. Therefore, the average annual growth rate of articles in this field was approximately 29%.

Then, a quality assessment was performed to ensure the relevance and credibility of the papers, and the selection was narrowed down to 50 papers. The shortlisted articles were examined further for eligibility on the basis of title relevancy and abstracts; a total of 26 articles were removed, and the remaining articles were assessed by a full article reading. After a critical analysis, we finally selected 17 papers for the literature review. Table 1 summarizes the number of articles after each step.

Table 1. Number of articles selected at each step.

Stages	Number of Articles
Initial results (using query)	83,700
After applying inclusion and exclusion criteria	16,800
After quality assessment	50
Based on the abstract and conclusion	24
Full article reading (Finally selected articles)	17

The proportion of selected research studies from each database is shown in Figure 2.

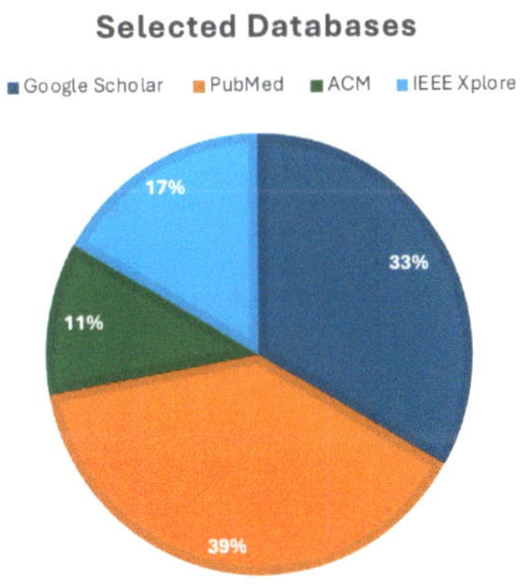

Figure 2. Proportion of the selected articles from each database.

Figure 3 shows the year-wise distribution of the selected articles. The year 2021 constituted the highest number of selected articles, preceded by the years 2022 and 2023. Moreover, the category of the selected articles is given in Table 2. A total of 12 journals, 4 conferences, and 1 doctoral dissertation were reviewed.

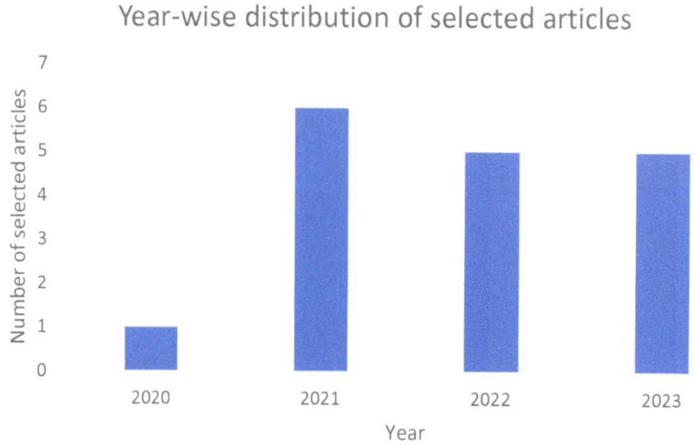

Figure 3. Year-wise distribution of the selected articles.

Table 2. Overview of selected article categories and count.

Category	Number of Articles
Academic Journal paper	12
Conference paper	4
Doctoral dissertation	1

3. Bias Mitigation via Synthetic Data Generation

Several techniques have been proposed in the literature to mitigate bias using synthetic sample generation. Table 3 summarizes the studies and the methodologies along with the dataset, modality, strengths, and weaknesses of each reviewed article.

Table 3. Overview of the methodology, dataset, modality, evaluation metric, strengths, and limitations of the reviewed research articles.

Refs.	Year	Methodology	Dataset	Modality	Evaluation Metric	Strengths	Limitations
[12]	2023	Analyses explainable artificial intelligence (XAI) methods and suggests metrics to determine the technical characteristics of the methods. Focuses on XAI methods such as LIME and SHAP, applied to machine learning models using synthetic data.	A large and heterogeneous corpus of one million Dutch EHR notes.	text data	Balanced accuracy and fairness scores to compare real and synthetic models, time-series metrics, and disparate impact metrics for representational bias and evaluating resemblance.	Auditing pipelines for robust evaluation under varying data, combines GANs, fairness metrics, and bias mitigation algorithms.	Focuses only on synthetic data generation and fairness, lack of datasets, and complexity in adversarial auditing methods.
[13]	2023	Focuses on generating synthetic data strategies for fairness assessment. Explores techniques for creating synthetic datasets that can be used to stress-test machine learning models and assess bias mitigation algorithms.	Healthcare data	Temporal and non-temporal datasets. Subgroup-level analysis of protected attributes such as gender and race	Metrics include faithfulness (correlation between feature and model predictions), monotonicity (correctness of feature), and incompleteness (effect of noise in feature).	Addresses the critical area of explainable AI, essential for user trust, provides insights into the evaluation of XAI methods, and guides future research.	The imperfection of existing XAI methods undermines user trust, does not delve into specific datasets, and lacks diverse data.

Table 3. *Cont.*

Refs.	Year	Methodology	Dataset	Modality	Evaluation Metric	Strengths	Limitations
[14]	2022	Utilized GANs. Interactive GUI tool to generate synthetic data. Integrated bias detection. Evaluated with LFR. Uses statistical fairness metrics including Statistical Parity Difference (SPD).	German Credit dataset, adult dataset	Tabular data	VP model-based clustering approach compared to clustering based solely on original patient data reduced biases by data from different hospitals with ARDS.	VP modeling approach mitigates biases by heterogeneous datasets and improves cluster discovery.	Depends on the availability of relevant observational data, and the complexity of use.
[15]	2022	Employs mechanistic virtual patient (VP) modeling to capture specific features of patients' states and dynamics while reducing biases introduced by heterogeneous datasets.	Observational data of mixed origin, including data pooled from different hospitals. ICU datasets like MIMIC or HiRID	text and tabular data	LFR improved fairness by 62% and 17.5%. Reduced SPD by 93%.	Interactive GUI, effective bias mitigation, improved fairness, comprehensive bias mitigation.	Specific to used datasets, generalizability issues, rely on specific metrics, limited to specific algorithms.
[16]	2021	DECAF framework. Structural causal model. Biased edge removal. Evaluated fairness. SCM focus on understanding causal relationships within data.	Tabular data	Tabular data	AUC, ROC, and Precision–Recall curves improved the representation of under-represented groups	Privacy preservation, effective bias identification, maintaining high data quality, and versatility for various medical datasets.	Dependence on initial dataset quality, methodological complexity, and parameter sensitivity may need adjustments for different dataset
[17]	2021	Data size reduction. Simulation of data biases. Bayes Boost approach for bias handling. Probabilistic models and synthetic data generation. Comparison with SMOTE and ADASYN for generating synthetic datasets	CPRD-based synthetic datasets (Synthetic CVD dataset) with 499,344 patients and 21 variables.	Tabular data	High-quality synthetic data, maintained utility of real data, fairness evaluated by demographic parity, equal opportunity.	Compatible with multiple fairness definitions, high-quality data, effective debiasing, and theoretical guarantees.	Requires causal relationship understanding, definition-specific results, focused on tabular data, and expert knowledge needed.
[18]	2020	GANs for generating synthetic biomedical signals using LSTM generator and CNN discriminator. Comparison with real signals to assess quality. Training using signal augmentation techniques.	Biomedical signal datasets like ECG, EEG, EMG, and PPG (17 types of ECG signals).	Time-series data (signal data)	Signal fidelity, noise levels, and usability. Signal similarity: high accuracy approx. 92%.	High-quality synthetic signals, reduce data scarcity issues, high accuracy, and versatility.	Computationally intensive, requires high-quality initial datasets, and model complexity.
[19]	2023	Review of GAN applications in medicine. Discussion on ethical security privacy conservation. Comparative analysis of different GAN architecture techniques with visual review.	Various medical datasets such as MRI, CT scans, and retinal images.	Structured and unstructured data	Accuracy, precision, recall, F1-score, and visual quality assessments. GAN metrics vary in each use case.	GANs generate synthetic medical images for datasets and new data patterns	Focus on theoretical aspects, limited empirical data, and ethical concerns.

Table 3. *Cont.*

Refs.	Year	Methodology	Dataset	Modality	Evaluation Metric	Strengths	Limitations
[20]	2022	Review of clinical papers from PubMed about AI-assessed disparities in dataset country sources, and clinical demographics (nationality, sex, expertise). Manually tagged a subsample of articles to train a model using transfer-learning techniques to predict. Studied transfer learning with the BioBERT model and automated tools like Entrez Direct and Gendarize.	--	--	Country metrics: U.S. 40.8%, Chinese 13.7%. Clinical Specialties: Radiology: 40.4%, Pathology: 9.1%.	A comprehensive analysis of 300,000 articles, highlights disparities in data, transfer-learning and automated tools to analyze the dataset.	Focuses on U.S. and China data only.
[21]	2021	Discusses the critical issues of fairness, bias, and the use of AI and ML in global health, specifically in Low- and Middle-Income Countries. It proposes a framework for appropriateness, bias, and fairness	Diagnosis clinical records of 200 consecutive patients at a clinic.	Text data	Disparate impact scores, fairness prediction from different groups, measure fairness in true positive rates across groups.	Addresses AI biases in underrepresented Indigenous populations, employing fairness metrics enhances transparency	Data specific to New Zealand, dependent on available health data.
[22]	2022	Analyzes data and algorithmic bias related to data collection and model development, training, and testing using health data collected in New Zealand. Measures fairness using DI scores, impact scores, equal opportunities and equalized tabular data.	Health data collected in New Zealand, including Maori populations. NZ-GP Harms and NZ-GDF Diabetes Mellitus (kaggle), PIMA, SACardio, MNCD-RED	Tabular data (NZ-GP Harms), Free-text	Accuracy was approximately 89.2% for both genders, models showed varying ROC for different groups.	A robust framework assessing fairness, bias, and appropriateness in AI/ML applications, offers clear guidelines for AI/ML fairness and reducing bias.	Heavily dependent on the quality and diversity of the training data, practical challenges in deploying AI/ML, and bias inherent in biological differences.
[23]	2023	Deep reinforcement learning framework for bias mitigation. Adversarial training to reduce biases during model development. Application on COVID-19 screening and patient discharge prediction	eICU Collaborative Clinical data Research Database	Text and structured data with multiple attributes such as patient demographics, diagnoses, treatments, and outcomes	Improved fairness and reduced bias in clinical AUC-ROC score of 0.818 to 0.875 using the XGBoost model and Random Forest (RF) model	Effective bias mitigation, application on real-world datasets, enhances clinical decision support.	Requires extensive resources, dependent on the quality of initial data. Limited dataset information
[24]	2022	Synthetic data generation to address the issues of small and imbalanced medical datasets. Algorithms containing tabular data of different sizes to test data, balancing using SMOTE, and ADASYN and data augmentation via Gaussian Copulas, and CTGANs	Eight medical datasets including MNCD, Bangladesh Diabetes	Tabular data	Synthetic data effectively maintained, improved synthetic data, and enhanced machine learning model training without the original dataset. Metrics: MNCD, PCD, KLD, MMD for statistical similarity and F1-score.	Evaluated multiple datasets, advanced synthetic data generation techniques such as CTGAN, and the effectiveness of Gaussian Copula in preserving data structure.	It can be time-consuming, errors encountered depend on the quality of original datasets, and challenges with CTGANs in maintaining balance and performance.

Table 3. *Cont.*

Refs.	Year	Methodology	Dataset	Modality	Evaluation Metric	Strengths	Limitations
[25]	2021	Neural language models (LSTM and GPT-2) for generating synthetic EHR text. Joint generation of synthetic text and annotations for NER with in-text PHI tag. User study for privacy assessment. Privacy was evaluated using ROUGE n-gram and BM25 scoring. Combining real and synthetic data to improve recall without manual annotation	A large and heterogeneous corpus of one million Dutch EHR notes.	Text-based (EHR data)	The accuracy of de-identification is 95%, The LSTM method produces synthetic text with higher utility compared to GPT-2.	Addresses privacy concerns, reduces manual annotation efforts and compares the utility of synthetic data to real data.	Privacy risks with synthetic text, challenges in evaluating privacy-preservation. The study focuses on Dutch EHR data.
[26]	2021	Discussed various AI models and algorithms for clinical outcome prediction. These models include decision trees, linear models, regression models, ensemble learning and neural networks.	Multiple clinical datasets include patient records (EHR), imaging, and genetic data.	Structured and unstructured data (mixed: text, tabular, images)	--	High predictive accuracy, robust model validation, personalized medicine, and effective data integration.	Model interpretability, and generalizability to diverse populations, require large datasets and lack privacy concerns.
[27]	2023	Synthetic data generation with controlled bias. Qualitative analysis of bias impact. Open-source toolkit. Controlled scenarios for bias studies.	Synthetic datasets with predefined bias	Synthetic data generation (open-source toolkit)	Qualitative analysis of bias impact.	Precise control over bias types, open source availability, flexibility to model various biases, contribution to fairness research	May not capture real-world complexities, generalization issues, requires expertise, scope of bias types might be limited.
[11]	2021	Synthetic data generation using various techniques. Comparative study. Analysis of bias reduction	Anonymized CPRD data. Large-scale datasets including real and synthetic data. Request-based access.	Tabular EHR data	Bias reduction by 15–20%, accuracy improved by 10–12%, privacy with <5% re-identification risk, and data utility retained by 90–95%.	Effective bias mitigation ensures privacy, scalable, and versatile.	Varying results and quality depend on models, resource-intensive, and metric reliance.

Detailed Analysis of the Reviewed Articles

This section provides a detailed analysis of the reviewed articles:

Hazra et al. [18] focus on creating synthetic biomedical signals by utilizing (GANs) to improve information accessibility of training data for medical students and machine learning models. The strategy includes an LSTM generator and Convolutional Neural Network (CNN) discriminator, prepared by utilizing flag increase strategies assessed against real signals for quality. Datasets incorporate Electrocardiogram (ECG), electroencephalogram (EEG), electromyography (EMG), and Photoplethysmography (PPG) signals. The ponder reports tall-flag constancy and similitude with accuracy signals, accomplishing roughly 92% exactness. In spite of its potential to moderate an information shortage, the approach is computationally complex and depends on the quality of initial datasets. Moreover, another approach named BayesBoost is proposed by [17]. It centers on taking care of the simulation of data biases through synthetic data generation. It employs probabilistic models and synthetic dataset generators like Bayesian systems and compares them with strategies like SMOTE and AdaSyn. The method employs Clinical Practice Research Datalink (CPRD)-based synthetic datasets, particularly the Synthetic Cardiovascular Disease (CVD) dataset that constitutes 499,344 patient records having 21 features. The results show an improvement in the Area Under Curve (AUC), Receiver Operating Characteristic (ROC), and Precision–Recall curves. The proposed model is effective in privacy preservation and bias identification. However, the approach is complex and relies on the initial dataset quality, requiring alterations for distinctive datasets.

Also, Breugel et al. [16] investigate the DEbiasing CAusal Fairness (DECAF) system that utilizes the Structural Causal model and one-sided edge expulsion to produce fair synthetic data. The consideration centers on data generation, guaranteeing high-quality synthetic data. Fairness is evaluated by demographic parity and equal opportunity. Decency is assessed by utilizing statistical equality and rise-to-opportunity measurements. The system is congruous with numerous fairness definitions, but it requires an understanding of causal connections and centers essentially on tabular data, thus requiring expert knowledge for further studies.

Gujar et al. [14] proposed a framework named GenEthos that utilizes GANs and Interactive Graphical User Interface (GUI) tools to produce synthetic data with integrated bias detection. The tool is assessed by using datasets, including the German Credit and Adult datasets. The framework is evaluated by factual fairness measurements like Statistical Parity Difference (SPD) and Disparate Impact (DI). Learning Fair Representation (LFR) has improved fairness by 62%. Reduced SPD by 93%. Despite its compelling Interactive GUI, effective bias mitigation, improved fairness moderation, and comprehensive assessment, the approach is particular to the utilized datasets and faces generalizability and specific algorithm issues.

Sharafutdinov et al. [15] utilize mechanistic virtual patient (VP) modeling to decrease biases in heterogeneous ICU datasets to identify acute respiratory distress syndrome (ARDS) using machine learning techniques. Utilizing observational information with mixed origin data from different hospitals, the VP model-based clustering approach, compared to clustering based solely on original patient data, makes strides in cluster revelation and mitigates bias. The approach depends on the accessibility of heterogeneous datasets, improved cluster discovery information, and relevant observational data, making it complex to use.

Paladugu et al. [19] audit the application of GANs in restorative imaging and AI preparation, emphasizing the generation of synthetic data information era and privacy conservation. It compares different GAN models utilizing restorative datasets like Magnetic Resonance Imaging (MRI), Computed Tomography (CT) scans, and retinal images. Measurements like precision, accuracy, review, visual quality assessments, and F1-score are utilized to assess the information that has been created. GAN metrics vary in each use case, whereas GANs appear guaranteed in making high-quality manufactured restorative pictures and design patterns. However, this approach centers on hypothetical perspectives with restricted experimental information and limited empirical data. Moreover, Celi et al. [20] explore how bias in AI emerges from clinical medication information, centering on the populace and data-source disparities. Utilizing PubMed clinical papers from 2019, it surveys aberrations about AI-assessed disparities in dataset country sources and clinical demographics (nationality, sex, expertise). They manually tagged a subsample of articles to train a model using transfer-learning techniques with the Bidirectional Encoder Representations from Transformers for Biomedical Text Mining (BioBERT) model to make predictions. The result of the survey highlights critical aberrations, especially in the US (40.8%) and Chinese (13.7%) information. Clinical specialties: Radiology: 40.4% utilize exchange learning with BioBERT, whereas a comprehensive analysis of 300,000 articles highlights the disparities in data. Transfer-learning and automated tools to analyze the dataset are mostly trained on US and Chinese datasets.

Also, Fletcher et al. [21] investigate a system for surveying fairness, bias, and the use of AI/ML in worldwide global healthcare, specifically in low and middle-income nations. Utilizing clinical records from 200 patients to train logistic regression models accomplished around 89.2% exactness for both genders; the ROC may vary for different groups, whereas the system depends on the quality and diversity of the training data. Additionally, Yogarajan et al. [22] analyze information and algorithmic bias in data collection and model development, training, and testing by utilizing healthcare records collected in New Zealand, centering on the Maori populations. Fairness measures, including impact scores, equal opportunities, and equalized odds, were utilized to assess bias and disparities among them. The results show evidence of bias when changes were made to algorithmic designs. However, employing fairness metrics enhances transparency to reduce bias in underrepresented populations.

Yang et al. [23] present a Deep Reinforcement Learning (DRL) system for bias mitigation that was acquired in the data collection process. The model is evaluated for COVID-19 predictions by eliminating any hospital and ethnicity-based biases. The technique includes Adversarial training to decrease biases during model development. The framework is also evaluated on the Electronic Intensive Care Unit (eICU) Collaborative Inquire Database to predict patient discharge status. The result reports an AUC-ROC score of 0.818 to 0.875 using the XGBoost model and Random Forest (RF) model.

Libbi et al. [25] explore the utilization of synthetic data information in healthcare, particularly for preserving privacy for individuals, by creating Electronic Health Record (EHR) data. Utilizing neural dialect models like LSTM and General-Purpose Transformers-2 (GPT-2), it aims to generate synthetic EHR content that incorporates in-text Protected Health Information (PHI) labels with annotations for Named-Entity Recognition (NER). Privacy was evaluated using a recall-oriented understudy for the Gisting Evaluation (ROUGE) n-gram and Best Match (BM25) scoring. The method utilized a dataset of one million Dutch EHR notes to train these models. The result illustrates that combining real and synthetic data information has accomplished a 95% exactness accuracy in de-identification, especially favoring the LSTM strategy for higher utility compared to GPT-2. However, the study discoveries are specific to Dutch EHR datasets.

Pettit et al. [26] discuss the application of AI, ML, and DL in healthcare, with a specific focus on the data processing model, clinical outcome prediction, utilization of data, and AI fairness. To reduce bias in the dataset, different AI models and algorithms have been discussed. These methods include linear and regression models, decision trees, ensemble learning, and neural networks, whereas the paper underscores accuracy, precision, recall, and the F1-score to measure the performance of the AI models.

Rodriguez et al. [24] examine synthetic data generation to address the issues of small and imbalanced medical datasets containing tabular data in different sizes. The proposed method utilizes techniques like Gaussian Copulas, Conditional Tabular Generative Adversarial Networks (CTGAN), and Synthetic Data Vault (SDV). The models are evaluated on eight different medical datasets, including MNCD, MNCD-RED, BANG, EarlyDM, HeartDis, Kidney, PIMA, and SACardio. The result shows that synthetic data effectively improved and enhanced machine learning model training without the original dataset. In spite of its evaluation on multiple datasets, advanced synthetic data generation techniques such as CTGAN and SDV are dependent on the quality of original datasets and are not time efficient.

Baumann et al. [27] present a strategy to generate synthetic data with a controlled bias to analyze the impact of bias on model performance. They proposed an open-source toolkit to generate synthetic data with different types of biases. The produced synthetic datasets with predefined bias are assessed to increase awareness of bias in AI and how it affects individuals and society. Even though the toolkit offers control over biases that need to be introduced, it may not capture real-world complexities. Moreover, Draghi et al. [11] compare different synthetic data generation methods to reduce bias in healthcare data. Utilizing anonymized CPRD informative large-scale datasets comprised of both real and synthetic data, the result illustrates a reduction in bias by 15–20% and precision accuracy changes by 10–12%, with privacy metric underneath 5% of re-identification. Overall, data utility was retained up to 90–95%. The approach is effective in bias mitigation and ensures privacy. However, the proposed approach is resource-intensive.

The next section analyses all these studies given our hypothesis and research questions.

4. Discussion

Based on our investigation, synthetic data generation provides opportunities to minimize biases in the data by generating artificial samples that are statistically similar to the real data. Therefore, we fail to reject our hypothesis, stating that synthetic data can be used to mitigate bias in medical datasets effectively. The previously formulated research questions are answered below:

RQ1. What are the methods or techniques to generate synthetic data to handle biases in datasets?

- Generative Adversarial Network (GAN): GANs use two neural networks, the generator and the discriminator, which compete to produce realistic synthetic data. This technique compares actual real and synthetic data. The generator creates data, while the discriminator evaluates it against real data, improving the generator's output iteratively. For example, SynSigGAN uses an LSTM as a generator and a CNN as a discriminator to obtain biomedical signal datasets to produce high-quality synthetic biomedical signals such as ECG, EEG, and EMG in time-series data signal data [18].
- Bayesian network: The Bayesian networks use probabilistic models to simulate data with controlled biases. They can model complex dependencies between variables, providing a framework for generating synthetic datasets. For example, the BayesBoost method employs Bayesian networks to generate synthetic datasets to address underrepresented group samples in healthcare data, showing improvements in AUC and ROC curve metrics [17].
- Structural Causal Models (SCM): SCM focuses on understanding causal relationships within data. They remove biased edges in the causal graph to generate fair synthetic data, ensuring that the generated data adheres to fairness criteria like demographics and equal opportunity. For example, DECAF is a framework that uses SCMs to create fair synthetic data, maintain high-quality data utility, and achieve fairness through causally aware generative networks [16].
- Synthetic Minority Over-sampling (SMOTE): SMOTE is an oversampling technique designed to identify data imbalance among the datasets. SMOTE is a kind of data augmentation approach that creates additional data points by interpolating between the minority class samples and one of its k-nearest neighbors. This method helps the model to make the data more balanced, which enhances the minority class's representation and reduces the bias in classification tasks. For example, if a dataset has 100 instances of class A and 10 instances of class B, SMOTE would generate additional synthetic data instances of class B to balance the dataset [28].
- Gaussian Copulas: Copula-based techniques simulate synthetic data by modeling the samples from different populations with similar marginal dependencies structure between variables separately from their marginal distributions. Gaussian copulas use the multivariate uniform distributions method to examine and compare the dependence between variables to represent the relation between various features and mitigate bias among them. This technique is especially helpful for producing high-dimensional data with complex dependencies, such as medical records with multiple variables like age, blood pressure, and cholesterol levels [24].

RQ2. What are the limitations of the existing techniques used for synthetic data generation?

Despite the vast application of synthetic generation models, there are still some limitations that need to be addressed. These limitations include

- Techniques like GANs, CT-GAN, and adversarial training require significant computational resources and high-quality initial datasets with meaningful data, which can be a barrier to the widespread adoption and implementation of this method [18].
- In Bayesian networks, the generation and effectiveness of synthetic data heavily depend on the quality of the original datasets. Poor-quality or biased input data can lead to synthetic data that are also biased [17].

- Structural Causal models require a deep understanding of causal relationships between variables and expert knowledge to be implemented effectively and to understand the definition of specific results. This complexity can lead to significant changes in the inferred causal relationships among data; also, this method focuses on tabular structured data [16].
- Techniques like SMOTE can overlap samples while interpolating between instance variables. SMOTE only focuses on tabular structured data. In high-dimensional datasets, the interpolation process to generate synthetic samples that lack accuracy among instances may lead to bias in the dataset [17].
- Copula-based methods, particularly Gaussian copulas, assume a specific dependency structure between variables captured by the copula remains consistent across the dataset. These methods often require a substantial large amount of data to model the dataset accurately without bias. These methods also require a good understanding of the relationships between variables, and they might go to dependency, which makes it complex to generate synthetic data without bias [24].

5. Conclusions

This article reviewed recent research studies to investigate the application of synthetic data to mitigate bias in healthcare datasets. For this purpose, different databases, including Google Scholar, PubMed, ACM, and IEEEXplore, were explored to find relevant research studies. A total of 17 articles were selected and reviewed, including conferences, journals, and a doctoral dissertation. For each article, the methodologies, dataset, modality, evaluation metric, strengths, and weaknesses were analyzed. The overall findings show that synthetic data generation can enhance the fairness and accuracy of datasets used to train AI models by artificially generating samples representing diverse patient groups. These models, when trained on unbiased datasets, can produce fair outcomes. Different techniques, including Gaussian Copula, SMOTE, the Structural Causal method, and GANs, are discussed in this review. Each data generation method has its own limitations. However, the efficacy of synthetic data is contingent upon the quality of the generation process and the synthetic datasets. Challenges such as ensuring high-quality initial datasets, managing computational complexity, ethical considerations, and privacy concerns need to be addressed to fully realize the potential of synthetic data generation. While the study provides useful insights into the application of synthetic data to mitigate bias, it is essential to highlight certain limitations that may have influenced the outcome. One significant limitation is the selection of databases; we have not included Scopus and Web of Science databases, which limits the scope of our study. These platforms provide a greater selection of research studies that could have enhanced the findings. Therefore, in the future, wider databases will be utilized to provide a more comprehensive analysis. Despite this, the current study lays out a strong foundation for future investigation in the area of artificial data generation to handle biases.

Author Contributions: Conceptualization: M.A.S.H., A.M.Q. and A.K. methodology: M.A.S.H., A.M.Q. and A.K.; writing—review and editing A.M.Q. and A.K. All authors have read and agreed to the published version of the manuscript.

Funding: This research was managed by the CREATE-DkIT project, supported by the HEA's TU-Rise programme and co-financed by the Government of Ireland and the European Union through the ERDF Southern, Eastern & Midland Regional Programme 2021–27 and the Northern & Western Regional Programme 2021–27.

Rialtas na hÉireann Government of Ireland | Arna chomhchistiú ag an Aontas Eorpach Co-funded by the European Union | Tionól Réigiúnach Tuaisceirt & Iarthair Northern & Western Regional Assembly | Tionól Réigiúnach an Deiscirt Southern Regional Assembly | HEA AN tÚDARÁS um ARD-OIDEACHAS HIGHER EDUCATION AUTHORITY

Data Availability Statement: No new data were created or analyzed in this study. Data sharing is not applicable.

Conflicts of Interest: The authors declare no conflicts of interest.

References

1. Tavares, S.; Ferrara, E. Fairness and Bias in Artificial Intelligence: A Brief Survey of Sources, Impacts, and Mitigation Strategies. *Sci* **2024**, *6*, 3. [CrossRef]
2. Jain, A.; Brooks, J.R.; Alford, C.C.; Chang, C.S.; Mueller, N.M.; Umscheid, C.A.; Bierman, A.S. Awareness of racial and ethnic bias and potential solutions to address bias with use of health care algorithms. *Proc. JAMA Health Forum. Am. Med. Assoc.* **2023**, *4*, e231197. [CrossRef] [PubMed]
3. Babic, B.; Gerke, S.; Evgeniou, T.; Glenn Cohen, I. Algorithms on Regulatory Lockdown in Medicine. *Science (1979)* **2019**, *366*, 1202–1204. [CrossRef]
4. Kiyasseh, D.; Laca, J.; Haque, T.F.; Miles, B.J.; Wagner, C.; Donoho, D.A.; Anandkumar, A.; Hung, A.J. A Multi-Institutional Study Using Artificial Intelligence to Provide Reliable and Fair Feedback to Surgeons. *Commun. Med.* **2023**, *3*, 42. [CrossRef] [PubMed]
5. Mandal, A.; Leavy, S.; Little, S. Dataset Diversity: Measuring and Mitigating Geographical Bias in Image Search and Retrieval. In Proceedings of the 1st International Workshop on Trustworthy AI for Multimedia Computing, Co-Located with ACM MM 2021, Virtual, 20–24 October 2021; Volume 21, pp. 19–25. [CrossRef]
6. Kordzadeh, N.; Ghasemaghaei, M.; Mikalef, P.; Popovic, A.; Lundström, J.E.; Conboy, K. Algorithmic Bias: Review, Synthesis, and Future Research Directions. *Eur. J. Inf. Syst.* **2022**, *31*, 388–409. [CrossRef]
7. Suresh, H.; Guttag, J. A Framework for Understanding Sources of Harm throughout the Machine Learning Life Cycle. In Proceedings of the 1st ACM Conference on Equity and Access in Algorithms, Mechanisms, and Optimization, Virtually, 5–9 October 2021. [CrossRef]
8. Naresh Mandhala, V.; Bhattacharyya, D.; Midhunchakkaravarthy, D.; Kim, H.-J. Detecting and Mitigating Bias in Data Using Machine Learning with Pre-Training Metrics. *Ingénierie Syst. d'Inf.* **2022**, *27*, 119–125. [CrossRef]
9. Raghunathan, T.E. Synthetic Data. *Annu. Rev. Stat. Appl.* **2021**, *8*, 129–140. [CrossRef]
10. Kandpal, N.; Deng, H.; Roberts, A.; Wallace, E.; Raffel, C. Large Language Models Struggle to Learn Long-Tail Knowledge. In Proceedings of the International Conference on Machine Learning, Honolulu, HI, USA, 23–29 July 2023; pp. 15696–15707.
11. Draghi, B.; Wang, Z.; Myles, P.; Tucker, A. Identifying and Handling Data Bias within Primary Healthcare Data Using Synthetic Data Generators. *Heliyon* **2024**, *10*, e24164. [CrossRef] [PubMed]
12. Oblizanov, A.; Shevskaya, N.; Kazak, A.; Rudenko, M.; Dorofeeva, A. Evaluation Metrics Research for Explainable Artificial Intelligence Global Methods Using Synthetic Data. *Appl. Syst. Innov.* **2023**, *6*, 26. [CrossRef]
13. Bhanot, K.; Bennett, K.P.; Hendler, J.A.; Zaki, M.J.; Guyon, I.; Baldini, I. Synthetic Data Generation and Evaluation for Fairness. Doctoral Dissertation, Rensselaer Polytechnic Institute, Troy, NY, USA, 2023.
14. Gujar, S.; Shah, T.; Honawale, D.; Bhosale, V.; Khan, F.; Verma, D.; Ranjan, R. GenEthos: A Synthetic Data Generation System with Bias Detection and Mitigation. In Proceedings of the International Conference on Computing, Communication, Security and Intelligent Systems, IC3SIS 2022, Kochi, India, 23–25 June 2022. [CrossRef]
15. Sharafutdinov, K.; Fritsch, S.J.; Iravani, M.; Ghalati, P.F.; Saffaran, S.; Bates, D.G.; Hardman, J.G.; Polzin, R.; Mayer, H.; Marx, G.; et al. Computational Simulation of Virtual Patients Reduces Dataset Bias and Improves Machine Learning-Based Detection of ARDS from Noisy Heterogeneous ICU Datasets. *IEEE Open J. Eng. Med. Biol.* **2023**, *5*, 611–620. [CrossRef]
16. Van Breugel, B.; Kyono, T.; Berrevoets, J.; van der Schaar, M. DECAF: Generating Fair Synthetic Data Using Causally-Aware Generative Networks. *Adv. Neural. Inf. Process Syst.* **2021**, *34*, 22221–22233.
17. Draghi, B.; Wang, Z.; Myles, P.; Tucker, A.; Moniz, N.; Branco, P.; Torgo, L.; Japkowicz, N.; Wo, M.; Wang, S. BayesBoost: Identifying and Handling Bias Using Synthetic Data Generators. In Proceedings of the Third International Workshop on Learning with Imbalanced Domains: Theory and Applications, Bilbao, Spain, 17 September 2021; Volume 154.
18. Hazra, D.; Byun, Y.C. SynSigGAN: Generative Adversarial Networks for Synthetic Biomedical Signal Generation. *Biology* **2020**, *9*, 441. [CrossRef] [PubMed]
19. Paladugu, P.S.; Ong, J.; Nelson, N.; Kamran, S.A.; Waisberg, E.; Zaman, N.; Kumar, R.; Dias, R.D.; Lee, A.G.; Tavakkoli, A. Generative Adversarial Networks in Medicine: Important Considerations for This Emerging Innovation in Artificial Intelligence. *Ann. Biomed. Eng.* **2023**, *51*, 2130–2142. [CrossRef]
20. Celi, L.A.; Cellini, J.; Charpignon, M.-L.; Dee, E.C.; Dernoncourt, F.; Eber, R.; Mitchell, W.G.; Moukheiber, L.; Schirmer, J.; Situ, J.; et al. Sources of Bias in Artificial Intelligence That Perpetuate Healthcare Disparities—A Global Review. *PLoS Digit. Health* **2022**, *1*, e0000022. [CrossRef]
21. Fletcher, R.R.; Nakeshimana, A.; Olubeko, O. Addressing Fairness, Bias, and Appropriate Use of Artificial Intelligence and Machine Learning in Global Health. *Front. Artif. Intell.* **2021**, *3*, 561802. [CrossRef]
22. Yogarajan, V.; Dobbie, G.; Leitch, S.; Keegan, T.T.; Bensemann, J.; Witbrock, M.; Asrani, V.; Reith, D. Data and Model Bias in Artificial Intelligence for Healthcare Applications in New Zealand. *Front. Comput. Sci.* **2022**, *4*, 1070493. [CrossRef]
23. Yang, J.; Soltan, A.A.S.; Eyre, D.W.; Clifton, D.A. Algorithmic Fairness and Bias Mitigation for Clinical Machine Learning with Deep Reinforcement Learning. *Nat. Mach. Intell.* **2023**, *5*, 884–894. [CrossRef] [PubMed]
24. Rodriguez-Almeida, A.J.; Fabelo, H.; Ortega, S.; Deniz, A.; Balea-Fernandez, F.J.; Quevedo, E.; Soguero-Ruiz, C.; Wagner, A.M.; Callico, G.M. Synthetic Patient Data Generation and Evaluation in Disease Prediction Using Small and Imbalanced Datasets. *IEEE J. Biomed. Health Inf.* **2023**, *27*, 2670–2680. [CrossRef] [PubMed]
25. Libbi, C.A.; Trienes, J.; Trieschnigg, D.; Seifert, C. Generating Synthetic Training Data for Supervised De-Identification of Electronic Health Records. *Future Internet* **2021**, *13*, 136. [CrossRef]

26. Pettit, R.W.; Fullem, R.; Cheng, C.; Amos, C.I. Artificial Intelligence, Machine Learning, and Deep Learning for Clinical Outcome Prediction. *Emerg. Top. Life Sci.* **2021**, *5*, 729–745. [CrossRef]
27. Baumann, J.; Castelnovo, A.; Cosentini, A.; Crupi, R.; Inverardi, N.; Regoli, D. Bias On Demand: Investigating Bias with a Synthetic Data Generator. In Proceedings of the Thirty-Second International Joint Conference on Artificial Intelligence (IJCAI-23) Demonstrations Track, Macao, China, 19–25 August 2023.
28. Chawla, N.V.; Bowyer, K.W.; Hall, L.O.; Kegelmeyer, W.P. SMOTE: Synthetic Minority Over-Sampling Technique. *J. Artif. Intell. Res.* **2002**, *16*, 321–357. [CrossRef]

MDPI AG
Grosspeteranlage 5
4052 Basel
Switzerland
Tel.: +41 61 683 77 34

Electronics Editorial Office
E-mail: electronics@mdpi.com
www.mdpi.com/journal/electronics

www.ingramcontent.com/pod-product-compliance
Lightning Source LLC
Chambersburg PA
CBHW041400210926
51850CB00013B/3133
* 9 7 8 3 7 2 5 8 3 8 9 5 0 *